MARIA THERESA
AND OTHER STUDIES

By the same Author

BEFORE THE WAR. 2 Vols.

COURTS AND CABINETS

STUDIES IN DIPLOMACY
AND STATECRAFT

FREDERICK THE GREAT:
The Ruler, The Writer, The Man

STUDIES IN GERMAN HISTORY

MARIA THERESA

MARIA THERESA

AND

OTHER STUDIES

G. P. GOOCH

D.Litt., F.B.A.

1724

LONGMANS, GREEN AND CO

LONDON · NEW YORK · TORONTO

LONGMANS, GREEN AND CO LTD
6 & 7 CLIFFORD STREET LONDON W 1
ALSO AT MELBOURNE AND CAPE TOWN

LONGMANS, GREEN AND CO INC
55 FIFTH AVENUE NEW YORK 3

LONGMANS, GREEN AND CO
215 VICTORIA STREET TORONTO 1

ORIENT LONGMANS LTD
BOMBAY CALCUTTA MADRAS

First published 1951

Printed in Great Britain by
NEILL & CO. LTD., EDINBURGH

PREFACE

THE two principal items in this volume attempt to bring the noblest of the Hapsburg rulers to life through the medium of her correspondence with her children. Like her son Joseph, and unlike her daughter Marie Antoinette, Maria Theresa was a born letter-writer. Though much of the material is lost, enough remains for us to visualise the great Empress, in war and peace, in her dealings with Ministers and Ambassadors, in the bosom of her family. It is an attractive picture, but it is hardly the story of a happy woman. The Silesian wars were a nightmare and the death of her husband in middle life was a shattering blow. Her numerous flock, devoted mother though she was, provided as little consolation as in the similar case of the widowed Queen Victoria. The two most celebrated members, indeed, caused more friction and sorrow than joy. Justly proud though she was of the abilities and the devotion to duty of her co-Regent and heir, and grateful for his unfailing affection, the ideological challenge to some of her deepest convictions was a source of ever-increasing grief. The trouble with Marie Antoinette, on the other hand, was that she had too little mind and too little personality, not too much. Flung into a dissolute and extravagant Court in her fifteenth year, the warm-hearted but empty-headed little Archduchess remained in her mother's eyes scarcely more than an irresponsible schoolgirl who declined to grow up, and whose incorrigible frivolities undermined the Austrian alliance. Though there is plenty of high politics in these pages and though celebrities, among them Frederick the Great and Catherine the Great, cross the stage, the main interest is to be found in the revelation of three very different characters. All of them helped to make history, the Empress and her son by the modernisation of Austria, the Queen of France by dissipating what little prestige the Bourbon Monarchy retained after the long and inglorious reign of Louis XV. Throughout the story there are more frowns and tears than smiles on the face of the most human of the Hapsburgs.

The main theme of the shorter items is the writing and teaching of history. *Modern Historiography* is reprinted, with trifling additions, from the 1950 edition of Chambers's *Encyclopædia*. *The Study of the French Revolution* is the third version of a brochure prepared for the *Helps for Students* series in 1920 and incorporated in a revised form in *Studies in Modern History*, 1931, now out of print. *The Cambridge Chair of Modern History* is reprinted, with additions, from the same work. It is followed by studies of the stern Catholic moralist Lord Acton, the most arresting figure among the holders of that high office, and of Harold Temperley, another ornament of Cambridge scholarship, who looked to Seeley and Ranke rather than to Acton for his inspiration. The former appeared in the American quarterly *Foreign Affairs*, the latter in the *Transactions of the British Academy*. *Historical Novels*, reprinted from the *Transactions of the Royal Society of Literature*, vol. 23, surveys the endeavours—in which a few professional scholars have taken part—to teach history without tears. *Our Heritage of Liberty*, an address to the Society of Individualists, pays tribute to the statesmen, the thinkers, and the stout-hearted citizens who fashioned our 'way of life' and bequeathed to us our priceless privileges. My thanks are due to the societies, editors and publishers for their kind permission to reprint.

G. P. G.

January 1951.

CONTENTS

CHAP.   PAGE

1. MARIA THERESA AND JOSEPH II 1

    I. The Young Reformer 1
    II. Friction on the Home Front 29
    III. Poland and Paris 55
    IV. The War of the Bavarian Succession . . . 77
    V. The Rapprochement with Russia 103

2. MARIA THERESA AND MARIE ANTOINETTE . . . 119
    I. From Vienna to Versailles 119
    II. The Dauphine and the Favourite 130
    III. The Temptations of Power 145
    IV. The Dismissal of Turgot 156
    V. The Years of Folly 168
    VI. Brother and Sister 184
    VII. Motherhood at last 193
    VIII. Journey's End 207

3. MODERN HISTORIOGRAPHY 219

4. THE STUDY OF THE FRENCH REVOLUTION . . . 259

5. THE CAMBRIDGE CHAIR OF MODERN HISTORY . . . 297

6. LORD ACTON: APOSTLE OF LIBERTY 332

7. HAROLD TEMPERLEY 348

8. HISTORICAL NOVELS 382

9. OUR HERITAGE OF FREEDOM 404

    INDEX 428

ILLUSTRATIONS

MARIA THERESA . . . . *Frontispiece*

Facing page

JOSEPH II 30

MARIE ANTOINETTE 40
   (from the painting by Mme Vigée Le Brun; photograph
by W. F. Mansell)

The portraits of Maria Theresa and Joseph II
are reproduced from Temperley's *Frederick the
Great and Kaiser Wilhelm* by permission of
Messrs. Gerald Duckworth & Co. Ltd.

I

MARIA THERESA AND JOSEPH II

I. *The Young Reformer*

THE publication of the correspondence of Maria Theresa with her many children was a landmark in late nineteenth-century historical research. Never before or since has there been such a generous and intimate revelation of the family life, the clashing personalities, the conflicting ideologies of an ancient dynasty at the summit of its fame. Though the tragic fate of Marie Antoinette lends peculiar poignancy to the exchanges with the youngest daughter, the three volumes dominated by the eldest son are of far deeper political significance. For while the Queen of France remained to the end in her mother's eyes scarcely more than an irresponsible child, the precocious heir to the throne was far too able and laudably ambitious to be kept idling in the wings, even had she been foolish enough to attempt such frustration. Though large portions of the correspondence have been lost we possess enough to pronounce that it reflects high credit both on mother and son. Each recognised the noble aims, lofty character and exceptional endowments of the other, and even the sharpest disagreements left their mutual affection and respect unimpaired. During Joseph's journeys abroad they sometimes wrote to each other every day. Almost all the letters are in French, since the Empress wrote her mother tongue almost as incorrectly as Frederick the Great, though she spoke German in the family circle. Some chronological gaps can be filled in from the voluminous communications between Joseph and his brother and successor Leopold, Grand Duke of Tuscany, for here too her venerated figure broods over the stage.

Maria Theresa married Francis of Lorraine, Grand Duke of

Tuscany, in 1736, and ascended the Austrian throne in 1740 at the age of twenty-three. Without any political schooling, she suddenly found herself the ruler of a territory whose provinces were connected neither by racial nor linguistic unity, geographical contiguity, historical tradition, nor similarity of institutions. That almost all her subjects were Catholics was a profound satisfaction to a woman of genuine though narrow piety, but the only direct bond of union between the scattered units of her realm was their allegiance to a common sovereign. Though its extensive area, its large population and its natural resources rendered it a Great Power, it was less formidable than it appeared, for the bundle of states was completely lacking in unity of sentiment and direction. The hereditary dominions, generally known as the Crown Lands, formed the core, while the outlying portions, Hungary, Lombardy and the Austrian Netherlands, to a large extent went their own way. The Grand Duchy of Tuscany, for which Francis had exchanged his patrimony of Lorraine, formed no part of the realm, though the dynastic tie ensured co-operation. That the rulers of Austria had been elected Holy Roman Emperors with a single exception for three centuries was a source of prestige rather than of political and military strength.

Plunged into eight years of desperate warfare from the first moment of her succession when Silesia, her richest jewel, was snatched away by Frederick the Great, Maria Theresa had little time to think of administrative reform; but on the return of peace the problem could no longer be ignored. The advantages of centralisation had been illustrated by the triumph of the Prussian robber, who never lost a battle during the War of the Austrian Succession. Yet decentralisation was not the only disability: every portion of her dominions cried aloud for dynamic leadership and radical reform. What other remedy was possible than the robust assertion of the royal authority on the lines of Louis XIV, and the creation of a benevolent despotism on the Prussian model of the Great Elector, Frederick William I, and Frederick the Great? The realm of the Hapsburgs could have little future unless a personal union could be transformed into a more or less centralised state.

A preliminary step had been taken by the Emperor Charles VI

when the Pragmatic Sanction of 1713, subsequently accepted by most European rulers, decreed the indivisibility of the Hapsburg possessions and implicitly announced the existence of a united Reich. Unification, standardisation, regimentation were as essential for external as for internal reasons. For two centuries the House of Austria had played its useful part as the bulwark of Christendom, and Prince Eugene, the hammer of the Turks, was still at the height of his fame. A task of such magnitude, however, as the modernisation of a Great Power required a far more vital personality than Charles VI. His only son had died in childhood and the heavy burden fell on the shoulders of his elder daughter. Happily for her subjects she was ready for the call. Combining a good average brain with a loving heart, an exalted sense of duty, astonishing powers of work, an imposing presence and exceptional charm, Maria Theresa, a true mother of her peoples, made the state not only a far more effective machine but something of a living reality. Her radiant womanliness appealed with special force to the chivalrous Magyar nobility, who gratefully accepted administrative and diplomatic employment outside the borders of Hungary. The European tide was setting strongly towards dynastic autocracy and centralised bureaucracy; particularist traditions were losing ground and the power of the Estates was broken, usually without a struggle. Conservative though she was by temperament and conviction, Maria Theresa had enough flair to realise that the old static order had outlived its day. Her reforms laid the foundations of the unitary system which, with numerous adjustments, lasted till the final crash in 1918. On her accession Austria was little more than a name; at her death forty years later the kingdoms and provinces were hardly more than empty forms. Hitherto the person of the sovereign alone embodied the unity of the realm; henceforth the omnipresence of Imperial officials and administrative boards reminded every citizen that even more significant than the ruler was the impersonal State.

Ever reluctant to part with faithful servants, Maria Theresa had retained Bartenstein and her father's other advisers after the peace of Aix-la-Chapelle [1]; now it was high time for a change

---

[1] The fullest account of Bartenstein is by Arneth, "Bartenstein und seine Zeit," in *Archiv für österreichische Geschichte*, vol. 46, Erste Hälfte, 1-214.

of *tempo* and therefore of *personnel*. The united efforts of the sovereign and of three younger Ministers seemed to open a new era. Haugwitz drew up a scheme of administrative reform, Chotek overhauled the financial system, and Kaunitz gave a fresh turn to foreign policy. Though a diplomatist by training, the advice of the latter was also sought by the Empress on all grave internal problems and family affairs. The support which she had vainly hoped to find in her husband was supplied during the minority of her son by the new Foreign Minister who, to the day of her death, was destined to stand in unswerving loyalty and friendship at her side.

Arneth's publication in 1871 of two comprehensive memoranda from the pen of the Empress revealed her firm grasp of the need of far-reaching reforms.[1] Undated though they are, they obviously reflect her mind and mood during the breathing space between the Eight Years and the Seven Years War, and they may be described as her nearest approach to a *Testament Politique*. After describing the untidy internal conditions at her accession, she concludes that the remedy is to be sought in the concentration of authority in the spheres of administration, legislation and finance. Only thus could the realm of the Hapsburgs rank with the other Great Powers. That the purpose of the memoranda was not only to clear her own mind but to encourage her successor to follow in her footsteps is revealed in the injunction that the second was not to be opened till after her death.

The most urgent need, it was clear to friend and foe, was in the military sphere. Austrian troops had fought with success against the French, but they had proved no match for the superbly drilled forces of Prussia. Hitherto the Austrian army had been raised and financed by the local Estates when troops were required for a campaign, and each province thought mainly of its own immediate needs. Thus the small number of troops in Silesia and Bohemia when the Emperor Charles VI died suddenly in 1740 encouraged Frederick to strike his felon blow. Every year the sovereign had to request supplies from the Estates; coercion was impossible. The two essential reforms were the assertion of the overriding authority of the Crown and the

---

[1] 'Zwei Denkschriften der Kaiserin Maria Theresia,' *Archiv für österreichische Geschichte*, vol. 46.

maintenance of a standing army strong enough to ensure respect beyond the frontiers. In the opinion of Haugwitz at least 108,000 soldiers were needed, involving an annual expenditure of 14 million gulden, an increase of 5 millions, to be settled for ten years. The Haugwitz plan, known as the Ten Years Recess, laid the foundations of the national army which was soon to win laurels in the Seven Years War. Virtual conscription was imposed, a uniform dress fostered *esprit de corps*, and Prussian methods of quick firing and rapid manœuvre were introduced. Training schools for officers were founded, but commissions, as in Prussia, continued to be reserved for the nobility. Such sweeping changes inevitably aroused opposition from the Estates which it took time to overcome.

No less drastic were the reforms in administration, where the creation of an over-all executive was urgently needed. At the centre the Chanceries of Austria and Bohemia were united to form a Directorium at the expense of Bohemian autonomy; district councils were created under the authority of the central government to which the control of the police was transferred; the exemption of the nobility from taxation ceased; internal tolls were abolished and roads were built; a High Court of Justice was established for the whole State; and the codification of the civil and criminal law was taken in hand, a lengthy process owing to the bewildering variety of systems. The Estates remained in being, but their wings were clipped. To enlarge their powers and to introduce a popular element was beyond the range of mid-eighteenth-century reformers, convinced as they were that feudal abuses could be dealt with only by the central authority. The smallest changes took place in the economic field, where the theory and practice of Mercantilism, with its high tariffs and monopolies, reigned supreme. It was a gallant attempt to infuse new life and vigour into the State, to cut out the dead wood, to overcome regional inertia; but the full success of such a comprehensive programme depended on a well-trained and zealous bureaucracy which did not exist. The task of raising the level of education in schools and universities was entrusted to van Swieten, the Dutch physician and friend of the Empress. She and her advisers desired to extend their schemes of renovation to Hungary, Lombardy and the Austrian Netherlands, but, unlike her impulsive successor, they were too wise to force the pace. The temptation to equalise the burdens of the Reich was strongest in regard to Hungary, the citadel of racial particularism, which, though larger and richer than Bohemia, contributed far less to the cost of national defence. She was grateful for such little help as she had received, but when she pleaded for more at the Diet in 1751 she only obtained half her modest request after promising to consider the redress of grievances. For practical purposes Hungary was a friendly independent state.

The Haugwitz reforms had hardly begun to take root when the Seven Years War diverted all thoughts to the problem of survival and revenge, and before the hurricane was over the heir to the throne had learned to think for himself. Born on March 13, 1741, at the height of the first Silesian conflict, Joseph made his first public appearance in his nurse's arms in the historic pageant when the radiant young Queen of Hungary appealed at Pressburg for aid in defence of her hereditary rights against the Prussian aggressor. She had him taught the Magyar language, clad him in the national attire, and chose a Hungarian tutor for him at the age of ten.

We make acquaintance with the precocious lad in the elaborate instructions[1] drafted by the loving but highly critical Empress for Count Batthyany in 1751: 'Since my son has been accustomed to great tenderness and affection from his cradle he has had too much his own way in many things. Owing to the flattery of his servants in particular he likes respect and obedience, regards opposition as distasteful and almost intolerable, denies himself nothing, and is often inconsiderate to others. Though these tendencies have been partially corrected by his zealous Abbé Weger, his first tutor, and though he shows many signs of a good heart, his great and increasing vivacity results in a vehement desire to get his way in every detail. He takes little notice of advice, forgets a thousand times like most young people, and it is often difficult to make him take trouble. The dry, sharp school-master's tone may compel obedience but can never be a success. In response to an appeal to his honour, on the other hand, he has often done more than he was asked. Thus his superior, whoever he be, must inspire both respect and fear. I do not add love,

[1] *Briefe der Kaiserin Maria Theresa an ihre Kinder u. Freunde*, iv, 5–13. Abridged.

because between my son, who has a good heart, and Batthyany that is assumed. The main thing is for the tutor to win the confidence and liking of the child; for this he must trouble less about the little daily failings and concentrate on general directives, rewards and punishments. The tutor can overlook minor faults of omission and thus avoid wrangling which my son, who is sharp enough, would turn to his own account. That has been the Abbé's method in teaching him French, reading, writing, etc. Moreover he is very reluctant to confess his faults. Since another of his failings is the urge to notice and satirise everyone's faults and peculiarities, the tutor must school him to avoid needless curiosity and to value solid worth. Every day must begin with prayer. The first thing for my son is to be humbly convinced of God's omnipotence, to love and fear Him, to derive all other virtues from Christian practices, beginning with love and reverence for his parents. The Abbé's help should always be enlisted as he knows both the strength and weakness of the child.' All matters of health were to be referred to van Swieten. His mother's searching analysis was to prove remarkably accurate: a good heart, a quick mind, an imperious will.

The most formative influence was that of Bartenstein, the chief Minister, who was selected as his director of studies and compiled a manuscript history of modern Europe for his pupil. His progress was frequently tested by examinations, at some of which the Empress was present. His religious training was entrusted to the Jesuits, who held a warm place in the ruler's heart, but his critical intellect owed more to the writings of the *Philosophes*, though he never shed his Catholic faith. The technical schooling for his future tasks was supplied by officials of the numerous departments and dominions of the House of Hapsburg. Despite his profound interest in military affairs his desire to join the army during the later phase of the Seven Years War was vetoed by the anxious ruler.

On October 6, 1760, Joseph was married to Isabella, daughter of the Duke of Parma and granddaughter of Louis XV. 'I am very busy preparing for my son's marriage,' reported the Empress to her close friend Maria Antonia, wife of the heir to the Saxon throne, in Dresden. 'I await my daughter-in-law with impatience. There is only one opinion about her—the most amiable character, highly intelligent, a charming figure. I think he is very lucky. I am satisfied with him. He has a good character, but he is not forthcoming; that will come in time.' Even these lofty expectations were to be surpassed. 'We have a princess who is charming in every way; she is my delight.'[1] The quiet and affectionate girl, whom she described as an angel, brought Joseph a measure of happiness such as he was never to know again, but it was too good to last. We come nearest to this adored princess who, though not unhappy, was possessed by a secret longing for death, in her letters to her closest friend and sister-in-law Marie Christine, to whom alone she confided her innermost thoughts.[2]

A lengthy Memorandum addressed to the Empress on April 3, 1761, the year in which the heir was appointed a member of the newly created Council of State, contained his first suggestions for reform. Joseph, like Frederick, had the pen of a ready writer. For an adequate reply to the points referred to him, he began, he would need much first-hand knowledge of the army and the commissariat, wide acquaintance with politics including the forces of Austria's neighbours, exact information on the merits and demerits of the old and new systems. All this, at the age of twenty, he lacked; yet, knowing the indulgence of the Empress, he would venture a few reflections suggested by a little common sense combined with much zeal and good will, just like a Capuchin monk at work in his cell. Despite this parade of modesty and inexperience the Memorandum is obviously the result of careful thought. Here already is the Enlightened Despot of twenty years later, sure of himself and his goal.

The question how many troops were needed for the security of the State in peace-time, he declared, was purely academic; the more the better. A reduction would discredit the Government and ruin the State. A year after demobilising a large part of his forces Charles VI saw himself assailed from all quarters, and lost Naples and Sicily. Yet he had been infinitely more powerful than the Empress. He had possessed Naples, Sicily and Silesia; his territories were not exhausted, since they had enjoyed a

---

[1] *Kaiserin Maria Theresa u. Kurfürstin Maria Antonia von Sachsen, Briefwechsel*, 1747–72, 83.
[2] See Adam Wolf, *Marie Christine, Erzherzogin von Œsterreich*, vol. i.

prolonged spell of peace; he had generals of great reputation and long experience; his enemies were not numerous, and the then King of Prussia was regarded as a friend. His allies, on the contrary, were strong in money, particularly the English and Dutch. 'Such reasons partly excused his reform, though it cost him two fine kingdoms. But when I think of our present situation, even the word reform makes me shiver. If we cannot compel the King of Prussia to evacuate Saxony, as seems to be the case since half a million men have been working at it for five years, what peace can we expect? The best we can hope is a return to the *status quo ante bellum*. Even then who would henceforth defend us from the insults of this formidable and implacable foe? Our allies? Certainly not. We witness the greatest monarchies in Europe vainly endeavouring to defeat him: an evil omen for the future.

'At one period people were so assured of the superiority of the allied monarchies—France, Russia, Sweden, the Empire and ourselves—that, without an appeal to arms, threats sufficed to secure justice from their neighbours. Yet now that the King of Prussia had demonstrated to all Europe—what he would not have believed himself—that he could not only stand up to their united foes but even force them to a disadvantageous peace, there is no hope that the power of these monarchies would enjoy respect. So we are at the mercy of the King of Prussia and the Turks. The former, who on principle is always armed and will not be disarmed by this conflict, will never miss a favourable opportunity of revenge; and with the Turks war begins directly it is declared. What shall we do, for instance, when we have them at Buda, which they can easily reach? Then we should need to balance the kingdoms of Hungary and Bohemia and choose which it would be the least misfortune to lose if it is impossible to keep both. For Your Majesty may be sure that when peace is made, if ever you are at war with the Turks, which is very probable, you will have the King of Prussia on your hands. And in this situation there is talk of reforming the forces! Even supposing we have nothing to fear from the Turks, will the French alliance last for ever? May not a storm blow up in Italy or the Netherlands or the Low Countries? If Bohemia and Moravia depend on the pleasure of the King of

Prussia, and Croatia and the Banat on that of the Turks, Tuscany
would suit the King of Naples, Lombardy the King of Sardinia,
the Netherlands the French and the Dutch.   Turkey keeps quiet,
and if France and England do not go to war, no one will attack
them.   They can contemplate a long peace, but not the countries
of Your Majesty which are so badly placed.

'However alarming this picture I believe it to be correct, and
I see no other remedy than the maintenance of an army capable
of impressing our neighbours.   We are deep in debt, it is true,
and the State is exhausted, but need we expose it to total certain
ruin in order to succour it?   To perish by reduction of expenditure, or, which is the same thing, to refashion our army in our
present situation, is the worst economy.   The better way is (i)
to foster commerce and agriculture, though that requires money
which we do not possess; (ii) to diminish extravagance and
retrench needless expenditure; (iii) to abolish sinecures and not
employ twenty persons where eight would suffice; (iv) to cease
large payments for doing nothing and rewarding failures as a
means of eliminating them, for my principle is that everyone can
be usefully employed in something, and if he is paid it is right
that he should work; (v) to put the finances in order; (vi) to
introduce a cheaper and well-arranged military system; (vii) to
utilise the considerable assets Your Majesty possesses.

'My idea would be always to keep the number of troops
absolutely required for effective defence, say 200,000 men.
That seems the only true means of defending the Monarchy and
securing a long period of peace while remaining ever on the alert.
All the other questions Your Majesty referred to me depend on it.
These are only thoughts jotted down without reflection.   Yet I
believe them to be very useful, and their application to be the only
remedy for the ills of the State, both to face our enemies and to
restore our finances, since we are on the verge of bankruptcy.   I
have not discussed the Bank, the Crown lands, the mines, etc.,
which are needed to pay the debts and expenses of the Court.
Being in a light fever we do not feel our weakness, but when calm
is restored we shall find that everything is lacking and only then
shall we realise our plight.   May God deliver us with honour as
a reward for Your Majesty's just intentions and immense daily
efforts for the welfare of the State.   I should rejoice to be of the

least assistance, and I would not spare myself to procure her more rest and relieve her burden. I beg her to make use of me as she thinks best.'

A few weeks later Joseph wrote a moving letter to the Empress. 'I cannot thank you enough, dear Mother, for your too gracious words. You know that I desire nothing more in the world than your favours and the friendship of my wife. You can judge of my happiness. Yes, I offer, if it pleases you, to make a vow, like the nuns, not to leave your side. Your Majesty will be my convent and her abode will be my cloister. It is without regret, though it costs me an effort, that I abandon once for all the plan of going on campaign or of travels to places where I could learn something, for instance in the mines or the Crown possessions; for why am I here but to repay as far as possible all the trouble you have taken for me? Thus to please you is to serve God and the public, and that is the only reputation I seek.' His offer of service was accepted in the sense that he was permitted to busy himself with the army and to suggest legal and administrative reforms, but he was not yet in a position to influence events. The death of his adored wife in November 1763, a few days after the birth of a second daughter, inflicted a blow from which he never completely recovered. The great sorrow seemed to bring mother and son even nearer to one another, and soon the Empress herself was to understand the meaning of bitter grief.

The ambitious policy of the Seven Years War had been a total failure, for Prussia retained the glittering prize of Silesia. Maria Theresa had had her fill of fighting: henceforth she stood for peace at almost any price. In the stress of the struggle the atmosphere of the Viennese Court had changed. In 1758 she had pawned her jewels, in 1760 a public subscription was organised and officials sent plate to be melted down. The anxious ruler could no longer bear entertainments and balls, card-tables disappeared, Court dinner-parties were reduced in scale. Religion was her comfort, long services and fasts the order of the day. The Haugwitz reforms had produced little result. Though the power of the provincial Estates had been broken, the transformation of a mosaic of largely autonomous provinces into a centralised autocracy and the creation of an efficient bureaucracy was a slow process. To accelerate re-

organisation Kaunitz suggested a Council of State to advise the
sovereign; not departmental chiefs like himself, but men with
knowledge of special provinces or special branches of the
administrative machinery were required.   With the Chancellor
an *ex-officio* member the Council was expected to render the same
support to the ruler in home affairs as was provided by Kaunitz
in the foreign field.   The Kaunitz plan was accepted by the
Empress, and the new State Council superseded the Directorium
of Haugwitz.   Daun was appointed president of an Army
Council, and each province was placed under a chief.   Joseph
attended the meetings of the Council of State from the start, but
he was little impressed.   Though loyal enough in sentiment,
Hungary clung too tightly to her historic privileges to fit into the
new centripetal system.   When at the close of the Seven Years
War the Empress pleaded with the Diet at Pressburg for more
revenue and army reform, so little help was granted that she
never summoned the Diet again.

The Treaty of Hubertusburg, which restored the *status quo*
before the bloody encounter of the Seven Years War, removed a
heavy load from the mind of the Empress.   'So peace is made
with the King of Prussia, which means the end of many anxieties,'
she wrote to Count Pergen in March 1763.[1]   'But I still have a
thorn in the flesh which I should greatly like to remove—the
election of my son Joseph as King of the Romans.   There is not
a moment to lose.   The Emperor and I are getting on in years.
If one of us goes, what would happen?   General tranquillity is
only just restored, and everyone desires and recognises at least
for a time the sweets of peace.   Would anyone try to thwart my
views and risk a new war?   To delay the election is to leave time
to enemies for cabals and intrigues.   So I greatly hope it will be
this summer.'   Happily the assent of Frederick had been secured
in the treaty, and the other Electors made no trouble.

How tender and trustful the relationship of mother and son
had become was revealed in the daily bulletins despatched by
Joseph during his journey to Frankfurt for his election as King
of the Romans in 1764.   Of her daily letters not one has survived,
but we can guess their nature by the warmth of his replies.
Every stage of the tour, on which he was accompanied by his

---

[1] *Briefe der Kaiserin Maria Theresia an ihre Kinder u. Freunde*, iv, 271–275.

father and his brother Leopold, is minutely described. His sense of duty was strong, but he went through the ceremonies with an aching heart. 'Full of sorrow though I am, I must appear enraptured by a dignity which I regard as a burden, not a delight. I who love solitude and find it difficult to make contact unless I know people well must be always in the crowd and must talk to every stranger.'

'Allow the Archduke to take his leave,' wrote Joseph after the ceremony of election, 'and, changing his name, allow the King of the Romans to beg you to forget all his dignities and to see in him merely a son inexpressibly attached to his mother, who knows no other pleasure than to deserve her approbation, and a subject absolutely ready to sacrifice himself for the least of her desires, for they are his laws. By regarding me in this light, dearest Mother, you make me the happiest King on earth, whereas if a difference occurred between us I should be the unhappiest of men. Such is the favour I ask, and I flatter myself that it will be granted.' Next day he wrote in the same loving strain: 'Do not trouble about my feelings, I beg you. Order, forbid, correct me as of old, for I need your guidance, and what little good there may be in me I owe entirely to your care. Fashion me as you will. It is already much when the learner feels the need of devotion and wishes to adopt in full the views of his teacher. That is my case. I do not examine what is or what seems good; I try to be exactly like you, and that will be enough for me, believing it to be the way of perfection both in public and private life.'

Almost every letter sounded the same note of loving gratitude. In thanking the Empress for 'her adorable letter', he writes on April 1: 'What an enviable fate is mine to have such a sovereign and such a mother! I am overjoyed that she deigns to approve my conduct; that is my sole aim in all I do. I beg you, dearest Mother, continue to tell me all your thoughts, for the more I learn of them the happier I shall be.' On returning from the coronation ceremony on April 8 the King of the Romans despatched a brief note to his 'adorable mother whose glance is more to me than all the kingdoms of the world'. There is no reason why we should not accept these emotional outpourings at their face-value. Never in his life was he prone to flattery, and he asked nothing from his mother but her love. Despite the immense acclamations he confessed that the image of his wife was never out of his thoughts. How successfully he concealed his grief we learn from a letter of Leopold to a friend: 'Our King of the Romans is charming, always in good humour, gay, gracious and polite, and he wins all hearts.' The constant strain it involved only his mother and brother could guess. His work was his salvation, and in the same year he paid his first visit to Hungary. Subsequent tours in various parts of the realm increased his determination to grapple with the poverty and ignorance of the downtrodden peasantry.

Little time was allowed to sorrowing young widowers of royal birth in the line of succession, and the question of remarriage fills a large part of the correspondence of mother and son during the Frankfurt episode. Isabella left an infant daughter, but the unhappy experiences of 1740 had emphasised the necessity of a male heir. Delay was unthinkable, but Joseph was far too depressed to indulge in dreams of equal happiness. 'Your wish is for my happiness,' he wrote on March 19 on the way to Frankfurt, 'but the choice must be good so that I can be happy, and the authorisation you extend to me I venture to return to you. Since I shall only marry to please you, I shall simply follow your advice. I confess, dear Mother, that my heart is cruelly torn these last few days. The loss of my adorable wife is still so deeply graven in my heart that it is never out of my thoughts. At every stopping place I expect to find news of her, but all is over. As I write these words I cannot restrain my tears.' Two days later he reported that the idea of remarriage became increasingly distasteful. 'I fear that the happiest moment for me, after having the pleasure of kissing your hands again, will be that when a poignard is plunged into my breast.' When the Empress strove to comfort him with the thought that his troubles would end with remarriage, he retorted that it would be the climax of his misfortunes. 'Forgive me, dearest Mother, for speaking so frankly, but that is how I feel. Even if I could obtain the person I should have wished I doubt if I could at this moment bring myself to it. Much time will be needed to heal the cruel wound, but your orders and a desperate effort on my part will prevail.'

On April 7 Joseph again poured out his heart to his mother.

'Yes, thanks to God and your good principles, I can claim to be pretty innocent, as you believe I am. I do not attribute this to my own strength, but only to my great trust in God, to respect for your orders, and to the inviolable love I once had and still possess—as if she were alive—for a woman who was torn from me at the summit of my happiness. This greatly altered my outlook. I have learned in some degree to know the world and mankind, and I have discovered that happiness can be found only in conduct beyond reproach. But enough of this sorrowful discourse. I laugh with my lips while my soul is in tears. Let us continue to conquer our feelings and to suffer alone, even without the consolation of pity. You, dearest Mother, enter into other people's sentiments too well not to understand my cruel plight. Were I not so fond of you, and if some experience did not make me know the world, I would remain a widower, or rather be united eternally with an angel in heaven. The conflict between the desire to please you and to follow my inclination is most cruel. I foresee that my affection for you will decide it, but please God it be not for my unhappiness and moral peril.'

On the day after this distressful letter Joseph was lectured by the Archbishop of Cologne, one of the Ecclesiastical Electors who had just made him King of the Romans. The whole Empire hoped he would remarry, and only one lady could fill the void—Princess Elizabeth of Wolfenbüttel. Joseph replied that he had not yet looked about for princesses, and that much time was needed before he could even think seriously about the question. When his visitor stressed the need for action, Joseph rejoined that he heard she was promised to the Crown Prince of Prussia.[1] She had a sister, was the reply, and the promise was not so solemn; the Bavarian and Saxon princesses were much less suitable. Joseph retorted that he knew nothing of them since the main question was unresolved. No one else had broached the subject, he reported to his mother, for he had not encouraged any approach.

Maria Theresa was as eager as the Elector of Cologne, and on April 1, 1764, she drafted a Memorandum in her own hand. She could never feel content till the matter was settled. She believed

---

[1] She was married in the following year to Frederick William, heir to the Prussian throne.

that the Spanish Infanta Marie Louise, daughter of Charles III of Spain, possessed all the needed qualities. Since that was unhappily impossible [1] the princesses of Saxony and Bavaria seemed the most suitable in view of their Christian education, their virtues and their character. 'They are Germans, members of leading families to whom we have obligations and who are of the same blood, with the same grandfather as myself.' There were complaints of their looks but reports differed. Joseph, on the other hand, preferred his sister-in-law, a girl in her fifteenth year who had had neither smallpox nor measles.

Though the Empress had little hope of success in this quarter she begged the King of Spain, as head of the Bourbon family, to grant her son's request. 'God has taken my daughter-in-law whom I loved like my own children. Her loss has so affected my son that he only consents to a second marriage from his love for me and in deference to my wishes. Both as mother and as sovereign I ardently desire his remarriage, but I also desire his happiness. He has a decided objection to all princesses older than himself, such as those of Saxony and Bavaria. His wishes are centred on Princess Louise of Parma out of respect for the memory of his wife and at her advice, for she had indicated her sister as the only person to take her place and make him happy. Your Majesty's wish that she might marry your son should prevent me from thinking of it, and I realise my indiscretion. But put yourself in my place. The happiness of my son and my peoples depends on it, so I look to you to restore a stricken family. That the princess is so closely connected with yourself and the King of France would strengthen the union of the House of Bourbon and my own which is so necessary for our holy religion and the preservation of the welfare of our states.' The King of Spain explained that the marriage of the coveted princess to his son had been arranged in the lifetime of his wife and that to abandon the project would be disloyalty to her memory. Joseph expressed his gratitude for his mother's effort and grimly resigned himself to the good-natured, plain and colourless Bavarian princess Maria Josepha, daughter of the Emperor Charles VII and sister of the reigning Elector Max Joseph and of Maria Antonia of Saxony. The marriage took place in January 1765.

[1] She married Leopold in 1765.

The childless partnership, in which there was no pretence of affection on the husband's side, ended with her death from small-pox two years later; even to show the outward respect for her which Frederick the Great displayed towards his unloved consort was beyond his power. Henceforth no one counted in his emotional life except his mother and his brother Leopold, and the vein of severity in his character developed from year to year.

The sudden death of the Emperor in Innsbruck from apoplexy in September 1765, on his way to attend the wedding of his son Leopold, ended the period of Joseph's apprenticeship. Father and son had meant little to each other; and except for their interest in the army they had nothing in common. Moreover the modest and kindly Francis knew as well as any of his subjects that he was a cipher. 'The Empress and my children constitute the Imperial family,' he remarked; 'I am only a private individual.' Henceforth the heir was not only Holy Roman Emperor but Co-Regent of the Hapsburg realm. For the next fifteen years it was jointly ruled by the widowed Empress, the Emperor Joseph and Kaunitz, who, despite wide differences of temperament, worked loyally for the interests of the dynasty. Though the heir was entrusted with the army as his special province and Kaunitz conducted foreign affairs, Maria Theresa, still under fifty, in good health, and with twenty-five years of experience, kept the final decisions, at any rate in home affairs, in her own hands. For mother and son hard work was the best antidote to domestic grief. Writing to Leopold a few days after his father's death Joseph describes his crowded day, including the morning report to the Empress and the midday meal with Kaunitz. 'The precious health of our august mother is excellent and she is beginning to recover; but I fear next week, when the six weeks will be over and she will see everybody again, and, I hope, go for an occasional walk.' The Co-Regency had been announced, the Court officials and Ministers had taken the usual oath, but not the army out of delicacy for the Empress. Leopold was urged to write to his mother regularly twice a week, even if only a few lines. 'My late wife always wrote thus to her father and I think you can do the same, particularly with such a good mother.'

Maria Theresa, like Queen Victoria, never fully recovered

2

from the loss of her husband, and when he was gone she seemed
to become an old woman.   In her early years she was full of the
joie de vivre, loving dancing, masked balls, riding, the theatre, the
opera, and even the gaming-table with fairly high stakes.   Now
she cut her hair, abandoned jewels, thinned her wardrobe, forbade
rouge, wore a widow's cap, and lived henceforth in rooms draped
with black or grey.   For years she continued to speak of *notre
admirable maître, notre grand Empereur.*   'Nothing but complete
acceptance of God's will can help me to bear this blow,' she
wrote to Leopold.   'You have lost the best and tenderest father.
I have lost everything, a tender husband, a perfect friend, my
only support, to whom I owed everything.   You, dear children,
are the sole legacy of this great prince and tender father; try to
deserve by your conduct all my affection which is now reserved
for you alone.'   She would be content with ten children, she had
written in 1748, but this generous target was quickly passed.
Yet sixteen of them, mostly of tender age, failed to fill the void
in her heart.   Henceforth her chief ambition was to prepare the
heir for his heavy responsibilities.   'I am very pleased with the
Emperor,' she wrote to Lacy.   'I hope to see my son follow just
and honourable courses and to be of use to him.   I think that
experience of the Aulic Council here and of the Imperial Court at
Wetzlar would earn credit for him at the opening of his reign and
gain the confidence of the Estates.' [1]

Reeling under the first shock of bereavement she exclaimed
that she had done with the world and would hand the reins to her
son and retire to a nunnery; but this mood of despair quickly
passed.   More than ever the faithful Kaunitz, who never lost his
head, became her friend and unfailing support, despite his vanity,
his eccentricities and his anti-clericalism.   So unreserved was
her confidence in his wisdom and loyalty that she never resented
unpalatable advice.   No ruler of her time possessed a more
devoted counsellor.   He was her Burghley, not her Bismarck, a
colleague, not a tyrant.

The family harmony was momentarily ruffled when Joseph
announced that he was sole heir under the late Emperor's will,
and Leopold was requested to forward the two million gulden
of his father's enormous fortune which was located in Tuscany,

[1] *Briefe an ihre Kinder u. Freunde,* iv, 286.

on which he would be paid interest at four per cent. for life.
Leopold replied that he had never received a letter with so much
pain: since the transfer of the sum would ruin Tuscany he
proposed an alternative. Joseph forwarded the letter to his
mother with a peremptory comment. 'I find the language very
strong and the tendency most improper. His proposals are
unacceptable. The money he has in his account in Tuscany
belongs to me.' The discord between her sons, replied the
Empress, who sought to pour oil on the troubled waters, concerned something too unimportant to disturb their friendship.
'It is a question of more or less, not of the ruin of the weaker
party. Your letter, written in haste, would have pained me did
I not know that reason and affection would prevail after time for
reflection. A young monarch, a little intoxicated by the incense
which envelops him and by his own temperament, resents everything, even the least obstacle he finds in his path. I must tell
you frankly that I find nothing in your brother's letter to deserve
your indignation, whereas I find a good deal of temper in yours.
I will return the letters this evening after reading them once or
twice more; if I can see Kaunitz I will talk to him about it, not
trusting to myself alone. Cultivate more magnanimity; we do
not want this additional trouble at this moment.' Maternal
affection never prevented Maria Theresa from roundly rebuking
her children when she thought them wrong.

Joseph replied on the same day that he had no thought of
discord with his brother. 'I only regret his weakness and I
condemn those who are pulling the strings. My letter was full
of the friendliest professions. I am not a bit angry with him,
and one has only to read his letter to see that it is not his style.
It is not a case of ruining the weaker party, but of utilising money
which is lying idle and of rendering service to the Monarchy.
The combination of these two objects does not appear to ruin or
incommode my brother. His proposals are unacceptable since
we need cash.' Despite these soothing phrases the Emperor
drafted a second letter to Leopold which pleased the Empress
scarcely better than the first. 'After this morning's talk I
expected something more friendly, more sympathetic, without
sting or humiliation. One does not correct others when we
please ourselves or our pride or petty spite.' The emphasis on

his posi￼ as elder brother was a mistake. 'That is indulging yoursel￼ d your great pride makes him feel he is nobody. If you al￼ s treated him on this footing of superiority it would be ine￼ able.' She confided to Count Franz Thurn, Leopold's friend￼ adviser, her dislike of the *hauteur* and impetuosity of her el￼ son. 'I tremble to think that this may be his character whicl￼ gradually taking shape and may involve him and all of us in￼ uble.' Though she rebuked her son for harshness, she had￼ lly little use for velvet gloves.

J￼ h's next letter assured Leopold that everyone consulted by l￼ elf and the Empress agreed that he had only demanded his due￼ d that not only the law but good sense and natural right we￼ n his side. 'The money is as much my own as the ducat in my￼ cket.' Equally obvious was the need of the State. 'You kr￼ dear brother, how our finances are still smarting from the cr￼ war. Since we cannot hope for succour, we must employ sa￼ gs. Trifles are merely a glass of water poured into the r￼ to make it navigable. Only by bold action and sound f￼ cial operations which sustain our credit and diminish ￼ nditure can we restore the State and make it some day ￼ nidable to its enemies. For that salutary purpose a certain ￼ is essential as a start. I have therefore given all I had, but ￼ re is needed. Would you deprive me of the sweet joy of ￼ ping the State to the utmost of my power? Without my ￼ oney in Tuscany all our projects would fail or be delayed. ￼ his explanation will surely convince your reason—and touch ￼ ur heart—that I must have it by the end of February. Think ￼ f the throne and forget the convenience of individuals. The ￼ uler of Tuscany will gain far more from wise financial operations which rescue the Monarchy and enable it to defend itself than from draining his marshes. Indeed I believe that as a prudent prince it would be your duty, even if I had no claim to it, to send these two millions.'

A week later Joseph added that he wanted to study problems and persons before reaching decisions. 'I think I shall create a Council which will deal with everything in my presence and then I shall decide. My chief preoccupation is our revenue.' Leopold now submitted with a good grace and harmony was restored. 'I am enchanted with your dear letter,' replied the Emperor, 'it is almost too submissive, for you forget the perfect equality that should exist between such sincere friends. I shall never suggest anything which is not to your advantage, which I shall prefer to my own.' Leopold rejoined that he could not express his joy on receiving 'this dear letter', and the year 1765 ended in Christmas mood. It was the first and last time that the harmony of the gifted brothers was seriously disturbed.

Two months after his father's death Joseph composed a Memorandum on the condition of the Monarchy more elaborate and far more censorious than that of 1761.[1] Then he had professed his ignorance and inexperience; now he was Emperor and Co-Regent. There is a new note of authority and urgency. Caring as little for pomps and vanities as Frederick the Great he dedicated himself afresh to his high calling as ' Le premier serviteur de l'état'. This massive disquisition ranks with the two Political Testaments of Frederick the Great among the classical utterances of the era of the Philosophic Despots.

Rejecting the rival creeds of innovation and a cramping traditionalism Joseph declares that the situation of the Monarchy demands prompt remedies. Novice as he was he could only start with general principles, hearsay and a little common sense. During the closing phases of the war he had been present at the deliberations of the eight departments of State. He had seen faces and wigs but had learned nothing, for only trifles were discussed. After a year of such experience he had joined the newly created Council of State. He expected to find himself among men of the type of Solon and Lycurgus, but his attention flagged. Even when he could find no reply to the financial experts he was not convinced. Since the Monarchy differed from every other state, past and present, common sense and reflection must decide. No Minister in recent years except Kaunitz had been of service. In the other departments there was too much paper work and too little decision. A compromise between opposing views was not a settlement. 'I do not believe that so many questions have been asked in a century as during the last three years, and yet we know less. To avoid petty mistakes large ones are committed: to discover and prevent a fraud of 50 florins, 80,000 are spent in a year. That four

---

[1] *Briefwechsel*, III, 335-361.

counsellors do not neglect certain Memoranda twelve are appointed which, with the notes, achieve less at triple cost. How many hundred thousand florins has brain-work cost the State, and how much common sense could have done with it!' Small changes would be merely a palliative; the evil must be attacked at the source if the whole edifice was not to collapse.

Passing to remedies, the Emperor begins with the Council of State. Instead of all the members attempting to survey the whole field—finance, the army, the law—without detailed knowledge, each should have a department. If two or more could not agree they should explain their differences in his presence and he would decide. Secondly, he would create a directorate to meet with the Chamber for the administration of the revenue. Thirdly, a Ministry of Finance, solely concerned with increasing the revenue, diminishing the burdens of the people, abolishing extravagance, paying off debt, strengthening the credit of the State and the provinces, and fostering commerce. Fourthly, the Department of Control should be joined to the Council of State. Fifthly, there should be a supreme Council of Justice and the army. The best men should be appointed and trusted and not burdened with writing reports. 'As for instructions I should simply say: "I confide to you this department, you will govern it in my name and with the same authority as if I were there. Your subordinates will depend exclusively on you. If some weakness or human failing influences you, tell me and I will bear the blame. You alone will have the honour of all your actions, and rewards will not fail. I shall never listen to stories so long as you serve me well. But remember that, allowing everyone, as I shall, to make complaints, if I find in you partiality or weakness you will hear about it. If it is a lack of capacity I shall be as much to blame for choosing you, and you will have another post; if you are unfitted for the first place you must be placed under someone else. But never let me find in you malice or injustice, selfish interests or deceit. Be assured that neither the purest blood, nor fifty years of service, nor your family would prevent me from punishing you for a single act in the most humiliating way and in the eyes of all Europe."'

The second part of the Memorandum outlines the programme of reforms. The first section, on education, reveals the standard-bearer of the *Aufklärung* and the sworn foe of clerical influence. 'Parents believe they have reached their goal and made their son a great statesman when he takes part in the Mass, tells his beads, makes his confession every fortnight, reads only what the limited intellect of his priest permits. Everybody says: What a charming young man and how well brought up! Yes, indeed, if the State were a cloister and our neighbours were monks. Our colleges are far from perfection, and their greatest weakness is that they are located in Vienna. In Brünn, Neustadt and Linz they would do much better: here there are too many temptations, and I should try to move them away from the tumult of the world. In my view the professors are too well paid. Elsewhere, outside their ordinary courses, they must earn by private tuition and therefore take more trouble, whereas here, being well paid, they deliver their lectures and do not care whether the pupils learn anything. I should regard the transfer of the University as useful for the State.'

II. 'To occupy youths of eighteen or nineteen who have finished their studies, have nothing to do and forget everything in a couple of years, I should make every young noble serve unpaid for at least three years in the army, without which he could hope for no appointment or honour.

III. 'To encourage service to the State, at my Court every chamberlain, official or officer—and their wives—should have priority even over their unofficial seniors. This incentive would animate many to devote their talents to the Monarchy. Neither recommendations nor the tears of all the beauties would induce me to relax this arrangement.

IV. 'To retain more able men capable of serving the State, I should decree—whatever the Pope and all the monks in the world might say—that none of my subjects should embrace an ecclesiastical career before coming legally of age at twenty-five. The sad results for both sexes often caused by an early vocation should convince us of the utility of this arrangement, quite apart from reasons of State. I do not deny that there would perhaps be fewer monks, but the genuine vocation of the others would make up for the reduction. I would authorise the Bishops to hold back some young people who choose this career in order to let them pursue the necessary studies, but no profession before

they are legally of age.   This is dictated both by common sense
and by our laws.   A young man cannot dispose of his property
before that date, and that is a trifle compared with his person
and his soul which he pledges for ever at fourteen or fifteen.

V. 'I would appoint an impartial Commission to examine all
existing foundations where the founder's intentions are being
ignored.   These I would reform or employ for pious purposes
which are also useful for the State, especially the education of
children who would be made not merely Christians but good
subjects.   Where there are too many foundations I should
reduce their number and employ the surplus for the above
purposes.

VI. 'For all these arrangements a good police is essential, and
the force should be organised in military fashion.   Abuses occur
every day which excite ridicule even beyond the frontier.   This
cohort of civil soldiers, besides committing a hundred excesses,
lacks the authority and discipline of the army.   Disabled men,
with their officers and some outside help, would do this job much
better.   The funds in all the towns earmarked for security and
night watchmen should be used to pay the disabled, thus
diminishing the burden of the State.

VII. 'Every department should try to fill posts with a State
pensioner or disabled man.

VIII. 'To make a country happy and agreeable it is necessary
to attract as many foreigners as possible who spend their money
and buy native goods.   But how are they to be attracted or kept
where studies have not advanced far enough to learn new things,
and where visitors have to change their habits?   Religion and
morals are unquestionably among the principal objects of a
sovereign, but his zeal should not extend to correcting and converting foreigners.   In faith and morals violence is unavailing;
conviction is needed.   The service of God is inseparable from
the service of the State.   He wishes us to employ those to whom
He has given talents and capacity for affairs, leaving it to Divine
mercy to reward the good and to punish evildoers.   As for the
censorship, we should be very careful about what is printed and
sold; but to search pockets and trunks, especially of a foreigner,
is an excess of zeal.   It would be easy to prove that, despite the
existing vigour, every prohibited book is available at Vienna, and

everyone, attracted by the veto, can buy it at double the price. Thus everyone, above all every foreigner, who only brings a single copy, may keep it, since the sovereign is not obliged to watch over individual conscience, but only over the general welfare.

IX. 'To foster our commerce I should exclude all foreign merchandise except groceries, above all rich fabrics and diamonds; clothes should be made within the country. I should start commercial lectures and make people feel that it is no disgrace for the nobility to enter business. Every business man who proves that he has brought 100,000 florins into the country should receive certain honours and privileges.

X. 'Since younger sons, and elder sons of modest means, cannot serve the State without payment, and since under the present system a man would be despised and regarded as scarcely capable of serving the State if he married beneath him, liberty of marriage should be introduced, even what are now called *mésalliances*. Neither the divine law nor the law of nature forbid it. Only prejudice makes us believe that I am worth more because my grandfather was a count and because I possess a parchment signed by Charles V. From our parents we inherit only physical existence; thus king, count, bourgeois, peasant, it is exactly the same. The gifts of soul and mind we receive from the Creator; vices and virtues come to us from a good or bad education and from the examples around us. Every woman would enjoy the prerogatives and honours of her husband, and equally a princess who married below her would have the same fate. I believe this would be one of the most essential things for the Monarchy, one of the most welcomed and useful measures for both sexes, since happiness is not found in pride.

XI. 'To curb extravagance I would forbid all gala days for individuals or Ministers, and only leave one at Court for the sovereign and the Royal Family; birthday fêtes should cease, and the announcement of the birthdays of the whole nobility must be forbidden. Officers must always appear in uniform. All other counsellors and secretaries must wear a coat of black cloth both in the Council meetings and at Court; elsewhere only black clothes, and for gala occasions a rich vest. The only exceptions

will be the higher nobility and the recipients of some Order.
High living is a grave abuse, and everyone is expected to possess
good Burgundy and a French *chef*; but since most of the victuals
are home-produced it does not matter much. Let the Court
and Ministers set the example and sensible folk will follow suit.
The import of wines and food should be absolutely forbidden.

XII. 'To diminish expenditure in time of peace the troops
should help with the fortifications, main roads, etc. Foreign
recruits should be sought regardless of cost. I would accept
not only tall but short men, women, children, any human being,
the most capable for service in the army, the others as settlers.
Not only Hungary but Bohemia and Moravia need population.
Millions for this purpose are a far more profitable investment
than paying off debt. Promotion must be by merit alone.

XIII. 'The pay of soldiers should be raised or that of civilians
reduced so that they are treated alike.

XIV. 'The extravagance and idleness of our Ministers is
beyond belief. Those with 400 florins run the State, and those
with 4,000 or 12,000 reap the advantage. Often they ruin
everything, thinking they know everything without reading or
experience; if they leave things to their secretaries they are
better done.

XV. 'Capable chiefs should train their successors, a sadly
neglected task. The Presidents prefer working with careerists
whom they treat like despots, and who aid them to cover
up their ignorance and errors, rather than employ well-born
assistants by whom they fear to be found out. From this lack
of suitable *personnel* flow the embarrassments and misfortunes of
the State.

XVI. 'Travel is indispensable for a sovereign who, on political,
civil and military grounds, must see what is going on. I do not
flatter myself that his presence will put everything right, but it is
worth the effort. Though we see things behind a mask and at
their best, by returning at intervals one notes changes, hears
complaints, meets people who may some day be employed, judges
the capacity and zeal of the Ministers. The old notion must be
abandoned that a sovereign directs everything when he has only
seen and learned through other eyes and ears, and that he has
done enough when he enjoys the phantom of glory. I, on the

contrary, hold that his duty is very different, that he must travel as a private citizen if he is not to do more harm than good.

XVI. 'It is as wrong to think everything before our time good as that everything needs to be changed. Everything can be good if one removes the faults and increases the advantages; the least pardonable of prejudices is to be afraid of attacking or diminishing them. Plenty of courage and still more patriotism are needed by an innovator in the present century. Nothing is easier than to leave everything as we find it, but one day we shall pay for our neglect.'

The survey closes with some general observations. 'I base it on my belief, my feeble lights, and on the example of the only department which serves the State and enjoys full confidence under the direction of Prince Kaunitz. I could say much more if I did not fear to be a bore, and I should say much less if I did not know the indulgence, the love of truth, and the desire to do good of her for whom I write. If I did not know that she possesses the courage and determination to carry out a decision, even if defective in parts, I should never dare to propose anything so bold. I suggest nothing which I should not perform, and I am confident of my ability to do so if fortified by her orders. Big things must be done simultaneously. It is best to explain all one's intentions to the public and, having reached a decision, to listen to no objection. Those who only see parts of the plan cannot and should not judge. If my ideas are not approved let us hear no more of them and not pick and choose, since their merit lies in their comprehensiveness.'

Such was the political philosophy of a young man of twenty-four and the programme for which he was to argue during the remaining fifteen years of his mother's reign and, so far as possible, to implement when he became master in his own house. This great state paper breathes the conviction common to all the Enlightened Despots of the eighteenth century that their responsibility extended to every sphere. The author's longing for the welfare and happiness of his subjects kindles every page. Everything was to be done for the people, nothing by the people; their interests, not their feelings, had to be considered. That he should invite their assistance never crossed his mind; their only right was to be well governed. Nobody counted except the nobility, the high officers and the bureaucracy. The bourgeoisie supplied the professions but possessed no influence. The Fourth Estate were mere beasts of burden, and there is no hint of the abolition of serfdom in this opulent list of reforms. Even if the proposal of mixed marriages were adopted, the caste system would remain virtually intact. Dynastic paternalism as expounded by Joseph was an exalted ideal, but it suffered from two congenital weaknesses of which he must have been fully aware but to which he makes no reference. It postulated a succession of supermen at the helm and provided no bulwark against the vagaries of an evil or incompetent prince.

Next to the major presupposition of a capable ruler and an omnipotent state, the reader is struck by the purely secular approach of the young Emperor who had been overdosed with religion as a child. The contemptuous references to the Church and the clergy must have grated on the pious Empress who, so far as religious matters were concerned, inherited the bigoted traditions of the Thirty Years War. This impatient child of the *Aufklärung* regarded the wealthy and obscurantist Church in Austria as one of the main obstacles to his plans for a well-governed, well-educated and enlightened State, and he was determined to clip its wings. To Maria Theresa the maintenance of the doctrine, the property and the prestige of the Catholic Church was as vital an obligation as the defence of her frontiers: compared with the dynasty and the Church, political, legal and social changes to which her son attached such importance were trifles. With the *étatisme* of the Memorandum, on the other hand, she was in full sympathy, for no eighteenth-century ruler had learned the alphabet of democracy. She was ready to consider many of the suggested secular reforms, but in the religious field she would not yield an inch. Here, indeed, we discern the first rift within the lute. In her eyes what came to be known as Josephinism or Febronianism—the Austrian equivalent of Gallicanism—was an abomination. Though her son was not a sceptic like Frederick, his attitude to ecclesiastical pretensions was identical: the State must be supreme. The Vatican was as much a Foreign Power as France, Prussia, or Russia. During the opening phase of the Co-Regency friction was avoided since national defence alone was placed in his hands. Yet his influence grew rapidly and the ideological collision between two strong personalities was merely postponed. Though the state chariot was drawn by two noble steeds, it was not easy for the conservative and the radical, the pious traditionalist and the rationalist reformer, to keep in step.

II. *Friction on the Home Front*

As Co-Regent—a status for which there was no precedent— Joseph promptly made his influence felt. No thinker or theorist, he was only interested in practical work. The primary task was to remedy the chaotic state of the finances. Without a moment's hesitation he transferred to the Treasury twenty million gulden —in property, shares, cash, works of art—inherited under his father's will, using it to convert the National Debt incurred in two long wars from six or five per cent. to four. The late Emperor's extensive game preserves were sold, and the wild boars, so destructive to agriculture, were killed off. To reduce the waste and overstaffing at Court was more difficult, for the Empress accepted the traditional etiquette and, though not personally extravagant, had no notion of balancing the national accounts. Despite a few retrenchments the debt continued to increase, till revenue and expenditure balanced for the first time in 1775. The burden of taxation lay heavy on the poverty-stricken population. At the close of the Seven Years War the realm of the Hapsburgs was not a happy place. The most popular act of the young ruler was the gift, with his mother's full approval, of the Prater to the citizens of Vienna.

How widespread was the suffering and discontent the young Emperor gradually learned as he travelled indefatigably over every part of his dominions. 'The internal situation is incredible and indescribable,' he reported; 'it is heartbreaking to see it all.' What little he could do in the sphere of financial reform was done, but the deeper causes of the trouble were untouched. Serfdom had outlived its day, but it was not till the birth-pangs of the French Revolution that it received stern notice to quit. Only in the field of military affairs did he possess a free hand. Here he co-operated with Field-Marshal Lacy in reorganising the army, ameliorating the condition of the troops, inspecting fortifications, and sharing in the manœuvres. While economising in civil expenditure he demanded a larger outlay for the army and therefore higher taxation, to which Kaunitz rejoined that a well-trained force of moderate size, strengthened by recruits in case of need, was all that was required. That a vigorous and consistent foreign policy was impossible without instant readiness for a major conflict was clear to everyone.

Hitherto the state had been governed by the Empress and Kaunitz; henceforth there were three rulers, all equally patriotic, equally industrious and equally determined to get their own way. With Frederick, as Voltaire remarked, it was Sparta in the morning, Athens at night: with Joseph it was Sparta all the time. The King was a blend of Stoic and Epicurean, loving the arts, literature and conversation; the Emperor, scorning delights, was at once the ruler and the slave of the state. The voice of the old Austria echoes through the seven volumes of the diary of the Court Chamberlain, Count Khevenhüller, the devoted servant of the dynasty, who respected the ability and energy of the young Emperor but found his innovations a sore trial. The glories of the Court, he complained in 1765, were waning, and the decline had begun before he took a hand. 'This unfortunate spirit of innovation which showed itself soon after the death of Charles VI and increased from day to day seems now to be in the ascendant. If it goes on like this there will soon be no more system and etiquette at Court. Only the Empress could prevent these deplorable innovations of her son who regards all old customs as vain prejudices; but she is partially inclined to them herself, and often she lacks the necessary courage and firmness to resist.' The people, added the ruffled Chamberlain, disapproved the abandonment of the old colourful ways, particularly the abolition of gala days, and regarded it as an evil omen. The Emperor's taste for simplicity in clothes also grated on the dignified official, ever mindful of the prestige of the House of Hapsburg.

Could such a novel system endure? The first explosion occurred in the early months of the new régime, when Kaunitz, misunderstanding his sovereign's well-meant proposal to appoint

JOSEPH II

Starhemberg, her Ambassador in Paris, as his assistant in the
exacting tasks of the Foreign Office, offered to withdraw. Yielding to her passionate appeal not to desert her, and convinced by
the assurance of her undiminished personal and political confidence, he withdrew his resignation and for some years the
triumvirate was reasonably harmonious. Joseph also expressed
his full trust in the resourceful and experienced Foreign Minister,
who now received the newly created title of Chancellor and was
described by his sovereign as Europe's greatest statesman.
That the Empress was the predominant partner was admitted
by both her colleagues, above all in the sphere of domestic
affairs. Joseph's partial subservience to his conservative mother
was facilitated by the unfeigned devotion which shines through
his correspondence. When she almost died of smallpox in
1767, and faced death with unruffled composure, he slept in the
next room, rarely left her side, and astonished the courtiers by his
bitter grief. 'There is but one Maria Theresa,' he exclaimed to
Kaunitz, 'and I admire her more than ever.' Her beauty was
largely destroyed by pock-marks, but the fine eyes were unaffected.

The epidemic relieved Joseph of his second wife, whom the
Empress esteemed for her solid qualities and whom she had
befriended in attempting to make up for her husband's studied
neglect. It would be easier for him, he had complained, to frame
a letter to the Great Moghul. That he never gave her a chance
is clear. 'Her piety and many other virtues,' comments Khevenhüller, 'were worthy of all praise. If the Emperor had got
accustomed to her appearance, and if he had not demanded such
a brilliant intellect as that of his first wife, she would surely have
proved worthy of his love in return for her affection and her
blind submission to his will. This he acknowledged when
informed of her death, and he let fall some words which indicated
regret that he had been so cold to her.' Having lost two wives
and banished for ever all thought of renewed domestic bliss, he
found an outlet for his affections in his mother alone: *Votre
Majesté* gave way to *Très chère Mère*. Leopold was a valued
friend, but he was far away in Tuscany and they rarely met.
The appearance in the Hofburg of the Angel of Death led to
one wholesome reform, for the Court abandoned the traditional
method of bleeding and closed windows in favour of inoculation

and fresh air. Three years later, in January 1770, Therese, the child of the adored Isabella, passed away, to the intense grief of her father and grandmother. It was all the worse, wrote the Empress to her Parma daughter-in-law, for she was an only child, the delight of her father and his only relaxation. He bore his loss like a Christian philosopher, but she feared for his health.

During the early years of the long partnership it sufficed for the sovereign to express her wishes. Shortly after his father's death Joseph yielded to her desire that he should avoid an encounter with 'the wicked man' during a visit to the Saxon battlefields of the Seven Years War. Writing to her from Reichenberg in June 1766 he reported that, firm in his resolution, above all when it was a matter of obliging the only person he respected and adored, he had missed the only opportunity he would ever have of seeing and knowing a man who excited his curiosity to the utmost. Her letter of approval rewarded him for the sacrifice. 'How easy it is to work for you,' he rejoined, 'and how richly is one recompensated by the kindness with which you recognise the slightest services.' While naturally eager to see the most celebrated performer on the European stage, he resented the idea of discipleship. 'The Ministers pay me an undeserved compliment,' he wrote to his mother, 'in saying I have taken the King of Prussia for my model. To imitate him is impossible for an honest man, a rôle I have no intention of abandoning for all the fine models if they are incompatible.' His desire for a meeting was to be gratified three years later with his mother's assent.

Maria Theresa never hesitated to tell her son his faults. He was too critical, she wrote after a year of the Co-Regency. 'I am very much afraid that, entertaining in general a very low opinion of people, you estrange also the few honest men by confounding them with the rest. Right-thinking men cannot incur suspicion nor can they be classed with the others; they will prefer to retire or will serve with less zeal. The basic motive is confidence; without it there is nothing left.' The rebuke was inspired by Joseph's criticism of an official who enjoyed her esteem and by a letter to Count Harrach, Leopold's chief adviser. 'I must tell you,' she added, 'that the tone of the note grieves me owing to the pleasure you take in chilling and humiliating people—the

exact contrary of what I have always done. I prefer the fulfilment of my wishes as the result of friendly words, of persuasion
rather than force. Now I fear you will never find friends. It is
not the Emperor nor the Co-Regent who exhibits biting, ironical,
ill-natured traits, but Joseph's own heart. That is what alarms
me; it will spoil your life and involve the fortunes of the
Monarchy and of us all. Though I shall not be here, I hope
that I shall live on in your heart and that your numerous family
and your states will lose nothing by my death but on the contrary
will benefit.

'But can I cherish such hopes if you adopt this tone which
eschews all tenderness and friendship? This hero, of whom so
many people talk, this conqueror, has he a single friend? Must
he not distrust everyone? What a life if humanity is banished!
In our religion above all charity is the great foundation, not
advice, not precepts. Do you think you are practising it if you
wound and alienate people, even those who have rendered great
services and only share our common failings, harmful neither to
the state nor to us but only to themselves, and who in their case
have only done their duty? Who would care to expose himself
to such criticism unless motived by the sheer necessity of describing to you things as they are? Whatever your talents it is
impossible for you to possess all the experience and knowledge
of past and present times; you cannot do things alone. A Yes,
a No, a clear refusal would be better than all this heap of ironies
which your heart has discharged. It is not bad but it will become
so. It is high time to cease enjoying all your *bons mots*, these
clever phrases which merely hurt and ridicule and which alienate
all decent people. The belief will spread that the whole human
race is undeserving of affection and esteem, since one's own
conduct has driven away all the good elements and opened the
door to knaves, imitators and flatterers. After this long sermon,
for which you will pardon my heart which is all tenderness for
you and my countries, I will give you, with all your talents and
charm, a comparison. You are a coquette of the mind. A *bon
mot*, a phrase strikes you, whether in a book or a person, and you
apply it at the first opportunity without reflecting whether it is a
suitable time. At the close of my letter I take you tenderly to
my arms and hope you will spare me the pain of such unpleasant

talk. I merely want to see you esteemed and beloved by every-body as you deserve. Always your good old faithful Maman.'

It speaks volumes for the trustful and tender relationship that this broadside left no wounds in the heart of the young Emperor. 'Penetrated by the kindness of these gentle rods, wielded by a mother's incomparable heart, I humbly kiss her hands. Do not imagine they have no effect. A heart like mine, a soul so sensitive, is more touched by the embrace with which you honour a son whom you believe to be at the moment unworthy of it than by the most terrible penalties or threats. I shed tears of gratitude, and I promise henceforth to avoid whatever could cause the least trouble, even if I had to miss an opportunity to shine.' The statements in the letter which had occasioned this chastisement, he added, were true, but he felt that the phrasing had been too strong. 'Pardon this fault, dear mother, of a son who loves you beyond all expression.'

After the brief idyll of his first marriage Joseph was never again entirely happy, but he found consolation in his work. 'Fortunately I have neither a wife nor any other attachment,' he wrote to Leopold in 1768, 'so I am free from anxieties and can dedicate myself to my task. Love of country, the welfare of the Monarchy, that, my dear brother, is my only passion and my only spur. I am so identified with it that my heart cannot rest nor my health be satisfactory unless I am convinced of its welfare and of the wisdom of our arrangements. Nothing seems to me small or trifling in this important matter, and I am equally interested in every aspect. I am not more drawn to the army than to finance. If I could feel that reduction was desirable, I would this very day turn all the soldiers into labourers, but circumstances forbid it.'

After three years' experience as Co-Regent Joseph felt in-creasing difficulty in running in double harness. The idea of thwarting his mother's will never occurred to him, but was it right for him to accept responsibility for policies which he notoriously disapproved? Surely not. A brisk exchange at the opening of 1769 reveals the tension and the suffering which it caused to both. 'The new arrangements made by the Council of State,' he wrote to his mother, 'which also affect myself, require an explanation. Henceforth all matters at the Council will have to be signed by whichever of us is present or by both. This change compels me to repeat the representations I once made in reference to the military department which I was desired to undertake. I am nothing, not even a thinking being, except in so far as I have to support all your orders and to reveal to you everything I know: that is the dictate of my conscience, my reason and my desires. If beneath the empty title of Co-Regent people wish to imagine something else, I hereby declare in all sincerity that no one will ever convert me to a different course. The additional signatures are so contrary to the laws of the Monarchy, of which the sovereign is the essence, and are so opposed to its welfare and to common sense, that I must refuse to sign. If, however, your convenience requires it, I will do so only with these two letters: E. C. Joseph, i.e. *ex consilio*, or Q. C. Joseph, *qua coregens*. I should never forgive myself were I not to do my utmost to avert sooner or later troublesome things which would darken my life if I ever found myself in your bad books or were ever to appear inconsistent.'

The Empress was in no mood for compromise. 'I promised to tell you my arrangement about the signatures—here it is. That is the only way I can meet you in a matter twenty-eight years old. If you decide to continue on the old footing observed till January 5 I should prefer it, though it would not bring me the relief I hoped to find. But you will not compel me to change a solemn convention to which I am deeply attached and which was the work of my heart on November 21, 1741,[1] and was renewed on September 19, 1765, the cruellest day of my life. Only the thought of finding in you a son worthy of such a father, and of proving useful to you, sustained me then and will sustain me now, not wishing to live a moment without possessing your affection no less than your confidence and esteem,'

Both parties had strong wills, and Joseph's reply combines firmness with affection. A singular and critical situation, he began, had unhappily led to his mother's displeasure. 'I will not go into the motives which have animated me and which compel me to maintain my course. You can be assured that reason and duty alone sustain me, and God knows I should have preferred strict obedience to your desires did not the refusal I find

---

[1] The date of Joseph's birth.

myself compelled to make involve my invariable respect and consideration towards my sovereign and my benefactress. Yes, I recognise the full scope and truth of this title. Do I not owe to you my existence, my education, and is not the little good there is in me the fruit of your care? Do you not labour without respite to assure me a happy fate many years ahead? Are you not my only friend in the world, for whom I would gladly make every sacrifice, the only confidant of my soul? Can you believe that, with all this ever present in my memory and graven deep in my heart, I could be so wicked and ungrateful as to offend you without the most compelling reasons? And do you think me too unintelligent to assess their importance at the price of the horrible sacrifice I am about to make of your favour which has been my delight for twenty-eight years? But is it possible, dear mother, that you demand at this price what is for you unimportant but for me of the greatest consequence? Grant me this new boon and you will make me happy and content. I request it on my knees.' The Empress, grieved but unshaken, replied on the same day: 'I know you can talk and write well; I still hope that your heart will speak, but your obstinacy and prejudices will prove your misfortune as they are already mine. You would despise me if I yielded in a simple matter which has always been the rule and which is now to be changed for your caprice and without you giving any valid reason. Return to your duty and you will hear no reproaches from me. God alone knows what I suffer. Yes, I am your friend, a devoted friend, who must do her duty and could not possibly yield, contrary to her conviction and experience.'

Two days later she was in gentler mood. Starhemberg, she reported, had reassured her on the chief points of her son's refusal to sign the minutes as before. 'He tells me you have assured him that it is not disapproval of the system, nor of the Council of State, nor of the method of conducting affairs. You have been wrong to behave like this and to cause me all this worry. One word from you would have secured my willing assent to any reasonable change you would have proposed. You know by a thousand proofs my readiness to please everyone and you above all. I only work for love of you; I cannot hope to gather the fruits of my labours; it is therefore for you that I undertake them willingly.

And now I find you in my way, carefully concealing the reason of your resolutions, so sudden and unexpected, so stubbornly maintained. Release me from this state of duress. The reason you gave me to-day is irrelevant.'

'I should have hastened to thank you in person,' replied Joseph on the same day, 'had you not expressed yourself in writing, so I feel I ought to follow suit. I am aware of all your favours and your heart which has never failed me. Moreover, if my truest devotion, combined with the greatest submission, count for anything, I do not think myself undeserving and I challenge everyone to do me justice. What a notion, dear mother! Could you believe that my refusal arose from discontent? Do I not know who you are and who I am? Have I not a hundred times by tongue and pen, respectfully but firmly, told you my feelings on different matters? Would not my duty and conscience compel me to do so? Hence my humble petition—to allow me not to sign, or only the papers of the War Council or in general like all the other matters with the name of Co-Regent, and thus to indicate to everyone what I feel and think. This would obviate misconceptions about my share of power and the disapproval and defeat of Your Majesty. That, I feel sure, will cause infinite inconvenience and intrigues which sooner or later will damage the Monarchy and perhaps disturb our happy intimacy. It is for these reasons that in these unhappy days I have forfeited your friendship. I can truly say that I have lost my sleep and rest. Wherever I go, even on horseback, this killing thought of your disfavour accompanies me. A hundred times at your feet I was ready to give up everything and to consent, from an almost abnormal affection, to all that my reason forbade. You ask me to diminish your burden; that is my sole ambition. But, if it is absolutely necessary, the more you increase my activities, the more I must demonstrate that I know what I am and what I owe you. Those are my invincible reasons. Every quarter of an hour by which you shorten my distress will be a boon. I submit to everything you may command; as for the past, if I have failed you, believe that the intention was not evil and accept my most sincere regrets. If you are good enough to pardon me, I shall redouble my affection if that is possible. I await your orders whether I am to recall the minutes signed as Co-Regent, and to

sign those I possess, hoping that you will grant my request and
that I may by this word present myself as your first subject and
servant.'

The harassed Empress asked for time to consider her reply. 'I
do not understand your letter. I only see in it sentiments which
have moved me to tears, all the more that I understand your
feelings by what I am suffering myself. I was on the point of
coming to embrace you and to terminate this cruel situation,
but the reiteration and firmness with which you insist on your
opinion restrains me, and you must leave me time to decide.
I do not wish you to bring back the papers signed against my
wishes; that would make too great a stir. Why do you not
simply sign the protocols as before till we decide together what
to do?' The controversy ended with a brief note from the
Emperor. 'I have the honour to declare my entire submission
in signing all the papers you have deigned to send me and which
I still had, too happy if I could thus please you and deserve that,
in granting my just demand which has no need of any arrangement, I am not under the horrible compulsion to return to the
same point in a few days, my conviction remaining the same and
my motives unchangeable.'

The affectionate letters to his mother written during the ensuing
visit to Italy prove that on Joseph's side at any rate the conflict
had left no scars. Accompanied by Leopold he revelled in the
sights of the Eternal City, but found the fair sex little to his taste.
'The ladies are mostly ugly and all of them are ill-educated and
unamiable. I am in no danger of losing my heart and I shall
return to your feet, dear mother, just as I left you.' Each of
them was guarded by her *Cavaliere Servente* and it was impossible
to get near them. Writing from Naples he sung the praises of
his sister Caroline, a striking contrast to Ferdinand, the feeble
king, who was completely dominated by Tanucci, a regular
Tartuffe. He was better pleased with Parma, where his sister
Amelia, shortly to marry Duke Ferdinand, could, he believed,
be happy if she were prudent. His impressions of Florence
would have to be reported verbally after his return, since Leopold
was very suspicious. 'I should certainly forfeit his friendship,
which I greatly prize, if he knew I was writing about him. I
have studied him thoroughly. I can assure you I have found an

excellent core, very wide information and incredible industry;
but he is not always happy in his choice of means and persons,
which often leads to depression and ill-temper.' To a lost letter
from the Empress during the Italian tour suggesting a third
marriage, Joseph replied that he could not oblige her. 'My mind
is made up, dear mother, and in this matter alone I venture to
appeal from your heart to your reason. Examine my character,
my person, my situation. Consider and analyse the marriage
state, its advantages and disadvantages, weigh the probabilities
of happiness and unhappiness, calculate the chapter of accidents.
Then condemn me, if you can, as sovereign, as judge, as friend,
but not as mother, to whose tender heart I confess my faults.
You fear for my soul and my health; you would like yourself
to survive in a hundred different branches. I feel it, but do not
stifle the voice of reason which I believe will tell you that I am
doing good work for God, for the State, for myself, for you, for
everyone.' Despite their differences she was justly proud of
her brilliant son. 'He has done wonders in Italy,' she wrote to
Lacy. 'Il faut dire qu'il est unique quand il veut.'

The riddle of joint rule was unsolved and indeed insoluble.
While the Empress fretted at opposition, the impatient Emperor
was pained by a sense of chronic frustration. 'You cannot
imagine how many difficulties everything meets with here,' he
complained to Leopold in November 1771, on returning from a
tour in Bohemia; 'one does not advance a single step without
wrangling, writing and preaching for hours. It is enough to
give one the spleen and I have my fill of it. Besides, the
weather is horrible; one cannot get out; and things decided
before my departure are not even begun.' Joseph possessed
a first-class brain and an affectionate heart, but he was too
highly strung to face the ceaseless wear and tear of public life
with equanimity.

An undated letter assigned by Arneth to the same month,
November 1771, reveals similar discouragement on the part of
the Empress. 'I prefer to write, for my heart is too oppressed
by all sorts of feelings for me to talk quietly and with self-control.
Your latest journey will also be one of your titles to fame, but
let us render it as happy for the thousands of people for whom
you sacrificed comforts and amusements and endangered your

health. Your intentions are beyond challenge, and they are always accompanied by convincing actions. Of mine you are aware. God, Who alone knows the secrets of my heart, sees that I have no thought but the public good, even at the expense of my own and that of you all. How comes it then that, despite these excellent intentions, things always follow a different course, that we often disagree and dispute? This has long occupied my thoughts and makes me more than ordinarily doubtful and depressed. Is it our own fault in being too positive, wishing others to think and act like us while we ourselves differ in our principles or methods of application? Both of us strive to fulfil our aims. We concentrate on each other's faults without seeking and correcting our own. We attempt to create a general system, to correlate and simplify all the parts. We wish every official to think and act in the same way and at less expense. Those are our thoughts day and night, and why does not the effect correspond to our intentions? I shall be grateful for your counsels and aid in this sad situation. My courage is beginning to fail; you are full of it. You are starting your career; mine is ending even more unhappily than it began. I desire to share the crushing burden with you. My experience may be useful, but I do not want to stop you doing what, after mature consideration, you think wise. So let us establish principles for the sake of our peace of mind and our conduct of affairs in order to render our peoples happier. For that we must be in agreement. Everything turns on it. Our good and zealous Ministers and officials will follow suit and will work with assurance and ease—very different from at present. Tell me frankly, by tongue or pen, as I have always begged you, my faults and failings. I will do the same, but in such a way that no one could suspect any difference. The first year, 1766, everything went well; only since then has it changed because our co-operation has slackened. You are so good at formulating principles; do so, for our tranquillity and the public good. Draw up maxims and rules for us; we will discuss them and decide. I too will turn it all over in my mind. I could not help relieving my oppressed heart by this explanation. I should utterly collapse without a son like you whom Providence has granted me; and so long as you do not fall into vice and abandon your faith, I can hope that you will be the saviour of

MARIE ANTOINETTE

your peoples. This thought encourages me to devote my whole strength to second you, only too pleased to see a son happier and more deserving of happiness than myself.' To Lacy she wrote that at bottom he was good, but his entourage was bad and unfortunately he was too able.

In Austria as in Prussia legal reform was in the air, for Beccaria's *Crimes and Punishments*, published in 1764, had set all the world thinking. Commissioners were appointed to prepare new civil and criminal codes, but the dead hand of tradition lay heavy on the State. The civil code promulgated in 1766 was so imperfect that it only functioned till Joseph came to the throne, and the criminal code, issued in 1768, retained the practice of judicial torture. The abolition of this antiquated penalty was vigorously pressed by Sonnenfels, the brightest ornament of the Viennese School of Law, but a direct appeal to the Empress merely provoked a sharp command not to mention the subject in his lectures and writings. The courageous jurist continued his campaign, and it was decided to procure the opinion not only of the Council of State but of the Governors and Chief Justices of Austria, Bohemia and Moravia. While the local authorities merely desired to limit the practice to eliciting evidence in charges of treason, robbery with violence, or false coinage, a majority of the Council demanded abolition. The conservative Empress was only ready for limitation, but at this point Joseph came out in support of the abolitionists; and when Kaunitz, whose advice even in domestic affairs always carried more weight with her than that of her son, took the same side, legal torture was abolished in 1776. Once again the eighteenth century had triumphed over the seventeenth.

The Partition of Poland, so ardently championed by the Emperor and so detested by his conscientious mother, left their nerves more frayed than ever, and once again the former poured out his heart to Leopold. 'Our uncertainties here have reached a pitch you cannot imagine. Tasks accumulate daily and nothing is done. Every day till five or six, except for a quarter of an hour for a solitary meal, I am at work, yet nothing happens. Trifling causes, intrigues of which I have long been the dupe, block the way and meanwhile everything goes to the devil. I make you a present of my position as eldest son, for I am in a mood of black

depression without hope for the future.   In every sphere things
are deteriorating to such a degree that advance is impossible, and
one cannot even hope ever to do any good.   Adieu reputation
and fame!   I take part unwillingly in this destruction, and my
patriotic heart is rent.   Adieu! I pour all my troubles into the
bosom of a friend.   Have pity on me.'

Despite his bouts of pessimism Joseph never dreamed of
throwing up the sponge.   After the Polish crisis, as after the
Seven Years War, his busy mind turned to administrative reform.
He was frantically busy, he reported to Leopold in April 1773.
The army had to be redistributed now that the threat of war was
removed.   The reform of the Jesuits raised problems; Prince
Kaunitz had drawn up a big scheme in 240 pages, full of verbiage
and commonplaces, on internal reform and plans for the new
Polish provinces.   'I am compiling four works for Her Majesty,
with a covering note on the reasons of the changes I propose.
Starting from the failings of the State Council, I suggest its transformation into a real Cabinet *in internis* and the creation of another
Cabinet *in politicis* to direct and inspire the State Chancery and
to survey the whole from a real centre.   Thus all the Cabinet
secretaries and Councillors of State will be united to the Court
and will work under the direction of Her Majesty and myself.
Then I must try to simplify the government of our provinces and
the departments in Vienna.'   The plan of scrapping the Council
of State was too ambitious, for it was the favourite child of
Kaunitz; but some new blood, including Joseph's chief adviser
Marshal Lacy, was added, and in May 1774 a statute reorganised
its work.

The impatient reformer was appalled by the slow *tempo* of
Vienna.   Big and little things alike, he complained to Leopold,
moved at a snail's pace.   '*Dum Romae consulitur, Saguntum perit*:
that is almost always our condition.'   A few weeks later he added
that he was the scapegoat because he told the truth and fought
abuses.   'What need I should have of you at such moments, my
only true friend!   What would I not give if I could tell you my
troubles and find in your counsels help and consolation!   Generally things are in such confusion that I see no issue.   Meanwhile
Prince Kaunitz wishes to resign though he will not go.   Yet
everything is in arrears, nothing is done, people kill themselves

for nothing, and affairs go from bad to worse.' On the same day, December 9, the Emperor once again explained, first in private talk with his mother and later in a lengthy letter, the difficulties of his position. That they would prove almost insurmountable he had long foreseen, since the Co-Regency was not intended to be an empty title. 'What have I done? I have tried to travel and to sacrifice the precious intimacy of your love. I took the same line about my signature, I have sought distraction, I have considered every idea as if I possessed influence, well aware that people would try to make me abuse it and that two wills can never remain so perfectly united as to avoid uncertainty and thus to open the door to intrigues. I have always acted on these principles, and it is you alone whom I have had to combat. If I have often carried my precautions too far, if, in making your happiness, service and tranquillity my sole aim, I have had the misfortune to displease you, I humbly implore pardon in pleading good intentions.

'I cannot conceal from myself that things seem out of gear and that the huge machine of Government does not function as it should. It is useless to tinker with the minor causes; allow me to say that, beginning with ourselves, I do not feel we are doing what our situation demands. Who am I? I hope I have never forgotten—nor who you are. But do you do the same? You think I am quite different from what I am and ought to be. You wrong me if you think me ambitious and anxious to command. You are blind if you think me talented enough for great affairs. Far from that, I am idle by nature, superficial, perhaps more froth on the surface than depth, and, apart from my zeal and uprightness in the service of the State, there is nothing very solid about me. But in these two points I am beyond challenge. Thus my opinions and counsels are only those of one of your servants who has no other right to give orders than by receiving orders from you; and they ought to count only if their reasoning is thought sound. It is for you to decide without appeal, for us to give what we think the best advice. I swear I have always acted in this spirit, but you have often avoided decisions. The reason is lack of self-confidence. That is unjust, for I can say without flattery that when you act on your own you never go wrong. If it is owing to divided confidence you are blind, for you cannot confound my inexperience with the reputation and talents of Ministers trusted by yourself and Europe.

'If you are afraid of hurting my feelings, believe that I am not obstinately wedded to my opinion, that I only wish for the best and for a clear conscience. Reject my ideas and I shall not mind; but if you ask me for them, permit my conviction and intellect to be my only guides. I ask one grace—to regard me and all your Ministers as your counsellors and servants; we have merely to inquire and to execute your orders. That is our sole duty. Everything must emanate from you. You alone can be the centre of everything. As we can only have opinions, not will, you can only have a will, not opinions. You will realise the confusion when it is thought or said that things are done against your wishes, or that you do not interfere in this or that department. If your present servants, myself included, cannot accept this situation, change them. If I am in your way, or if you see danger in receiving my views, if my person keeps from your side men a hundred times more useful and capable than myself, I crave in God's name and for your reputation, duty and affection, the withdrawal I desire. No heir among my predecessors or contemporaries has been thus employed, so why should I? Leave me to the Empire, to books, to honest amusements. I desire nothing more. Why hurl me before my time into all the worries of government? Why saddle me with the cruel doubt whether perhaps I, unwittingly and to my own unhappiness, am a cause of your worries, of confusion and disorder, discontent and disgust, perhaps of losing your Ministers? I love you and the State alone; decide. If I thought only of myself, I well know what I should do.'

Confronted with the distasteful alternative of giving her son greater influence or forfeiting his services, the Empress chose the former. Though still under sixty she felt her will-power and resilience waning. 'I have been thinking how to take advantage of this moment when you open your heart to me to organise our internal affairs which are in a sad state. I am ready to hand over everything and to retire, but you have so often told me you cannot entertain the idea. Once again I make the offer as the only way to secure tranquillity and comfort. Do not fear I shall feel regrets. I have seen too much of the world not to quit it

with the greatest satisfaction.   Two things restrain me—your
opposition and the condition of our affairs which I think so bad
that I should not like to burden you all alone at this moment
against your wishes.   Discouraged as I am, I feel revived if I
can count on your help and counsel.   I must confess that my
faculties—eyesight, hearing, quickness of apprehension—are
declining very rapidly, and that the failing I always dreaded is
want of resolution, accompanied by discouragement.   Your de-
sertion, that of Kaunitz, the death of all my intimate counsellors,
irreligion, the decay of morals, the jargon of the day which I can
scarcely understand: all these things are more than enough to
overwhelm me.   I can think of nothing better than to charge
you to work with whoever you wish in arranging a Council of
State capable of relieving me by returning to the idea of formulating principles of government without changing the personnel,
starting from your two Memoranda on administrative reform.
If you wish to keep me, that is the only way.   I cannot see the
State perish owing to my unhappy situation, and I can only find
a solution with your aid.   I promise you my entire confidence,
and I beg you to give me prompt warning if you think I am going
astray, not willingly but through lack of comprehension.   Tell
me what you wish me to do; nothing will hurt me in my cruel
situation of the last six years.'

The campaign against the Jesuits by the Catholic sovereigns
of Europe during the decade following the Seven Years War
raised an issue which might have been expected to provoke
violent dissension between mother and son.   Their wealth,
political influence, far-reaching commercial activities, and the
feeling that they were agents of a foreign Power, led to the
closing of their establishments in France, Spain, Portugal and
the Bourbon Courts of Naples and Parma.   Maria Theresa was
as stout a champion of the secular authority as any other
eighteenth-century ruler, Catholic and Protestant, and in 1767
the reception of Papal briefs in the Hapsburg dominions was
forbidden without the consent of the Crown; yet the attack on
the Jesuits, the traditional champions of the Hapsburgs, filled
her with grief.

The election of Ganganelli in 1769 as Clement XIV installed a
Pontiff who detested the Order and announced his readiness to

suppress it if the Catholic Powers were unanimous in such a demand. Its only hope lay in the pious Empress, whose sympathies were notorious. That Joseph and Kaunitz desired suppression was only to be expected, for they loathed clerical pretensions in all their forms; but there was no need for them to take an active part in the campaign. What finally decided her to yield were considerations of high policy. The corner-stone of her system since the making of the French alliance in 1756 had been the maintenance of Hapsburg-Bourbon solidarity, and it was to this overriding necessity that she now sacrificed her feelings. Declaring her neutrality in the quarrel, she announced her willingness to accept the decision of the Pope, who, to the delight of the Emperor and the Chancellor, proceeded to suppress the Order in 1773. All she could achieve was to soften the blow by securing the provision of pensions and other alleviations. 'The fate of the Jesuits is decided to-day,' she wrote to Count Pergon; 'I am very sorry for them but there is nothing to be done. Every month I feel weaker and more depressed.' 'Our poor Jesuits,' she informed her son Ferdinand, ' have accepted their fate in all submission and humility.' For the next two years the uneasy partnership continued without an explosion, but in 1776 the agonising conflict of ideologies broke out again. This time it was not the problem of the machinery of government but an issue which touched the deepest springs in the soul of the Empress. Pious she had always been, and since her husband's death religion in the only form she recognised became an obsession. Though regretfully conscious of belonging to a vanishing age, she scorned all thought of compromise in regard to her inherited faith. At the close of 1775, writing for once in German, she declared that the grant of free exercise of religion was forbidden to all Catholic princes, and the talk of freedom in everything made her anxious. 'I am too old ever to adopt such principles, and I pray God that my successor never tries it on. Neither he, nor, still less, his successors, would be the happier.' Never would it have occurred to her to follow the lead of her devoted friend Maria Antonia in appointing Protestant as well as Catholic ladies in her household on the ground that Saxony was a Protestant country.

To this brief but pregnant communication Joseph replied gravely at length on Christmas Eve. 'Since my duty to God,

my Fatherland and Your Majesty has always been the sole
criterion of my actions and counsels, I am at last compelled to
inform you of my considered ideas. In so many instances I
observe an ineradicable mistrust on the part of Your Majesty
which I have incurred either through my principles or my
declarations. Since I have no cause to reproach myself, I accept
it as my fate in silent subjection, but the consequences lead me
to my present step. What is the use to you of a person whose
principles you disapprove, both in his duty to God and in justice
to his family, in matters of state hasty, prejudiced, thoughtless,
full of false formulas gathered from books or dangerous company,
full of prejudices, etc.? Nothing except to try your patience
whenever he has to express his honest but perhaps erroneous
opinion. That is precisely my situation. You have made your
attitude clear by tongue and pen, so what remains for me to do?
Change my principles? Gladly enough if I were to be converted.
I should not mind continuing my work, onerous and distasteful
as it is, but for the prospect of damaging the Fatherland and
giving you offence. These two things are too much for my
usual tolerance. If you hold this opinion of me, justly or unjustly, I am not only useless but harmful. If you find in all my
writings and conversation such dangerous principles, all the good
I might perhaps do is thrown away. Such a conflict brings
disorder and vacillation into my department, however careful
I am. Moreover I am faced with the loss or at least the drastic
diminution of the favour you have shown me for thirty-five years.
Does that make sense? Could I remain longer when I realise
that I am useless and dangerous to the public welfare? No
remedy is at hand; the longer it lasts the worse for me. What
I have always foreseen and for years have kept to myself has now
become so strong a conviction that I cannot be moved. In a
word, deliver your son, a young man without experience, from
the cruel burden, to which the world can show no parallel, of a
Co-Regent. A woman like you, who has reigned in glory for
so many years, has no need of such a being. Everything has
gone worse since then. Let me be your true servant and son;
remove this fetter which prevents me from defending my
principles and you will not hear from me another word. Everything will go better and I shall live happier, more tranquil and

perhaps more usefully than now. Do not trouble about the
method. The moment I get your written discharge it will go
through without much publicity. Gratitude will fill my heart
and I hope to deserve your favour twice as much. I can obey
but I cannot change my convictions.'

On Christmas Day the Empress sent a sorrowful but unyield-
ing reply: 'With the best will we do not understand each other.
Perhaps I am too overwhelmed with chagrin that I see neither
the confidence nor the frankness which I thought I deserved;
that is the trouble of my life. I can say that for thirty-six years
you have been my only concern. Twenty-six of them have been
happy, but I cannot say the same to-day, for never can I accept lax
religious and moral principles. You exhibit too clearly your
antipathy to all the old customs and to all the clergy, and lax
principles in morals and conduct. I am justly alarmed about
your delicate situation; it makes me shudder for the future. It
has all leaked out and people know how to exploit it. The
glorious Christmas season is not the time to deal with the decision
you ask of me; I will give it in the New Year. You can imagine
how heavy my heart is in seeing yours so little in unison and
preferring your old prejudices. I hope they make you happier
than myself.'

Joseph replied that he would await the decision with profound
respect and submission. 'I long to return to the position whence
you summoned me ten years ago. I feel hopeful since you
recognise the cause of the frequent troubles arising from the
performance of my duties which in the long run would spell
misfortune for the state as well as myself. Get rid of my scruples,
my peculiar principles; let me obey the promptings of my heart
which is tenderly attached to you, and I believe I shall merit your
entire satisfaction.' A lost letter from the Empress evoked a
reply regretting the postponement of the decision. 'In reiterating
all my arguments I renew my request: the welfare of the State,
yours, mine, even our consciences and our reputations require it.'
The Empress forwarded the correspondence to Kaunitz with
the words: 'Herewith the sorry *débris* of what has passed. The
Council to-day went better than I expected, but one senses the
strain in everything. I am very low.' Joseph confided to
Leopold that it was the Church which held the first place in his

mother's heart.   Since no further documents on the Christmas crisis remain, we may assume that the matter was settled in conversation, for the Co-Regency continued.

At the age of sixty Maria Theresa was no longer her old resolute self.   Joseph reported to his brother that she was longing to see him and to embrace his children at Gorizia.   She insisted on living in the same house, able to see them rise, dress, dine, go to bed; resistance to her plans would upset her.   She was coughing a little, which was hardly surprising in view of the crowds who came to talk to her.   Only four days later he forwarded a letter from his mother reporting that she was unwell.   'Do not worry about her health,' he added; 'her cold is nothing, but she has been talked round and is afraid she may die.   It is inexplicable.   I urged her not to cancel her plans, but to let you and your children await her at Gorizia.   At this she went to bed in order to seem ill.   She says she will start on May 3, but I do not believe it.   Intrigue and defeatism in her *entourage*, I fear, will frustrate my efforts.   I shall, however, train my batteries and appeal to her *amour propre*, so perhaps she may still consent.'   A week later she decided against the journey.   'She says she is sorry, but in reality she is greatly relieved, for they had inspired her with an almost incredible dread.   Seeing that she would have gone unwillingly, perhaps have upset everyone by her apprehensions, and had no peace of mind, it was best to give it up.   She is in excellent health.   My dear brother, I will not describe my feelings.   Knowing my friendship, you can imagine my regret.   But it is much diminished now that I have seen that her journey would have been no advantage to you, for she would certainly have been in no humour for it.'

In the summer of 1777, during Joseph's absence in France, the old religious antagonism flared up more fiercely than ever when several thousand Moravian Catholics became Protestants. Appalled at what she regarded as a monstrous apostasy, the Empress asked her son for advice and received a dissertation which excited her wrath scarcely less than the incident itself.   'In regard to the affairs you wished to discuss with me,' he replied, 'the open declarations of irreligion in Moravia confirm my principles: liberty of belief, and there will no longer be only one religion guiding equally all inhabitants for the good of the state.

Without this method we shall not save more souls and we shall lose far more useful and needed bodies. Half and half methods are not in my line. Either full liberty of worship or the expulsion of all who do not share your beliefs and practise the same forms of worshipping the same God. That souls may not be damned after death it is proposed to expel them and to forfeit all the advantages we could derive from excellent cultivators and good subjects during their life. What power are you claiming? Do you wish to usurp the prerogative of divine mercy to save people against their will, to issue orders to consciences? If service is rendered to the state, the laws of nature and society observed, your Supreme Being not dishonoured but respected and adored, what have you to do with other things? It is for the Holy Spirit to enlighten the heart; your laws can only challenge its operations. That is my conviction, as you know, and I fear I shall never change it.'

The reply of the Empress to this eloquent confession of faith was uncompromising; 'This will reach you in Switzerland; those people do not realise the price of your presence. In that refuge of all the cranks and criminals there are two women whom I hope you will not see. They will be impudent enough to try, and I must reluctantly confess that there is nothing left to spoil in matters of religion if you persist in admiring this general toleration which you tell me is your unalterable principle. I shall not cease to pray—and get others worthier than myself to pray—that God may preserve you from this misfortune, which would be the worst the Monarchy had ever known. In thinking of having cultivators, keeping them, even of attracting them, you will ruin your state and cause the loss of many souls. What is the good of possessing the true religion if you value it so little that you scarcely care about its preservation and extension? I do not observe this indifference in all the Protestants, and I wish we imitated them, for no state permits this indifference within its boundaries. You see it in this wretched Switzerland. They observe and experiment in what goes on in the Empire, England, Saxony, Baden, Holland, etc., but is the country the happier? What is needed is good faith, immutable rules: where will you find or keep them?'

The Emperor returned to the charge in a letter from Freiburg.

The misunderstanding, he explained, arose from the word toleration. 'You took it in quite a different sense. God save me from thinking it is a matter of indifference whether subjects become Protestants or remain Catholics, still less whether they believe or at least observe the inherited cult. I would give my possessions if all our Protestants turned Catholics. Toleration, in my view, simply means that, in purely temporal affairs, I would employ and allow the possession of property and the rights of citizenship to those who bring benefit to the state. Those who are unfortunately of a false faith are far further from conversion if they remain in their countries than if they settle where they see and hear the striking truths of the Catholic faith. The free exercise of their cult makes them better subjects and saves them from an irreligion much more dangerous for our Catholics than their observances. If Protestants do not generally adopt this method it is because their Ministers flee from the truth and wisdom of ours, and also because republics find it particularly difficult to make such changes. If I had more leisure than a letter affords I think I could prove that, in my approach, I could face a tribunal which would determine my future life. No one would become Lutheran or Calvinist; there would be fewer unbelievers in all religions and the state would greatly gain. I cannot feel that all this would render me guilty in the sight of God. At any rate that does not seem to me in conformity with His perfection, nor with the task He has set me in placing me at the service of fifteen million human beings.'

Maria Theresa's lengthy rejoinder was a spirited performance. 'Without a predominating religion!' she began. 'Toleration and indifference are the best way of undermining everything. It was not the Edict of Nantes which ruined those French provinces; there was no edict at Bordeaux and there the country is no richer. It is the miserable forms, the bad administration, the feeble or intriguing Ministers who ruined that kingdom, so favoured by its position; it is the want of religion of these people who think only of their interests or passions which ruins everything. How can these sort of folk be constrained? There is no way, neither gallows nor the wheel, except religion or cruelty. Now I am speaking as a politician, not as a Christian; nothing is so necessary or salutary as religion. Do you wish everybody to manufacture

one for himself?   No fixed cult, no obedience to the Church!
What would become of us?   That will not bring peace and con-
tentment: the era of *Faustrecht* would return.   Such a declaration
on your part might cause disaster and saddle you with responsibility for thousands of souls.   Imagine what I am suffering to see
you with these erroneous principles.   It concerns not only the
welfare of the state or the preservation of a son who has always
been the sole object of my actions, but your salvation as well.
By hearkening to this spirit of contradiction you ruin yourself
and drag the Monarchy down with you.   You waste all the
efforts of your ancestors, who have won for us these provinces
and then improved them by introducing our holy religion—
unlike our adversaries—without force or cruelty.   No persecution, but still less indifference or toleration!   That is my
programme.   I wish to live only so long as I can go to the grave
like my ancestors with this consolation—that my son will be as
great and as religious as his predecessors and abandon his false
reasoning, evil books, such as those which exalt the mind at the
expense of everything holy and worthy of respect, and desiring
to introduce an imaginary liberty which can never exist and which
degenerates into licence and total revolution.   Pardon this long
letter.   I love you and my estates too tenderly not to think of
these things, especially now that I can only communicate with
you every fortnight.   I am glad it is July, the last month without
seeing you.   I greatly need that consolation, for my faculties are
beginning to fail.'

While Joseph was still on his travels Maria Theresa called the
Moravian offenders to heel with a sharp crack of her whip.
Meetings were forbidden, emigration vetoed, leaders arrested,
men ordered into the army or sent to forced labour, ringleaders
exiled, heretics under fifteen assigned to the priests for re-
conversion.   On learning of these draconic regulations after his
return to Vienna the horrified child of the *Aufklärung* let himself
go.   'My duty and my devotion to your service and your glory
compel me to say that the recent orders about the Protestants in
Moravia are so contrary to what has always been regarded as
the principles of our religion, good administration and even
common sense, that I feel sure you will apply a remedy directly
you see them.   Can one imagine anything more absurd?   To

convert these people by making them soldiers, sending them to the mines or to public works! That did not occur in the time of persecutions at the beginning of Lutheranism. I could not exaggerate its significance. I must declare very positively, and I will prove, that whoever suggested this rescript is the most unworthy of your servants and as such deserving of my contempt. I beg you in this important matter to consult others than the authors of such things, and to apply a prompt remedy in revoking the rescript. I must humbly declare that if such things are to occur during my co-regency, I must withdraw from affairs and thus announce to the whole world that I have nothing to do with it. That is demanded by my conscience, my duty and my reputation.'

The Empress replied in the same tone of injured innocence. His complaint was a great surprise. She had followed neither her head nor any Minister. It had all been dealt with by the Bohemian department of the Chancery and by the Council of State. 'I hope, when you know the details, you will change your views in your own interest. But I must confess how upset I am that at the least difference between us you repeat this odious and painful proposition about the Co-Regency. I do not think my actions and orders have compromised you. Your mind moves too quickly. Activity is admirable in a private citizen, but a ruler must take time to reflect and must follow the maxims and statutes of the country, only abandoning them for something better not only in his own eyes but in the opinion of all. We owe account to Him alone who placed us in our posts to govern His peoples according to His holy law, which we must cherish and sustain.'

The rebuke strengthened Joseph's desire to throw off the almost intolerable burden of responsibility without power. 'I felt sure this rescript could not be approved, much less ordered, by you, but I see I am wrong. There is nothing for me but to keep silence and humbly beg pardon if my words, written under this misconception, transgressed the limits of affection and respect. I should not think of using a pretext to obtain your consent to my wishes. Relief from my duties, or what I regard as such, is not a pretext, a straw fire, a grimace; it is my dearest, indeed my only, desire. You have issued an order which I consider unjust and harmful, and which will kindle a fresh and lasting flame. In the Council I have either to be continually opposing or forced silently to swallow in long draughts a slow and deadly poison. Since I am unfortunate enough to disagree with you I am no more use. In consequence you will permit me to withhold my opinions by pen or tongue, which would merely upset you and perhaps cause you to mistrust your own principles and advisers. Withdrawn from affairs and my repulsive task, it would be infinitely less difficult to deserve your favours. My rôle as a good son has always been easy, for I had only to follow my instincts; that of Co-Regent, which might be tolerable, I can only imagine. After twelve years of study I have still not learned the art and I never shall.' This time his mother's reply was brief. 'Your letter has not consoled me. It is cruel for us to love and taunt each other without doing any good. I hope you will not resist reason.' His reply was equally terse. 'The matter is so clear and my conviction so firm that I can expect nothing from the arguments of other people but a truce and silence on my part.'

There was indeed nothing to be done, for the Empress was no less determined to harry the Protestants than to refuse her son's petition to withdraw. Resignation without her consent was unthinkable since the spectacle of discord in high places would have damaged the interests of the State. Once again he confided his troubles to Leopold who shared his views on the issues at stake. 'The only important item in internal affairs is that of the Protestants in Moravia. Her Majesty had begun with gentle methods, changing the Ministers and the indiscreet missionaries, but recently she has resolved to force the pace. I have energetically opposed, but that has merely served to postpone the execution of a lot of penal laws directed against anyone who would not at once declare himself a Catholic and go to church and confession. I will send you the details when I have time, but I shall stand fast in such an important matter. If I have to yield I must let the whole world know that it is against my will.' The Pope described him as the best Catholic in the world and his orthodoxy was impeccable. Yet on two matters his convictions exposed him to the charge of anti-clericalism or at any rate in-difference. The first was the unchallengeable supremacy of the

State.   The second was the toleration of religious minorities, for they too could be good citizens.

Though he failed to secure the complete withdrawal of the intolerant decrees, Joseph's protests were not in vain, for when the conflict with his mother was at its height the cool-headed Chancellor came to his aid.   The arrest of delegates from Moravia who came to Vienna to beg the Emperor for liberty of conscience convinced Kaunitz that it was time for him to intervene.   The true faith, he argued, was a gift of God and should not be imposed by force.   Confronted by a combination of the heir and the Chancellor, the angry sovereign yielded, the persecutions ceased, and the heretics were allowed to worship in their own homes.   It was the fiercest encounter between mother and son that had ever occurred.   Joseph's sole consolation was that in a few years he would be undisputed master of the State.   The Co-Regency had been rendered tolerable only by mutual affection and a tacit division of authority.   In domestic politics the Empress remained supreme to the end; in foreign affairs the Emperor's power increased from year to year and long before her death it had become irresistible.   Yet in both spheres fundamental differences of temperament and policy were the cause of bitter grief.   Judged by the ever-increasing friction which it generated the well-meant experiment must be pronounced a failure.   Long afterwards the cold war between Francis Joseph and his nephew Francis Ferdinand confirmed the lesson that the division of responsibility between the ruler and the heir is a source of confusion and of weakness to the State.

III. *Poland and Paris*

THE principal motive for concluding the French alliance in 1756 had been the prospect of recovering Silesia.   Since the expectation was not fulfilled, it might have been plausibly argued not only that the Seven Years War had been fought in vain but that the partnership itself was a mistake.   Yet no one in Vienna dreamed of its cancellation, which would have humiliated France, left Austria without even a nominal friend, and encouraged

Russia and Prussia to fresh aggression. But to what purpose could it be turned in the days to come? Joseph had been too young to take a hand in its creation, and he was always far less Francophil than his mother and the Chancellor; yet he agreed with them that its potential value was not entirely exhausted and that a comrade in the West might perhaps some day aid Austria's ambitions in the East. The sprawling and ill-governed territories of her Polish and Turkish neighbours were a tempting bait, and Kaunitz, the ingenious author of the *renversement des alliances*, was the acknowledged master of the tricks of the diplomatic game. If Silesia was indeed irrecoverable, as seemed to be the case, it was plain common sense to seek compensation elsewhere.

That any far-reaching plans might involve the risk of war was equally clear to the three directors of Austria's fortunes, but here their agreement came to an end. 'Le bon Dieu aura à la fin pitié de nous et écrasera ce monstre,' the Empress exclaimed in 1758 at the height of the Seven Years War; but 'le bon Dieu' had declined to intervene. Now she had had her fill of bloodshed and longed to end her days in peace: all thought of revenge was laid aside for ever in 1763. Joseph and Kaunitz, on the other hand, held that there was no need to remain indefinitely in the rôle of passive spectators, since the European situation was as changeable as the weather. Here was the germ of another acute antagonism between the Co-Regents when the Hapsburg realm began to recover from the ravages of war. In domestic affairs, as we have seen, there was an unceasing struggle between the clericalism of the seventeenth century and the rationalism of the eighteenth. In foreign affairs there was a no less stubborn conflict between the instinct of adventure and the slogan of safety first. Had her dominions been attacked the stout-hearted woman would have been as resolute in their defence as in 1740, but in the absence of such an improbable event she had no intention of drawing the sword again. The psychological cleavage which emerged during the Co-Regency in practical form in regard to Poland and Bavaria was to cause the ageing ruler poignant grief, not only because she had a spotless reputation to lose but because she discovered to her horror that her will was no longer supreme in every sphere.

When Joseph succeeded his father as Emperor and became Co-Regent in 1765 Frederick the Great was the most celebrated sovereign in the world. He realised that the Empress would cause him no more trouble, but the reforming zeal of the young Emperor in the military sphere gave warning of storms ahead: an interview, he felt, could do no harm and might conceivably do good. Joseph needed no pressing, and a projected tour of the battlefields of Bohemia and Saxony in 1766 offered an opportunity. Maria Theresa, who detested 'the wicked man' not only as the robber of Silesia but as a *libre penseur*, was deeply distressed at the idea. 'What shall I do?' she wrote to Kaunitz. 'Shall I write to my son or not? It would grieve me deeply if this meeting, which the Emperor desires, were to take place. I cannot reconcile myself to it.' The Chancellor, though for other reasons, was inclined to agree. People, he calculated, would put it down to Joseph's admiration for the King, and this would diminish his dignity: all Europe would wonder and speculate. When, however, the Austrian Minister in Berlin was officially informed that the King greatly desired a meeting, Kaunitz changed his mind and argued that its benefits might perhaps after all outweigh its disadvantages; since Frederick presumably disliked his dependence on St. Petersburg, some benefit might perhaps be obtainable for Austria. He proceeded to draft instructions for the expected interview, but at this point the Emperor, resenting the idea of leading-strings, abandoned the project, to the delight of his mother. 'The meeting is not taking place,' she wrote to a friend, 'because Providence forbade it. *L'homme propose, Dieu dispose.*'

Two years later, in 1768, the wind changed in Vienna. Frederick had swallowed the disappointment of 1766 and Joseph's eagerness to meet the superman had revived. This time the initiative came from Austria with the assent of the Empress, and was warmly welcomed at Berlin, for glittering prizes were now at stake. In December 1768 the ingenious Kaunitz proposed to the Empress and Joseph an alliance of Austria, Prussia and Turkey, with the object of securing Courland and Polish Prussia for Frederick, who, it was hoped, might then be willing to return Silesia. When the Emperor commented that the King would decline such a bargain the project was dropped; but some form of temporary co-operation with Berlin remained in the Chancellor's programme, and Joseph felt no moral scruples about a profitable deal with 'the wicked man'. The first task was to discover his intentions, and for this purpose he was the best instrument. Instructions were drawn up by Kaunitz, and sanctioned by the Empress on the assurance that the visit was to be purely exploratory.

For each of the rulers of Eastern Europe it was an axiom that neither of the others should become strong enough to upset the balance of power: if one were to secure new territory the others would claim compensation. The Tsarina hoped to keep the whole of Poland in her grasp through a subservient ruler or, if it were deprived of independence, to secure the largest slice of the cake for herself. Frederick's territorial desires were limited to the acquisition of West Prussia, which for over two centuries had separated East Prussia from the core of his dominions. If Austria were to have a share, it could only be in the south. But at this point, when partition was in the air, a sharp disagreement emerged between mother and son. While Joseph, supported by Kaunitz, had no inhibitions in his longing for territorial aggrandisement, and indeed would have deemed it treason to the State to neglect favourable opportunities, the pious Empress detested the notion of pillaging her defenceless Catholic neighbour. That she had to give way was her bitterest experience during the earlier phase of the Co-Regency. Hitherto her son had been forced to witness much that he disapproved in home affairs. Now it was her turn to yield, for in foreign affairs the heir, backed by the Chancellor, was irresistible. It was the first time that he really asserted himself and that the Co-Regency became something more than a phrase.

'I am grateful to you for proposing to the Prussian Minister that I should visit Neisse,' wrote Joseph from Como during his Italian tour on June 21, 1769. 'It will certainly be extremely interesting for me to see this King and his troops. It will be much more worthwhile than the interview with the Pope of which you speak.' Needless to say he was supplied with instructions by Kaunitz, who took an artist's delight in the composition of lengthy memoranda. After a brief halt in Vienna he set out for the three days' rendezvous at the old fortress

town in Silesia, whence he despatched full and vivid bulletins.
'The King has overwhelmed us with friendly courtesy,' he reported on August 29. 'He is a genius and a marvellous talker,
but one senses the rogue in every sentence. I believe he desires
peace, not from goodness of heart, but because he sees he could
not wage war with advantage. I asked him all sorts of questions.
I enclose a journal of the chief matters, but to tell the whole story
would be impossible since we talk for at least sixteen hours a day.
His fear of Russian power, which he wishes us to share, colours
everything. In regard to religion he has been very discreet.
He has spoken with all respect of Your Majesty and with high
esteem of Prince Kaunitz: you can guess if I contradicted him.
His health is still very good. He is unlike any of the portraits
you have seen. The servility of his brother (Prince Henry) and
his nephew (the heir) is beyond belief; at the dinner-table they
do not say a word. I enclose the letter he wrote me. You will
see the reasons which made me accept the change he so desires. I
gave him a scrap of paper containing the important words, and he
gave me the enclosed. I should have liked to retrieve my little
note, but to show my confidence I left it in his hands. He cannot
make mischief with it, and I did not wish him to think me capable
of such a thought. My reply was written in haste during the
night. I confess I was not sure whether I was more pleased to
arrive or to depart.'

The exchange of letters fulfilled the desire of the host.
'After the inestimable happiness of receiving Your Imperial
Majesty nothing could have been more precious than the letter
you have been good enough to write me. I find in it the most
certain proof of your friendship and above all, what I most
desire, the perfect reconciliation between two houses unhappily
so long estranged. Yes, Sire, I repeat in writing that it is impossible for my heart to be the enemy of a great man. Heaven
grant that this first step may lead to others which will unite us
still more closely. I promise, by the faith of a King and on the
word of a man of honour, that even if war is renewed between
England and the Bourbon houses, I will faithfully preserve the
peace happily restored between us; also, if some other unpredictable conflict breaks out, that I will observe the most scrupulous
neutrality for your present possessions, as you will do for mine.'

The Emperor's letter, to which that of Frederick was supposed to be a reply, was in reality written after its receipt, and echoed its substance, though with greater reserve. 'Now that we are so sincerely reconciled, I see nothing which could reasonably prevent the establishment and maintenance of as much confidence and friendship as hitherto there was mistrust. These odious sentiments, I hope, will now disappear for ever.' Joseph proceeded to repeat the formula of neutrality in the King's letter. Both parties realised that a reciprocal promise of non-aggression was as far as they could go, for neither cared to renounce explosive ambitions elsewhere.

The accompanying diary filled in the outlines. On the day of arrival, at Joseph's suggestion, the King had spoken very modestly of the battles of the Seven Years War. Both affirmed their peaceful intentions, though the old warrior frankly confessed that as a young man he had been ambitious and had acted wrongly. Those times were over, as was proved by his refusal of Russia's suggestion that he should invade Saxony on the suspicion that the Elector was intriguing in Poland against King Stanislas. What should he say to Russia about their meeting? Might he express his wish for a prompt peace in Poland and mention Joseph's praise of the Tsarina? Neutrality in all future wars would be difficult to guarantee, for he was the ally of Russia; he could promise it in respect of any war in Germany, but he could not answer for what Poland, Sweden, or Russia might do. Joseph replied that he had no wish to embarrass him and that the letter containing the promise could be dropped. Again and again the host reverted to the theme of Russia: to arrest her advance all Europe would have to raise its shield because she would strike out in all directions. He expected an attack on Sweden, and she was determined to have Azov. In regard to Poland, so long as her honour was saved, Catherine would not be too rigid in her demands. The more the King tried to alarm Joseph about the Russians, the more reserved his visitor became. In the event of a general conflagration, he observed, Prussia would be in the front line and Austria could sleep quietly: fearing no intervention in the south, he could do what he liked with the Russians. This Frederick denied, adding that he feared them: the Russian alliance had been a necessity, but it was extremely uncomfortable and the Prussian subsidy in lieu of supplying troops was burdensome. The monarchs parted with friendly words but with distrust in their hearts. 'The King was almost too polite, and full of friendly assurances,' reported the Emperor, 'but one feels that the old mistrust lingers in his soul and even more in his character. It has been most interesting to see him once, but God preserve me from a second meeting. He threatens to return the visit at Kolin.'

An undated letter to his mother summarised his impressions of the three eventful days at Neisse after taking time to digest them. On several occasions the King appeared to be speaking with complete sincerity, and in dealing with the past he was absolutely frank; on military matters his talk was enchanting. Joseph's task, as he saw it, was to win his confidence, to remove any suspicion of a desire for aggrandisement at Prussia's expense, to exhibit Austria's desire for peace and her complete indifference to his Russian ties. The King was eager for the neutrality of the two states, for instance in a war between England and the House of Bourbon. The Emperor proposed an exchange of letters, and agreed to his host's suggestions on its terms. The core of the declaration was the promise not to attack each other in any unpredictable emergency. For the time Austria and Prussia needed one another, firstly in order to clip the wings of the Russian eagle, secondly to snatch the prizes which neither was strong enough to secure alone.

The wound inflicted in 1740 had been plastered over at Neisse, not healed. While Joseph's suspicions of his host's good faith were unabated, Frederick guessed that Silesia was unforgotten. 'I feel he is devoured by ambition,' he reported to his Foreign Minister, 'and is brooding over some great plan. He is temporarily held in leash by his mother but is fretting to throw off the yoke; when his arms are free he will start off with a big *coup*. Beyond doubt there will be a flare-up when he is in control.' To his Minister in Vienna Frederick used the striking phrase: 'Il est tout feu.' On the other hand the Seven Years War was too recent and too costly an experience for either side to envisage fresh conflicts for the moment. While reserving the future they might profitably co-operate in the spoliation of a defenceless neighbour. A return visit was paid in the following year when

the Emperor received the King at Neustadt, in Bohemia. But
on this occasion it was Kaunitz who expounded the policy of
Vienna, and no letters between mother and son are preserved.[1]

Though the amputation of Poland was discussed neither at
Neisse nor at Neustadt, the occupation of the mainly German-
speaking County of Zips in Galicia by Austrian troops with the
assent of King Stanislas shortly after the former meeting gave
the signal for the First Partition three years later. It had once
belonged to Hungary and had been mortgaged to Poland in the
fifteenth century; but Joseph now announced that the mortgage
was to be paid off, and argued that a mortgage was not a transfer
of sovereignty. When, however, neighbouring districts not
covered by such shadowy claims were occupied at the close of
1770, the Poles had a right to object. Though Maria Theresa
and the Chancellor recognised the justice of the complaints, they
were overruled by the ardent Emperor, who vetoed an inquiry
into the legal aspects. When the news reached St. Petersburg,
Catherine exclaimed to Prince Henry of Prussia, then on a visit
to Russia, that if Austria helped herself, Prussia could follow
suit. Frederick had already flown a kite at St. Petersburg and
was biding his time. The fate of Poland was sealed, and it only
remained to agree on the respective shares of her greedy
neighbours.

While the Emperor and Kaunitz were ready to take an active
part in the game of grab, the Empress was torn between her
scruples and the material interests of her realm. 'In all my
painful career,' she wrote in January 1771, 'I have never faced a
harder decision. I agree with the Emperor about not going to
war with the Russians. I cannot put everything to the hazard
in present circumstances, which I consider even worse than does
the Emperor, for he forgets the plague, the maladies, and the
immense cost of transport in the devastated provinces. But my
chief reason is that the Turks are the aggressors, that the Russians
have always shown me every consideration, that they are
Christians, that they are the victims of an unjust war. All these
and many other reasons determine me not to march against

---

[1] The full report of Kaunitz to the Empress on the Neustadt meeting was
published by Adolf Beer, 'Die Zusammenkünfte Josephs II und Friedrichs II
zu Neisse und Neustadt,' in *Archiv für österreichische Geschichte*, vol. 46, 383–527.

Russia. So there must be no menaces. But equally I could never join the Russians in the expulsion and destruction of the Turks. These two points being settled, we must inquire what to do.' She proceeded to criticise, not only certain points in a lost memorandum of her son, but the spirit of the document itself. 'My maxim, which I owe to Prince Kaunitz, is honesty and candour; no double-dealing.' She could only allot a limited sum. 'This decision will be called feeble and timid. I admit it, but I lack the strength of mind to decide on a war which I think unjust and therefore opposed to my conscience. At my age one no longer thinks calmly; after the terrible wars I have had to wage I know the dangers of plague and famine, particularly in this country.'

Joseph was unmoved. His plan, he declared, would be ruined by her conditions. 'The King of Prussia must be subjected to embarrassment and his credit with the Porte destroyed; that alone can make him act and play our game. The regiments must come from the Low Countries to increase our forces and to arouse his just suspicions. In the event of a total destruction of Poland we must get a good morsel, and we must succour the Porte in case of real need. The King of Prussia, if he wished to take action, must know that we should attack him. Thus a pronounced determination for peace would be even worse than war. I beg you either to do everything and leave to me the execution of my project, which cannot be watered down without destroying it, or to do nothing at all. Forgive the liberty I am taking, but I should fail in my duty were I not to speak with the utmost energy when it concerns you, dear Mother, and the country.'

A few days later, on January 24, 1771, Joseph confided his troubles to Leopold. 'We are wallowing in uncertainty. Her Majesty will not make up her mind. I wrote a long Memorandum but am not sending it as the hour has not struck. Kaunitz has drafted a decisive letter for me to send to the King of Prussia. He thinks we should say that, if he promises to keep quiet, we will make war alone against the Russians in Moldavia. I, on the other hand, have a thousand reasons for thinking that we ought never to fight Russia alone, but that we must be ready to take advantage, promptly and without risks, of any moments of Russian weakness, or at any rate to get our quota, and, if we cannot prevent their aggrandisement, to preserve the equilibrium by corresponding gains. Those are our views. The Empress invents a third and is convinced, even after other conquests by Russia, that war against them is unjust and violates her conscience, since they are Christians and the Porte is Turk. I leave you to judge the validity of this argument, but time is being lost. I have arranged about internal measures, but every day's delay is of the greatest importance, and we shall lose so much time that we shall ultimately have to leave the Russians a free hand. You can imagine how my zeal for the well-being of the state is tried. I cannot abandon my system; I feel it is a good one, either involving the King of Prussia in the game or for ever ruining his credit with the Porte. If war is decided I will wage it, but I shall proclaim in writing all the unhappy consequences I foresee. If it is decided to do nothing, to leave everything to chance, to exhibit such weakness, I shall have to make a row and thus inform the public that it is not my doing. Only yesterday we received a report, ordered last September, on the lack of grain in Bohemia. It is so badly presented that one cannot make it out except that there is a lack of almost everything. We shall strive to put things straight, but trying to get something done in our country is like drinking the sea.'

The Polish problem was complicated by the Turkish factor. The Ottoman Empire, which had ranked among the Great Powers ever since the conquest of Constantinople, had passed its zenith, and the chancelleries were considering how to fill the vacuum in South-Eastern Europe left by the receding tide. Since the victories of Prince Eugene the Hapsburgs rightly regarded the southward thrust of Russia as a far graver danger, and in July 1771 a defensive treaty with Turkey, then at war with Russia, was signed. Kaunitz, indeed, was prepared to join her in the field if Frederick promised neutrality in the event of an Austro-Russian clash. This plan proved impracticable, for the King was negotiating with the Tsarina for a partition of Poland. The Turkish flirtation was soon over, and the conclusion was reached by Kaunitz and Joseph that more was likely to be obtained from co-operation with Russia than from attempting to thwart her ambitions on her southern border. These intricate manœuvres were detested by the Empress, who had no desire to despoil Turks, Poles, or anyone else. The wisdom of the new orientation was to be justified in the eyes of its authors by the acquisition of Galicia from Poland in 1772 and of Bukovina from Turkey in 1777.

The year 1771 passed in wearisome negotiations between Berlin and St. Petersburg, but at the opening of 1772 the sluggish wheels of diplomacy began to revolve more rapidly. When Frederick at last dropped his demand for Danzig, which Catherine refused to concede, the chief obstacle to agreement was removed. But what would Austria do? Though neither Prussia nor Russia had any cause for tenderness towards her, she was too powerful to be ignored. Everyone knew that there were two wills and two voices in Vienna: which would now prevail? On January 25 the Empress once again reminded her son that her reputation was dearer to her than any acquisition of territory. Though Russia and Prussia were on the point of agreement as to their share of the Polish booty, she still desired to take no part. 'I am too obsessed by our critical situation not to set it forth once again in all its clarity and to seek the least evil remedy. We must above all reach peace on both sides as quick as possible; prolonging the conflict makes our situation ever worse. We cannot undo our errors since November 1770, when troops were summoned from Italy and the Low Countries. The unhappy treaty with the Turks, the threatening tone to Russia, our mysterious conduct towards both our allies and our foes— all this comes from trying to use the Russo-Turkish war as a lever to extend our frontiers and secure advantages of which we never thought before the war. The Prussian model was followed while trying to retain the appearance of honesty. It may be that I am mistaken and that the events are more favourable than I think. But even if they won for us Wallachia or Belgrade itself, I should regard them as too dearly purchased at the expense of the honour and glory of the Monarchy, of good faith, of our religion. During my unhappy reign we have at least tried to practise good faith, moderation, fidelity to our engagements. That earned us the confidence, I might even say the admiration, of Europe, the respect and veneration of our foes; for the last year all that is gone. I can hardly bear it, and nothing has pained

me more than the loss of our good name.   Unfortunately I must
confess that we deserve it.   That is why I wish it to be remedied
by rejecting as evil and ruinous the whole principle of profiting
by these troubles, and why I wish for a way to escape as soon as
possible from this unhappy situation, the least bad, without
thinking of acquisitions, but to restore our credit and good
faith, and, so far as possible, the political balance.'

It was too late.   The signing of an agreement between Russia
and Prussia in St. Petersburg on February 2, 1772, made it
imperative for Austria to obtain compensation if the balance of
power was to be maintained.   When Kaunitz explained that there
was nothing to be done but to specify what Polish territory was
desired, the Empress reluctantly concurred.   'I cannot look on
quietly at the aggrandisement of these two Powers,' she wrote
on his letter, 'but still less do I wish to join them.'   At last he
was authorised to state the demands of Vienna, and on August
21 the three Powers signed the final treaty in St. Petersburg.
'Elle pleure mais elle prend,' commented Frederick in a cruel
phrase.   'She carved territory from Poland with one hand,'
sneered the French Ambassador at Vienna, 'and used her handker-
chief with the other.'   She had been overborne by her son and
the Chancellor who acted on the time-honoured principle that
no opportunity of enlarging one's territories should be lost.
No other ruler of the eighteenth century would have held out
so long.   Hers were at least honest tears when Galicia, with its
three million inhabitants and its precious salt mines, were added
to the Hapsburg realm.   To her son Ferdinand, who ruled in
Lombardy, she confided, in September 1772, that this unhappy
partition had robbed her of at least ten years of life.   'How often
did I strive to dissociate myself from an action which sullies
the whole of my reign!   God grant that I shall not be held
responsible for it in another world.   It weighs on my heart,
tortures my brain, and embitters my days, which are sad enough
in any case.'

A year after the Partition Treaty was signed Joseph decided
to visit Austria's latest acquisition.   'However disagreeable it
will be to leave you and what are called the amenities of life,' he
wrote to his mother in June 1773, 'I cannot help wishing to see
this Galicia.   I believe I can render real service to you and the

state by my journey of inspection. Perhaps we may be missing
certain advantages which others now enjoy. So I should like to
see what can be done.' That the nerves of the Empress were
still frayed is clear from her emotional reply.

'My peace of mind and good spirits did not last long. The
same evening I wrote playfully to you I received the letter which
has greatly upset me. I cannot regard this terrible journey as
you do, nor any of those made at the cost of so much fatigue,
for which you sacrifice your health and strength, while robbing
me of the few moments which remain to me and filling me with
bitterness. Help me instead to put in order the provinces you
have already visited and which are under our eyes. If that is
accomplished, Transylvania and Poland will follow; but in
dealing with these there is not the same great object to be obtained.
Forgive me, it is for me to tell you the truth. Even with all your
sagacity and industry it is impossible in these journeys of two or
three months to see everything and draw conclusions, particularly
in Poland, where no one can tell you anything, least of all the
Poles themselves. And what chaos will you find! Neither the
Tsarina nor the King of Prussia has been there so far. You
saw in the winter that he was not inclined to this journey, and
you have been cruel enough to ask my consent. You count only
on my indulgence which is always on your side against my own
heart: I realise that you wish for it. Being unable to decide
against my conviction I have consulted Kaunitz. Here is his
reply, in consequence of which I have sent the papers. May God
accept the sacrifice I make to Him, not to you, to Him alone, that
He may bless your intentions and enterprise. As usual, you will
hear neither complaints nor murmurs from me. I keep it all to
myself. Despite the rumours of the past fortnight that this
journey would take place I alone was without anxiety. Now it
is authorised I will say nothing more, but that is not the end of
my troubles. Forgive this outburst. I am not in the least
angry, but I am sad and feel I must warn you for your future.'
'His journey will take at lest ten years off my life,' she wrote to
her Parma daughter-in-law. 'He overtires himself; in a few
years he will be old and broken. It is suicidal.'

The visit to Galicia was carried out according to plan, and the
traveller reported from Lemberg that there was much to be done.

'The inhabitants showed good will, but the unfortunate peasant possessed nothing except the shape of a man. The minor noble was also poor, but trusted to our justice for protection against his grandee oppressors. Doubtless the latter were discontented but they put a good face on it. I try to be equally polite to everyone.' Joseph had fulfilled his dream of enlarging the Hapsburg realm without firing a shot, and he no more regretted his share in the pillage of Poland than the cynical robber of Silesia or the greedy Tsarina herself.

Despite his substantial success in the acquisition of Galicia, Joseph surveyed the political and military situation of the Monarchy without much satisfaction. A Memorandum to the Empress in 1774 on army reorganisation revealed the impatient reformer in his usual pessimistic mood.[1] Had the Monarchy gained or lost in strength and solidarity since the Seven Years War? The latter, he feared, was the case. Poor harvests, a superfluity of officials, and crazy proposals had impoverished the State. The frontiers had been extended but not secured, the fortresses were neglected or incomplete. The far-flung Hapsburg territories rendered them a tempting bait to aggressors. Their enemies, on the other hand, had increased in strength. Prussia had made good use of her annexations. Russia had gained to an unprecedented degree in pride and prestige, in resources and power, and she regarded her alliance with Prussia as the corner-stone of her policy. The Turks, with their wretched constitution, were more likely to follow Russia, of whom they were most afraid. France had so grievously declined in power and prestige that for some years she had played a melancholy part in Europe. Even if the situation were to improve under the new King, she was certain to shirk all positive implementation of the alliance. What then could Austria do? Either she must show a soft front to the world in order to preserve her scattered territories, or she would have to make fresh associations in which she would be subject to the convenience of two other Powers. Such an arrangement could not endure. Consequently, unless she possessed an army which, though divided up, could hold its own against Prussia, Russia, Turkey, France, Spain, Sardinia, and the whole Empire, all internal measures would be of no avail.

[1] Benedikt, *Joseph II*, 253–263.

The King of Prussia had recently increased his army. Austria must follow suit, the expense being met by internal economies and the exploitation of the newly acquired province of Galicia.

Could anything else be done to strengthen the Monarchy? Could the ties with France, for instance, be drawn a little closer? The Emperor had talked of a visit to Paris as long ago as the leave-taking of Marie Antoinette, but the first documentary reference occurs in a letter of Maria Theresa to Mercy in the autumn of 1773. He had spoken to Rohan, the French Ambassador, and hoped to travel after Easter, 1774: he was full of it and Mercy would doubtless hear direct. 'You will of course say if you think it undesirable, but in that case you will have to give your reasons.' The expected letter, dated September 30, 1773, explained his objects: to see the Dauphine, to meet the King, to study the resources, administration and armaments of France. He had no wish to share in the frivolities and amusements which drew people to Paris: no meetings of societies, no dinners, no suppers, no fêtes! The visit would be very short, very simple, and in the strictest incognito. Mercy approved the project, not only for political reasons, but in the interests of the Dauphine herself.

The Empress, on the other hand, was full of apprehension. 'Except in regard to my daughter,' she wrote on January 3, 1774, 'I greatly dislike this journey and I anticipate no advantage from it. Their contempt will grow when they see the levity, the absurdity, and the intrigues of that nation.' The four selected members of her son's suite, she added, were all enemies of France. He hoped to leave in Easter week and to be back in July. He even thought of returning *via* Switzerland to see Voltaire, Haller, 'et tous ces extravagants'. It hurt her, she confessed: there was too much vanity about the whole thing. While Joseph admired the celebrities of the *Aufklärung*, his pious mother detested the sound of their names. The Ambassador soothingly replied that he would doubtless begin with a feeling of pitying contempt for some of the persons who were governing France, but he would urge him to suspend judgment. 'Gifted as he is with so much intelligence and knowledge, I feel sure I can convince him that, despite all its sufferings, this nation possesses great and fine qualities as well as astonishing resources. I predict with confidence that the journey will give satisfaction to Your Majesty in regard both to the Dauphine and to politics. I will only add that he will be received by the Parisians with extraordinary marks of respect and enthusiasm.' The visit to Voltaire in Switzerland, he believed, would not materialise. She hoped with all her heart, rejoined the Empress, that the Emperor would listen to him, for he was surrounded by Francophobes.

When everything seemed settled Joseph suddenly decided to postpone his departure for a fortnight, and on April 5 he begged his mother to decide whether he should go at all. She had not been consulted about the project, was the reply, and she could not now decide. Generally speaking she was not in favour of these journeys which took him away from Vienna, but she felt that to abandon so widely known a project would cause a sensa-tion. Just for that reason, commented Joseph, he would not go, so that the public should not make these premature decisions. The French Ambassador in Vienna, added the Empress, would doubtless return to the charge. The real reason of her son's change of plan, she guessed, was the King of Prussia, who seemed unable to believe that he could go to France without having other projects such as the Low Countries in view. The Emperor wrote to Mercy that at the moment he could not leave Vienna; would the late autumn be a suitable time? The Ambassador replied that the announcement of the coming visit had made a great impression; the King and still more the Dauphine and the public were eagerly looking forward to it. The autumn would do very well, for the Court would be at Fontainebleau where he could be quieter than at Versailles. Assuming that he had decided to visit France, the sooner the better in order to avoid disappointment.

Shortly after this exchange Louis XV died, and there was no more talk of a visit in 1774. 'I am anxious about my sister,' wrote Joseph to his brother Leopold; 'she will have a difficult part to play. If only she does not get mixed up in the affairs and intrigues of the Court!' A week later he commented on the news that the du Barry had been sent to a convent and Maurepas called to the helm. 'I hope our sister will not meddle in Court intrigues: that would be her undoing. I have given her advice, and I do not like this punishment of the du Barry. What is the good? She should be left at liberty and in oblivion.' It would not be easy for the Queen to stand aloof, he added; that would need a constancy and system of which so young a person was hardly capable. Despite these anxieties he wrote a week later to say that she was doing splendidly and he thought it might last.

In January 1775 the Empress learned that her son had written a German letter to his sister and had charged his youngest brother Maximilian on his approaching visit to talk German with her. She had, however, so far forgotten her mother tongue that she asked Mercy to translate it. The Emperor's letter, reported the Ambassador, was witty but rather severe, though it closed with some very kind words. After reading it the Queen remarked: 'We might quarrel about this, but that I will never do. I shall send a jocular reply.' A further letter from her brother, she reported to her mother in March, had given her great pleasure, and she now definitely expected a visit. She had replied accepting his conditions so far as it depended on her, and for the rest he would find that he would be almost entirely his own master. The Emperor, reported Maria Theresa to Mercy, was very pleased with the Queen's last letter, and was more and more inclined to pay his respects in the spring of 1776. In May she reported that the correspondence with his sister was now once more on terms of confidence and affection.

The welcome *entente* was interrupted when the Queen's two letters to Rosenberg, describing her reception of Choiseul during the coronation ceremonies at Rheims, came into the hands of her mother and brother, who made no attempt to conceal their indignation.[1] 'How could you wish me to come and see you in present circumstances?' wrote Joseph. 'You appear to be meddling with an infinity of things which do not concern you, which you do not understand, and in regard to which the cabals who flatter you are getting you into hot water. In diminishing the friendship and esteem of the King you are forfeiting the good opinion of the public and all the consideration which you have built up astonishingly well. What are you doing, my dear sister, in dismissing Ministers (Turgot), sending one to his country estates (d'Aiguillon), getting a Ministry for someone,

[1] See pp.158–160.

winning a lawsuit for another (Guines), creating a new and expensive post in your Household (Lamballe), and using language unseemly in your position ("le pauvre homme")? Have you ever asked yourself by what right you meddle with the government? What studies have you made that you imagine your advice or opinion is any value, especially in matters which need considerable knowledge? You, an amiable young person who thinks merely of frivolity and your amusements all day; who neither hears nor reads sense for a quarter of an hour in a month; who never reflects or meditates, nor thinks of the consequences of your words and deeds. The impression of the moment is your sole guide. Could anyone frame anything more imprudent, unreasonable and improper than you wrote to Count Rosenberg about your arrangements for a conversation at Rheims with the Duc de Choiseul? If ever such a letter went astray, if ever, as I fear, such phrases escape your lips among your intimates, I can only predict misfortunes. I confess it causes me the deepest grief. They are your enemies who urge you to these steps. Believe me, believe the voice of a friend who you know loves you. No one can tell you the truth like me. Drop all these performances, leave politics alone, remove or resist those who would drag you into them. Strive to deserve the friendship and the confidence of the King; that is your only duty to the state. Study his tastes, spend time with him. Never speak to Ministers about affairs. When you are pressed for something merely report to the King without importuning him and then convey his decision. For the rest, read, occupy yourself, enrich your mind, cultivate talents and find resources in yourself for later years or if, as is inevitable, you lose your popularity. That is the rôle of every woman in her own home.' This tactless lecture was too much even for the Empress and was never despatched. The writer was persuaded to send a milder version which has not survived.

In October 1776 the Empress informed Mercy that her son was planning his journey for January 1777: she hoped rather than expected that all would go well. A month later she reported that he was resolved on the visit. 'I am not mixing myself up in it. I hope it will be a success, but only the event will reassure me. I greatly fear he will overdo his reproaches to my daughter. He likes to please and to shine; probably he will not be insensible to her display of friendship and her charm.' At this point in the dictated letter she added in her own hand: 'Imagine my dis-agreeable situation; here is an example. The last four days the Emperor seems—or pretends to seem—to find great difficulties about the journey. He wishes to leave the decision to me, but, unhappily familiar as I am with such turns, I am not responding. Tell me if he writes to you about it. I confess I should be easier if he does not.'

'My visit to France, so often planned, is now likely to come off,' wrote Joseph to Leopold on October 29, 1776. 'I cannot say anything definite, and any trifling circumstance could prevent it; if I go it will be in the winter. I should like to spend the last week of the carnival at Paris and then visit the provinces.' On November 24 he again submitted the decision to his mother. 'It would be useless to detail the reasons why I hope it might be useful. I should study the Court and the country. It ought to be very interesting to make the acquaintance of the King and the leading men, and to see the government machine at work. I will not speak of my desire to see my sister and of the importance of judging of her position and of the advice my friendship may suggest. I shall try to appear as a reflective and rather reserved person, to talk as little as possible, to listen much, to be very polite, only desiring to see my sister and satisfy my curiosity about the interesting things there. I believe that in the eyes of sensible people a very natural and simple conduct, with complete incognito, will do no harm to my reputation. These are the principles which I submit very humbly to the approbation of Your Majesty. I shall try to turn my absence to good account. I am certainly not out for pleasure or aimless amusement. On political matters I shall talk as little as possible, as I am acquainted with your system.'

A letter to Mercy at the close of 1776 suggested that at last he had made up his mind. He would live in the Embassy, not at Versailles, the Trianon, or any other place belonging to the Court; when away from the Embassy he wished to pay for his quarters. 'I would rather return every night to Paris than drop my incognito. Kindly engage two rooms in the town at Versailles.' Mercy sent the Empress a copy of this letter and of his reply. Despite all precautions, he reported, the Emperor would find it difficult to avoid demonstrations, but that would not matter if his visit were of advantage to his sister. 'I see more clearly than ever that, despite her genuine pleasure in seeing him again, she feels great embarrassment about his impressions of the Court and her way of life.'

1777 opened with a brief letter of advice from Maria Theresa to her daughter. 'In a month you will see the Emperor, an interesting occasion for you. You know his heart and his sagacity. On the first you can count; he will not fail you, for he is really anxious to see you. You can learn much from him. I hope you will talk to him with the confidence and tenderness which he deserves, and which should permanently strengthen the ties not only of our Houses but the most tender friendship between the sovereigns—the only means of securing the happiness of our states and families. I hope that he will get on with the King and that friendship and confidence will prevail when the first stiffness wears off. Think of your Maman when you are together.' To Mercy she wrote by the same courier authorising him to speak freely to the Emperor about the Queen's undesirable *entourage*, but she was in no sanguine mood. 'I am not expecting good results from the journey. Unless I am mistaken either my daughter will win the Emperor by her charms or he will offend her by playing the schoolmaster. The first seems more probable, but in neither case can one hope for a miracle.' The Queen replied on January 16 that she was longing to see him, and only regretted that he would not be her guest. 'It will cause surprise, but I bow to his wishes. I count on his friendship and he can reckon on mine. I feel sure his journey will do good in every way. I know his discretion and I will talk frankly. After the first moment of embarrassment the King will be glad to see him and converse with him; only good can result both for public affairs and for myself.'

Once again the journey was postponed, ostensibly on account of the snow, but really owing to anxiety about Prussian plans in Bohemia. Louis XVI now wrote to the Emperor expressing his regret at the delay, his pleasure at the forthcoming visit, and his assurance that 'Count Falkenstein' would be his own master in France. That the Empress learned of this letter from Mercy and not from her son was a real grief. 'You can see how little consideration he has for me in a matter which would have given me pleasure.' Even as late as the middle of February she was hoping that the visit would fall through. In March, Mercy reported that the Queen was becoming more and more embarrassed; he was doing his best to restore the confidence in her brother which alone could render the visit of use. In April he described a distressing talk of two hours which revealed the fear and suspicions generated by mischief-makers. 'Accustomed to open her heart to me, she told me things so revolting that I let myself go and launched into one of my most terrible attacks against the favourites, male and female, depicting them one after the other without sparing a single detail. She was deeply moved and closed the audience with the words: "I see how attached you are; you have always given me proofs and I fully recognise it."'

The Emperor's attitude to his sister, added the Ambassador, would be a very delicate matter, all the more since, despite his representations, she might try to mislead him on several topics. If, however, he would listen, he would be informed on all the most essential points, such as her passion for gambling, the influence of the favourites of both sexes, and the abuse of her favour. 'I shall devote particular attention to the most important item of all—the little pains she takes to get closer to the King, to seek and increase the opportunities of his company and of making the marriage a reality. Negligence in regard to the latter would be fatal. I know that in this perverse Court whirlpool there are wretches who plot to make the King a libertine; indeed they have dared to mention to him an actress of the Comédie Française. These horrible tentatives have produced no effect and I am morally certain they never will, but the Queen must be on her guard. I have told her everything and I shall tell the Emperor too.'

Joseph reached Paris on April 28, 1777, and Mercy's first letter (May 7) was in cheerful vein. 'Though I counted on good results, what I have seen surpasses my expectations. He has so perfectly understood how to make an impression on his sister that his suggestions cannot fail to take root. The best is that she is reassured and confident. He attacks her prejudices tactfully, explains his arguments, draws parallels, and thus dominates her mind. Though it is too early to judge of his influence on the King, his conversation and good example are sure to implant ideas which will bear fruit in due season. In particular the Queen is now more convinced than ever of the necessity of getting closer to the King, to win his affection and confidence, to be with him as much as possible, to feel that this will in the long run determine her credit.'

The main purpose of the visit, in regard to which not a single letter between mother and son is preserved, was to fortify the alliance by confidential advice to the royal pair. The King had to be persuaded to face an operation which would enable him to secure the succession, the Queen to be convinced that her frivolities were not only destroying her popularity but damaging the prestige of the throne. In the first aim he succeeded, and in the following year the first of four children was born. In the second he failed, for the gambling habit and the influence of greedy courtiers were too strong to be broken by fraternal admonitions. His distinguished personality and the simplicity of his bearing inspired general respect, but not even he could breathe new life into the Austro-French partnership. The Seven Years War had been a grievous disappointment to both parties, and the French government was determined not to be involved in a fresh conflict between Vienna and Berlin. Vergennes had had no share in the making of the alliance, and he regarded it with complete detachment. In a striking Memorandum dated April 12, 1777,[1] on the eve of the Emperor's arrival, the influential Foreign Minister argued that to destroy the power of the King of Prussia would be to remove the only barrier against Austrian ambitions and to open the way to the frontiers of France.

The comparative failure of the journey hurt the Emperor more than the Empress, who had never encouraged the plan and shrank from further political or military adventures. Moreover to the end of her life she dreaded the effect of her children being exposed to such undesirable contacts as Protestant communities or sceptical *philosophes*. The English, she complained, were nearly all deists, infidels and freethinkers. Every journey of her eldest son caused her anxious heart a pang, and despite the wearing

[1] Printed in Benedikt, 327–331.

friction she would have preferred to have him always at her side. 'He is thinner,' she reported to her Parma daughter-in-law on August 4. 'He seems very pleased with the French, particularly with the Royal Family and his sister.' How little he had been able to achieve in the realm of high politics was to be revealed to the world a few months later when the War of the Bavarian Succession tested the vitality of the Bourbon–Hapsburg alliance and revealed the rift within the lute.

IV. *The War of the Bavarian Succession*

IF the pillage of Poland had been hard for the high-principled Empress to bear, Joseph's Bavarian gamble was an even more grievous trial. In the former case there was no serious risk of an appeal to arms; in the latter a terrible conflict seemed inevitable. The older she grew the more she dreaded the horrors and the hazards of war. The news of the death of Maximilian Joseph, the childless Elector of Bavaria, on December 30, 1777, was received by the Co-Regents with very different feelings. For Joseph it was the longed-for opportunity to secure some compensation for the loss of Silesia; for Maria Theresa it was the harrowing prospect of a new round in the boxing-match with the 'wicked man'. For how could anyone expect the King of Prussia to witness a major aggrandisement of Austria with folded arms? The story of this painful disagreement fills half the second and half the third volume of the correspondence between the Co-Regents, for in 1778 alone have almost all the letters of both parties been preserved.

The annexation of Bavaria by conquest or exchange was a familiar conception at Vienna. As early as 1772 Kaunitz had instructed a jurist to prepare a *dossier* on Austria's claims, and the Emperor independently ordered the Chancery to collect the relevant material. At the opening of 1777 Karl Theodor, the Elector Palatine, the heir to the Bavarian throne, fearing that the King of Prussia would use the approaching change of ruler to seize his duchies of Jülich and Berg, approached Vienna for protection. The response was friendly, but he was surprised to learn that Austria had claims to certain lordships amounting to about one-third of Bavaria on the ground that they were lapsed fiefs of the Bohemian, Austrian and Imperial crown.   Here then were the elements of a deal.

'The issue of the Bavarian Succession is at hand,' wrote Joseph to his mother on March 31, 1777.[1]   'If we do not at once decide what military measures are needed it will be too late.   I think we should consult Field-Marshal Lacy.'   By the end of the year a convention between Austria and the Elector Palatine was in sight.   On New Year's Day, 1778, when the news of Maximilian Joseph's death reached Vienna, the Emperor informed Kaunitz of his plans.   'Since we have no time for detailed discussion I am in favour of immediate occupation of Lower Bavaria.   I advise you to say nothing to Her Majesty in order not to spoil to-day's ceremony.'   She was aware of the negotiations with the Elector Palatine, but it had never occurred to her that her son would support his shadowy claims by force.   That he could decide on a step of such vital importance is the best proof that in the sphere of foreign affairs he had come to regard himself as the captain of the ship.   He felt no more sentimental tenderness for Bavaria than for Poland, for had not the Wittelsbachs done their worst throughout the critical years of the War of the Austrian Succession?

The first reaction of the experienced Empress was to warn her son against uninsurable risks.   'The present situation,' she wrote on January 2, 'far from offering me a happy prospect, overwhelms me with apprehensions which I cannot shake off and could never forgive myself for not passing on.   It concerns the happiness and tranquillity, not only of the peoples committed to my care, but of the whole of Germany.   This consideration alone should prevent hasty action on our part.   It is all the less necessary since it will always be quite easy to undertake after mature reflection what we are now about to do in a hurry by sounding the tocsin, opening the door to all the unhappy consequences, incurring censure and indignation for causing perhaps wholesale confusion, and making numberless people unhappy.   Our territories, hardly yet recovered from past misfortunes, will be the chief sufferers.   Even if our claims on Bavaria were better

[1] Benedikt, *Kaiser Joseph*, 280.

founded, we should hesitate to start a universal conflagration for a particular convenience. We shall never score as much as the others, shall incur immense expenditure, shall have to impose new burdens on our peoples to pay our debts and to maintain an ever-increasing army proportionate to our growing possessions. We should lose all our prestige now so happily re-established, replacing it by force, bidding farewell to tranquillity, peace and happiness, which is only won by good faith and public confidence. From the sovereign down to the peasant we are only too well aware of this situation since the King of Prussia introduced his maxims, thirty-six years ago. Civil and political ties no longer hold. We see men and provinces in growing decadence and distress, and this deterioration will increase if we follow suit. I speak from my experience in politics and as a good mother. I am not opposed to the settlement of these affairs by negotiation, but never by force of arms, a method which would rightly turn everyone against us from the start and would alienate those who would have remained neutral. I have never seen such enterprises prosper except when I lost Silesia in 1741.'

The warning fell on deaf ears. On January 3, Karl Theodor, Elector Palatine, the feeble heir of the Elector of Bavaria, consented to a treaty recognising Austria's claims to Lower Bavaria, a territory bordering on the Hapsburg dominions and forming about a third of the Electorate. Having no legitimate children, it was his dynastic duty to consider and consult his nephew and heir, Karl of Zweibrücken, but any scruples he might have possessed were overcome by the promise of money and titles for his bastards. Austrian troops promptly crossed the Bavarian frontier, and within a week of the Elector's decease the stage was set for a new Austro-Prussian conflict. Frederick had expected Austria to move, for Joseph's ambitions had long filled him with alarm. 'I keep my eyes on him,' he remarked as he glanced at the Emperor's bust; 'he is a young man whom I must not forget. He has brains and could go far.' He had recently squeezed Bukovina out of Turkey, but that was merely a *hors d'œuvre* before the more substantial Bavarian meal.

In transmitting the newly made pact to Leopold, and announcing the despatch of the troops, the Emperor added cheerfully: 'The circumstances of Europe appear favourable. Everyone is occupied, so I think this *coup* will succeed without war, and the acquisition, though not complete, will be a boon which costs us nothing.' A week later he was slightly less complacent. 'I cannot guarantee success, but if it comes it is a real stroke and a rounding off of the Monarchy of incalculable value. Her Majesty, as you can imagine, is a little troubled about it, but she is good enough to admit the valid reasons with which she is supplied.' Leopold expressed his approval, but on January 29 Joseph reported the ominous silence of the King of Prussia. 'He is in a very bad temper and is knocking at every door to inquire if they will make common cause. If he finds them shut, he will need patience, not daring to advance alone, and I think this affair, to everybody's surprise, will pass off very quickly. We had to act promptly and resolutely; otherwise we should not have secured a single village.'

The comments of *ce diable de Frédéric* when they came were described by Joseph as pretty impertinent: the old Prussian poacher had turned gamekeeper. On February 26 he wrote in a more chastened tone : 'There is hardly any chance of avoiding war. The wine is drawn and we must drink it. You can imagine my difficulties with Her Majesty and all the Ministers, but it is necessary to put up with a great deal for the good cause. The Duke of Zweibrücken, who was ready to accept our convention and to receive the Golden Fleece for which he had asked, has been talked over by Prussian emissaries. He has gone to Zweibrücken without signing and without the Fleece; it is inconceivable. In fact, things look bad all round, but one must have courage.' His mother, he must have felt at times, was the better prophet.

The bankruptcy of the French alliance was a shock. 'They tell us that they cannot mediate or supply the stipulated support even if we are attacked, and they wish to inform the King of Prussia of their desire to maintain complete neutrality. This is a breach of the ties of the alliance. At the moment we shall have to hide our feelings but we must bear it in mind, for it is a bit strong. The communication was wrapped up in stale compliments and blandishments.' Marie Antoinette was pressed into the service, but her amateur efforts were in vain. France had the American War of Independence to think about, and it was no part of the policy of Vergennes to make the Hapsburgs masters of Southern Germany. The dream of an easy and bloodless triumph had soon vanished, and Joseph found himself in deep water. Frederick's demand for the return to the *status quo*, which reached him on March 9, sounded like an ultimatum; he thought war practically certain though not actually decided. He would ask France for mediation and for the 25,000 men stipulated in the alliance in the event of being attacked; her reply would show exactly where she stood. He almost succumbed under the burden, and found it difficult to sleep. He was now turning over a new and daring plan in his mind which had been suggested by the Elector Palatine, and he asked for Leopold's views. 'Do you think it possible and suitable to exchange the whole of the Austrian Netherlands for the whole of Bavaria and the Upper Palatinate? It is a difficult problem and deserves your consideration. The revenues of the Netherlands, I believe, exceed those of Bavaria by a million, but that could be arranged by a loan. I should not like to do anything without your advice.' Leopold's reply is not preserved and no formal negotiations took place; but the Emperor never lost sight of this tempting project and before long he was to try again.

Leopold received confidences from his mother no less than from his brother. The situation, she wrote on March 12, was more than critical and unhappy, as she had always foreseen. The Emperor would never admit it, but would wait for something to turn up. 'I hope it will before we are forced to put everything to the hazard, for I am expecting one of the King's usual strokes early in May. If we lose, that is the end; if we win, nothing is gained. Such is our cruel plight, and the Generals are as alarmed as myself. It is not cowardice but experience and reflection, love of the Monarchy and mankind. We cannot withdraw our troops or admit our mistake, so war is inevitable. No other Power will mediate; there are only France and Russia, both of them fully occupied and both more Prussophil than Austrophil. We cannot blame them; in their place we should do the same. We shall do our best, and I am ready to compromise my name and show weakness in order to save the Monarchy. This idea alone sustains me; but when once the sword is drawn I fear it will not so soon be sheathed. The

6

most atrocious methods will be employed by our adversary, who sticks at nothing. You can imagine my situation, alone, without advice. Since I transferred the army to the Emperor in that unhappy year (1765) I know nothing beyond what he tells me, as I do not wish to complicate matters by my doubts and fears, still less to furnish an excuse if things go wrong. I am so old, worn out and deeply agitated that I can answer for nothing. If war comes I shall need support, and to whom can I look but to you?'

Two days later, on March 14, a long and ably argued letter from the Empress to Joseph, the first that has survived since the invasion of Bavaria, struck the note of 'I told you so.' 'The inconveniences and dangers foreseen when we marched into Bavaria have been only too fully realised: indeed they are mounting so rapidly that I should be unworthy of the name of sovereign and mother were I not to take suitable measures without a thought of myself. Nothing less is at stake than the destruction of our House and the Monarchy, even turning all Europe upside down. No effort is too great to avert these misfortunes. I will reconcile myself to everything, even to the disgrace of my name. Let them accuse me of senility, weakness, pusillanimity: nothing will stop my efforts to rescue Europe from this perilous plight. I could not employ the remainder of my unhappy days in a better way. I admit this sacrifice is hard, but I shall know how to bear it.'

The writer proceeded to explain the reasons for her acute anxiety. 'Our army is inferior to that of the King of Prussia by thirty or forty thousand, particularly in cavalry. He has the advantage of interior lines; we have double the distance to defend. He has fortresses; we have none. Possessing vast territories, we evacuate them and expose them to invasion and revolts. Look at Galicia, where there are only two hundred horses and seven battalions of elderly men. It is an open country, newly conquered, not yet consolidated; the spirit of liberty is only slumbering; the nation has shown it has feelings. Hungary is also denuded of troops, and the Russo-Turkish War is about to flare up again on her borders: Prussia is pulling strings in Constantinople. The King's latest letter to his *chargé d'affaires* shows that nothing will be neglected to mobilise this enemy who could seize whatever he liked in Hungary which possesses neither soldiers nor fortresses. If our forces were stationed in Saxony, Silesia, or the Upper Palatinate we could not succour Galicia or Hungary and should have to abandon them to their unhappy fate, to the mercy of a barbarous enemy, to ravages which would ruin them for a century. I say nothing of our lands in Italy or the Netherlands and of our new possessions in Bavaria. All these would have to be abandoned.

'Where then should we find resources to sustain this cruel war which at the outset would involve the abandonment of five such important countries? What confidence and credit could we enjoy in the search for allies and financial aid? What would be our prestige in our own countries, already oppressed and taxed in time of peace for the purposes of defence, if we abandoned them at the first sign of a war which, once begun, will only end with our total ruin? I cannot consent; everything is at stake. Do not let us delude ourselves. Even were our armies to be victorious it would lead nowhere. Two or three battles would not win us a Circle in Silesia; many campaigns and many a year would be needed for success. We learned in 1759 that our enemy is not so easily overcome. Even with luck we should have to fight for three or four years, during which the whole of Europe would intervene to stop us becoming too powerful. I know of no friend or ally on whom we could rely. We must therefore estimate our resources in relation not to the King of Prussia alone but to all who frown on our aggrandisement. That means all Europe, and how could we stand up to it? Time is against us. The longer the war, the more numerous our enemies. At the start it is undesirable to risk a decisive battle; we must play for time to wear down the King and to train our army, over a third of which consists of inexperienced troops. Even this interval, so useful for military operations, will from another point of view be to our disadvantage. His superiority in light forces will overwhelm our provinces and exhaust our resources. Meanwhile, egged on by his intrigues and by the same motives for which we invaded Poland and Bavaria, our neighbours will treat us in a similar way. Thus we have everything to lose and nothing to gain. With all our forces concentrated at one point, if we are beaten there we are finished.' The situation became still more alarming when Prussia and Saxony signed a convention of mutual support on March 18. With his mother in such a mood the Emperor thought of bringing Leopold to Vienna. 'At such critical moments,' he wrote in April, 'it is impossible to leave her to herself and exposed to her *entourage* who would ply her with false news and sabotage all our essential preparations.'

The Empress was ageing rapidly and was losing her resilience, but there was still plenty of fight in her when thoroughly roused. That she loved her son made political disagreements the more painful. The full gravity of the crisis was revealed when, on April 6, Frederick left for Breslau and five days later Joseph set out to join his troops in Bohemia. 'If it comes to war,' she wrote to Leopold, 'I shall be in great need of help, from you above all.' But the Grand Duke of Tuscany was far away and without influence. The faithful Kaunitz was at her side, but the absence of the Emperor was a sore trial in such anxious times. 'I cannot refuse myself the consolation of worrying you with my scrawl,' she wrote the day after his departure. 'We are entirely without support and when the war starts everyone will move. I am not sanguine, but I hope God will soften the hard heart of your adversary and bless your good intentions. You have left behind you a terrible vacuum and sadness; imagine a mother's feelings at my age. Two sons and a son-in-law are torn from me. How often have I thought of poor women who are forcibly deprived of their children, whereas mine go at their own wish and are as far as possible shielded from danger. What a wretched business is war, the foe of humanity and happiness!' Easter was a sad time. 'These great days of salvation will be hard to bear without my sons, and in such a situation. I implore you to take care of yourself; all the news petrifies me with fright. Fritz is furious and will vent his rage everywhere. Finding his army in low spirits he orders numberless executions and promises free pillage to the soldiers, which would be horrible.'

Contrary to the advice of Kaunitz the Emperor wrote to Frederick on April 13 reminding him of their two meetings and suggesting a discussion of the question at issue in preference to an appeal to arms. The King replied that no one desired peace in Europe more than himself, but that it was his duty to defend the rights of the members of the Reich against Hapsburg ambitions.

When Joseph forwarded the autograph letter to his mother she gloated over her discovery that he could not spell. 'So this monster is not such a universal genius after all, and on such occasions he needs somebody to wash his dirty linen.' [1] For once she was in a softer mood. 'You know, and I repeat, that you possess and deserve my entire confidence. The matter concerns you more than me, particularly if it comes to war. That might finish me, and then the State would be yours: I am sure it would be in better hands than mine. I only wish you better luck, but that will be as Providence decides. Take care of yourself. There is only one Joseph for his loving mother. Every day I pray God, if He wishes to punish me with war, to keep you safe.' Kaunitz, she reported, confessed that the situation was very grave, adding that they had to keep their heads and play for time.

Joseph's dream of exchanging the Austrian Netherlands appalled the Empress. 'If we abandon the Low Countries,' she commented on May 1, 'it would be a greater loss than Silesia. What a miserable bargain! It concerns you more than me. It is hard to lose one's heritage so painfully acquired. I do not wish to thwart you; do as you think best.' The thought of her son's labours and perils oppressed her hardly less than his adventurous policy. 'Good God, what a situation!' she wrote on May 2, 'and you in the midst of it all, distracted and worn out! It cannot last, and everything depends on your preservation. To-day I have seen Caramelli (Vice-President of the War Council), who is in ecstasies at the way you work and think of everything. Tears came into our eyes when we spoke of you.' Joseph's task was to sustain his mother's courage. 'The army, so far as I can see, need have no fears if it comes to the worst,' he reported on May 2. 'I think our defensive plan will avoid all the misfortunes and devastations you seem to dread.' The morale, both of soldiers and civilians, was excellent, and there had been no desertions. 'It is a real tonic to get your news,' replied the Empress, 'even a few lines, but I beg you not to steal time from your sleep. It is comforting to know you find a good spirit everywhere; it is the same in all the provinces. Never have people worked with such zeal, owing to the master's eye and to

---

[1] An allusion to the rôle of Voltaire in bygone days.

seeing you everywhere. I hear there is a lot of illness. I beseech you not to expose yourself. A son like you is irreplaceable.' In reply to a birthday greeting she wrote: 'I only live for you. If I can be of use to you, I am willing to bear these sad days which are only made tolerable by your love.'

Maria Theresa was obsessed by the horrors and hazards of war. 'God preserve us from playing a humiliating rôle; better fight than that. But even with a force equal or perhaps superior to the King we gain nothing by fighting four times: that is what is so depressing. If we were in his situation I should not think of peace. We can no longer count on the loans from the Low Countries and the subsidies from France which alone enabled us to sustain the last war. The dry hot weather points to a poor harvest, and remaining too long in one spot is bad, especially for the horses. I do not think there is now any question of exchanging the Low Countries for the whole of Bavaria. The part we already possess is quite unsuitable; every day reveals the drawbacks. The Monarchy, my dear son, is in tatters; it will need all your assistance and activity, and for that we require peace. You cannot be in two places at once, and you will be badly seconded from here in case of war, for men and resources are lacking. I am sorry to paint such a picture; unfortunately it is only too correct. Nothing is so bad as to expose oneself without the least chance of advantage and to risk the life of so many brave men, the *élite* of the Monarchy. These sad truths make one wish for peace at any price short of humiliation. Steps towards this goal will be the only means of preserving your Monarchy which in your hands will be more fortunate.'

In vain did the Emperor suggest the summoning of Leopold to Vienna: Maria Theresa was inconsolable. 'I am terribly afraid of the first encounters. The King is believed to have a new weapon—a murderous long-range gun—which he is keeping very secret. All these inventions for the destruction of humanity make me shudder. One cannot trust this sub-human creature. You see he is out for an alliance with France and Russia. He has his agents everywhere, while we have none. We are honest, he the reverse. He impresses everyone, we are the dupes. I confess I am sometimes quite exasperated, not for myself, for my career is over, but for you. The great thing, my dear son, is to establish the confidence in you that you deserve, and that is not gained by arms. Greed does more harm than good. The example of Galicia proves it; that success has been our misfortune ever since.' The Emperor's reply was in his usual resolute vein. 'The essential point is to hold fast; the prestige of the Monarchy demands it. It would be a hundred times better to yield after several defeats than before. I cannot answer for events, but if, as I expect, we have to fight alone, I flatter myself that he will have to pay dearly for any victories. I believe pretty well everything has been thought of. I am ready for almost all emergencies, and I still feel he will think twice before he issues the order to march. If he gives way, it will be a triumph.'

The exchange of letters between the Emperor and the King continued, but they had taken up their positions and refused to give way an inch; each reckoned on the disinclination of the other to fight. 'Make peace, my dear Joseph,' implored the Empress on June 2; 'be the father of your peoples. Do not sacrifice them for an object which may involve their and our destruction. Keep them for better times, and preserve for me two dear sons about whom I am so anxious ; let me enjoy their presence during my few remaining days. Never forget that a moderate peace is better than a successful war. I authorise you to make peace on the field of battle on any terms you like. If war occurs I do not know if you will see me again. I am utterly done. Only submission to God's will supports me, but even so I cannot hold out for long.' A phrase in Joseph's letter of June 8 reporting that all the troops were in their places and that the rest must be left to chance shocked the pious Empress. 'It is not chance but God's blessing which will decide our fate. We must ask it with insistence and humility and must deserve it by our actions and fidelity.' Her letters were a blend of affection and poignant grief. During June she wrote almost every day. 'My heart is full, yet full of confidence in your wisdom and perspicacity. I am anxious about this precious Joseph to whom you scarcely give a thought, and without whose preservation everything goes to pieces. I recommend to you this dear son, if you love me and the state. If I had been told twenty-one years ago that I should be threatened on this anniversary [1] with

---

[1] The Austrian victory at Kolin in 1757.

a third war and that I should still be alive, I think I should have succumbed. It is the most critical of the three and assuredly the most cruel.'

Once again the Emperor tried to comfort his mother by the assurance that, if they stood firm, the King of Prussia would give way. 'We must show that we are not afraid of war.' She ad heard all this before and, knowing Frederick's ways, refused to indulge in wishful thinking. 'I cannot persuade myself that there will be no war, and I do not see how it will end. You will not be able to sustain the burden of body and mind for the next five months which you have had during the last three. Our troops under good leadership have always done their duty, but three-fourths are recruits or have no experience of warfare. They would need to get used to it, but that is not the game of the King, who always starts off with a general engagement. That is what I fear for all our brave officers and men—that our losses will be in vain, for we shall obtain nothing more and the Monarchy will go to its doom. I felt just as you did when this rascally King humiliated himself to approach Kaunitz, hoping to find him more pliable than you. Such is this great man who is considered a Solomon; if one has watched him long and closely he is very small, a pure charlatan hiding behind his power and his luck. I do not want to be proud, but my Joseph is very different and works in a very different way.'

Both armies were manœuvring for position before venturing a blow, and on June 21, scared by rumours of new destructive cannon balls, the distracted Empress once more pleaded for peace. 'The monster is furious that you have spoiled his game and that he cannot attack you with advantage, so he must employ other horrors to destroy us. Make peace. This district of Bavaria is surely not worth all the expenditure already incurred and all the fatigue which neither you nor anyone can stand in the long run. My God, what an unfortunate idea is this Lower Bavaria! I cannot believe that the exchange of the whole of Bavaria for the Low Countries, another disastrous idea, is still being seriously considered. Looking around I see nothing but sadness, which will get worse, and you in the midst of it in the greatest danger. It is almost unbearable.' War, retorted Joseph, was indeed a great evil, but to accept Frederick's demands would be worse.

'Either we shall have war in a week,' he wrote on June 28, 'or he is merely bluffing. The time is critical, I agree, but we can pursue no other course. It is no longer a question of Bavaria but of the prestige or humiliation of the Monarchy. The war may be unfortunate, but it can never be so destructive as yielding to his threats.' The news that agents had been despatched to poison the water and the wells, declared the Empress in alarm, would be incredible if he were not Frederick. 'You are already in his way, and he wishes to destroy the Monarchy or at any rate inflict all the harm he can; that is why I am so afraid of a devastating war. I believe in our armies, but just because they are good after all the training, ought we to risk them for so disproportionate an object? If war occurs our poor countries will be ravaged and pillaged. Where shall we be at the close? He will stick at nothing and he will succeed, for you cannot do everything. He is striving for friendship and commercial agreement between France, himself and Russia, and we are doing nothing.'

The correspondence between Joseph and Frederick led to nothing. The King was prepared to sanction the transfer of a fraction of South-west Bavaria in exchange for a small equivalent to the Elector Palatine elsewhere; more he could not approve. At the end of June, Kaunitz confessed that further negotiations would be fruitless, and on July 5 the long-expected blow fell. 'Dearest Mother,' wrote Joseph, 'I have just heard the news. This morning the King of Prussia entered Bohemia near Nachod. I have no details, but I hasten to tell you, though I feel anxious about the shock it will be for you. May God bless the just defence of Your Majesty and my fellow-countrymen. I shall certainly neglect nothing, and in a few days we may be able to see more clearly.' The reply of the Empress was eloquent in its brevity. 'Some situations can only be felt, not described. I am grateful for you thinking of me. For a *fait accompli* there is no remedy. What is humanly possible you and your fellow-countrymen will do. So long as you are there, everything can be mended.'

The Emperor reported daily on the military situation without attempting to conceal his growing anxieties. He had little sleep. 'When one closes one's eyes, what terrible reflections on our plight!' The Empress was not in the least surprised at the turn of events. 'I have foreseen all this for six months, hence my depression. God save us from a rout; a lost battle is a great evil but it does not decide the issue. God is my only support. May He give you, me and the army strength. Reverses test men. I have seen you so often in this predicament that I hope you will keep your health and your nerves, more necessary now than ever before. Against this enemy there is no point in fighting: only time wears him down. If you can make peace on the battlefield, do so on any conditions you like; that would not be weakness, or, if it were, throw the blame on my grey head. I will try to second you and to extricate you as quickly as possible from this cruel and dangerous situation. Do not fear on my account; I feel my own strength and with God's help I shall come through. The essential is to save Joseph, and I feel the same fire as at twenty-five.'

A letter from the front on the same day, July 11, heightened her alarms. 'Our situation is certainly very critical; the enemy is everywhere stronger than we, well trained and bold. If we cannot hold out here, we must evacuate Bohemia. Only a happy moment, a little divine grace, could put things right. We wait patiently but with great anxiety, as you can imagine. If there was any chance of peace on fairly honourable terms, it would be a blessing, but I see none.' Next day Joseph, who had never witnessed a battle, confessed that the evils of war were much worse than he had thought. If there were a chance of shortening it, or of persuading France and Russia to mediate, that would be best. 'I say this not as a coward, but as a man and a citizen, for it is horrible to see what they have been suffering this week.' While he was writing these words his mother's spirited letter arrived from Vienna. 'I could not reply if I would,' commented Joseph; 'I can only say it touched me to tears, and my admiration for your attitude equals my gratitude. What luck to have such a mother and such a sovereign! How I should reproach myself if I proved unworthy of the precious blood in my veins. Believe me, I will redouble my efforts and courage to serve you as you deserve; but I must repeat, our utmost efforts are needed to stand up to this enemy. Once again I see before me the great, the incomparable Maria Theresa, who will discover and employ the necessary means to sustain her armies, her states, and her glory.'

At the very moment Joseph was applauding her fortitude the Empress, convinced that he was galloping headlong to destruction, decided to seize the reins. Hitherto he had conducted the negotiations and forwarded copies of the documents to Vienna. Now, for the first and last time, she acted behind his back though with the approval of Kaunitz. On July 12, a week after the outbreak of hostilities, she addressed a letter to 'the wicked man' himself. 'The withdrawal of the Prussian Ambassador and the entry of Your Majesty's troops into Bohemia fill me with concern at the outbreak of a new war. My age and my desire for the preservation of peace are known to all, and I could not give a more striking proof than by taking this step. My mother's heart is justly alarmed to see two of my sons and a cherished son-in-law [1] with the army. I am acting without informing the Emperor, and I beg that it remain a secret whether or not it succeeds. I desire to renew and conclude the negotiations, hitherto directed by him and, to my great regret, broken off. Baron Thugut has full powers from myself.' Her plan was to purchase Prussia's consent to the retention of a small corner of Bavaria by recognition of her claims to the reversion of Bayreuth and Anspach. A postscript on the following day added that she was about to tell the Emperor, though without entering into details, in order to avert hasty action.

On the day of her envoy's departure the Empress confessed to her son: 'If I had received your letter of July 11 I should have sent Thugut with much greater peace of mind. I cannot express what it has cost me to have dealings with this monster and how I fear your disapproval. So you can guess how comforting it was to get your letter expressing a wish for peace, and to find that I had anticipated your wishes without committing you in any way. May God bless my intention to save you and the Monarchy! I must warn you that having undertaken this task I shall carry it through in my own way; for you and the Monarchy, indeed everything, are at stake. My grey head is ready to bear all the blame.' No wonder that, as she confessed to her Parma daughter-in-law, she could think of nothing else, even in church.

Joseph reacted as if a bomb had exploded under his feet. 'Never have I had such a shock. Who can have given you this

---

[1] Albert of Saxe-Teschen.

advice at this moment, and what will be the effect on your reputation and the prestige of the Monarchy? Of course the King, elated by this step, will make ridiculous and intolerable propositions. It is a confession that all the forces of the Monarchy are as nothing, and that, if he wishes for anything, we have to obey. Impossible! It would be far better to withdraw and to abandon Prague. The war has begun and the peasants have been pillaged, but our armies are still intact; retreat and surrender would be the worst policy of all. If there had been time I should certainly have stopped Thugut *en route*. This step shows your utter condemnation of my action. What can I do but throw up everything and go somewhere in Italy, without passing through Vienna? Your Majesty cannot possibly have reflected; it is crushing. The luckiest thing would be if the King's reply were to close the incident. Can my letters possibly have suggested it? I described the dangers in order that all practicable measures should be taken. I spoke of the wish for peace, but through foreign mediation; your idea would never have occurred to me.

'I am now in the most terrible predicament. The honour of the Monarchy, its prestige and my own, are compromised. If I am to rescue them, I must reluctantly announce our difference of opinion and reveal Your Majesty's flabbiness in order to preserve a consistent policy. All the money wasted, our public credit diminished, the power of Prussia doubled! I leave you to imagine my feelings, and I cannot yet tell what I shall do. If the good God were to bury it in oblivion that would help the state more than a victory; its honour would be intact instead of being destroyed for ever. What a contrast from one day to another! One letter reveals you in all your vigour, your courage, your determination to wage war with all your might. The next speaks of the most humiliating surrender. My brain is in a whirl as I reflect on all the consequences. I cannot mention it to anybody. You can imagine my cruel uncertainty after this thunderbolt for which it was impossible to be prepared, and which I shall never understand.'

An undated letter from Marshal Laudon tactfully endeavoured to calm the agitated Emperor.[1] 'I can quite understand how this wholly unexpected news has upset Your Majesty. It may be

---

[1] Benedikt, *Kaiser Joseph II*, 280.

some consolation that the army, and indeed the whole world, has
seen how you have reacted, and that this step is entirely due to
the mild heart of Her Majesty, who in accordance with her lofty
views prefers peace to any increase of her power, and would
rather preserve it by a magnanimous surrender of her rights than
trust to the uncertain arbitrament of arms. Forgive me for
saying I feel it would be a mistake to bypass Vienna and make
straight for Florence, which would be the talk of Europe and
above all of the Monarchy. This, I think, is the moment for
Your Majesty to display a truly elevated soul by wisely giving
way and then, directly peace is assured, gaining more than during the last sixteen years [1] by putting the army on a footing to
meet our powerful neighbour at any time. Till then we should
avoid a new war and quietly await the more favourable moment
which is sure to come.'

The Empress, though grieved and anxious, was wholly un-
repentant. 'We must wait for Thugut's return, then we shall
see more clearly what to do. My idea was to save you and the
Monarchy, not in any way to tarnish your glory or disavow your
course. I would do the same again. A speedy conclusion is a
necessity, for time is not on our side.' Joseph's exasperation
was all the greater because the military situation seemed to him
promising. 'Deserters in considerable numbers report sufferings
in the Prussian camp. In a few days, if this unfortunate negotiation comes to nothing, we might have the honour of compelling
the great Frederick to retreat without a battle. The deserters
all say that a Russian envoy has arrived there, but I fear it is
Thugut. Can one imagine such a thing? What a shock it
would be for Europe, what humiliation for the Monarchy and
its army!' In reporting to Leopold on the first two weeks of the
war he ignored the Thugut mission but revealed his anxieties.
'War is horrible—the devastation of the fields and cottages, the
lamentations of the poor peasants, the ruin of so many innocent
people, the anxiety by day and night. It is a dog's life.' The
Empress was grieved that he should think she needed encouragement. 'I hoped to have convinced you long ago that my
greatest wish is to please you, but we must do what promises
success, not failure.'

[1] From the close of the Seven Years War.

Delighted to discover the sharp divergence between mother and son, Frederick replied that the mission of Thugut, who travelled under a Russian name, was being kept a profound secret. 'It was worthy of Your Majesty to show magnanimity and moderation in this controversial issue after having defended your heritage with heroic firmness. Your Majesty's tender attachment to the Emperor and the princes deserves the approval of all sensitive souls and increases, if that is possible, my high respect.' He added a few articles to the draft agreement prepared by Kaunitz for Thugut, which he thought too vague. Pending her reply he would do nothing to cause her alarm for her family. On July 22 she received her envoy's report and forwarded it to her son. Though he had naturally welcomed the prospect of the evacuation of part of the recently occupied Bavarian territories, the wary Frederick was on his guard. Joseph seemed relieved that nothing definite had been arranged, and urged his mother not to lose a moment in strengthening and supplying the army, but his wrath continued to burn. 'Your Majesty began this incredible negotiation without consulting me. You have concluded it, finding the King's propositions and desire for peace in conformity with your own. What more can I say? The affair is past mending, and I have only to think of rescuing what is left of the honour of the State and my own.'

Reproaches left the Empress unmoved, for she had always regarded victory as unattainable. 'We were a Great Power but we are so no longer. We must bow our head, save at least the *débris*, and render the peoples who remain to us happier than they have been during my unfortunate reign. Begin yours by restoring calm, peace and happiness to those who so richly deserve it. Their happiness will be yours, even at the price of your personal grandeur. I know your heart: save your peoples and earn greater fame thereby than by any title of conqueror. Thugut should return to the King; if you approve I should like to send him to you *en route*, to explain our ideas, for we ought to agree on the principles. As regards method I will meet your wishes. I am not ashamed of my *démarche*. Time passes. I pray God to touch your heart and enlighten your mind. I shall never cease to regard our situation as requiring peace whatever the price.' If Thugut turned up, retorted Joseph sharply, he would not receive him. 'You possess the power and can do what you like, but I cannot pretend to approve what I shall always regard as the disgrace and ruin of the state.' At peace with her conscience, the Empress quietly but firmly restated her attitude. 'What a horrible war, worse than all the others! We must get out of it with honour and without leaving the suspicion that we have tried to trick people, to which I will never consent. You have long known my maxim: I would rather be deceived than deceiver.'

Joseph continued to smart under the shock and humiliation. 'For the last week,' he reported on July 30, 'the many deserters say that in the Prussian camp there is talk of my having asked for peace and an armistice and that an envoy had arrived to negotiate. The hussars even say they have received orders not to fire unless our troops begin. You can imagine the effect on the army and on my position. Everyone believes I am in the secret. I have had my full share of unpleasant experiences and humiliations, but never have I known and never could I have imagined anything like this. Well, such is my fate. Reflection has taught me to bear what is beyond remedy and in regard to which one's conscience is clear. A reasonable being should be able to take things calmly, and it is merely with slight impatience that I await the conclusion of this incredible affair. How honour and peace-making are to be combined I cannot make out.'

Maria Theresa was quite capable both of holding her ground and of pleading her case with undiminished vigour. 'For the last four days I have been brooding over my cruel situation, and thinking much more about you than about our common enemy. Till you told me of our critical situation I kept my fears and feelings to myself in order not to trouble you. You must admit that, despite my disapproval, I have acted as if it were my own policy, and I was able to bear it for your sake. But now you say you will have to abandon Prague and Bohemia if forced to quit your present position, as the King could compel you if he wished. To defend Bohemia, you say, is almost impossible. If there was a means of making peace on fairly honourable terms, you add, it would be a blessing to make it a short war and to end the sufferings which are beyond imagination. You say our armies are hardly 80,000 and that the King has at least 50,000 more than we. And with things in such a state you do not wish me to try to stop a conflict which at the very start may lose me the kingdom whence I derive most revenue and men, and which the enemy will ruin for half a century if he establishes his winter quarters there! The future is even darker. Our resources and our armies will be diminished; recruits will not fill the gaps; there will be misery and depression; all sorts of events can worsen our plight, and I shall be forced to make peace. We shall have to do so some day, and I see nothing humiliating in proposing it at the present time when nothing has shown our great inferiority, above all when the initiative comes from me, and you retain the liberty to disapprove my action and to declare that only out of consideration for me do you, as Emperor and heir-presumptive, accept what I have arranged. If I had not acted thus I should feel bound in conscience and affection to do it now. I shall have to send Thugut back if I am not to expose myself and the King who has summoned his Ministers post-haste from Berlin, which causes a lot of talk. All I ask is that, if I obtain reasonable conditions, you will concur. Think it over quietly, I implore you; the safety of the Monarchy and your own glory depend on it. In case you refuse, I must tell the King that I have to break off negotiations because you reject our agreement. Without the assent of the Emperor and heir it is impossible for him to settle anything with me or for me with him.'

On the same day the Empress poured out her heart to Mercy, her devoted Ambassador in Paris. He would see how she had been rewarded for seeking to save the Monarchy and to extricate her son with honour. 'I am used to being contradicted and my proposals always being disapproved. This was not exclusively my idea. Kaunitz suggested it to console me, and I would have knelt at the King's feet if that would have secured peace. For the last six weeks the Emperor has ceased to correspond with Kaunitz who is now in disfavour—I do not know why. I have no other Minister or adviser. I deserve pity and I do not know how it will all end.'

The family duel continued to rage throughout August, the Empress clamouring for peace on any terms, the Emperor wrathfully sounding the note of Hapsburg prestige. In forwarding Frederick's reply, on August 2, she argued that in view of the political and military situation of Austria it would be desirable to end the war even without any gain so long as appearances were saved. This time she consulted her son before despatching Thugut with her reply, once again beseeching him to reflect. 'At this hour the fate of your states is in your hands, but you are answerable to yourself and to God. The happiness of so many thousands is at stake. The first sufferings of war have touched you, but have they softened you? Think it over quietly and without prejudice: you will find a tender mother, a reasonable and straightforward friend, and a just sovereign who fulfils her duties towards God and man. Your decision will be carried out. I will give you all the support I can. If you wish to continue the war please obtain the written opinion of your four marshals on the military situation.'

Joseph was far from happy, for Prince Henry had just crossed the Bohemian frontier. This would compel him to retreat, and the better half of Bohemia would be occupied by the Prussians without a battle. If she was determined to negotiate it would have been better to do so before they had lost their strategic position. 'All I beseech you once again is not to involve me in your transactions, for I cannot alter my convictions.' He added that he could take no part in the proposed negotiations, for he had not been told of the initiative; the consequences had always seemed and always would seem to him dishonourable and disgraceful. He therefore returned the documents. 'Your Majesty alone must and can decide. If it is to be war to the last man and the last coin it must be waged à outrance. You have fine subjects and resources, and a resolute will could retrieve the situation. If, on the other hand, you are unwilling to play for high stakes, you should make peace as soon as possible and on any terms, for war cannot be waged with a faint heart. You know which alternative I prefer, but it is for you to choose. I know my duty, and you know my respect. Whatever you do will be law for me. I could only manifest my sorrow and take steps to prevent an unfortunate difference of opinion inflicting further damage on the state.'

The news that Prince Henry's army had entered Bohemia confirmed the profound conviction of Maria Theresa that the struggle was hopeless, and made her more anxious than ever not to sacrifice her subjects without saving the state. 'If we fight now, it is pure loss—but about that you will do what you think best. The essential point is to preserve your life; all is lost if you act in desperation, as I fear you may, for a victory we cannot expect. While you are alive everything is capable of remedy. Without you, all would be lost. With God's grace we can do and bear all. He owes us nothing. If we bow before Him, He will have pity on us. Then the ending of the war will fall on my unhappy head, only too happy if I can save you and our dear countries from measureless calamities. Then I shall joyfully go to my grave, even perhaps in disgrace, on condition that I save you and what is left of our countries, that I can count on your affection, that you pity me and do not hate me, that you recognise that you are my favourite child. Bless you. God keep you.'

While grateful for his mother's expressions of affectionate anxiety for his health, Joseph gloomily pictured Frederick gloating over the Thugut *démarche*. 'It would be a real comfort,' he wrote on August 7, 'if I learned that all idea of negotiation is abandoned and that Your Majesty will take every step to oppose the King; or, if not, that you have at least found a way of making this step more compatible with my honour. The indecision, the doubt in which I have been living for three weeks, is the most cruel experience I know. No philosophy helps.' Never had he written so sharply to his mother as during these agonising weeks while the outcome of her fateful initiative was trembling in the balance. Military prospects, he added next day, were not so hopeless as she supposed. Frederick had mobilised to the last man, including veterans and youths. 'If he suffered a reverse he could scarcely find recruits in his own country—so I can merely await with resignation the result of the terrible step you are taking. You will see what the world says about it and I shall be the butt. Your indifference to such talk will have to be paid for by the state and by your successors. All our work, and even the credit we have gained abroad in sixteen years, is annulled and destroyed for ever or at any rate for a very long time. It is an unhappy fate to have to live in such an epoch and, like myself, to have to play a part.'

Once again Joseph poured out his heart to his brother. 'I

note that you are aware of Her Majesty's action in writing to the King and sending Thugut to him.   You will, I think, have shared my view though you will not have felt it so deeply.   Nothing more dishonouring, detrimental and destructive could occur.   I was not consulted and I almost collapsed at the news; so I have refused and always shall refuse to know anything about it or to take a hand.   If to the ignominy of begging when one has been the victim of the most cruel aggression is added a disadvantageous peace, I shall have to speak to the whole world in order to save in part the prestige of the state and my own deeply compromised honour.   In that case I should leave here and, avoiding Vienna, come to you, my dear friend, tell you of my troubles, and at the same time renounce all activities during Her Majesty's life.   It is my misfortune to have a different approach to affairs: perhaps for that reason I have unwittingly made trouble.   Henceforth I assure you that my name will no longer appear and that I shall exert no influence.   To be a dupe for sixteen years is too much. Now it must stop, and it will be a service to the state to end the embarrassment resulting from conflicting wills.   Perhaps my visit will not be very welcome, but I flatter myself that, when I have told you everything, you will feel that I am acting solely in the interest of the state and yourself and the children.   If Vienna would provide the necessary support I could remedy everything; but with this wrong-headed and unhappy idea of peace they will do nothing.   Apart from lamentations they cannot decide either on war or peace.   What a situation!   Picture my state of mind and the figure I cut.   I was prepared for plenty of reverses and misfortunes, and I do not lack courage, but this I never expected. If I could ever have imagined it I think I should have chosen to become a hermit.   Pray God that this horrible peace be avoided and that we may wage war with success.'   The anguish of the Empress was equally keen.   'Your situation breaks my heart,' she wrote on August 9, 'as I am the innocent cause, hoping to deliver you from your critical situation even at the price of my name being bandied about.   If I have failed in my purpose I am doubly an object of pity.   My only consolation is that my intention was pure and that we are merely the instruments of Providence; but it is very hard on those who are used as hostages to torment all they love most.   I am in despair at having lost for ever the friendship and confidence of my only support for thirty-six years.'

The episode of secret diplomacy terminated as the Emperor had hoped. To test the attitude of Austria Frederick forwarded suggestions allotting her a slender slice of Bavaria. Thugut returned with a new offer from the Empress to restore the occupied portion of Bavaria and to cancel the treaty with the Elector Palatine if he would promise, for himself and his successors, not to unite the Hohenzollern Margraviates of Bayreuth and Anspach with Prussia. The suggestion was promptly declined by the King on the ground that the Margraviates were not a matter for dispute since his right to them was clear. A meeting at Braunau between his Ministers and Thugut broke down on August 16, and on August 20 the Empress reported the return of her envoy and the collapse of the negotiations. 'Your wishes are fulfilled. Yet I am impenitent, and I should never have forgiven myself if I had not made almost superhuman efforts to save so many thousands of lives and our poor ravaged countries. My affection has been ill requited, and I will merely say that my sole object was to rescue you from this terrible predicament. Now you will no longer be troubled and I shall spare my own feelings. I wish you as much happiness and satisfaction as I have chagrin and sorrow.' Joseph was touched by her grief at the rupture, but his own wounds still rankled. 'Now we must save the state and the fatherland, throw in everything we possess. My life, my blood, my efforts, all my faculties are nothing in comparison. If I were to feel that your favour, which has been throughout life my happiness and my sole aim, would be diminished by the truths which I have ventured to express so forcibly, I should forfeit a large measure of courage but I should not despair. You forbade me to attack and you actually informed the King of Prussia of this order; and he replied that he would try to avoid bloodshed.'

Now that her direct attempt at peace had failed, the Empress returned to her previous tactics and implored her son to continue the quest. 'This time the enemy does not risk battle, but he is utterly ruining our countries and thus acquiring more than in all his other wars. It is useless to compare our resources with his, for ours diminish from day to day while his increase. If you find the moment to make peace, seize it; I accept in advance any arrangement you may make.   A month less of calamities would be a great boon; if they continue, famine and illness will finish us. Do not imagine I am neglecting anything, but you must have no illusions about our situation.   If Bohemia remains in his power two months longer, we could not possibly wage war for more than a year.'

After two months of limited liability belligerence Joseph had lost his first enthusiasm, but he saw no reason for despair.   'I begin to believe,' he reported on September 3, 'that perhaps we shall be able to get out of this fairly well.'   The Empress, on the other hand, remained an incurable pessimist.   The King, she declared on September 5, held all the cards.   'You are always preaching that everyone must give up everything: easier said than done.   Small economies at Court and elsewhere would be useless.   You think as a statesman, I as a mother and a woman. I confess that time increases my eagerness to finish this unhappy war, so destructive for everyone.   Do not fear that I shall renew negotiations.   I undertook them solely to extricate you and our poor people from a highly critical situation.   My conscience is clear, and nothing else matters.   But I shall neglect no means, as you say yourself, to secure by the co-operation of France, Russia and the Empire—if its head is willing to assist—the restoration of peace this winter since the conflict is without purpose.   If not, this year of war will cost as much as two in the last struggle.'

Throughout the autumn the armies watched each other and went early into winter quarters.   Both rulers were awaiting an opportunity to end hostilities without loss of face, for they realised that a military decision was impossible.   Even Joseph knew that he could hope for nothing beyond a minute portion of Bavaria.   'The Russians have declared for him and against us,' lamented Maria Theresa in October to her daughter-in-law Marie Beatrix.   'I always expected it, but it is scandalous! I do not think their troops will intervene this year, but surely next.   I never doubted their ill-will, but this is definitely dishonourable.' The only way out, it was clear on both sides, was through third parties, 'France acting for Austria and Russia for Prussia.'   After some sharp exchanges between the Empress, the Emperor and

Kaunitz, it was decided to leave the settlement in the hands of the two mediating Powers. France, as expected, proved a very lukewarm champion of her ally, and the lead was taken by the Tsarina, whose proposals were adopted as a basis for a congress summoned to meet at Teschen in Austrian Silesia. The making of peace was a wearisome process, for Saxon and other interests in addition to those of the two protagonists had to be considered. When the main difficulties seemed to have been overcome, Maria Theresa wrote to Lacy, on February 13, 1779: 'For fourteen months I have not gone to bed so happy. God be praised. I preserve my children, my friends, my brave troops, and I avert the total ruin of my good provinces.' Even now, however, the stream of appeals and warnings from Vienna frayed the Emperor's nerves. 'Her Majesty is always in alarm,' he reported to Leopold on April 14; 'she torments herself and everyone who has anything to do with it in a distressing manner. I play the part of Job. Perhaps they are only cheating us, and we might be caught unawares, since we are utterly unprepared for another campaign.'

The Treaty of Teschen was signed on the birthday of the Empress, May 13, 1779. The Emperor had to content himself with a crumb from the Bavarian loaf, the so-called Inn Quarter, and consented to the merging of Bayreuth and Anspach in Prussia on their childless ruler's death. Neither his dreams of glory nor his mother's fears of catastrophic defeat had been fulfilled. After a separation of four centuries the Palatinate was reunited to Bavaria. But the real victor was Frederick, who emerged as the successful defender of the German princes against the resurgent ambitions of the Hapsburgs. The Emperor's stock in the European market had fallen, and he knew it. 'When one thinks of what it might have been,' he reported to his mother after a visit to his new territory in October, 'it is a trifle; yet it is good so far as it goes and is most conveniently situated for Upper Austria. There are about 80,000 souls and the yield is perhaps half a million florins. Nearly everyone appears content and friendly. The disorder which existed there is beyond expression.' How deep was his disappointment he was to reveal six years later when, as Frederick expected, he made a second and equally unsuccessful attempt to seize Bavaria. The Empress, on the other hand, had no regrets. 'To-day I have gloriously ended my career with the *Te Deum*,' she wrote to Kaunitz. 'Dearly though it may have cost me, I took part in it with joy at the thought of the peace which, with your help, I have brought to my countries.' Fortunately for the sorely tried ruler, she was spared a repetition of the grief and anxiety which poisoned the closing years of her life.

V. *The Rapprochement with Russia*

JOSEPH was not the man to abandon his ambitions at the first rebuff. During the War of the Bavarian Succession the King of Prussia had enjoyed the moral support of his Russian ally, while the chilly neutrality of France had shown that for all practical purposes the partnership fashioned by Kaunitz and Choiseul was at an end. The lesson of the whole transaction was clear enough: before a second bid for Bavaria could be made with any prospect of success the approval of Catherine must be secured. In no other direction could he look for effective support. The necessity of a new orientation had become obvious even before the war. 'The disagreeable and odious King of Prussia,' he wrote to his mother on March 31, 1777, 'needs careful watching; if we could trip him up it would be a sin to miss the opportunity. Russia is in quite a different category. Without her we shall never do anything worth while. With her everything is possible, above all against our arch-enemy.' [1] Fortunately for Austria the Russo-Prussian treaty ran out in 1780 unless renewed: now was the time to act. The two rulers had already collaborated in the spoliation of Poland; now perhaps they might repeat the experiment at Turkey's expense, for the Tsarina longed to extend her dominions to the Black Sea.

The Emperor's first task was to propose a meeting and to make a favourable impression, not by Frederick's technique of flattery, to which he never stooped, but by sheer force of personality. It was entirely his own idea to engineer a second *Renversement des Alliances*, to substitute Austria for Prussia as the ally of Russia; if that were to prove impossible, at any rate he might well loosen the tie, which had never been very strong, between St.

[1] Benedikt, 279.

Petersburg and Berlin. On February 1, 1780, he paid a private visit to the Russian Ambassador Prince Galitzin at his house in the Prater. After a few moments of general conversation he asked if the rumour in the papers of an approaching visit of the Tsarina to her western provinces was correct. When the Ambassador replied that he knew nothing of it, the Emperor remarked that, if the rumour were confirmed, he would be glad to extend his own forthcoming journey to Galicia and to make her acquaintance on Russian soil. That was his only purpose: there was no political aim and he did not dream of negotiating with her. He merely wished to see her. The Ambassador was requested to report that this was a purely personal approach. The reply to this flattering proposal was prompt and cordial: she would be happy to receive him at Mohilev, where she expected to arrive on June 7. Only now did the Emperor inform Lacy, his friend and counsellor. 'If only I could in this way rouse the beloved Frederick to a pitch of excitement which would finish him off!' Kaunitz was not a little hurt when he learned of the plan, not from his sovereign but from the Russian Ambassador. He had long wished to talk about the matter, explained the Emperor to the Chancellor not very convincingly, but he saw him so seldom and in their brief conversations he had forgotten it. Now he proposed to visit him so that they could draft a reply.

The consent of the Empress, so Kaunitz was informed, had been obtained, but her sanction would be more accurately described as the reluctant acceptance of a *fait accompli*. The Emperor, she reported to Mercy, had jestingly spoken during the winter of his desire to meet the Tsarina on her projected visit to Mohilev when he would be visiting Bukovina. 'You can imagine how little it appealed to me, partly owing to the impression which such a meeting would produce among the other Powers, partly on account of the detestation which such a character as the Empress of Russia inspires in me. The Emperor, however, always so sure of himself, and without consulting Prince Kaunitz, approached the Russian Ambassador.' Though the Tsarina had promised that she would keep the secret even from Count Panin, her Foreign Minister, she was sure to tell the King of Prussia. 'Here is another proof how little I

am able to veto my son's projects, though I always have to share
in the blame.   He paints the rosiest picture of all the advantages
of such a meeting, and is already gloating over the shock to the
King of Prussia.   I am by no means convinced, and I regret to
see that new material is always being accumulated to accentuate
his embitterment and to upset our allies.'   All that Kaunitz
could do was to persuade the Empress to keep her disapproval
to herself.   'This long journey in this season is a great worry,'
she wrote to her beloved daughter-in-law Marie Beatrix; and to
Mercy she confided that it was one of the saddest events of her
life.

The Chancellor was in his element when a new international
situation required comprehensive memoranda in the drafting of
which he was an expert.   The King of Prussia, he assumed,
would do his utmost to sow suspicions in regard to the journey,
and Prussophil influences in the Tsarina's *entourage* would
complicate the traveller's task.   His first duty would therefore
be to explain to his hostess the motives of his visit and to counterwork Prussian stratagems.   He must declare that he desired not
only that he should make her acquaintance but that she should
learn to understand him.   The real object of the journey was for
the two rulers to make friends.   This would be practicable so
long as she had not pledged herself—which he did not believe—
to support Frederick in aggression.   Further he should not go
unless the Empress or Potemkin gave the lead.   He should deny
Frederick's charge that Vienna was meditating an attack on
Prussia or scheming to place an Austrian prince, such as Prince
Albert of Saxe-Teschen, the son-in-law of the Empress, on the
Polish throne.   Austria was ready to collaborate with Russia
in Poland, where her only interest was to prevent the election of
a foreign king.   If the Tsarina raised the question of an Austro-
Russian front against Turkey, the Emperor should neither
commit himself nor close the door.   A second and shorter
Memorandum contained advice on how to deal with Potemkin.
Before leaving Vienna on April 2 the Emperor wrote to Cobentzl,
the Austrian Ambassador at St. Petersburg, to explain that he
would travel as Count von Falkenstein and did not want any fuss
to be made.   He hoped the Empress would not make him any
presents.   The only jewels which would be welcome, he added

facetiously, would be the Silesian fortresses of Schweidnitz and Glatz, Neisse and Kosel.

Joseph approved the Kaunitz memoranda, which he supplemented with one of his own for the consideration of the Empress and the Chancellor.   If Russia and Austria were henceforth to walk hand in hand it was essential to loosen the ties of the former with Prussia and to convince the Tsarina that certain rumours concerning his schemes were false.   If this could be achieved her confidence in the persons who had supplied such misleading information, the King of Prussia at their head, would be shattered. Since it was possible that she had mentioned the approaching visit to Frederick and that she might report the conversations, it would be wise to avoid political themes, and, in the event of a Russian initiative, to be cautious in his replies.   If Frederick were told that politics had been avoided on both sides, he would never believe it, and the conviction that he had been tricked by the Tsarina would go far to shatter the alliance.   The visitor's rôle would be that of the intelligent traveller seeking information about such subjects as the army and the educational system and leaving high politics alone.

Passing to Kaunitz' Memorandum on how to deal with Potemkin, the Emperor declared that he would enter into no discussions with him, powerful though he remained.   For the Austrophobia of his rival Panin, the Foreign Minister, would be intensified if he saw the visitor negotiating with the Favourite behind his back.   The more consideration shown to Panin, the better the prospect of weakening his attachment to Prussia.   A further motive for avoiding close contacts with Potemkin was the Grand Duke Paul's aversion for the Favourite and his friendship for Panin; for though the heir counted for nothing while the imperious Catherine was alive, it was desirable to look ahead and to win his sympathies in advance.   After studying her son's Memorandum the Empress forwarded it to Kaunitz, who proceeded to comment in his usual ample style.   While agreeing that to make a favourable personal impression on the Tsarina and her advisers was of supreme importance, it would not suffice. Formal declarations of Austrian friendship were also required, and, if the hosts avoided the initiative, the visitor should find the right moment to speak.   The proposal to avoid political discussion with Potemkin was approved, but if he intervened he should be treated with every consideration.

Such elaborate preparation for the journey on the part of the rulers of Austria was justified by the fact that the Emperor's mission was to be the most important of his life. The meetings with Frederick had not been designed to lead, and had not led, to any change of direction, and the visit to France had a limited objective. Now there seemed to be a chance of transforming the whole landscape of Eastern Europe and of opening the way to the realisation of projects unattainable without Russia's good will. Joseph had always loved travelling, and he looked forward with the keenest zest to the rendezvous at Mohilev, not far from the Galician frontier. 'I am truly anxious how I shall find everything there,' he wrote to Leopold. 'Obviously the country has changed out of all recognition since the beginning of the century and has, so to speak, been reborn. It is rich in territory and resources, and its situation is impregnable. Well, I will tell you more when I have seen it.' To his mother he wrote from Lemberg, the capital of Galicia, that he would strive to deserve her approbation in the delicate enterprise, and to Kaunitz that he would try to follow his wise counsels. He took with him Philip Cobentzl, the favourite disciple of Kaunitz and his destined successor at the Foreign Office. The traveller's reports were sent both through the regular post and by his own couriers. Since the former, as he was well aware, were opened and the contents were communicated to the Tsarina, graceful compliments could be paid to his hostess in an unobtrusive way. His real thoughts, needless to say, were to be found in the sealed correspondence.

On his arrival at Mohilev 'Count Falkenstein' was met by Potemkin, then at the height of his power, who presented a flowery autograph letter of welcome from the Empress. Joseph replied that he had long desired to make her acquaintance. Their first conversation after her ceremonial entry into the town took place at a large dinner-party and was general in character. He was pleased with his reception, he reported to his mother, but, as she knew, he had no taste for functions. Four days later he summarised his first impressions of the talks at meals, at the card-table, at balls, and at the opera, never alone with the sovereign yet frequently beyond the range of listeners. 'She seems pleased with me and our exchanges become daily more natural and more interesting, for confidence is springing up. She appears disinclined to intensive political discussion, and one has to seize one's opportunity to slip in a word. Not till yesterday could I refer to the false and sinister interpretations which the King of Prussia has spread about me. She replied that it was mere gossip, that he was ill informed by minor personages, that he was no longer believed even when he spoke the truth, and that his hermit life and advancing years had soured him. She hopes for the end of the American war and desires the independence of some of the colonies.' The most unexpected turn in the conversations was a suggestion that Italy, and above all the Papal states, might be suitable as the patrimony of the Holy Roman Emperors. 'I responded in a jocular manner, but then I remarked that the *status quo* in Italy was of lively concern to so many Powers that I could not secure recognition even of the rights derived from Augustus himself. Her Rome, namely Constantinople, on the other hand, was much easier for her to conquer. She seemed embarrassed at having raised the question, assuring me that she only desired peace and had no thought of such a conquest.'

The guest found it difficult to get in close touch with his hostess, who was never alone. It would be different, she assured him, if, as she hoped, he would come to St. Petersburg. Only in the capital could he form an impression of the achievements of Peter the Great and herself; there, too, he would see three squadrons of warships ready to sail. Joseph needed no pressing, not only because he was eager to see the youngest of European capitals but because an arrangement could be reached nowhere else. Moreover it would indicate to Frederick and other interested observers the success of his journey, and would allow him to meet the Grand Duke Paul and Count Panin. It would also help to weaken the impression of the approaching visit of the Prince of Prussia. It was accordingly decided that he should accompany the Tsarina as far as Smolensk and then branch off to Moscow, where Potemkin would be in charge. The Empress proudly described the most celebrated of her many lovers as her pupil, adding that she had found such harmony of ideas in no other man. So far he had not talked politics, but he would certainly do so before long; perhaps the visit to Moscow had been arranged for that purpose.

The first prolonged conversations with the Tsarina, who proved very friendly and well-informed, took place during the long drive to Smolensk.   Since the whole purpose of the visit to Russia was to loosen the ties between St. Petersburg and Potsdam Joseph began with the King of Prussia's reported utterances about himself, and Catherine reiterated that she did not believe what he said.   He then declared that at Vienna they were firmly resolved to inform her of their views on all important occasions and to ask her advice.   Highly pleased, she promised to give the best advice and, if so desired, to carry it out herself.   The conversation now reached the critical point: she complained of Austria's penchant for Turkey, Joseph of the Prussian alliance. She explained that at the moment of her accession she had no choice but to make peace, since she had found everything in a state of collapse.   She seemed about to indicate a remedy, but merely observed that her visitor possessed no capital city.   'These reiterated references to Italy make me think she has something up her sleeve, but so far I have not got to the bottom of it.   Whenever she talks to me of Rome, I always mention Constantinople with a smile.   Once, however, she replied that if she had ever conquered it she would not have kept it but would have used it for some other purpose.   This brings me back to the notion that she is still thinking of dividing up her empire and of giving the Eastern Empire to her grandson Constantine when she has conquered it.   I assume Prince Potemkin will talk about it at Moscow and perhaps enter into detail.   I shall keep my ears open, and perhaps greater privacy at Tsarkoe-Selo will bring her out.   Already the strongest prejudices seem to have been dispelled: Her Majesty appears to like me.   That will smooth the way to further proposals which I must not make prematurely. Too much haste would do more harm than good, all the more because all this may perhaps be a trap to provoke indiscretions. I trust no one here and apparently they have no confidence in each other.'

Moscow fully realised the traveller's anticipations.   He had never seen so vast a city, far surpassing Paris, Rome and Naples, but palaces and hovels jostled one another.   Contrary to expectation Potemkin had avoided politics. 'He is too indolent, too cold for sustained effort, too indifferent. Apart from his position at Court, I feel he could only be of service to prevent something at a particular moment, not for anything requiring system, principles, application.' St. Petersburg was still more impressive; it had to be seen to be believed. 'I am not prone to enthusiasm or exaggeration, but any tourist anxious to see fine and inspiring objects who does not include this in his itinerary is making a great mistake. Her Majesty continues to shower favours on me and I never cease to delight in her conversation. The Grand Duke is far above his reputation abroad, and his wife [1] is as pretty as she is suited for her position. It is a perfect union, and there are two nice little princes. So far I have seen very little. The Court absorbs my time, but I do not regret it, for that is my sphere of action. Though I am not much of a courtier, my life here is much more agreeable than I dared to hope.'

Three days later, on July 8, he summarised his numerous conversations with the Tsarina. She was now almost inclined to treat Austria on the same footing as the King of Prussia, but she would avoid a breach with the latter as she desired to be courted from both sides. She regretted the sorry plight of England, liking the English but despising the weakness of the King and the follies of his Ministers. As regards France it was just the contrary; she approved the conduct of the King and the choice of his Ministers but had no love for the nation. In Sweden she disapproved both the people and the King. These observations were largely academic, but Turkey was a live issue. 'She is undoubtedly hostile to the Turks, and the notion of an Eastern Empire occupies her head and heart: it is constantly peeping out. For instance, she said she did not understand why the French were so keen on having Moslems at Constantinople and why some other nation should not suit them. She positively assured me that she would never ally herself with the Turks, not even by a commercial treaty. The King of Prussia was often a blunderer in politics; he cherished incompatible designs and was deceived by his Ministers. All this was due to his lonely and melancholy way of life which exposed him to the most extravagant ideas. She added with emphasis that she would not begin a war,

---

[1] A Württemberg princess.

not even against the Turks, but would stoutly resist any attack.
To the observation that they would not be so foolish after their
rough lesson, she replied that one could never be sure of them;
as neighbours they could always find little incidents if they wished.
Whenever Italy, and above all Rome, was mentioned, the
Empress warmly declared that that was my capital; there I should
have a vast field for glory and fame.' These advances evoked
no response as he had from the first made his position clear.
Potemkin had spoken to Cobentzl, who made light of it as something possible and even easy, but without entering into details.
'All this may be ruse, or falsity, or chimeras which I can hardly
imagine Her Majesty takes seriously.'

Potemkin and the Tsarina worked together, and the Favourite
was employed to take soundings through the Austrian Ambassador. He assured Cobentzl of his zeal for the reunion of
the two Courts. Now that he understood the views of the
Emperor, the time had come to end the estrangement and restore
the old confidence and intimacy. Since no details were
mentioned, Joseph instructed Cobentzl to suggest, as if it were
merely his own idea, that one of the first steps, the most innocent
and generally acceptable, would be for the two Powers, as Kaunitz
had suggested, to guarantee each other's possessions. That
would be purely defensive, and Russia could arrange with the
King of Prussia in the same way. To avoid the impression of
importunity Joseph reported that he hoped to find an opportunity
to make a similar observation to Panin. 'Then we must await
their response. This first step might lead to others. Anyhow,
no harm would be done, since the matter is quite simple, cannot
hurt anyone and is only put forward as a suggestion.'

Potemkin consulted the Tsarina, who inquired whether future
conquests would be included in such a pact. That, it was
explained to him, was impossible, for there would be no re-
ciprocity. He rejoined that Russia would guarantee all Austria's
future conquests except in Germany and Poland, but this was
also dismissed as unreasonable. The Favourite now reduced
his demands to a verbal promise from the Emperor that Austria
would never conclude an alliance with the Turks against the
Tsarina in return for a similar assurance. Joseph observed that
the drafting would have to be left to the Ministers. 'All this,'

he reported, 'took several days of comings and goings between Potemkin and Cobentzl, the former consulting the Tsarina at every step. That is the present situation. If Her Majesty speaks to me I shall assure her that we have no wish to join the Turks against her, and we would both undertake not to join in any offensive against each other. The shorter and simpler the phraseology, the better.'

A second and totally unexpected suggestion was made by Potemkin to Cobentzl which the Tsarina could not well make for herself. She was dying to ask the Emperor for the Golden Fleece. She knew it was against the rules, but she passionately desired such a public declaration of his friendship; she hoped an exception would be made in this special case. 'I was greatly embarrassed,' confided Joseph to his mother. 'I think I understand Her Majesty, whose only fault is vanity. The thought of being the first female recipient delights her beyond measure. To refuse it would be to disoblige her. I replied that it would be very difficult and almost impossible, but that if Her Majesty met us in other ways the impossible might become possible. I am curious to see if she will speak of it herself; if so it cannot be refused, and it would have to be sent by one of the existing Knights—a rich little Fleece, well mounted but not too large, which she can wear on her coat.'

The Tsarina was far too vain and selfish to inspire genuine friendship, but the more Joseph saw of Grand Duke Paul and his wife, the more they pleased him. 'He seems quite at ease with me, and I am enraptured with the Grand Duchess. If I could have found or imagined such a princess ten years ago I would have married her without hesitation. They are two most interesting people. They are intelligent and well informed. They affect or possess—I cannot say which—sentiments of the greatest probity and justice, placing peace and the happiness of humanity above everything. Their relations to Her Majesty, especially those of the Grand Duke, are rather strained; the cordiality without which, dear Mother, I could not live, does not exist. The Grand Duchess is more at ease. She dominates her husband, shows interest in him, and manages his household to perfection. She is a princess who might some day play a leading part. Both show me friendship, but I must be on my guard

since too close an association with them would be unwise.   So
far everything seems to have gone very well.   Her Majesty has
told me all about the revolution which brought her to the throne,
and spoke of the madness of Peter III.   The Grand Duke has
talked of his frustrations and of Her Majesty's natural son.   All
this indicates confidence; but it is not easy to satisfy both parties,
since each desires exclusive consideration.'

The Emperor left St. Petersburg with regret.   'I have been
overwhelmed by marks of confidence and affection and I am
grateful.   During my short visit to this empire I have seen great
things done, planned and executed in the grand style; nowhere
does one sense doubt or half-heartedness or cramping economies.'
The situation had been explored and the atmosphere improved
but no commitments were made on either side.   No official reply
was made concerning the reciprocal guarantee which Cobentzl
had proposed to Potemkin.   Fortunately the Tsarina herself
had not spoken about the Fleece, and her guest, mindful of his
own dignity and his mother's feelings, never dreamed of offering
it.   'The same ideas are always cropping up.   They want to
save Germany and to give us a bit of Italy so that they can do what
they like with the Turks.   They have never put it into so many
words, but all indications point that way.   We shall see if they
become vocal before I depart.   I can see that she is on fire, but
I shall leave it to her to speak; all this may only be a stratagem.
I have told her many times that we desire no aggrandisement in
Germany or elsewhere, but also that we will never allow the King
of Prussia to make fresh acquisitions nor exchanges of territory,
since his enmity to us has always been unconcealed.   Once she
quoted Peter the Great's observation to the father of King
Stanislas Augustus that they could do more in an hour than the
Ministers in a month.   That showed her wish to talk of plans, but
either her pride, or her courage, or her *finesse* prevents her.   Thus,
in these two matters I quietly wait and see.   If one adopts a
serious tone, she changes the conversation as though she herself
had not been speaking seriously.   We must let her take her time
and not give her the satisfaction of becoming her dupe.'

Though no definite decisions of any kind had been reached
when the Emperor left the capital on July 18 he was entitled
to regard his visit as a success.   Its object had been strictly

8

exploratory.   When he was invited to keep up a correspondence he merely promised to write on great occasions. 'You will see, dear Mother, that despite all the fine words and most friendly demonstrations I am not altogether the dupe. I shall never entirely trust their sincerity. They think they have blinded me and consequently, as they take less pains to wear a mask, I see them more naturally and profit thereby. The Empress really touched me by her affectionate farewell. She embraced me; so did the Grand Duke and the Grand Duchess, and if one could believe this race I should be regretted by everyone.' That was not strictly true, for the Prussophils, with Panin at their head, were glad to see him go. Warm expressions reached the traveller from the Tsarina at various stages of his return journey. Now the ice had been broken the friendship had to be kept in repair.   Only with time and patience, wrote Kaunitz to Cobentzl, could they gradually attain their goal of a friendship and a guarantee treaty.   That it would be easier to reach when Joseph should become the sole ruler of Austria was not mentioned but was generally understood.   Yet even Maria Theresa seemed pleased and relieved at the results of the mission.   'I can assure you,' she wrote to Marie Antoinette, 'that no negotiations have taken place, but he seems to have succeeded in dispelling the unfounded prejudices against us which were very deeply rooted.' A flattering reference to Leopold in one of Catherine's letters led the Emperor to advise him to write to her direct. 'It is our interest to consider her in every way, and a grateful letter from you will suffice.   Forgive this burden, but it is grist to my mill.'

Two years later the Emperor summarised his impressions of the Tsarina in conversation with Keith, the British Ambassador in Vienna.[1] 'Whoever has to deal with her must never lose sight of her sex nor forget that a woman sees things and acts differently from one of our sex.   I speak from experience in saying that the only way to keep in with her is neither to spoil her nor to cause offence; to give her her way in matters of little consequence, to render every refusal as palatable as possible, to let her perceive a constant desire of pleasing, yet at the same time firmly to adhere to certain essential principles and a just sense of one's own rights. When she expresses a wish for a thing that can be granted without

[1] Temperley, *Frederick the Great and Kaiser Joseph*, Appendix III.

departing from these principles, indulge her with that complaisant attention which is ever due to a lady; but when she insists on what ought not to be complied with, indicate that though she may often lead she cannot drive. In this manner one may hope to live upon a fair footing with her, guarding against the heat and impetuosity of her feelings, and convincing her that in essential points every sovereign has an unquestionable right to draw the line of his own conduct and to adhere to it strictly. The singular misfortune of the Empress is that of having no person about her who dares to restrain, even to depress, the first effusion of her passions.' As a rule Joseph was a poor psychologist, but he had read the mind of Catherine the Great and dispelled her suspicions of Vienna. A year later the two sovereigns became allies, and in 1787, at the Tsarina's invitation, they met for the second and last time.

Soon after the Emperor's return from Russia the great Empress passed away. Incessant childbearing, the burdens of government, the excitements and anxieties of war, and the painful friction with her gifted heir had worn down her strength. It had been no mere figure of speech when she complained in her letters of failing powers. Corpulency, a yellow skin, breathlessness, a craving for open windows day and night, an insatiable thirst which even iced lemonade could not quench, all pointed to incurable heart trouble. Drenched by a rainstorm during a drive in an open carriage she developed a temperature, but on account of her breathing she could not go to bed. The day was spent at her desk, the night in an armchair. She reminded her doctor of his promise always to tell her the truth as she desired to prepare for the end while her brain remained clear. On November 25, 1780, she made her confession; the next day she received the Sacrament. On November 27 hope was abandoned. On November 28 she received Supreme Unction in the presence of her children. Everyone was in tears except the dying woman, who blessed and kissed them and bid them farewell. Speaking without the slightest tremor she declared that all she had done had been inspired by good intentions; she hoped God would be merciful. Her only grief was to leave her children. When Joseph begged her to sleep she rejoined: 'I do not want to be caught by death unawares; I wish to see it approach.' She ordered her doctor to close her eyes, adding that it would be too much for the Emperor. In the evening of November 29 she passed away. For forty years she had striven, in war and in peace, for the good of her subjects as she conceived it. Though she inspired little affection among them, no eighteenth-century ruler had won such universal respect. She did honour to her throne and her sex, declared Frederick the Great. Anchored in the past and terrified by the clamour of an age which she failed to understand, she made the common mistake of moving too slowly, as her son, the apostle of reason and the enemy of privilege, was to make the almost equally common mistake of charging impetuously ahead. It is only fair to both to remember that the ramshackle empire was less easy to govern than a unitary state.

'I am so overwhelmed by the horrible ceremony that I can only send you a single word,' wrote the Emperor to Leopold on December 4. 'This is the most cruel experience imaginable. An attachment of forty years, the object of my life and of gratitude for all her favours—to lose it is almost enough to unbalance me. My whole scheme of life is upset and I find myself almost alone in the world, since Providence has taken my wives, my child, my father and mother. Only your friendship and my work will enable me to bear up. I cannot tell you how it has all affected me, and all my previous troubles do not approach this.' Leopold's grief increased his own. 'I cannot get used to this misfortune; every minute I feel I ought to be sending her papers or going to her. A sweet habit of forty years, a blend of duty, inclination and gratitude, is not forgotten or effaced. I am still feeling quite stunned. Naturally my heavy burdens divert my thoughts, but the moments of reflection are terrible. And the weather is too bad to go out. It all makes me feel an old man.' To Kaunitz he wrote that he had ceased to be a son, which had been the best side of him. Among the letters of condolence was one from the Tsarina with fervent wishes for health, glory and a happy reign.

At last the reformer—the Categorical Imperative on the throne, as his latest Austrian biographer, Ernst Benedikt, describes him—could do what he liked. When the first pangs of filial grief were over the predominant feeling must have been one of intense relief. For twenty years there had been not only a union of hearts but friction and frustration. In the protracted contest of wills both scored victories and both suffered defeats. Kaunitz remained at his side, but the Emperor was now the master. 'A despot in the noblest sense,' declares his Russian biographer, Mitrofanoff. *Sic volo, sic jubeo*, was the order of the day. With his impulsive temperament a quicker *tempo* was to be expected, but there was a new philosophy as well. Even if he had known that he had only nine years to live, and that he would die before he was forty-nine, the first servant of the state could not have driven himself harder. His friends were few and he had no hobbies. Many rulers and statesmen with only a fraction of his gifts and virtues have possessed a certain horse sense which saved them from gross miscalculations. This instinct was lacking in Joseph, who was forced to learn by bitter experience the truth of the Bismarckian aphorism that politics are the art of the possible. In the famous phrase of Frederick, he always took the second step before the first. By the time he was beginning to learn his lesson he was at death's door. The lifelong apprehension of Maria Theresa that her brilliant son—the ablest though not the wisest of the Hapsburgs—might endanger or even destroy his splendid inheritance by his scorn for tradition and compromise was not wholly without justification. Few sovereigns who have worked so hard and so unselfishly have left such a store of resentment behind them. Yet no one could fairly argue that Joseph's striving for a brave new world—for a powerful, unified, well-governed Austrian state—had been wholly in vain. Without the drastic modernisation inaugurated by the great Empress and developed by her successor the realm of the Hapsburgs could scarcely have survived the storms and stress of the Napoleonic Wars.

Bibliographical Note. — Maria Theresa must be studied in her correspondence: *Maria Theresia und Joseph II, Ihre Korrespondenz*, 3 vols.; *Correspondance Secrète du Comte Mercy d'Argenteau avec l'Impératrice Marie Thérèse*, 3 vols.; *Briefe an ihre Kinder und Freunde*, 4 vols. The story of her reign was compiled from the archives by Arneth in 10 vols., 1863–79. Guglia, *Maria Theresa*, 2 vols., 1917, is the fullest and most important of the later biographies. Mary Moffat, Kretschmayr, Tschuppik and Kurt Pfister cater for the general reader: of these Kretschmayr is the best. The volumes on Maria Theresa and Joseph II by J. Franck Bright in the *Foreign Statesmen* Series are admirable summaries. On Joseph II there is no satisfactory work on a large scale. Mitrofanoff's *Joseph II* (German translation, 2 vols.) is a detailed study of his reforms, not a biography. The best short biographies are by Ernst Benedikt (with an appendix of new material) and Padover. Redlich, *Das Österreichische Reichs- u. Staatsproblem*, vol. i, opens with a masterly analysis of the constitutional and administrative changes carried out by the two rulers. The seven volumes of the diaries of the Court Chamberlain, Count Khevenhüller, the Austrian equivalent of Dangeau's *Journal of the Court of Louis XIV*, record the daily round at the Hofburg and Schönbrunn.

2

MARIA THERESA AND MARIE ANTOINETTE

I. *From Vienna to Versailles*

NO eloquence of tongue or pen is needed to adorn the moving story of Marie Antoinette. Among all the unhappy women who have worn a crown not even Mary Stuart nor the last Tsarina was offered such a cup of bitterness to drain. No actor on the crowded stage of the French Revolution has held the imagination of mankind to such an extent as the warm-hearted, pleasure-seeking, vivacious Archduchess, whose character ripened in the fires of affliction. The purpose of this study is to depict her fortunes during the first decade of her public life with the aid of a series of letters unique in historical literature.

Amid the vast array of evidence on the closing phase of the *Ancien Régime* no single item compares in significance with the *Correspondance Secrète entre Marie Thérèse et le Comte de Mercy-Argenteau, avec les Lettres de Marie-Thérèse et de Marie Antoinette*, published in Paris by Arneth and Geffroy in 1875. In these fifteen hundred pages, printed, with a few omissions, from the originals at Vienna, are recorded, sometimes from hour to hour, the emotions of a mother and daughter compelled to play leading parts in the hazardous international game. Our understanding of the two chief actors is quickened by the far more voluminous parallel correspondence between the Empress and Count Mercy d'Argenteau, the Austrian Ambassador in Paris since 1766, of which Marie Antoinette never knew. So completely did this wise and devoted diplomat enjoy the confidence of his sovereign that no secrets were withheld from him, and his advice was sought on all personal no less than on all political issues. Long afterwards, when a prisoner of the Revolution, the Queen told Mme de Tourzel, governess of the royal children, that she had regarded him as a father. He was, indeed, her guide, philosopher and friend. He was often consulted both on the drafting of the maternal admonitions and on the replies from Versailles. In addition to the reports which her son the Emperor Joseph and Kaunitz, the Foreign Minister, were permitted to peruse, many others were marked for her alone. The Empress, for her part, often added confidential passages in her own hand to the letters dictated to her secretary. The whole exchange was in French, though it was the mother tongue of the Ambassador alone, for Mercy belonged to an old noble family of Liége. As a picture of the atmosphere and personalities of the most sumptuous Court in Europe it rivals that of Elizabeth Charlotte of the Palatinate, sister-in-law of Louis XIV and mother of the Regent Orleans, nearly a century earlier, and the personal interest is far greater. Liselotte, with a thicker skin than Marie Antoinette, was well able to take care of herself. Her subordinate position saved her from the temptations which confronted a Dauphine and a Queen, and she had no political tasks to fulfil. Her letters to her family are the entertaining gossip of a Court. Those of the Empress and Marie Antoinette are the revelation of two sorely tried souls.

The ninth child and youngest daughter of Maria Theresa was born on November 2, 1755. Her father, the Emperor Francis of Lorraine, a good-natured mediocrity, pious, frivolous, extravagant, less interested in public affairs than in the chase, died when she was ten. Her mother, respected and admired for her character and courage even by her lifelong enemy Frederick the Great, set an example of the strenuous life to her sixteen children. Immersed in the exacting tasks of ruling her far-flung dominions and needing every penny for the ruinous Silesian wars, she had little time or thought to spare for the younger members of her family, while it was particularly regrettable that the education of Marie Antoinette should be neglected, since she was destined from the nursery to a marriage of the highest political significance.

After a century and a half of conflict between the Bourbons and the Hapsburgs for the hegemony of Europe the rapid rise of Prussia produced the historic *renversement des alliances* during the breathing space which followed the close of the War of the Austrian Succession in 1748. Locked in a deadly embrace with

England for domination in the far places of the earth, France now seemed less of a menace than the ambitious Protestant power in Northern Germany whose ruler had seized Austria's richest province on the death of the Emperor Charles VI in 1740. When the first two Silesian wars proved that she could never hope to recover her stolen property without a powerful Continental ally, Maria Theresa accepted the advice of Kaunitz to make friends with her ancient foe. France, sadly fallen from her high estate, was ready to grasp the proffered hand. The treaty was signed in 1755 and was implemented in the Seven Years War which broke out in 1756. The whole face of Europe had been changed. Though the effort to regain Silesia failed once more, hope was never abandoned by the Empress, her son Joseph and Kaunitz, for the French alliance remained the corner-stone of Hapsburg policy for almost forty years. What then could be more natural than a dynastic union? *Bella gerant alii, tu felix Austria nube.* The plan, which originated in 1764, soon after the close of the Seven Years War, was warmly welcomed by Choiseul, the Foreign Minister, and informal discussions with the Austrian Ambassador ensued. Mme Antoine, as she was called, was selected as being of the most suitable age for the Dauphin, one year her senior. We hear of special attentions—such as presents of fruit out of season—paid by the French Ambassador in 1767, on her twelfth birthday, and a symbolic dolphin (dauphin) played a prominent part in the fête. She had learned a little Italian from Metastasio, a little music from Gluck, and a smattering of French. A tomboy and a mimic, she was restless and indolent, easily distracted from her lessons, and preferred romping in the woods with her dogs. Temperament she had, and heart, but little brains.

In November 1768, on the morning of her thirteenth birthday, the Empress instructed her Ambassador to select a French priest capable of forming the character and developing the intelligence of the destined bride. 'I am impatient to know who will be chosen as the confessor of my daughter,' she wrote; 'I should also like a *friseur*, but I leave everything to Choiseul.' The choice fell on the Abbé de Vermond, a man of thirty-five, Librarian of the Collège Mazarin. Tactful, conscientious and reasonably cultivated, he did his best for the little pupil, who speedily won

his affection.   It was uphill work, for she had no desire to learn.
His reports describe a girl who detested reading, knew practically
nothing of history and geography, and was unable to spell.   Her
French was a jargon full of German words.   He began with an
hour a day devoted to French conversation, and soon added
reading lessons in history.   Though by no means stupid she
found it difficult to concentrate and loved to make fun of her
entourage.   Eager to know more of the destined bride of his heir,
Louis XV despatched an artist to Vienna and sent a portrait of
the Dauphin.   In the summer of 1769 the Empress imported a
coiffeur from Paris, and the girl was instructed in the curtsy.
'Tout va bien pour notre petite,' exclaimed Kaunitz, 'pourvu
qu'on ne la gâte pas.'   The marriage contract signed on April 4,
1770, fixed her allowance and promised her jewels worth 200,000
crowns.   On April 15 the French Ambassador arrived with a
large suite to ask for her hand.   Four days later the Papal Nuncio
officiated at the marriage by proxy, the Dauphin being represented
by a brother of the bride.   On the previous evening she had
written her first letter to the King of France at the dictation of her
mother, who added a private appeal : 'May Your Majesty be
good enough to guide her.   She is full of good will, but at her age
I beg for indulgence for any mistake.   I commend her as the
most tender pledge of the happy union between our states and
dynasties.'   On April 21 the Archduchess drove away from the
Hofburg.   Taking her daughter in her arms the Empress
whispered : 'Be so good to the French that they can say I have
sent them an angel.'   Sobs broke her voice, and the half-fainting
girl had to be helped into the carriage : both of them realised
that they would never meet again.   Joseph, her elder brother,
accompanied her as far as Melk.

Her mother's parting gift was a length memorandum in French
which she was exhorted to study at intervals of a month.   'You
will begin by saying your prayers on your knees and by a few
minutes of devotional reading.   Everything depends on a good
start of the day and on the intentions with which we face its
duties.   On this point you will be very strict.   Its execution is
solely in your hands, and your happiness, spiritual and temporal,
may depend on it.   It is the same with your evening prayers and
examination of conscience; but I repeat that those of the morning

and the little devotional readings are the most vital. You will always tell me which book you are using. You will practise meditation as often as possible during the day, above all at Holy Mass. I hope you will hear it with edification every day, and twice on Sundays and fête days if it is the custom of the Court. But you must not think of introducing new customs nor should you ask for the adoption of our Vienna ways. When in church display the greatest respect and do not look around. All eyes will be fixed on you; do not give cause for scandal. Read no book, not even a brochure, without the approbation of your confessor. This is all the more necessary in France because among the flood of publications many are hostile to religion and morals beneath a veneer of respectability.' Passing from the religious duties the anxious Empress draws on her experiences of thirty years of rule. 'Do not ask for favours; listen to no one if you wish for peace. Do not be inquisitive. Avoid all familiarity with humble people. Always ask M. and Mme de Noailles what you should do in every case, since it is your wish to please the nation, and let them tell you if there is anything amiss in your talk or conduct. Reply affably to everyone, with grace and dignity, but you must also know how to refuse.' She would hear from her mother once a month and should reply by the same courier. She could correspond with her brother Joseph and her sister Caroline, Queen of Naples, whom she might well take as a model. 'Her example should be a guide and encouragement, her situation having been and still being in every way much more difficult than yours.'

The first letter to her daughter, dated May 4, combined delight in the reports of her affability *en route* with further motherly advice, 'So now you are in the place assigned to you by Providence. In view of your circumstances you are the luckiest of your sisters, indeed of all princesses. You will find a tender father (Louis XV) who, if you desire it, will also be your friend. To give him your full confidence will involve no risks. Love him, obey him, try to anticipate his thoughts as much as you can. It is this father, this friend, who is my whole consolation amidst my grief, in the hope that you will follow my advice to await his directions in everything. Of the Dauphin I say nothing. You know my delicacy on this matter. The woman is subject to her husband in everything, and she should have no other occupation than to please him and do his will. The only true happiness on earth is a happy marriage; I speak from experience. Everything depends on the woman. My only anxiety concerns negligence in your prayers and readings. Bestow affection on your family, your aunts, your brothers-in-law and sisters-in-law. Allow no bickering; you can silence people or avoid it by moving away.' The Empress enclosed a letter to the King, and there was also a line for Mme Adelaide, the eldest and ablest of the King's daughters. 'These princesses are full of virtues and talents, happily for you, and I hope you will deserve their friendship.' She was to tell the Choiseuls that she had received instructions to pay them special consideration. 'Do not forget a mother,' concluded the letter, 'who, though far away, will be thinking of you till her last breath. Blessings on you.' In the blend of genuine piety, maternal affection and political strategy the letter is characteristic of the noblest of the Hapsburgs.

At Kehl, on the French frontier, Comte de Noailles, the envoy of the King, carried out the customary observances in a wooden house constructed on an island in the Rhine. The girl exchanged her Austrian attire for French garments, and her suite was replaced by ladies of her French household with Comtesse de Noailles, her *dame d'honneur*, at their head. The same evening she was rapturously acclaimed in Strasbourg, and Mercy reported that her *début* had surpassed all expectations. Similar scenes were witnessed at Nancy and other cities *en route*. On May 14 she was welcomed at Compiègne by the King, Mesdames his daughters, the Dauphin and his brothers, and Choiseul. Louis XV was delighted with the graceful and lively girl with her blue eyes and dazzling complexion; 'J'ai ma Duchesse de Bourgogne,' he exclaimed, alluding to his mother, 'the rose of Savoy,' who was the delight of Louis XIV in his closing years. The Dauphin, a fat and clumsy lad not yet sixteen, was tongue-tied and shy; his voice was disagreeable and he was slovenly in his clothes. Stupid he was not. He liked history and geography, and knew some Latin, Italian, German and English, but he had been kept so much in the background that his appearances at Court were an ordeal. He was afflicted by an inferiority complex and a resulting paralysis of will which he was never to overcome. His character was beyond reproach, but the graces were lacking. He was happiest in physical exercises, hunting, swimming, the felling of trees, the sawing of wood, and in occupations of a manual kind. With these vigorous activities went the ravenous appetite of the Bourbons. He was almost terrified at the sight of a woman, and his experienced grandfather sarcastically observed: 'Ce n'est pas un homme comme un autre.' Of the *bonhomie* of Henri IV and the dignity of Louis XIV there was not a trace. The nearest precedent in the royal house was the equally blameless and equally colourless Louis XIII. The only entry in the meagre diary which he had kept since his thirteenth year for the day on which he saw his future wife ran: *Entrevue avec Madame la Dauphine.*

Two days after the welcome at Compiègne the Court drove away, stopping for a little time at St. Denis to visit Mme Louise, the youngest of Mesdames the King's daughters, who, on the promotion of Mme du Barry, had exchanged the foul air of Versailles for the peace of a Carmelite nunnery. The night was passed at La Muette, a royal hunting lodge in the Bois de Boulogne, and that evening the Dauphine made the acquaintance of a very different woman. Mme du Barry had never appeared at formal gatherings, but on this occasion, to the general surprise, she sat beside the King at the *Grand Souper.* It was inconceivable, wrote Mercy, that he should have chosen this moment for an honour hitherto withheld. The bride, who innocently inquired what was the function of that pretty woman, was told that she had to amuse the King. She was soon to learn the truth from his scandalised daughters. Next morning the Court reached Versailles and at midday the marriage was celebrated by the Archbishop of Rheims. After supper the Royal Family and the Court dignitaries accompanied the young pair to their bedroom, the Archbishop pronounced a blessing on the bed, and the King handed the Dauphine her chemise. For the first time they were alone together. Everyone had been struck by the indifference of the bridegroom. The only entry in his diary for his wedding day was *Rien*. Having had no part in the choice of his wife he had gone through the ceremonies like an automaton. Mercy reported that he scarcely spoke a word, and the Abbé Vermond was equally distressed. 'While I was with her this morning,' he reported, 'the Dauphin came in. "Have you slept?" he asked. "Yes,"

was the reply.   He left without another word, and the Dauphine
amused herself with her little dog.'

The coldness of her husband and the presence of the Favourite
cast a shadow over the first phase of her new life, and no one
could describe the Court of the elderly *roué* as a happy place.
Shortly before her arrival most of the leading figures had been
removed by death—the neglected Queen Maria Leczinska, the
respected Dauphin Louis, his excellent wife Maria Josepha of
Saxony, and Mme de Pompadour, the ambitious *maîtresse en titre*.
After a brief phase of disconsolate boredom the King filled the
vacuum with Mme du Barry.   His three unmarried daughters,
Adelaide, Victoire and Sophie, lived frustrated lives in the vast
palace which housed five thousand souls.   His five grandchildren were the Dauphin, the Comte de Provence (later Louis
XVIII), the Comte d'Artois (later Charles X), Mme Clothilde,
and Mme Elizabeth, an attractive little girl of seven.   Choiseul
was still at the helm, but his position was threatened by the anti-
Austrian clique, led by Marshal the Duc de Richelieu, First
Gentleman of the Chamber, which had pushed the Favourite into
the King's arms.   The illegitimate daughter of an untraced father
and the mistress of Comte du Barry had attracted the King's
notice in 1768 at the age of twenty-five and was formally presented
in 1769.   Henceforth the Court and the Government were
divided into two camps—her friends and her foes.   That she
was the prettiest and most elegant woman at Versailles was
conceded on both sides.

The French marriage was avowedly a political expedient, and
a mother's anxieties are revealed in her monthly letters.   'I fear
her tender age,' she wrote to Mercy before hearing of her arrival,
'the excessive flattery, her indolence and want of application.
Keep watch, I beseech you, lest she fall into evil hands, for you
possess my entire confidence.'   The first bulletins were reassuring.   On June 15 the Ambassador reported the Dauphine's
opinion that her husband appeared to be a good man and that his
timidity and coldness were doubtless due to his education.   The
King, he added, was very pleased with her, and she caressed him
in a most touching manner.   'Vive et un peu enfant,' he remarked,
'mais cela est bien de son âge.'   Mesdames de France were also
enchanted.   'The whole Court and the public praise her affability

and grace. Yet, as Your Majesty bade me express my opinions, I must confess that, despite her well-merited success, I reflect that in so lively and superficial a nation and in such a tempestuous Court it is easier to win favour at the outset than to preserve it.' A few minor errors, such as making jokes about people, are attributed to youth and high spirits. 'The most important point is to induce her to overcome her extreme repugnance to serious occupation, above all reading, for only thus can she escape the dangers of her station. When I have spoken to her she manifests so much love and respect for Your Majesty and so great a desire to please that, if Your Majesty thinks well to stress these points, it would have much more effect than all representations from other quarters.'

On July 9 the Dauphine reported her first impressions. 'The King is full of kindness to me and I love him tenderly, but his weakness for Mme du Barry—the most stupid and impertinent creature imaginable—is pitiful. She has joined in our play every evening at Marly. Twice she sat next to me but did not speak to me, and I did not enter on conversation with her, though I spoke to her when it had to be. As regards my dear husband he has greatly improved. He is most friendly to me and he even begins to show me confidence.' Three days later she confessed that her mother's letters brought tears to her eyes, 'quoique je suis très bien ici.' She then described how she spent her day, as the Empress had asked her to do. But there were graver matters in her mind than the routine of the Court, and on July 14 Mercy reported a conversation which gave the Empress keen satisfaction, for the young couple at last discussed their situation. He was aware of the marriage state, began the Dauphin. From the start he had formed his plans, and now the time had come and at Compiègne he would make their union a reality. Since they were to live together, rejoined the Dauphine, they should talk freely about everything. For the first time he spoke of the Court, explaining that he knew and saw many things but had never allowed himself to talk about them. This intimate exchange reached the Ambassador through the Abbé Vermond, who received it from the Dauphine herself. The tutor had become the *Lecteur*, and he was never far from her side.

The Dauphine confided the good news about Compiègne to

Mme Adelaide, who thoughtlessly passed it on, and it was soon the talk of the town. When in consequence the sensitive lad, who loathed publicity, shrank back into his shell, wagging tongues inferred that a quarrel had occurred. In reply to the King's reproaches for his frigidity his grandson explained that he found his wife charming and loved her, but he needed time to overcome his timidity. Mercy was not seriously alarmed; with patience, he reported, everything would come right. The Empress was relieved, adding that her only anxiety came from Mesdames. Indeed, the more the Ambassador saw of the Dauphine the more he found to praise. 'She is acquiring a judgment and insight so far in advance of her years that I am often surprised. To these qualities she adds something more important still—a character of frankness and truthfulness which even in the smallest matter has never failed. There is still something to desire in her reading; but, to make up for it, the conversations with Abbé Vermond are becoming longer, more serious and more instructive. By his wise methods, his frankness and his zeal, this priest continues to render service beyond all price. She gives him her full confidence, and never has confidence been better deserved. The lies of the du Barry clique have had no result but to display their impudence and malice.'

The Ambassador, as he assured his sovereign, learned through his various informants at Court what the Dauphine said, did, or heard every hour of the day. 'Thus I can unhesitatingly affirm that it is absolutely false that the King is growing reserved and embarrassed; on the contrary, she increases in favour. That she insults the Favourite is equally untrue; there has never been anything but a little talk which Mesdames always began. Now she is more on her guard, and weeks pass without a critical word. Finally, she is adored by her *entourage* and the public. So far there has not been a single serious mistake, and I guarantee there never will be so long as I retain the help of Abbé Vermond and the confidence of Her Royal Highness.' Her praises were sung in the salons where the opinion of the capital was largely formed. 'Il n'y a qu'une voix sur Mme la Dauphine,' reported Mme du Deffand to Horace Walpole, 'elle grandit, elle embellit, elle est charmante.'

No sooner had Maria Theresa received these comforting

bulletins than a bomb exploded under her feet: on December 24, 1770, Choiseul was dismissed. He had been elevated by one royal mistress and was overthrown by another. For twelve years the indolence of Louis XV had made him the real ruler of France, but his unconcealed contempt for the Favourite was his undoing. 'Elle est jolie, elle me plaît, cela doit suffire,' the King had remarked, and Choiseul had to recognise defeat. The du Barry had more power than the Pompadour had ever possessed, reported Mme du Deffand to Horace Walpole, more even than Cardinal Fleury. For a moment the Empress was almost in despair. 'The dismissal of Vermond I regard as inevitable, and the fall of my daughter as well. Your access to her will be restricted and people will not dare to give you all the news. This abominable clique will ruin her and turn her against wise counsellors. I feel this blow is decisive for her though not for the alliance, which is as useful to France as to us. Tell me everything, above all the talk and bearing of the Dauphin, whom I do not regard as a fool but who is under the thumb of this clique.' To her daughter she wrote with rather more self-control. 'More than ever you will need the advice of Mercy and the Abbé, but have nothing to do with any faction. Observe neutrality, please the King, obey your husband. Be more reserved than ever, particularly with your aunts.' The Dauphine, who never concealed her feelings, sharply resented the fall of the Austrophil Minister and visited her displeasure on his successor, the Duc d'Aiguillon, nephew of the Duc de Richelieu, the leading champion of the Favourite.

The Empress's letters to her daughter usually contain more blame than praise. 'At your age,' she wrote on February 10, 1771, 'it is permissible to enjoy oneself. But to make that one's sole occupation, to do nothing solid or useful, to kill time with walks and visits—you will one day recognise its emptiness and regret not to have made better use of your time. I must also observe that the style of your letters grows ever worse and more incorrect; in these ten months you ought to have perfected yourself. You should get the Abbé or someone else to form your handwriting.' To Mercy she wrote by the same courier with even greater severity. 'I confess that my daughter's situation makes me very anxious. Her nonchalance, her distaste

9

for all serious tasks, her lack of discretion resulting from youth and vivacity, her contacts with her aunts, above all Mme Adelaide, perhaps the greatest intriguer of the lot—all this causes me alarm.   Everything depends on your skill in arranging occasional conversations with my daughter and in keeping Abbé Vermond at his post.   Perhaps she would welcome the removal of a man who might stand in her way in moments of dissipation.'

No one expected immediate results from a boy and girl marriage, but as the months melted into years all the world began to speculate about the succession.   When Louis XV ordered an examination of his grandson by the Court doctor the mystery was explained.   A slight physical defect existed, and the young husband lacked the courage to face a little pain.   'I try to persuade him to a small operation which has been spoken of and which I think necessary,' wrote the disappointed wife. Years of frustration left deep furrows on the character of both partners, accentuating the inferiority complex of the one and driving the other into senseless frivolities.   Indeed this freak of nature produced consequences far transcending the unhappiness of a married couple.   A Dauphin—and then a King—apparently unable to have children became the butt of satirists, while some people whispered that his wife sought consolation elsewhere. Among the many reasons that the *Ancien Régime* fell with a crash in 1789 the declining respect for the Royal Family comes high on the list.

II. *The Dauphine and the Favourite*

MARIE ANTOINETTE had been despatched to France in order to keep the Austrian alliance in repair, a task which demanded above all the favour of the King.   This, in turn, necessitated tolerable relations with the Favourite, who was *persona ingratissima* at Vienna on the dual ground of her character and her association with the anti-Choiseul clique.   Louis XV greatly preferred the Dauphine to his unloving daughters, whose loathing for the du Barry was unconcealed, but as she grew to maturity it became increasingly difficult for the monarch to tolerate a virtual boycott of the *maîtresse en titre*.   The intimacy with the aunts, above all

with Mme Adelaide, filled the Ambassador and the Empress with
alarm. In the summer of 1771, more than a year after the
marriage of his grandson, the King decided to act. Mme de
Noailles was informed that the Dauphine talked too freely and
that such conduct might produce evil results in the Royal Family.
The message was delivered to the fair offender, who promptly
informed her aunts and the Abbé. The latter passed it on to
Mercy, and Mercy to the Empress. At this point Kaunitz himself felt it necessary to intervene, for grave issues were at stake.
'To fail in consideration for one enjoying the favour of the King,'
he wrote to the Ambassador, 'is to fail in consideration for the
King himself, and offensive remarks would be even worse. Such
persons should be regarded simply as objects of the confidence
and favour of the sovereign—one should not inquire whether
rightly or wrongly. Prudence points to the same tactics, for they
can make mischief. I cannot believe that the Dauphine, gentle
and sensible as she is, has not grasped all this, so I feel she has
been blamed to excess. Since, however, the King believes it, I
think she should see him at once and tell him she is ready to do his
bidding.' When this letter was read to the Dauphine she replied
that an interview was needless; she would be so careful that no
further cause of complaint would arise. Such a negative attitude,
however, was not enough, and the tension increased from day to
day. Though she continued to meet the Favourite at balls, at
cards, and at the royal table, not a glance indicated that she was
aware of her existence. The indolent ruler had always detested
scenes, and he dreaded a talk in which the future Queen of France
would be commanded to speak to his mistress. Accordingly
Mercy was summoned by the Foreign Minister, and, to his surprise, was received in the apartments of the Favourite herself.
After a few words the latter entered the room and explained that
it was a calumny to attribute to her hostility to the Dauphine.
A few minutes later the King appeared, remarking to his visitor:
'Hitherto you have been the Ambassador of the Empress, but
now I beg you to be mine for a time.' The Dauphine, he continued, was charming, but young, impulsive, and married to a
man incapable of guiding her. She gave ear to the evil counsels
of certain persons and allowed herself to be mixed up in all
sorts of intrigues. The Ambassador was urged to work for a

change.   Mesdames were not mentioned, but for that there was no need.

In reporting this momentous interview Mercy played his trump card: the alliance, he argued, was at stake.   Capitulation was inevitable, and the angry girl promised to follow his advice. A day or two later, the scene having been prepared by the Ambassador, she was on the point of speaking to the Favourite when Mme Adelaide intervened with the words: 'It is time for us to go and await the King in the apartments of my sister Victoire.'   The Dauphine's nerve failed, and she subsequently apologised to Mercy, alleging her fear of displeasing her aunt.   Conversations with the Favourite, reported Mercy to the Empress, convinced him that, though mindless and frivolous, she was not malicious, and that a single word from the Dauphine would remove many difficulties.   The Ambassador's frequent references to her indeed are by no means unfriendly.   Her appearance and manners were reasonably refined, and unlike the Pompadour she was politically unambitious.   The King was as hurt as the Favourite who had been publicly snubbed.   'Well, M. de Mercy,' he exclaimed, 'your counsels have not borne fruit.   I must come to your aid.' But the Dauphine had a will of her own, and months passed before her surrender.

Marie Antoinette was more afraid of her mother than of the King, and the next letter from Vienna, as she expected, brought a stinging rebuke.   'The aunts have never won the respect of their family or of the public, and you choose to follow their lead. This fear and embarrassment about speaking to the King, the best of fathers, and of speaking to persons to whom you are advised to speak!   This fear of saying even *Bon jour*!   Even a word about clothes, about some trifle, causes you to make a wry face.   You have allowed yourself to be enslaved to such an extent that your reason and sense of duty are numbed.   I cannot keep silence after Mercy's conversation with you about the King's wishes and your duty.   You failed him, and what good reason can you allege?   None.   You must regard the du Barry merely as a lady admitted to the society of the King.   As his first subject you owe him obedience and submission.   You owe an example to the Court and the courtiers that the will of your master should prevail.   If degradation or familiarity were demanded of you,

neither I nor anyone would suggest it.   But some commonplace
word, some little attention, not for the lady but for your grandfather, your master, your benefactor!   And you fail him in such
a marked manner at the first opportunity of obliging him and
displaying your attachment, which will not so soon recur!   For
whose sake?   For a shameful complaisance for people who have
subjugated you by treating you like a child, in arranging rides
for you, playing with children and dogs, etc.   Such are the ties
which attach you to them in preference to your master, and which
in the long run will make you an object of ridicule, neither loved
nor esteemed.   You made such a good start: your judgment,
when not dominated by others, is always for the true and the
good.   Follow Mercy's advice.   What interest has he or I except
your happiness and the welfare of the State?   You are afraid of
speaking to the King but not of disobeying him.   You may
postpone verbal explanations with him for a short time, but I
demand that you convince him by every action of your respect
and affection and by seeking every occasion to please him.'   She
authorised Mercy to withhold her letter if he thought best, but
he decided to present it.

The Dauphine's reply displays praiseworthy self-control.
'Firstly I am in despair that you believe all the lies you are told
from here in preference to Mercy and myself.   I have several
reasons for believing that the King does not really wish me to
speak to the du Barry, apart from the fact that he has never
mentioned it to me.   He is friendlier than ever since he learned
that I had declined.   If you were here and could see everything
which goes on, you would realise that this woman and her clique
would not be content with a word but would always press for
more.   Be assured that I am in no need of being led by anyone
in matters of honour.   To show you the injustice of the friends
of the du Barry I must tell you that I did speak to her at Marly.   I
do not say I never will, but I cannot agree to do so at a fixed time
in order that she may announce it in advance and put a feather in
her cap.'   The reference to the Ambassador reveals her ignorance
of the fact that her mother's strictures were based on his reports.

Mercy now despatched a reassuring bulletin.   'In certain ways
she improves from day to day—in her deportment, in a little more
application, infinitely more in her French.   Everything denotes

a fine character, truthfulness, sound judgment.   Only the vivacity of youth and the unreasonable insinuations of Mesdames cloud these excellent qualities.'   Despite this testimonial the next note from Vienna returned to the charge.   'What troubles me is your silence about the aunts, which was the main point in my letter and is the cause of all your mistakes.   Does my advice and affection deserve less return than theirs?   I confess this thought pierces me to the heart.   Compare their rôle and reputation with mine.   So you should believe me in preference when my advice conflicts with theirs.   I am not comparing myself with these respected princesses, whom I value for their solid qualities, but I must repeat that they have won neither the esteem of the public nor the affection of their family.   By letting themselves be led by others they have rendered themselves odious, disagreeable and bored, the object of bickerings and cabals.   I see you going the same way and am I to keep silence?   I love you too much for that.   Your studied silence has hurt me and gives little hope of change.'   Her daughter quietly replied that she did not follow their lead, and that their faults were exaggerated.

At the close of 1771 there was encouraging news of the Dauphin.   'In the last few weeks,' reported Mercy, 'his attitude has improved out of all recognition, and his attentions amount to gallantry; little caresses, an eagerness to be with her and to anticipate her wishes, a tenderness which seems to increase from day to day.   Recently the King observed jokingly in the family circle that his only hope for the succession was the Comte d'Artois.   The Dauphin turned to his aunt Mme Victoire and said with a smile: "My grandfather does not think much of me, but he will soon be proved wrong."'   It was also good news that the King had lunched with the Dauphine, had made a long stay, and seemed in excellent spirits.   In discussing with the Ambassador her mother's reproaches, she confessed to little failings of hastiness and levity, adding that if she could see everything which went on she would forgive her.   She was well aware of the faults and shallowness of her aunts, but they were all the society she had.   Far more important was it that a measure of affection for her husband had been gradually added to respect.   One day, after a scene with the Comte de Provence, she embraced him with the words: 'I feel I love you more every day.   The more I compare you with others the more I realise your superiority.' After eighteen months of matrimony they were at last beginning to be friends—friends but nothing more.

It was the custom at Versailles for the ladies of the Court to pay their respects to the Royal Family on New Year's Day. Learning that the du Barry proposed to follow that practice the anxious Ambassador hurried to the Dauphine on the last day of 1771. 'I tried every imaginable means of persuading her not to snub the Favourite,' he reported, 'and it was only with great difficulty that I secured her promise. The main point was that Mesdames were not consulted.' Next day, when she appeared with two other ladies, the Dauphine, looking at her visitor without embarrassment, remarked to her: '*Il y a bien du monde aujourd'hui à Versailles.*' It had been a severe ordeal. 'I followed your advice,' she remarked to Mercy; 'here is the Dauphin to bear witness.' The young man smiled but said nothing. 'I have spoken once,' she continued, 'but I am resolved to stop there, and that woman will not hear my voice again.' Her vow was impossible to keep literally, but never again was a remark addressed directly and solely to her. Mercy expressed his congratulations and advised his sovereign to do the same. The incident, he added, had produced the expected benefit. The same evening the King embraced her, while Mesdames reproached her so sharply that she almost repented her act. Her mother's satisfaction, as usual, was decidedly grudging. 'Your agitation after these few words and your saying that it cannot be repeated alarms me. Who can give you better advice or better deserve your confidence than my Minister who knows everything about France? His sole object is your welfare. I repeat, my dear daughter, if you love me, follow his advice *without hesitation* in everything. If he wishes you to repeat your attentions to the lady or to the Comte and Comtesse de Provence, remember that he knows best how to avoid trouble.' Alike in her high sense of public duty, her authoritarian ways, and her inability to realise that her children were growing up, there was a good deal of Queen Victoria about the Empress Maria Theresa.

The best news for Vienna in the opening months of 1772 was that the Dauphine, as Mercy reported on February 20, 1772, resolved to shake off the yoke of the aunts. 'She is now on terms of easy friendship with them, but she reflects and decides for herself. No one leads her.' She was reading more and her excellent memory retained what she read. She enjoyed books on French history and would remain two or three hours in her apartments. At times the Abbé read aloud while she busied herself with needlework. She took dancing lessons and gave time to her music. Yet there were still moments of boredom which drove her to the society of her aunts, who seized the occasion to win support for the ambitions of their protégés, some of whom the Ministers could not possibly approve. 'I explained to her that all this was visibly compromising her reputation and even her sense of justice. In many cases, yielding to importunity, she allowed the use of her name to support this or that request without knowledge of the details. I strongly disapprove of such surprises, and in two or three little instances I was so successful in making her feel the dangers of such abuses that she is resolved to abstain. I am continually reminding her that to maintain her position she must absolutely avoid any request contrary to good order or to the interest of a third party, since in favouring one person there is a risk of disobliging others, committing injustices, and embarrassing the Ministers.' Those chiefly concerned were the Ministers of Finance and War, both of whom bowed to her requests. For the Duc d'Aiguillon, the Foreign Minister who had succeeded Choiseul, she could scarcely hide her dislike, and the Ambassador who was the guardian of the alliance advised a little more consideration.

Marie Antoinette loved and reverenced her mother but found her admonitions a sore trial. 'All Your Majesty's letters,' wrote Mercy in June 1772, 'have been received with respect, but at least as much with fear. No mother has had so much right to speak with authority, and on several occasions I have recalled this great truth when the letters upset her. She admitted it in principle, but she felt she was not much loved and would always be treated with severity. The latest letters have removed this prejudice, and Your Majesty can rely on guiding her in all the essentials of her position.' Her influence on the Dauphin, he added, was clearly increasing; she talked to him quite naturally about his faults and with excellent results. There was nothing more to desire except that the union should bear fruit. Meanwhile she was prudent and patient. That she spent less time with the aunts and more with the Count and Countess of Provence was good news. The King was very fond of her, but she might well be a little more considerate. More serious was her inability to resist pressure from or on behalf of unworthy applicants for favours.

On the last day of 1772 the Empress fired another broadside. She had often expressed disapproval of her daughter's riding to the hunt for fear of accidents, and scolded her for evading the desired response. It was the silence, more than the riding, which hurt her. 'Why should I wish to deprive you of such an innocent pleasure, I who would sacrifice my life to give you pleasure, if I did not fear the consequences? Since the King and the Dauphin approve, I have nothing more to say.' Passing from personal to political topics the Empress, ever mindful of the fragility of the alliance, returned to the most unsavoury topic of all. 'With the old year I conclude my sermons. You will do me injustice if you do not take them as the greatest mark of my tenderness and lively interest in your future welfare which is always in my thoughts. I am hoping to hear the result of my counsels about your attitude to the Favourite. You must not content yourself with abstaining from attacks. You must treat her with courtesy and speak to her as to any other lady received at Court. This you owe to the King and to myself; you owe no account of your actions to anyone else. I do not wish you to be degraded or dominated by others. Take care! The balance, once upset, is impossible—or only with great effort—to restore; and for that I do not think you are much inclined, being too much addicted to your convenience.'

The reply opens with an exasperated appeal to abandon 'cette vilaine ombre sur ma confiance; il ferait le malheur de ma vie.' Passing quickly to less controversial matters, she had learned that her sister Caroline, Queen of Naples, was *enceinte*, and there was hope of a son. 'When shall I be able to say the same?' When Mercy once again reminded her that the Empress was her best friend, tears came into her eyes. 'I have not a thought which I would wish to hide from her,' she exclaimed, 'but writing is an effort, and I am afraid of upsetting her by unpleasant tidings. I have told her that it was only to please the King and the Dauphin that I occasionally rode with the hunt; you know that is true.'

As regards the Favourite, she explained that the position was complicated by her husband's growing detestation of her. The Dauphin, she added, had a marked instinct for justice, order and truth, good sense and judgment; but she feared his nonchalance, his lack of response, his want of nerve. The Ambassador's advice to her to encourage him to make better use of his time and to show more friendliness in his personal contacts bore fruit, and for the first time she actually urged him to treat the Favourite in a way which would not displease the King. He followed her advice, and at the New Year reception in 1773 he astonished the courtiers by speaking to her in a friendly way. To Mercy's surprise the Dauphine on the same occasion said not a word to the Favourite or the two ladies who accompanied her; when he remonstrated she replied that she had treated all three alike and had therefore given no cause for complaint. The Favourite was distressed, but when Mercy explained that the Dauphin's *beau geste* was due to his wife's prompting she sent a message of gratitude.

Smarting under her mother's lash, Marie Antoinette told Mercy that there was nothing she would not do to prove her love, but that she was afraid of her. Even when she was writing to her she was never at ease. She was not the only one of the daughters to go in fear of her formidable parent. Many years after her death Queen Caroline of Naples, on revisiting Vienna, confessed that her children respected her profoundly but were very afraid of her. On learning that her daughter's affection was mingled with fear the Empress adopted a softer tone. 'Do not say I scold and preach. Say, Maman loves me and is always thinking of me and my welfare; I must believe her and comfort her by following her sound advice. You will feel the better for it and every shadow which has troubled you will disappear from my confidence.' Despite all such attempts at explanation mother and daughter drifted ever farther apart. The Dauphine sometimes wondered whether she was really loved; she supposed she would be treated like a child till she was thirty or more. She talked most freely with the Abbé Vermond and at times she let herself go. 'Regardez cela, M. l'Abbé,' she cried on one occasion, showing him the latest lecture, 'si on voyait cela, cela me ferait un tel honneur.' One day she read him an extract

complaining that she needed serious reading more than anyone.
'For two months I have been waiting for the Abbé's list.   I am
afraid horses and donkeys have taken the time destined for books.
Cultivate this occupation in winter, since you have not yet fully
mastered any other—neither music, nor drawing, nor dancing,
nor painting, nor other forms of art.'   'Elle me ferait passer
pour un animal,' exclaimed the culprit.   The Abbé reported to
Mercy: 'Ma charmante princesse était piquée.'   He knew even
better than the Ambassador that the Empress had taken the wrong
line.   'I feel sure,' he wrote, 'that if her Majesty would make
allowance for the weakness of youth and accustom her daughter
to regard her as her friend, all would go well.'   Similar advice
came from Kaunitz, the cynical man of the world, who urged his
sovereign not to waste her efforts in reprimanding her daughter,
which only vexed her.   It was all in vain, for at sixty the Empress
was too old to change.

It was an ancient custom that the Dauphin and Dauphine
should pay a formal visit to the capital shortly after their marriage,
and Marie Antoinette eagerly desired to see the sights.   For three
years the King had turned a deaf ear, but on May 18, 1773, she
asked him point blank and extracted permission to go as soon as
she liked.   Ever since the nightmare of the Fronde the Court
had frowned on Paris.   Louis XV had rarely seen it, his wife and
daughters not at all.   Unable to await the appointed day, the
young pair, accompanied by the Comte de Provence, appeared
incognito at a masked ball at the Opera.   At last, on June 8, Paris
saw the smiling girl and took her to its heart.   'Mon Dieu,' she
exclaimed, as she gazed at the shouting crowd from a balcony of
the Tuileries, 'Mon Dieu, que de monde!'   'Ah, le bon peuple,
Madame,' gallantly replied the Duc de Brissac, Governor of Paris,
who was at her side, 'n'en déplaise à M. le Dauphin, ce sont deux
cent amoureux de votre personne.'   On reaching home she went
straight to the King, tactfully exclaiming: 'Your Majesty must
be greatly loved by the Parisians, for they have given us a fine
welcome.'

The story was told in a happy letter to her mother.   'Last
Tuesday, a day I shall never forget, we made our entry into Paris.
We were received with all the honours imaginable.   That was all
very nice, but what touched me most was the affection and

enthusiasm of poor people who, despite their crushing burden of taxation, were in transports. When we walked in the Tuileries Gardens, there was such a gathering that we stood for three-quarters of an hour, unable to advance or retreat. Several times we ordered the guards not to strike out, and this produced an excellent effect. The enormous crowd which followed us everywhere was so orderly that no one was hurt. Then we stood for half an hour on a terrace. I cannot tell you, dear Maman, the transports of joy and affection they displayed. Before retiring we waved to the people. What happiness in our station to win the friendship of a whole people at so small a price! Nothing is so precious; that is how I felt and I shall never forget it. Another joy on this happy day was the Dauphin's conduct. His replies to all the addresses were marvellously apt; he felt the enthusiasm of the people and showed them his good will. To-morrow we go to the Opera, and I expect two other days to the Comédie Française and Comédie Italienne. I realise more every day what my dear Maman has done for me. I was the youngest and you have treated me as the eldest; my heart is filled with the most tender gratitude. My dear Maman praises me beyond my deserts for my affection. I could never repay half what I owe her. I embrace her with all my heart.' It had been the happiest day of her life and it was the happiest letter the anxious mother had ever received. That the visit had been a triumph for the Dauphine was recognised on all hands. 'The public was seized with enthusiasm,' the Ambassador reported. 'They said that in her grace and kindness they recognised the daughter of the august Maria Theresa. Wherever she went she smiled at them, and when after dinner she walked in the Tuileries Gardens, where there were over 50,000 souls, people had climbed into the trees. She ordered the guards not to hold them back and several times she was cut off. There was clapping of hands and exclamations: How pretty! How charming! Before leaving she appeared on the great balcony, saluting right and left to the crowd, who cheered with delight. The Dauphin, who played his part excellently, was only regarded as an accessory to the fête: everyone talked of the Dauphine. This visit was of great significance in shaping public opinion.' Never before nor after did Marie Antoinette and the French people come so close to each other

as on this bright summer day in her eighteenth year.   What a
fund of loyal affection the Monarchy still possessed had been
shown during the grave illness of *Louis le bien-aimé* in 1755; it
was shown again—for the last time—in 1773.

On April 29, 1774, Louis XV developed smallpox, and on
May 10 he died at the age of sixty-four.   The critical nature of
the illness, which had carried off so many of the Royal Family,
was recognised from the first, and all eyes turned to the heirs.
Fearing that Mme du Barry might ask for orders whether she
should remain at Court, Mercy advised a reply that it was not their
business; if the sufferer recovered he would resent her expulsion.
Whatever happened, the Ambassador assured his sovereign that
she need have no anxiety about the conduct of her daughter, and
a week later he added that in this delicate situation she had
behaved like an angel.   'I cannot express my admiration for her
piety, her prudence, her judgment; everyone is enchanted, and
rightly so.   She has kept in the background, and except for the
Royal Family she has seen only the Abbé and myself.   I have
told her all I could think of regarding both the circumstances
of the moment and the possible future.   I believe she is well
warned and prepared for everything.'

Marie Antoinette had come victoriously through her apprenticeship.   She had earned the sincere respect of the Ambassador and
had gradually won the affection of her diffident partner.   Paris
was at her feet.   Even Mme du Barry, who fled from Versailles
when her royal lover was on his death-bed, felt no bitterness
towards her.   The living embodiment of the alliance could
hardly be *persona grata* with men like Marshal Richelieu, who had
evicted Choiseul and thrown the Favourite into the King's arms,
but she had made no serious blunders.   She had won the liking
of the King under trying circumstances, and had kept on good
terms with brothers-in-law for whom she could feel little respect.
Mme Adelaide's friendship, never very genuine, had waned with
her diminishing influence.   The devotion of Mme Campan is
reflected in her memoirs.   With the significant exception of her
childlessness, for which no one held her responsible, everything
pointed to a bright spring after what Carlyle in his drastic way
describes as the era of harlotocracy.   'I saw her just above the
horizon,' wrote Burke many years later in a famous passage,

'glittering like the morning star, full of life, and splendour, and joy.' Her popularity seemed the greatest asset of the Monarchy. Mercy described her as '*une belle âme*.' But the sterner tests were to come. Would the Queen repeat the success of the Dauphine? Had her indolent nature the strength to resist the temptations of flattery and power? Would her husband overcome his diffidence and restore the tarnished prestige of the crown? At the accession of Louis XVI and Marie Antoinette few onlookers would have argued that it was too late for the Monarchy and the *Ancien Régime*, once so honoured and so powerful, to make a fresh start.

So impressed was the Ambassador by her new status that he proposed to turn it to political account. 'I see the time approaching when important destinies await her. The King is ageing. He finds himself isolated, helpless, without comfort in his children; there is neither affection nor fidelity in his motley *entourage*. In his old age he has no resource except in the Dauphine, who combines character and intelligence. He knows it as I can see from his conduct to her. But there is one matter to which I always return. She understands things with the greatest facility but she is terribly afraid: she dares not allow herself to think that she will one day possess power and authority. She tends to be passive and dependent, timid and fearful, even on the smallest occasions. She is afraid of speaking to the King, fears the Ministers, fears even the members of her household. It is vital that she should learn to recognise and implement her powers. I would answer with my life that if she only resolved to exert her influence with the King, no Favourite or Minister could resist. Despite his excellent qualities the Dauphin will probably never have the force nor the will to reign by himself. If she does not govern him others will, and such a disagreeable development must be averted in good time. All my conversations with her turn round this great project, and the Abbé Vermond seconds me with a zeal beyond praise. Yet in a matter of such importance the results of our efforts will be slow and uncertain unless supported by the voice of Your Majesty which alone can make a deep impression.'

The reply of the Empress poured water into the Ambassador's wine. 'I must tell you frankly that I do not wish my daughter to gain a decided influence in affairs. I have learned by experience

what a crushing burden it is to rule over a vast monarchy. Moreover I know her immaturity and thoughtlessness as well as her
lack of application; she might fail in such a dilapidated monarchy
as present-day France. If she could not restore it, or if its condition became still worse, I should prefer that some Minister
should receive the blame. I cannot talk politics to her unless
you judge it suitable and tell me precisely what I am to write.'
The next letter returned to the theme of her daughter's political
insufficiency. 'I recognise how she manœuvres to reach her
goal; she yields only in secondary matters. This she admitted
to you in declaring that when one has adopted a system of conduct
it is difficult to change. Her attitude towards the Favourite, her
riding, her confidences to the Comte and Comtesse de Provence,
etc., are proofs of her unreflecting character and persistence in
her own ideas. Despite her fine qualities and her intelligence I
am always apprehensive of the effects of her thoughtlessness and
obstinacy.' It was well that the Dauphine never saw nor guessed
the existence of these letters, for those she received herself were
about as much as she could bear.

At the close of 1773 the marriage of Artois turned the attention
of France once more to the problem of the succession. Though
the Empress was always complaining of the danger of her
daughter's rides, after more than three years she can have had
little expectation of good news. Since the Comte de Provence
was also childless, the marriage of his younger brother to another
Savoy princess gave rise to a conversation between the Dauphin
and the Dauphine which the latter reported to Mercy and Mercy
to the Empress. He talked of the approaching wedding and of
the sensation it would make if the new member of the Royal
Family became *enceinte* before his wife. He then embraced her
with the words: 'Mais m'aimez vous bien?' 'Oui,' she replied,
'et vous ne pouvez pas en douter; je vous aime sincèrement et je
vous estime encore davantage.' The Dauphin appeared to be
very touched, caressed her tenderly, and told her he hoped all
would go well. Like similar promising conversations, however,
it wrought no change in a situation which was beginning to
darken her life.

In his last report of 1773 Mercy sang her praises once again.
In her personal qualities no less than by her rank she eclipsed

everyone at Court, for her sisters-in-law lacked charm and the young princes seemed to possess little heart. Everyone, including the Favourite, coveted her favour and protection. The Controller-General told Mercy that he would always obey her orders, but begged him to advise her against any requests manifestly unjust or too onerous for the Treasury. This, he assured the Empress, he had already done, and no trouble had arisen for a long time. 'Though the other Ministers, from the nature of their offices, have fewer occasions to obey her, I find them no less eager to please her, in contrast to the position of the other members of the Royal Family. With the exception of the Dauphin, who has never asked for anything, his brothers and still more Mesdames daily support the most unreasonable demands which are constantly refused and which merely reveal the total discredit of these princes and princesses. Pursuing a completely different course, she is winning more and more political consideration.' Her high standards and kindly heart were illustrated on the wedding-day of the Comte d'Artois when the King played cards with the Royal Family, the principal personages of the Court, and the Favourite. Her gain of 1,200 louis embarrassed her and she tried to lose it, with only partial success, for the game closed with a net gain of 700 louis. Next day she sent 50 louis each for the poor of the two parishes of Versailles. She consulted Mercy on the distribution of the remainder, explaining that she would keep nothing for herself, and at his advice she divided it among her staff. The stress laid by the Ambassador on this incident—the first reference in his correspondence to the hazards of the gaming-table—suggests that she had so far resisted the contagion.

The first letter of the Empress to Mercy in 1774 opened with a sharp complaint, not of her daughter but of the heir to the throne. 'The frigidity of a young husband of twenty towards a pretty woman is beyond belief. Despite all the assertions of the doctors, my suspicions concerning his physical constitution increase. Almost my only hope is in the intervention of the Emperor who, when he reaches Versailles, may perhaps find the means of bringing this indolent husband to his duty.' Unfortunately the projected journey of Joseph II had to wait for three years, and meanwhile the Ambassador continued to stress the con-

trast between the Dauphin and his brothers. The Comte and
Comtesse de Provence, he reported, had always been friendly
to the Dauphine; his behaviour had always seemed to hide
projects in regard to which she should be on her guard, as she
well understood. 'She is now quite safe from danger in that
quarter, and with their agreeable manners they help to make up
her circle. With the Comte and Comtesse d'Artois it is different,
for his ways are becoming increasingly disagreeable and unseemly,
to the disgust of the whole Court. The young Prince has no
consideration for the Ministers, to whom he announces his orders
in a violent and peremptory tone. He shows no regard for
anybody. There have been signs of intemperance, he loves
gambling, and recently he arranged a game for very high stakes.
I have felt it my duty to beg the Dauphine not to lend herself in
any way to such disorders. She thoroughly realises the danger
and disapproves them.' The Ambassador was equally hopeful
about the Dauphin. 'Under a somewhat rough exterior there is
frankness, character, regularity of life, a disposition to do good
in his particular sphere. The Dauphine pays the greatest
attention to all that concerns him, and is always suggesting how
to make the best of himself. I try to give her hints, and the
Dauphin, who is aware of it, has always shown his gratitude. His
deference to her proves how much he values her counsels, and his
gratitude binds him to her ever more closely.'

III. *The Temptations of Power*

'LE roi est mort! Vive le roi!' The familiar cry echoed through
the gilded corridors of Versailles on May 10, 1774. Mme
Campan describes the stampede of the courtiers towards the
apartments of the new rulers, aged nineteen and eighteen, who
fell on their knees with the words: 'Que Dieu nous protége!
nous régnons trop jeunes.' It was not merely their youth and
inexperience which made their task so difficult. Other young
rulers, such as the Great Elector and Francis Joseph, Charles V
and Queen Victoria, soon learned their difficult trade. The root
of the trouble was that neither of them possessed the qualities

10

needed for their calling. The glamour of the monarchy was almost gone and the sands were running out of the hourglass. Louis XVI changed too little, remaining to the end a blameless, colourless, tongue-tied and well-intentioned mediocrity, without grace or dignity, more like a peasant taken from the plough than a king—in a word, a royal misfit. Marie Antoinette, on the other hand, changed too much. The pursuit of pleasure, hitherto her pastime, became her passion. She never took life seriously— indeed, hardly began to grow up—till it was too late to repair the mischief she had wrought in her first four years on the throne. As Dauphine she was a spectacular success, as Queen a distressing failure. Since the full-blooded intriguer Marie de Medici the consorts of France had been shadowy figures, producing the desired heir to the throne and then hustled off the stage. Here at last was a pretty, vivacious, friendly young woman who in the first flush of radiant girlhood had taken Paris by storm. 'It was impossible to see anything except the Queen,' reported Horace Walpole after witnessing a ball at the marriage festivities of Mme Clotilde. 'Hebes and Floras, and Helens and Graces, are street-walkers to her. She is a statue of beauty when sitting or walking, grace itself when she moves.' Yet not every good starter can stay the course. Her mother's ineradicable conviction that she was a lightweight was confirmed, for power and money proved too much for her.

The first letter of the new Queen was written on May 14 at Choisy, once the home of La Grande Mademoiselle, whither the Court had fled from the germ-infested palace of Versailles. The end of Louis XV, she reported, had been most edifying. The new King seemed to possess the heart of his people; two days before the death of his grandfather he had given 200,000 francs to the poor, and it had produced a great effect. He was working hard and wrote many letters in his own hand. 'He has a taste for economy and is eager to make his peoples happy. He desires and needs to educate himself. I hope for God's blessing on his good intentions.' The public, she added, had expected great changes, but he had confined himself to dismissing 'the creature'. The letter ended on a cheerful note. 'I cannot help admiring the ways of Providence which has chosen me, the last of your children, for the finest throne in Europe. I feel more than ever my debt to the affection of my august mother who took such pains to procure this fine position for me. Never have I so longed to embrace you, to pour out my heart, to let you see how it is filled with respect, affection and gratitude.' The King added a few lines of thanks for the gift of her daughter, who was everything he could desire. Mercy's bulletins were full of praises of the modest demeanour of the young couple. Mesdames, he reported, were still a danger, for though the Queen realised their failings, her good nature might make her too inclined to submit to their whims. The King possessed solid qualities but lacked personality, and business might bore him. 'The Queen must learn to put up with it; her happiness depends on so doing. He loves her. With tact, kindness and caresses she will acquire absolute power over him, but she must govern him without seeming to do so.' The least hopeful observer was the austere and industrious Empress herself. 'The position of the King, the Ministers and the State makes me anxious,' she confided to Mercy. 'She is young, she has never shown any application and never will, or only with great difficulty.' Her first letter to the happy Queen was in a sombre strain. 'I shall not compliment you on your dignity which is dearly bought and will cost you still more if you abandon the quiet and innocent life of the last three years, which has won for you the approval and love of your peoples. That is a great advantage for your present situation, but you must know how to keep it and use it for the benefit of the King and the State. You are both very young and the burden is heavy. Without the support of your adorable father I should never have come through, and I was older than either of you. Do not rush things. Follow Mercy's advice; he knows the Court and the capital, is prudent and deeply attached to you. Regard him as your Minister as well as mine, though there is no antagonism between the two rôles. Your glory, your welfare, is as near my heart as our own. Those unhappy times of jealousy are over. Our holy religion and the welfare of our States demand that we remain closely linked in heart and interest, and that the world should realise the solidity of the tie. I will do my utmost, and my closing days can only be tranquil if I see both my dear children happy.'

At the opening of a new chapter in the life of Marie Antoinette the Ambassador forwarded an elaborate characterisation by the

Abbé Vermond, the man who knew her best. He had found her hurt by the apprehensions of her mother and brother. Their exhortations had turned principally on two points—the danger of political interference and of patronage. In neither respect was she conscious of fault; the gossip of Vienna, she felt, must be as ridiculous as that of Paris, and it was more dangerous because it was too far away to expose. The problem of recommendations, continued the Abbé, was very difficult. To forbid them was impossible in France, where from time immemorial three-quarters of the places, honours and pensions were accorded, not for services, but according to birth, favour or intrigue—in the army, the civil service, and the Church. Indeed, some posts, in accordance with custom, were only obtainable after a request from royalty. As Dauphine she had never exceeded her proper functions. 'By character and principles the Queen shrinks from recommendation; if she has on rare occasions yielded to importunity it was in cases of minor importance. Moreover, if she declined to take action, other members of the Royal Family would fill the vacancies with less worthy candidates.' Passing to the second theme Vermond reported her annoyance at the charge of political interference. Since she had always held aloof, both by principle and inclination, she could not understand the fears of Vienna. 'For myself I desire rather than hope that she should concern herself with affairs sufficiently to discuss them with her husband and thereby increase his trust. Since his accession he has busied himself with them, and he cannot feel much confidence in her unless he talks to her about them. She told me she would grieve at any dissension between the two Courts. How could she prevent it, she asked, if she took no part in affairs? I know she must never take a hand in the intrigues of individuals, but I think she ought to know how the machinery works. Your Majesty, like the public, knows that none of her ladies dominate her.'

This reassuring analysis produced little effect at Vienna. 'I fear her indifference,' replied the Empress, 'her disinclination for serious occupations, her dislike of any effort and constraint.' This indolence might sometimes lead her to yield to the importunities of her aunts, and her affability would not long preserve the affection of her subjects or the authority due to her rank. The same courier, however, carried an unusually affectionate letter to her daughter which for once contained counsels without rebukes. 'I cannot express my comfort and delight in all I hear about you; everyone is in ecstasies. And there are good reasons for it—a King of twenty and a Queen of nineteen, their every action breathing humanity, generosity, prudence and judgment. Religion and morals are not forgotten. I pray God to keep you thus for the good of your people, for the universe, for your family, and for your old maman. I long to see you, my dear children, always loved and respected and full of kindness. How sweet to make one's people happy, if only for a time! How I love the French at this moment! What resources there are in such a responsive nation! One could only wish they were more constant and less frivolous. Think of me not only as your tender mother but as your intimate friend. Try to be the confidant and the friend of the King; everything depends on it, his happiness and yours. If I have pressed you to avoid recommendations, it was only because I know the goodness of your heart and fear you may be taken unawares.'

The new reign opened with a clean sweep of the leading Ministers of Louis XV—Maupeou, d'Aiguillon, and the detested Abbé Terray. The appointment of such a lightweight as the frivolous septuagenarian Maurepas to the first place was a serious error, for his chief qualification was that his official career had been wrecked by Madame de Pompadour. Four of his colleagues, on the other hand, were men of character and ability—Vergennes, an experienced diplomatist, at the Foreign Office, Saint-Germain at the War Office, the universally respected Malesherbes as Minister of the King's Household, and Turgot, the dynamic Intendant of Limoges, at the Treasury. At last there seemed a real prospect of national recovery. What was required—and what was in doubt—was security of tenure; in other words, the steady support of the King.

A few weeks after the change of ruler the Ambassador reported on the prospects of the new régime. He was no longer afraid of the aunts, who now lived at Bellevue, once the home of the Pompadour. 'The Queen has received Mesdames in a friendly way, but has indicated that the time of their domination is over. Madame Adelaide seems much less inclined to interfere in everything.' In the princes, on the other hand, he found little to praise. The King's dislike for his brothers was unconcealed, but the Queen, with her frank and friendly nature, should be more on her guard. 'She allows them too much familiarity. Her supreme position requires dignity; any appearance of equality, even in her own family, should cease.' The King's confidence in her was growing; she could learn all she wished to know and she could secure the adoption of her ideas. 'She advances with sure tread towards the greatest influence, and it will prevail whenever she cares to use it. The Ministers are taking note and all of them, especially Maurepas, seek her favour.' Mercy's only anxiety was her *penchant* for dissipation, but this left him no peace. Long before her accession she had pined for a little home of her own in the country. Now when she mentioned the Petit Trianon the King replied that he was delighted to present it, and the Ambassador approved. But her thoughts now centred on making an English garden, which would be entirely harmless if it left room for serious thought. She neglected her reading, and in that direction no change was to be expected. 'She has not yet thought out a system of conduct suitable to her brilliant position. Isolated objects, often useless, sometimes harmful, set her in motion; then she asserts herself, makes use of her credit, and gets her way, while more important and really useful matters are ignored. Beyond doubt she possesses great influence over her husband, witness the dismissal of the Duc d'Aiguillon and the termination of Choiseul's disgrace. It is now proved that when she really wishes for anything it is hers. But if in the long run her credit is employed merely for her whims, if, instead of making herself useful and indeed necessary to the King by giving him sound advice and dispelling his doubts, she only makes unexplained requests; if, while continuing her distaste for all that is serious or requires some reflection, she shows herself bored or inattentive when the King talks to her, it is only too probable that he will seek advice elsewhere. Her influence would disappear, others would gain it at her expense, and nothing would be left of her present brilliant prospects. Her Majesty, who invariably listens to me with the same friendliness, agrees with my arguments; but since dissipation always effaces the serious impressions, I only obtain results in particular cases, never anything systematic or consecutive.' Her rôle, he added, was particularly important since the King was so weak. She could easily govern him if she took the trouble and devoted the necessary time. This possibility brought little comfort to the Empress, who doubted whether her daughter, owing to her lack of application, would ever take much part in affairs.

Maria Theresa's next letter, dated July 17, 1774, mingled warnings with compliments. Everyone was in raptures and looked forward to a happy reign. The King was regarded as well-intentioned but weak; she must help him. There was talk of millions spent on building, though it was not a time for such expenditure. Some people thought her too familiar with the members of the Royal Family, and in particular the Comte d'Artois was said to be too forward. 'Every consideration for all, but no familiarity! In this way you will avoid annoyances and recommendations. You really must concern yourself with serious things; it may be useful if the King asks for your advice or talks to you about affairs as a friend. Do not lead him into great expense. Do not let his first charming gift (the Petit Trianon) cost him too much. Everything depends on this happy *début*—happy beyond all expectation—being followed up and on your finding your happiness in that of your people who look to you alone for their welfare. Steady justice, blended with kindness and suitable economy, will ensure respect for this monarch by friends and foes. In my thirty-three years on the throne I have not achieved what this dear prince has done in thirty-three days; but it is necessary to live up to this splendid and marvellous start. He must remove the intriguers and have friends who dare to tell him the literal truth. With God's help there is every ground for hope; your own idleness and dissipation are the only things you have to fear.'

The Queen agreed that her husband was praised on all hands. He well deserved it by his sincerity and desire to do good, but would the enthusiasm last? 'The little I understand of affairs shows me how difficult and critical they are. It is generally recognised that the late King left things in a very bad way. There was no unity, and indeed it would be impossible to content everyone in an impatient country which wanted everything done in a moment. What you say about forming principles and sticking to them is quite true. The King will not have the same failings as his grandfather. I hope, too, he will not have a favourite. But I fear he may be too gentle and yielding, as when Maurepas made him give half a million francs to the Duc d'Aiguillon. My dear Maman may rely on me not to lead him into great expense. On the contrary, I decline to support requests to him for money. He has no idea of spending millions on buildings; that is an exaggeration, as is the talk of my familiarity. I cannot judge myself, but I am conscious only of an atmosphere of friendship and gaiety natural at our age. It is true that the Comte d'Artois is very lively and giddy, but I know how to make him aware of his mistakes. As for my aunts no one can now say that I am in their hands. As for Monsieur and Madame (the Comte and Comtesse de Provence) I am on my guard. I must admit my dissipation and disinclination for serious things. I wish and hope gradually to correct it.' As usual, we learn more from the confidences of the Empress to Mercy than from the carefully phrased letters to her daughter. 'I am more and more convinced,' she wrote on July 31, 'that I am not mistaken about her whole character and her *penchant* for dissipation. I have noticed that, despite her deference to your remonstrances, she none the less goes her own way when her wishes are involved. I place all my confidence in your zeal and wisdom, but I cannot conceal my fear that some day she may try to get rid of the Abbé Vermond on some plausible pretext in order to be relieved of an embarrassing observer.'

The anxieties of the Empress were increased by Mercy's bulletin on September 11 on the plight of France. 'The deplorable lapse of the late King during his last four years disgraced his reign. The State was in the power of a low creature with a disgraceful *entourage*. Decent folk kept away and were replaced by rascals. There was nothing but disorder, scandal and injustice, neither morals nor principles; everything was a gamble. The Government had no resilience left in it. The country felt ashamed and dispirited. Only the black sheep remained on the stage; nothing was respected.' He described the position so that she might discount calumnious rumours about her daughter. The cause was to be sought in the confusion of the closing years of the reign: with such deep roots it would take long to remedy,

whatever the new ruler might do.   Yet the French nation must
not be confounded with the few who were foam on the surface
and were generally abhorred.   Happily the character of the
Queen was beyond reproach.   She had never deviated from the
highest standards; of that no one was more fully convinced than
the King.   Her rare qualities were known to the public, whose
adoration was unfailing.   Her only dangers were lack of application, excess of vivacity, unwillingness to turn to account the
finest position ever occupied by a Queen of France.   A little
experience and the passing years would remedy these disadvantages.   The grave tone of this letter was partly due to a
scurrilous pamphlet, attributed to Beaumarchais, which declared
that the King could not have a child, and cautioned the heirs to
the throne against some dark intrigue by the Queen.

The next bulletin was more cheerful.   The Queen spent
several hours daily at her music and enjoyed playing the harp.
To induce her to read was impossible, but she was showing
interest in the state of the country.   The King talked to her about
it, and she listened attentively.   Mesdames had lost all influence,
but the Comte d'Artois continued his unwelcome familiarities.
The Empress, always more difficult to satisfy than her Ambassador, continued to criticise.   Her daughter's latest letter, she
complained, contained, as usual, little of interest.   'Her taste for
dissipation and her nonchalance increase my fear that she is losing
the only chance of gaining some influence in affairs.'   Mercy's
last bulletin of 1774, dated December 18, was again in the major
key.   Everyone was enchanted by her kindness and charm.   Her
main occupations were music and dancing, with very little reading.
Her daily lengthy talks with Abbé Vermond, and his own audiences
once or twice a week, were the only occasions on which she heard
serious matters discussed.   Harmony in the Royal Family was
complete.   Mesdames played no part; Monsieur and Madame
behaved themselves.   The Comte and Comtesse d'Artois had not
changed their ways.   In a letter of the same date, intended for his
sovereign alone, he added that the credit of the Queen had recently
increased more than at any previous time, though without any
striving on her part: circumstances favoured her.   'I continually
remind her that such a brilliant position demands more attention
and more system in order to make it solid and durable.   She

deigns to listen, and understands the reasoning very well; but dissipation always returns to weaken the effect, and it is only little by little that it begins to bear fruit.'

The Queen had made a good start, but 1775 witnessed a darkening of the sky. The first letter of the Empress on January 3 declared that, except for want of application and a distaste for reading common to almost all her children, she was pleased with her daughter. The family and Court life and the conduct of the royal pair were satisfactory; the vital point of conjugal life was the only worry. Mercy's first bulletin of the new year reported that the weekly balls revealed her as the perfect hostess; each day added some new degree of perfection to the Court. Everyone was enchanted by their reception, and even Artois was mending his ways. The Empress responded with a handsome tribute to her Ambassador. 'I confess that the progress of my daughter surpasses my expectation, and I recognise it as your work.' It was too good to last, for in February Mercy reported that the succession of festivities claimed the whole of the Queen's time and menaced her health. The Empress gently reproved her daughter for her attire, about which the papers had much to say. Her hat, for instance, was reported to be thirty-six inches high. 'You know I always believed in following the fashions in moderation. A pretty young Queen has no need of all these follies; simplicity is more impressive and more suitable to her rank. She should set the tone, and everyone will follow suit. I, who love my little Queen and follow her every step, cannot help warning her about this little frivolity, all the more because I have so many reasons to be satisfied and even proud of your doings.' 'It is true,' replied her daughter gently, 'that I concern myself to some extent with my dress. Everyone wears plumes, and it would seem very strange if I did not. Since the end of the balls they are not nearly so high.'

In March Mercy expressed his satisfaction to the Queen that the carnival was over. 'Then I went in great detail into the excess of dissipation it had involved and its consequences. Despite his great tolerance, the King disliked lengthy and noisy amusements. Moreover, the public would think that the Queen, caring only for frivolity, would never try to gain credit in serious matters, an opinion which would in itself suffice to deprive her of part of

the immense advantages she enjoyed.   I confess to Your Majesty
that I painted too dark a picture, but such are the ravages of
recent dissipations that only shocks can make her reflect.   I
noticed that she resented my remonstrances; she seemed sad and
pensive, but she was kind enough to listen and to discuss her
difficulties.   She explained that she had to seek diversion and
that the only way was to multiply her amusements.   I replied that
she would make fresh trouble for herself if she failed to fortify
her credit.   My representations seemed to take effect, for she
promised to resume her serious occupations.   Since the end of the
carnival she has been reading a little again, but nothing solid or
useful.   The Abbé Vermond tries to make up for it.'

The Empress could be more outspoken than the diplomatist,
and every letter brought reproaches and advice.   'All letters from
Paris,' she wrote on June 2, 'report that you do not share the
King's room and that you possess little of his confidence.   That
strikes me all the more because, with the day given up to dissipation, this friendship, this habit of being together, will cease.
I foresee misfortunes and chagrin for you in the brilliant position
which it depends entirely on yourself to preserve, since the King
loves and respects you.   Your only task should be as often as
possible to spend the whole day with him, to keep him company,
to be his friend and confidant, to try to understand things in order
to discuss them with him, to comfort him so that he need never
seek his pleasures elsewhere.   We are in the world to do good.
Your task is of the greatest importance.   We are here not for
ourselves or for amusement; heaven is not a gift but must be
earned.   Forgive this sermon, but I confess these separate rooms
and your excursions with the Comte d'Artois have worried me all
the more since I know the consequences.   I cannot portray them
too clearly to save you from the abyss into which you are falling.
Attribute my alarms to my affection, but do not dismiss them as
superfluous.'   Marie Antoinette gently indicated that things were
not so bad as her mother believed.   Her letter of June 22 began
by describing the coronation of Louis XVI at Rheims in which,
according to precedent, she took no official part.   'It was quite
perfect.   Apparently everyone was delighted with the King.
The ceremonies in church were interrupted at the moment of
the coronation by the most touching acclamations.   I could not

control my tears. I did my best throughout the journey to respond to the enthusiasm of the people, and though it was very hot and crowded, I did not mind the fatigue. It is astonishing and gratifying to be so well received despite the high price of bread which unfortunately continues. It is an extraordinary feature of the French character to be led astray by evil suggestions and then quickly to revert to good ways. Seeing the people who despite their misfortunes treat us so well compels us to work even harder for their welfare. The King seems to be penetrated by this truth. For myself I shall never forget coronation day even were I to live to a hundred. My dear Maman, who is so good, would have shared our happiness.' Passing from this happy experience to her mother's complaints she explained that her husband had only slept in his own room because she had a cold. 'I am grieved that my dear Maman judges of my promenades from the papers, which are often false and always exaggerate. On the days I spent in the company of the Comte d'Artois the King was out hunting. Besides, he always knew of these promenades, and there were always plenty of gentlemen and ladies of the Court.' The same courier carried two letters from the Ambassador, the first destined for the eyes of the Emperor and Kaunitz describing the coronation, the second for the Empress alone, once again analysing the character of the Queen. She always received him in the friendliest way, but her impressions were transient. Only time and experience would help, but help they would. Till that happy moment dissipation and vivacity would injure her position. 'I am far from suggesting that she will ever make big mistakes, but she will be subject to continual petty failings which it will be necessary to overcome and to render as little harmful as possible.' Unfortunately things were to become very much worse before taking a turn for the better.

IV. *The Dismissal of Turgot*

As Dauphine, Marie Antoinette played no part in politics, but she was a woman of vehement likes and dislikes, and as Queen she promptly made her influence felt. It was natural that she should hate the Duc d'Aiguillon, who as a leading member of the

du Barry clique had helped to overthrow Choiseul and had
succeeded him as Foreign Minister.   She had forgotten all other
resentments, reported Mercy, but against him and his wife she
had hardened her heart.   On receiving the ladies of the Court on
her accession she had shown herself affable to everybody except
the Duchess, to whom she said not a word.   The incident was
interpreted as a preliminary notification of the Minister's disgrace.
She pressed the King to dismiss him, while his relative, Maurepas,
the chief Minister, strove to avert his fall.   The nerveless monarch
had no desire for a change, but his importunate wife prevailed.
Without waiting to be dismissed he resigned on June 2, 1774.
Unlike Choiseul, he was not banished to his estates, and he was
allowed to retain his post as Captain of the Light Horse, which
qualified him to appear at Court.   Smarting under his dismissal,
he made his house in Paris a focus of intrigue.   The feud came
to a head in the following year.   On May 31, 1775, at a review
of the King's Household, the Duke, at the head of his Light
Horse, was about to salute the Queen when she brusquely drew
down the blind of her carriage.   Furious at this public affront, he
announced that he was preparing to accompany the sovereigns to
the coronation at Rheims in the following week.   Here was the
Queen's opportunity, and Maurepas was summoned to her
presence.   She had long had grounds for disapproval of his
nephew, she began, and the cup was now full.   He must be
forbidden to go to Rheims and must withdraw to his estates.
'May I say that it is the will of Your Majesty,' asked the old
Minister, 'and not that of the King?'   'I consent,' was the reply;
'I take full responsibility.'   When Maurepas raised the question
with the King, the latter refused to intervene and left the date
and conditions of exile to his wife.   'What shall I write to him?'
inquired Maurepas in a further audience with the Queen.   'Whatever you like,' was the reply, 'but let him be off.'   D'Aiguillon
left next day, but it was not merely his friends who censured her
conduct.   'It was her action in this affair,' wrote her brother-in-
law, the Comte de Provence, long afterwards, 'which gave her
the reputation for malice and implacability.   The enthusiasm
she had aroused on her arrival in France lasted unimpaired till
1775, when it started to wane, and soon it disappeared.   It was
then that the libels and verses against her began to appear and

that they dared to compare her to Messalina for debauchery and cruelty.'

The well-known Choiseul episode at Rheims a day or two after the banishment of d'Aiguillon was no less of a blunder, though here she was an agent, not a principal. She had secured his recall from exile at the opening of the reign, and he received permission to attend the coronation. The King, like his father, had never admired him and never dreamed of his return to office, and even Maria Theresa had ceased to want him back; but his friends, with Artois at their head, resolved to use the Queen as a lever in their strategy. She was to receive him and hear his views, thus identifying herself with his claims and helping to overcome the resistance of the King. But how could his permission for such an interview be obtained? Here a little diplomacy was required. She would be very glad to talk a moment with her old friend, she remarked in the most innocent manner, but owing to numerous engagements she could not suggest a time. The King fell into the trap and suggested the morning of the following day. The audience duly took place, lasted an hour, and became the talk of the European Chancelleries. Without directly begging for his reinstatement, Choiseul confined himself to cultivating her favour and advising her on her attitude to the King. The authors of the plot, however, had overshot the mark, for their unconcealed rejoicing aroused his suspicions. At the next reception of the Queen Choiseul's fate was sealed. When he came to kiss the King's hand the latter withdrew it, turned his head away, and made a terrible face. The ex-Minister took the hint and retired to his estates.

This was by no means the end of the Choiseul incident, for a storm blew up in Vienna when Count Rosenberg, a trusted Austrian diplomatist who had recently tutored the eighteen-year-old Maximilian on a visit to France, thoughtlessly communicated to the Empress two letters he had received from the Queen very different in tone from her correspondence with her mother. The first, which was harmless enough, was dated April 17, 1775. 'I shall never worry about gossip in Vienna so long as they tell you what is said. You know Paris and Versailles, you have seen and judged. If I needed a defence I should look to you. I will confess more than you say yourself. My tastes are not the same as those of the King, who only cares for hunting and mechanics. You will agree that I should be out of my element in a forge. I should not be Vulcan, and the rôle of Venus would displease him much more than my tastes, which he does not disapprove.' A second letter, dated July 13, was more explosive. The dismissal of d'Aiguillon, she began, had been entirely her work: that contemptible person engaged in espionage and scandal. Then there was the audience she had granted to Choiseul at Rheims, which had been so much discussed. 'You may be sure that I did not see him without telling the King, but you will not guess how cleverly I avoided the impression of asking his leave. I told him I wished to see M. de Choiseul and that I was only engaged in daytime. I succeeded so well that the poor man himself arranged the most convenient hour. I think I made use of a wife's rights.'

On reading this incautious utterance Maria Theresa let herself go. The Emperor, she confided to Mercy, was also shocked by its tone, particularly the reference to *le pauvre homme*. The letter, which she enclosed, had struck her to the heart. 'What a style, what an attitude! It confirms my anxieties. She is galloping to her doom. If Choiseul returns as a Minister she is lost. He would take less notice of her than of the Pompadour, to whom he owed everything and in whose overthrow he took the lead. Rosenberg has placed me in a most cruel predicament by telling the Queen that he has shown me her letter. Here is my reply and I have no hopes it will do good.' The most fulminating rebuke ever administered from Vienna, dated July 30, 1775, was omitted from the correspondence published by Arneth and was utilised for the first time in Stefan Zweig's biography.[1] 'I must confess that a letter written to Rosenberg has thrown me into the greatest consternation. What a style! What levity! Where is the heart, so good and so generous, of this Archduchess Antoinette? All I see is an intrigue, low hatred, vindictiveness, persiflage; intrigue such as a Pompadour or a du Barry might have practised to play a part, not like a queen, a great princess, a princess of the House of Lorraine and Austria, full of kindness and propriety. Your easy triumph and your flatterers

---

[1] It is printed in *Correspondance entre Marie-Thérèse et Marie Antoinette*, 1933, 155–156.

have always made me tremble for you since that winter when you plunged into pleasures and ridiculous attire. All this pleasure-hunting without the King, this knowledge that he does not care for it and that out of pure complaisance he accompanies you or allows you to do everything you like, made me mention my just anxieties. I find them all too confirmed by your letter. What language! *Le pauvre homme!* Where is the respect and gratitude for all his complaisance? I leave you to your own reflexions, though there would be plenty more to say. Your happiness can easily lapse and can plunge you into the greatest misfortunes. This terrible dissipation leads to your letting everything slide. What do you read? And then you dare to meddle in the most important matters, such as the choice of Ministers! What are the Abbé and Mercy doing? It seems to me you have turned against them since they are not base flatterers; they love you and wish for your happiness, not to amuse you or turn your failings to account. You will realise this some day, but it will be too late. I do not wish to survive this misfortune, and I pray God to shorten my days now that I can no longer be of use to you and cannot bear to witness the unhappiness of my dear child whom I shall love tenderly to my last breath.'

The Queen's reply, dated August 12, was brief and dignified.[1] 'I should never venture to write to my august mother if I felt half as guilty as she thinks me. I wrote a letter to a man of merit (Rosenberg) who possesses your confidence and to whom therefore I felt I could give mine. As he came to this country and knows the value attached here to certain phrases I am not afraid of any unpleasantness. My dear Mother judges differently. It is for me to bow my head and to hope that in other circumstances she will judge me more favourably, as, I venture to say, I deserve.' She showed both her mother's letter and her own reply to Mercy, unaware that he had already seen the former. 'My Mother,' she added quietly, 'sees things from a distance and is too hard on me. But she is my Mother, she loves me, and when she speaks I can only bow my head.'

A scolding from her brother Joseph, on the other hand, aroused

---

[1] Only the latter part of this letter, announcing the confinement of the Comtesse d'Artois, was published by Arneth. The whole is printed in *Correspondance entre Marie Thérèse et Marie Antoinette.*

her anger, and for half an hour she poured out her heart to the kindly Ambassador. Surprised at his silence she bade him express his views. Having seen so little result from his previous conversations, replied Mercy, he could only keep his apprehensions to himself: he faced the unpleasant alternative of grieving the Empress by exact reports or of concealing or toning things down. Hitherto he had chosen the latter alternative, in the belief that the difficulties would pass. Now that he saw them increasing, he must consider his position and ask her advice how to reconcile his two desires—not to displease her and not to fail in his duty to his sovereign. 'She seemed both embarrassed and pained. I went on to say that from the point of view of her real welfare everything was going badly. Since she never troubled to examine anything and acted only on impulse, was swayed by the passions of her *entourage*, and spent all her time on dissipation, useless or dangerous things, she risked forfeiting not only the confidence, veneration and love of the public but her influence over the King. I then recalled many particulars. Your Majesty will notice that I painted the picture much darker than it is, for it is less a question of actual evil than the absence of all the good there might be; but I felt it my duty to make an impression. I think I succeeded, though I cannot predict how long it will last.' Never before had the respectful Ambassador used such plain words.

The Queen's gentle rejoinder turned away wrath, and the next letter of the Empress was in her usual vein, blending affection with reproof and advice. 'Your situation appeared to me to justify the comparison which you justly describe as horrible. It pained me to make it, and imagine my alarm at seeing you succumb in the midst of temptation and adulation. My comparison had nothing personal about it: God preserve me from any doubt. It related to the intrigues and patronage in regard to which your offences would be worse than theirs. For you are stationed by Providence while they had to make and keep their position. I feel I must offer this explanation, and I am truly touched that you are distressed. None will be more ready another time to do you justice, for my heart always beats in unison with you and suffers doubly if it cannot speak.' The Empress had shown herself a bad psychologist, and her letter of

July 30 might well have broken down the bridges; but her daughter's answer shows that not even the most unmerited charges could destroy her love. 'Your dear letter has restored me to life. The thought of being in disgrace with my tender Mother weighed on me, and I hope I shall never deserve a similar suspicion. As regards patronage I believe it is unavoidable in this country: indeed it is the etiquette that persons of rank in my household require my favour in special cases. The important thing is for me to use my patronage wisely, and I will always do my best.'

The eviction of d'Aiguillon from the Foreign Office, however justifiable on personal and political grounds, had caused bad blood, and her failure to restore Choiseul to power should have warned the Queen not to meddle in matters outside her competence. Yet her third intervention was of far graver significance. 'I have already told my dear Maman that M. Turgot is a very honest man,' she wrote, 'and that is most essential for the finances.' The new Controller-General, reported Mercy, was considered virtuous, firm and enlightened, and had already made economies though time would be needed before they bore fruit. 'He seems a little frightened by the immensity of his task, as he has reason to be, but he is expected to succeed.' In character and abilities he towered above his colleagues, was anxious to win the good opinion of the Queen, and was an old college friend of the Abbé Vermond. Mercy and the Abbé co-operated in persuading the Minister, in view of the generous provision for the brothers and sisters-in-law of the King and for Mesdames, to increase the provision for the Queen. They were pushing at an open door, and Turgot willingly undertook to advise the King, as if it came from himself, to double her allowance. This transaction took place without the knowledge of the Queen, who willingly consented to the economies proposed in the Royal Household.

No one watched the wielding of the broom with greater approval and anxiety than the Ambassador, for vested interests were difficult to overcome. Writing a year later, in August 1775, he reported that the new Minister of the King's Household, Malesherbes, was a novel and admirable type. 'The identity of his views with those of M. Turgot will result in a great reform of abuses if they are allowed a free hand, which is very doubtful.

I foretell that it will not be easy to keep M. de Malesherbes long. Perhaps M. Turgot will remain longer if the price of bread falls and if his measures are not thwarted. These two men are of rare virtue and disinterestedness. As to their talents, only events will show. The present Ministers are working in general agreement for good ends; there is little intrigue among them, but there is all the more among the courtiers and that always ends by involving the Ministers.' Mercy's compliments were fully deserved. Never had France possessed a better team, but their virtues were their undoing. The *Ancien Régime* had reached the condition of the Roman state as described by Tacitus—incapable of bearing either the evils or the remedies.

The first friction arose over the remuneration for the Princesse de Lamballe, at this period Superintendent of the Queen's Household. In October 1775 Mercy reported that her claims were not easy to satisfy at a moment when the Government was striving to economise. Maurepas seized the opportunity of gaining the favour of the Queen, which he had never fully possessed, and undertook to obtain the assent of the King. She was also very satisfied with Malesherbes, who supported the demand. 'Only the Controller-General is coldly treated. But I hope that at Fontainebleau it will prove possible to recover her favour for a Minister who has given her no cause for complaint and who on every occasion has shown his zeal and respectful attachment.' These hopes were soon to be disappointed. Never was a French Minister less of a courtier than Turgot, whose austerity was an unspoken rebuke to the gilded throng. On his appointment the King had promised him to stop the *ordonnances au comptant* which were paid without inquiry. Before long, however, a note signed by the King for half a million livres was presented to the Treasury in the name of 'a person of the Court', who was in fact the Queen. Hurrying with it to the King he asked: 'What shall I do?' 'Do not pay,' was the reply. The Queen was indignant, and though a settlement was reached she retained a bitter memory. A year later there was a fresh conflict over the lucrative supervision of the postal service which she wanted for a friend, but which Turgot suppressed on the ground of economy: henceforth she ceased to speak to him. The next trial of strength arose when he challenged the Polignac clique by vainly opposing the pension extracted from the King for an aunt of the Queen's new friend. When the latter wrote to thank the Minister he acidly replied: 'Madame, you owe me no thanks since I did my utmost to oppose it.' Thereupon the Polignac circle, in the presence of and with the approbation of the Queen, drafted an impudent letter which was shown to Maurepas before being despatched. 'Madame,' commented the old man, 'if ever you are dissatisfied with me, give me two blows but do not write to me like that.'

Since the overthrow of the austere Minister required a concentration of forces the Baron de Besenval and Mme de Polignac decided to win over Maurepas. The Baron was to approach the Minister, while the favourite would deal with the Queen. The cynical old statesman, jealous of Turgot's prestige and anxious to curry favour with the omnipotent Queen, was quite ready for a fight. Mme de Polignac, hitherto his critic, now began to sing his praises to her royal friend, who at once received him in the friendliest way. During the talk the King, who had been told of this effort at reconciliation, entered the room, and was informed that they were now good friends. Knowing nothing of the sinister purpose of this partnership, he expressed his delight, and all that was now needed was a pretext for the knock-out blow. It was found in the affair of the Comte de Guines, an old *protégé* of Choiseul and friend of the Polignac circle who was recalled from his post as Ambassador in London by Vergennes with the approval of Turgot and Malesherbes. He had used his official position to engage in contraband transactions and to speculate on the Stock Exchange, and by injudicious utterances had endangered the Spanish alliance on the eve of the war with England. The evidence of these grave offences was supplied by his secretary, who, however, was pronounced by a court to be a caluminator.

At this point the Polignac circle rallied to the defence, and the Queen joined in the campaign to save the 'victim', not because she was interested in him, but in order to vindicate the authority of her friends. While she deliberately kept in the background, the foes of Turgot employed every weapon, including forged letters. Furious at the supposed utterances of the Minister she besought the King with tears to rehabilitate Guines by bestowing the title of Duke, and to dismiss Turgot on the day of the announcement.

The feeble monarch capitulated, and the letter announcing the Dukedom was drafted under the eye of the Queen. Turgot's requests for an audience were ignored and he received orders to leave Versailles at once. Malesherbes was dismissed the same day. The Polignac group had won a spectacular victory. Though the Queen took no part in their loud rejoicing, it was common knowledge that her hand had struck the blow. That de Guines was welcomed to the Court told its own tale.

That Marie Antoinette lied to her mother suggests that she was not very proud of her handiwork. In announcing the dismissal of the two Ministers she added: 'I confess to my dear Maman that I do not regret their departure, though I had no hand in it.' Mercy's report told a very different story. 'I cannot conceal from Your Majesty that in recent weeks things have gone contrary to the true interests of the Queen: one day they may subject her to just reproaches from the King and the whole nation. In the affair of the Comte de Guines the King is in manifest contradiction with himself. By his conflicting letters to Vergennes and Guines he compromises all his Ministers. The public knows all about it and realises that he has yielded to the will of the Queen. The Controller-General, aware of their hatred, has decided, largely for this reason, to withdraw. Her plan was to demand not only his dismissal but his commitment to the Bastille on the same day that the Comte de Guines became a duke. The strongest representations were necessary to stop the effects of her anger at Turgot's attempt to recall him. Since the Controller-General enjoys a great reputation for honesty, and is loved by the people, it is regrettable that his retirement is partly her doing. She would also like to dismiss Vergennes on account of the Comte de Guines, and I am not sure if she can be prevented. Your Majesty will doubtless be surprised that the Count, for whom she can have no personal affection, should be the cause of such commotions. The reason is to be found in her *entourage*, which is solidly in his favour. She is besieged by them and wishes to get free. They play on her *amour-propre* and run down those who in the public interest resist her wishes. All this occurs during drives and excursions or in evening talk. They succeed in intoxicating her, and, in view of the extreme complaisance of the King, there are at times no means of bringing her to reason.

I believe this is only a passing storm, for at bottom her good character, her intelligence, her fine qualities are intact. Abbé Vermond and I agree that we must work cautiously. We have just witnessed her resentment at our remonstrances which she seeks to evade, and we are unpopular with the whole of her circle.'

The comment of the Empress had to be diplomatically phrased, for she dared not give her informant away. 'I am very glad you had no hand in the retirement of the two Ministers who enjoy high reputation with the public and who are guilty, in my opinion, merely of undertaking too much at once. You say you do not regret them. Doubtless you have your reasons, but the public no longer speaks so well of you and attributes to you many little tricks unsuited to your position. The King loves you and the Ministers should respect you; in requesting nothing contrary to the general welfare you win respect and love at the same time. My only anxiety for you—young as you are—is too much dissipation. That you never liked reading nor any application has often worried me. I was so glad to see your interest in music, and I have so often bothered you to let me know about your books. For over a year there has been no mention of them or of music. I hear only of horse races and hunting parties, always without the King and with a mixed lot of young folk which, loving you tenderly as I do, makes me very anxious. Your sisters-in-law act quite differently. All these noisy pleasures in which the King takes no part are unsuitable. You will tell me he knows and approves. I shall reply that he is good and for that reason you must be more careful and plan your amusements jointly. In the long run you can only find happiness in this tender and sincere union and friendship.' To Mercy she wrote, as usual, with greater freedom. 'I regret to see that events fully justify my apprehensions about the taste of my daughter for continual dissipations, encouraged by the frivolity of the Comte d'Artois who keeps in her good books, while she is chilly to his brother who is too clever to show his hand. I realise the danger of her course, for her domination of the King rests on no solid foundations and can easily be destroyed by her attempts to make him accept her crude ideas. The affair of the Comte de Guines is a striking example. I recognise your zeal and that of Abbé

Vermond, and I know that it is not your fault that your remonstrances have been in vain.   I agree that you must show reserve,
while never concealing your disapproval of errors occasioned by
her levity or the pressure of her favourites.'

Stung by her mother's rebuke the Queen replied to the indictment point by point.   'It hurts me that my dear Maman believes
reports which are often false and almost always exaggerated.   I
cannot guess what is meant by little tricks unsuitable to my
position.   I witnessed the nomination of the Ministers without
taking the slightest part.   I frankly told my dear Maman that I
did not regret their departure, since they alienated almost everyone.   My conduct and intentions are well known and have
nothing to do with tricks and intrigues.   Some people may
speculate on what passes between the King and myself, but I
shall not give them the pleasure of jeopardising the confidence
which should exist between us.   Moreover, public opinion is
not so hostile to me as my dear Maman has been informed.   My
taste for music has not ceased.   Till the visit to Marly I had a
concert in my apartments every week.   Some time ago I resumed
the reading of Echard's *Roman History*.   There have been no
horse races for two months.   The King hunts twice a week at
Saint-Hubert; I go and sup with him regularly and sometimes
I hunt with him.   I pay attention to elderly people when they
come to pay their respects.   I admit there are not many of them
in my circle; but should my dear Maman be told that it consists
of unselected folk, they are people of birth and nearly all of them
hold posts and are of 35 to 40 or more.   I have nothing to say
against my sisters-in-law, with whom I am on good terms; but
if my dear Maman could see things at close range the comparison
would not be to my disadvantage.   The Comtesse d'Artois
possesses one great advantage in having children, but that is the
only thing she has and it is not my fault if I lack that merit.   As
for Madame, she has more brains but I would not exchange
reputations.'   The Queen scored on minor points, but to the
most serious charge she could make no truthful reply.   Her
ardent championship of an unworthy representative of the Crown,
of whom she knew nothing, advertised the supremacy of the
Polignac clique, exhibited the King as a pawn in their selfish
game, and revealed her readiness to sacrifice competent Ministers

to the whims of her friends. With the fall of the most courageous reformer France had produced for generations went one of the last chances of averting a catastrophe. Among the shining qualities of the Queen political insight and foresight were never to be found.

V. *The Years of Folly*

FRIENDS and foes of Marie Antoinette agree in describing the period between her accession in 1774 and the birth of her first child in 1778 as the years of folly, but they differ in the severity of their verdict. To some observers her dissipations were the natural outcome of an indolent and frivolous nature, destitute of intellectual interests, indifferent to the welfare of her adopted country, unmindful of the prestige of the Crown, careless of the character of her *entourage*. 'Que voulez-vous?' she exclaimed to Mercy; 'j'ai peur de m'ennuyer.' Gentler critics maintained that the pretty butterfly was not the real woman, that her frivolities were merely escapism, and that the chief responsibility for her failure rests on the unsuitable husband who for seven years denied her the satisfaction she craved. In proof of the thesis that she was more sinned against than sinning, they point to the transformation effected by motherhood and to the revelation of noble qualities when faced by calamity. With her children around her, the dross melted away and the shining gold emerged.

Of these rival interpretations the austere Empress leaned to the former; the Ambassador, who was in a better position to judge, to the latter. Perhaps the fairest verdict is that of the Marquis de Ségur, one of her latest biographers: 'She lost her reputation but preserved her virtue.' Here at any rate we are on firm ground. Till Fersen came into her life at a later period she seems never to have been seriously attracted by men. When the elderly Swiss officer, Baron de Besenval, was momentarily carried away by his feelings, he was promptly put in his place. That she enjoyed the company of the fascinating Duc de Lauzun for a season is true enough, but we need hardly accept the statement in the memoirs of that notorious Don Juan that on one occasion she was ready to surrender had not his chivalrous instincts held him back.   'There is an epidemic of satirical verse,' she wrote to her mother in December 1775, 'and I am not spared. They credit me with two tastes—for women and for lovers. Though malignities go down in this country, these are so dull and vulgar that they have fallen flat.'   Yet when the gravest charges are swept aside enough remains to make the angels weep.   Living as she did in a glass-house she set a deplorable example by her passion for clothes, jewels and cards.   Her eyes were partially opened when, to her horror, after a decade on the throne, she discovered that her popularity was gone, that she was surrounded by enemies, that their damaging version of the incident of the Diamond Necklace could be widely believed, and that by that time it was too late to recover the lost ground.

After four years of repression and frustration as Dauphine, Marie Antoinette found herself in her twentieth year able to do as she liked, to break the hated fetters of etiquette, to buy what-ever tempted her fancy, to choose her circle of friends, to amuse herself to her heart's content.   The King—for seven years a husband only in name—made no attempt to train or restrain her, and until the closing years of sorrow he counted for little in her life.   In his halting way he strove to perform the duties of his office while she seemed unaware that she had duties to perform. That her brothers-in-law were no help was not her fault.   Artois was a disgrace to the family, but though she despised his character she found a certain pleasure in his giddy company.   It was the carnival of youth; elderly people—whom she called '*les siècles*' —felt out of place.   'I can't understand,' she petulantly exclaimed, 'how anyone over thirty dares to show himself at Court.'   But to what other members of the Royal Family could she turn?   'Je suis assez bien avec le roi,' confided Monsieur to Gustavus of Sweden in June 1775, 'pas mal avec la reine'; but his relations with the Royal couple were never cordial.   The elder sister Clothilde married the Prince of Piedmont in 1775, and left the country for good.   Elizabeth, later a friend and comrade in misfortune, was still a child.   The Italian sisters-in-law possessed little heart or brains, and Mesdames faded out of the picture on her accession to the throne.   Starved for love, destitute of resources in herself, and lacking suitable occupation, Marie Antoinette lived for the hour and threw discretion to the winds.

In the midst of the most critical and scandal-loving people in Europe the warnings of the Empress, the Ambassador and Abbé Vermond fell on deaf ears. Some of her diversions—riding, dancing, tennis, billiards and amateur theatricals—were innocent enough. English fashions were in vogue, and in 1775 horse racing and the betting which accompanied it was introduced. Mercy reported her delight in the weekly fixtures, and complained that it was difficult to preserve a semblance of dignity amid the motley throng on the racecourse. The King had enough of it after a single visit and expressed his disapproval to his wife. No one could blame her for loving the enchantments of Paris, but her appearances without the King at the masked balls at the Opera, when she amused herself by talking to anyone she met, bred stories of amorous intrigue. One night, returning with Artois at two in the morning, she found the palace gates closed. It was the express order of the King, she was informed, and she had to enter by a private door. Next day her husband reminded her that he always went to bed at eleven, and did not want his first slumber to be disturbed. The scene ended in the usual manner with his surrender and the order to the gatekeeper was revoked. With the sole exception of the reinstatement of Choiseul in power he could never say her nay.

Far more compromising for herself and the monarchy were the extravagant habits which became the talk of the town. As Dauphine there had been no sign of profusion, and she could justly claim that she had never been in debt; but her good resolutions on coming to the throne to eschew useless expenditure were soon forgotten. Hitherto she spent little on her toilette; now the temptation of dress and ornaments proved irresistible. The magnificent crown jewels were not enough for her. In January 1776 she bought a sprig of diamonds for 400,000 francs, and the seller was asked to wait for years for the money. Six months later she purchased a pair of bracelets for 250,000 francs, though this, according to Mercy, was the result of pressure by her *entourage*. Since her purse was empty she sold some jewels and reluctantly asked her husband to fill the gap. 'These stories,' wrote her anxious mother, 'break my heart, especially in view of the future. This French levity, with all these extraordinary ornaments! My daughter, my dear daughter! I cannot bear to think of it.' When the offender pleaded that the bracelets were a trifle, she sharply replied: 'A sovereign degrades herself by adornment, still more if it involves large sums and at such a time. I observe only too much of this spirit of dissipation. I cannot keep silence, loving you for your welfare and not wishing to flatter you.' Even worse was the intoxication of the gaming-table. Playing for high stakes was an established tradition at Court. Money had flowed like water at the parties of the Montespan and other Royal mistresses, but the Queens of France had held aloof. The Dauphine had shown distaste for gambling, and for the first year of her reign she held her ground, but in 1776 and 1777 she cast off the brakes. The evil example of Artois, the Duc de Chartres and her own intimates proved irresistible. 'She is playing for high stakes,' announced the horrified Mercy in September 1776. Once the King himself played for a few evenings, lost 1,800 louis [1], and, like the younger Pitt, never played again. When he was expected in the circle of Princess de Guéménée the cards were hidden and brought out again after his departure. In addition to her clothes, jewels and gambling debts the Queen poured out money on other objects: whence it came she never stopped to ask. Where Marie Leczinska had possessed 150 horses, she had 300. The embellishment of the Petit Trianon cost a fortune, and at a later stage the palace and park of Saint-Cloud were purchased for her by the King from the Duke of Orléans. Stories of her extravagance spread through the country and earned her the sinister title of ' *Madame Déficit* '.

The faithful Ambassador and the Abbé were almost in despair, and the latter only remained at his post at the urgent entreaty of the Empress. 'My daughter is racing to her doom and needs your help. Mercy and I hope you will at any rate hold on till the winter. Then, if things do not change, I could not ask you for fresh sacrifices.' Mme de la Marck reported to the King of Sweden: 'The Queen is always going to Paris to the Opera and the Comédie, runs up debts, wears plumes and top-knots, and laughs at everything.' Tired of tendering unheeded advice the Empress decided, as she grimly expressed it, to confine her letters to the weather. The Abbé Vermond usually reported to the

---

[1] The standard coins were the gold louis, worth 24 francs or livres, the silver écu, worth 3 francs or livres. The franc or livre was a standard, not a coin.

Ambassador, but on October 17, 1776, the '*lecteur de la Reine*' was asked to write direct to the Empress. 'The Queen's *entourage* have it all their own way and muffle my voice. I have swallowed my bitter mortifications so long as they only affected myself, but I cannot surrender the hope of becoming once more useful to the Queen. She has more insight and judgment than all those who beset her. Her youth and her taste for skimming the surface of things are the source of her errors. She will recover from them. For over a year she has listened very little to me, but she still confides her ideas to me and opens her heart— on certain matters to me alone. My character and my duty forbid me to soften the truth in my replies, but, while avoiding importunity, I can be of use when time and circumstances lead her back to herself. I am obsessed by the thought of the trouble she may be laying up for herself; if they occurred I should be her confidant, perhaps the only one to whom she can talk with perfect safety. My heart and soul are with her; I shall be at her service so long as she permits.'

The good Abbé's letter did nothing to allay the anxieties of the Empress. 'My daughter's conduct towards you and Vermond is just like her,' she wrote to Mercy. 'Eager to dodge those who try to turn her from her errors, she goes her own way and skilfully finds excuses to colour her doings. I am glad to see from his letter that Vermond appears for the time to have abandoned his idea of resignation, but I think he has nothing like so much influence with her as I should wish.' The same courier brought a sharp reproof to her daughter. 'Your excuses for forgetting my name-day (St. Theresa) are fully accepted; but, my dear daughter, it is not only once a year that I should like you to think of me, but that every month, every week, every day, you should recall my affection and advice. This life of continual dissipation, of excursions such as were never indulged in by other queens much older than you, though still young and accompanied by their husbands! What worries me most is that all this goes on without the King. Some day it may end, especially if extraordinary expenses are incurred. It is on such occasions that I should wish you to think of me. I am sure—and I know your heart unless it is entirely changed by flattery and frivolity—that it would restrain you to recall the pain these levities would cause me.   They will come to an end, but perhaps too late for your happiness and glory, which are and will always remain my motive.'   The Queen briefly replied by asking how she could ever for a moment forget what her dear Maman had done for her.

How little the good opinion of the Empress meant to her in this hectic phase appeared in the voluminous despatches of the Ambassador dated November 15, 1776, which contained particularly unwelcome news.   During the annual visit of the Court to Fontainebleau the Queen was seized by the desire to play at faro, the most hazardous of games, and begged permission to summon banker-players from Paris.   The King replied that in view of the prohibition of games of chance, even in the apartments of princes of the blood, it was a bad example to admit them to Court; but with his usual good nature he added that it would not matter just for one evening.   The banker-players arrived on October 30.   Gambling continued all night and during the morning of October 31 in the apartments of Princess de Lamballe, where the Queen remained till four A.M.   The game was renewed the same evening and continued well into the early hours of November 1, All Saints' Day.   The first night she lost 90 louis and Artois won 500.   On the second she played till three A.M., only losing a few louis while Artois lost 100.   Monsieur, who played unwillingly, lost 400.   The King, as usual, remained in his room.

It was forcibly represented to the Queen, continued Mercy, that such late hours were dangerous, if only by leaving her husband alone for a purpose he disapproved.   'In this whirlpool, so damaging to the welfare of the Queen and so distressing to myself, I could be little more than an onlooker.   The items of dissipation followed each other so rapidly that it was very difficult to find time for serious talk.   Yet I snatched a few moments and was relieved to note that her zeal for frivolities changes neither her mind nor the foundation of her character; that both of them, tending naturally to goodness, will prevail in quiet times; in a word, that her great qualities are only suspended by unmeasured dissipation, not irrevocably destroyed.'   The bulletin for the eyes of the Empress alone added a few details.   The Queen had been particularly friendly to him, but she often closed their brief conversations about serious matters by gaily remarking that reason would come but that it was necessary to amuse oneself. The Abbé had passed days without once having a talk, for never had there been such systematic dissipation. The worst feature was that she tried to palliate the breach of faith in prolonging the game of faro for thirty-six hours on the ground that the King had authorised a session without fixing its duration. The feeble King laughed at this shameless paradox and actually authorised a second visit from the Parisian tempters.

The Empress was deeply distressed but in no way surprised, for she had almost given up hope. 'My daughter's conduct at Fontainebleau,' she replied, 'is a new proof of her character. It would be superfluous to reiterate my reflections; you know them only too well from all my letters, and you also know my method of dealing with her. Moreover, you will see by her laconic and nonchalant reply to three of mine how little she cares to discuss with me the subjects about which I wrote and that this indifference towards me will become chronic. Like you I deplore the excessive indulgence of the King. I am glad Vermond seems to have renounced the idea of resignation, but his plan of shortening his stay at Versailles makes me anxious in view of the critical situation of my daughter who might often need such a wise and admirable man.' The letter to her daughter despatched by the same courier was brief and cold. The episode of the bankers was ignored. 'I am glad to learn of your return and of a quieter time in the winter. In the long run your health will not stand these late hours. If the King were with you I would keep silence; but, always without him and in company with the worst and youngest elements of Paris, the Queen, this charming Queen, is almost the oldest member of the company. The papers, which were my delight, used to record the good actions and the most generous traits of my daughter; now that one finds nothing but horse races, gambling and late hours I no longer care to read them. Yet I cannot prevent people talking to me about them, for everyone who knows my affection for my children tells me what they say. Often I avoid company in order to avoid distress.' Once again the Queen quietly defended herself. 'Truly I might pity myself for the different judgments passed on me. While people tell my dear Maman that my society consists merely of persons as young as myself, for the last year the very young folk have felt themselves ill-treated and kept at arm's-length; only a fortnight ago there was talk of a little conspiracy not to come to my balls. However, they all turned up, some of them looking as if they had just left college. Our balls have started this month. I like dancing, but I do not tire myself so much as in recent years.' For the anxious mother in the Hofburg the year 1776 closed in almost unrelieved gloom, while her light-hearted daughter, deaf to warnings and appeals, was having the time of her life.

Marie Antoinette reverenced her mother and respected her husband, but in the absence of children she sorely needed friends. Thrice and only thrice in her life did she seem to find her heart's desire. Her romantic attachment to Fersen lies outside the chronological limits of this study, but the names of Princess de Lamballe and Countess Jules de Polignac are inseparably connected with her own. Both women at first deserved her love and gave her their own in return, yet neither partnership brought enduring happiness. Though no greedier than most other courtiers, neither of them could withstand the temptations of power. The early honeymoon with the Lamballe lasted till her star paled before the rising sun of her more accomplished competitor. Neither association ended with a violent break, and the Lamballe, after a long eclipse, was to seal her loyalty with her blood; but in both cases, though no one could fairly describe Marie Antoinette as a fickle friend, the bloom gradually wore off. When the storm burst over her head in 1789 the threatened Queen found herself without an intimate friend except the absent Swedish nobleman. Her children brought her an inner peace deeper than she had ever known; but even here there was bitterness in her cup, for two of the four were snatched away in early years.

Princess de Lamballe, a member of a younger branch of the House of Savoy, had married a degenerate French nobleman whose vices left her a widow at the end of a year. Living in the house of her respected father-in-law, the Duc de Penthièvre, at Versailles, she reappeared at Court when her period of mourning ended. Though by no means a beauty she possessed grace and charm, and her expression of youthful innocence was like an open letter of recommendation. That she lacked brains was no

disqualification in the mindless circle where pleasure was the
business of life.   That she had a heart goes without saying, for
no one else could win the love of Marie Antoinette.   As a guest
at Compiègne with her father-in-law she had witnessed the
arrival of the little Archduchess, but their first meeting was at a
ball given for the Dauphine by Mme de Noailles in 1771.   The
girl-wife and the young widow of twenty-three instantly became
friends, sharing in their walks and all the festivities of the Court.
The Ambassador's first reference in March 1771 was distinctly
favourable.   'For some time Mme la Dauphine has been greatly
attached to the Princess de Lamballe.   Gentle, amiable, and
enjoying the prerogatives of a princess of the blood, she is well
placed to pay court to her and to cultivate her favour.'   Long
before the accession three years later they had become inseparable.
'I am glad Mme de Lamballe is not leaving you,' remarked the
new King with a smile; 'you are very fond of her?'   'Oh, Sire,
she is the joy of my life,' was the reply.   It was an excellent choice,
declared Mercy, for, though a Piedmontese, she had no contacts
with the sisters-in-law of the King.   He had, however, advised
the Queen to keep her favours within bounds in order to prevent
trouble.   The comment of the Empress, always inclined to
alarmist views, was that her Piedmontese birth was a warning
against unlimited confidence.   A rumour in July that she was
to be appointed Superintendent of the Queen's Household upset
the Comtesse de Noailles, the Dame d'Honneur, till Mercy was
able to assure her that no such idea was entertained.   In September
he reported the Queen's unchanging affection for her friend, but
added that it remained within bounds.

In his last bulletin of 1774 the Ambassador reported that the
Queen was once again thinking of making the Lamballe Superintendent of her Household, but he had persuaded her to wait.
The post had been created by Mazarin for his niece, was suppressed in 1741, and had at all times been a sinecure.   Her
increasing power, however, was manifested when, at the instance
of the Piedmontese princesses, she begged the Queen to procure
a large pension and a regiment for her brother, the Prince de
Carignan.   The King consented without consulting his Ministers,
but the incident made a bad impression at a moment when Turgot
was struggling to reduce expenditure.   When Mercy told the

Queen that the friendship had already caused umbrage she made
the usual reply that she would take more care, and he believed
that his warning would at any rate postpone her promotion.
Moreover, the Lamballe was subject to fainting fits and convulsions, which, if they continued, would present a disqualification
for the office.   A year after her accession, however, the Queen
had her way.   In July 1775 she wrote to Count Rosenberg that
Mme de Lamballe was to be her Superintendent.   'Imagine my
happiness; I shall make my intimate friend happy and I shall
rejoice even more than she.'   Mercy promptly informed his
sovereign of the news, which was not yet public.   She was still
very young, and it remained to be seen whether she would continue to be the quiet, gentle, decent person she had always been.
In any case, he feared the decision would create difficulties in the
Queen's circle.

The bulletin of August 16, 1775, which announced the
approaching nomination of a Superintendent of the Queen's
Household, contained Mercy's first reference to the woman who
was destined to play an even larger part in the life of Marie
Antoinette.   The Lamballe, he reported, had already lost a good
deal of favour with the Queen, who for a time had preferred the
company of the Comtesse de Dillon; 'but the latter has just been
supplanted by a young Comtesse de Polignac, for whom she has
developed an affection much stronger than for any of her predecessors.   These various affections cause embarrassment and
inconvenience.   In fulfilling her engagements to the Princess the
Queen would like at the same time to bring her into contact with
the present favourite by making the latter *dame d'atours*.   For this
the Princess de Chimay would have to become *dame d'honneur*.
Here, however, there are major difficulties, for she declares that
she is not rich enough for the entertaining it involves.   It
cannot be given to the Comtesse de Polignac, who is only twenty
and has never held a post at Court.   All the palace ladies are at
sixes and sevens, and the Queen does not see the way out.   I go
to the limits of importunity with my advice, but in such matters
the whim of the moment prevails.'

Yolande de Polastron, born in 1750, had married Count Jules
de Polignac at seventeen, and was now twenty-five.   The young
couple, who being poor spent most of the year in the country,

12

were rarely seen at Court till the Countess Diane de Polignac, sister of Count Jules, was appointed to the Household of Comtesse d'Artois and received apartments in the palace. The Queen's pleasure in her company was so marked that she was invited to the *salons* both of the Lamballe and the Comtesse d'Artois. Soon they were inseparable. Even her exquisite portraits, we are assured by contemporaries, failed to do justice to her indefinable charm. Her blue eyes, her caressing voice, her air of kindness and simplicity, were irresistible. The Lamballe had given more love than she received, but to the Polignac Marie Antoinette for the first time in her life gave her whole heart. With her—and her alone—she felt absolutely at home, remarking 'j'y suis moi.' For seven years—till she succeeded the Princesse de Guéménée in 1782 as Gouvernante of the Enfants de France—she held no official post, but her influence was supreme. Against such a formidable competitor the Lamballe, with far less personality, had little chance. After a long and painful battle she accepted defeat and withdrew from the Court.

On September 15, 1775, the Queen informed her mother that Mme de Noailles had resigned; that Mme de Chimay, hitherto *dame d'atours*, would succeed her; and that Mme de Lamballe would be Superintendent. What were to be her functions, her salary, and her authority? No one had held the post since the death of Marie Leczinska. Mercy urged the Queen to keep down expenditure and to avoid encroachments on other departments of her household. The advice was the more necessary since unsuitable demands had recently been put forward from various quarters and granted, but at the last moment the Lamballe intervened in tears. Her father-in-law, the Duc de Penthièvre, she declared, opposed acceptance of the post unless it carried the same dignity and emoluments as in the past. The Ambassador implored the Queen to stand by her first resolutions, and he anticipated endless trouble with the two other office-holders, the *dame d'honneur* and the *dame d'atours*. His exhortations were fruitless, for the old confusion of authority and the high salary remained. A month after the appointment he reported that the new Superintendent was too new to the work to be judged, but her attitude on rights and emoluments was not encouraging.

Mercy had disapproved the appointment from the time it was

mooted, and his apprehensions were speedily confirmed. As Dauphine the chief danger had been the influence of the aunts; as Queen it was that of her own household. Three groups existed, for in addition to the two favourites there was Mme de Guéménée, who held the post of *Gouvernante des Enfants de France*, though there were no royal children to serve. Of this undesirable woman Mercy disapproved more than of the Lamballe. 'The Queen,' he reported in October 1775, 'is becoming very fond of the Princess de Guéménée, who gathers round her a noisy circle, mainly of young people. She spends many evenings with her, and as I am in touch with her I can during this sojourn at Fontainebleau keep my eye on this new habit and try to remedy the disadvantages I anticipate.' The Princess was a daughter of Marshal Soubise, the head of the great House of Rohan, but she was separated from her husband, and her *liaison* with the Duc de Coigny was notorious. Another short-lived friendship was with Mme Dillon, whose relations with Prince de Guéménée were unconcealed. Though strict enough in her own practice Marie Antoinette was regrettably tolerant with her *entourage*. How marriages were arranged and how little the legal tie interfered with the pleasures of either party we may read in the memoirs of Lauzun.

Mercy disliked the Comtesse de Polignac from the first. His bulletin of September 18, 1775, reported that by his advice the Queen had abandoned the plan to give her one of the two highest places in her household. He was collecting evidence that she lacked the intelligence, the judgment, and even the character needed to earn her confidence. Invited to Fontainebleau for the annual autumn sojourn of the Court the Ambassador could study the two favourites at close quarters. The Lamballe, he reported, had good qualities, but was too young and inexperienced. The Polignac, a person of very little intelligence, was subject to very undesirable influences. The Empress replied with her usual pessimism that the new friends were obviously unworthy of her daughter's confidence. 'Young as she is, unreflecting and indolent, the only way of avoiding trouble is to keep your eye on her. To be with her as much as possible, always ready to counsel and to warn, is the best service you can render me.' The complications arising from the emergence of a new favourite were described in a lengthy despatch on November 15. 'The Queen finds it extremely difficult to keep the peace between them. They are very jealous and each complains of the other. I have told her that, after public demonstrations of her friendship for both, she should treat them well but not listen to their complaints, thus shielding herself from many importunities.' Each possessed highly undesirable champions. 'The Princess de Lamballe is supported by the Comte d'Artois, the Duc de Chartres, her relative, and all the Palais Royal set whose intrigues fill me with alarm. The Comtesse de Polignac's partisans include Baron de Besenval, several young people of the Court, an aunt of evil reputation, and other equally dangerous elements. It would be difficult to say which of the two parties might do the most harm. It would be best if they hold each other in check. This is my aim, though I seize my opportunities to attack them both. After long experience I find the best method is to tell the Queen everything I hear and let her draw her own conclusions. I have recently succeeded with one of her great favourites, the Chevalier de Luxembourg, whose ambition and bad character made him very dangerous. Now he is nothing, and I hope that the other favourites, male and female, will share his fate. The most critical moment of the day is after supper, when she goes for the rest of the evening to her Superintendent or to the Princess de Guéménée. Every day from these two sources flow so many insinuations and requests that I could not tell Your Majesty even a part of them without going into endless detail. Baron de Besenval, for instance, is instigated by the Duc de Choiseul (as I discovered from various soundings) in favour of his *protégés*. Directly or indirectly I have been very well informed about these *soirées*. The Queen told the Abbé Vermond and myself something, and we then tried to counterwork what seemed to us undesirable pressures, with success beyond our expectations.'

Mercy's last monthly bulletin of 1775 reported that the Polignac had lost ground which the Lamballe had gained. Following his tactics of striving for an equilibrium he had vigorously combated certain projects of the latter, not altogether without success. When she begged the Queen to secure a pension for the Comtesse de la Marche after separating from her husband, the Ambassador explained to the Queen that her Superintendent cost the state annually over 100,000 crowns, including the pension to her brother, and should therefore be more careful not to abuse her favour, above all by interfering in matters outside her department. 'All my remonstrances did not prevent the Queen on several occasions from yielding to the importunities of the Princess de Lamballe, but I persuaded her to defer her decisions.' The struggle between the favourites continued throughout the winter. The Queen's letters to her mother made no reference to it, but Mercy's bulletin of February 28, 1776, reported the general surprise that the Superintendent gave no balls and therefore lost an opportunity to give the Queen pleasure. 'If she goes on like that her favour, now somewhat diminished, may well disappear. Fortunately, since the Queen's affections are divided, they lose in force what they gain in scope, and I have always felt it essential that she should not be ruled by a single person. That is not the case at the moment. Yet she has partial affections for several people, and when they all combine for a special purpose resistance is impossible.' In April he reported that the Lamballe was losing much of her favour and indeed lacked the means of keeping it. 'I believe she will always be well treated by the Queen, but the intimate confidence is gone. Moreover, her health, which is very poor, necessitates frequent absence from the Court. Next month she will go to Plombières or Vichy for the waters for six or eight weeks. Comtesse Jules de Polignac is more successful in retaining her credit and is more cautious. Happily I have had some opportunity of urging the Queen to be on her guard with her favourite.' A private letter added that the latter was now guided by Maurepas.

In May, Mercy reported a further decline in the fortunes of the Superintendent, whose tactless efforts to regain her footing made things worse. 'By multiplying her pretensions and her haughty attempts to sustain them she causes commotion in the Queen's household, which complains of her despotism. She had continual disputes with the *dame d'honneur* and the *dame d'atours*. The Queen had to listen to these complaints and to decide; everyone was discontented. The Princess de Lamballe, who is almost always at fault, is steadily losing favour, and I see the time coming when Her Majesty will regret having revived a useless post.' An attack of smallpox in July revived her affection, though not

sufficiently to arrest the gradual decline of favour. Despite
her drawbacks, he added, he would welcome a partial recovery
at the expense of the Polignac, who constituted a greater danger.
To preserve an appearance of equal treatment the Queen granted
the wish of the Lamballe that her relative the Duc de Chartres
should be appointed to the government of Poitou. After her
return from Plombières, reported Mercy in August, he anticipated
further scenes of jealousy and complaints which would weary
and annoy the Queen. The best result of the rivalry of the
favourites was that she was too taken up with them to form new
attachments. 'I am delighted to witness the diminution of her
taste for the Princess de Guéménée, whose influence is nearly
gone.'

Mercy's voluminous bulletin, dated September 17, 1776,
intended for the eyes of the Empress alone, spoke with severity
of the influence of the Polignac. 'I have always regarded the
Queen's favourite as dangerous. She has little intelligence and
is controlled by her aunt, Countess d'Andlau, of evil reputation.
This influence has led her astray and made her scorn what
degenerates call prejudices. She sports a lover. Her attitude
to dogma is no less equivocal, and the Court doctor, Lassone,
who knows her, told Abbé Vermond that he feared she might
endanger the Queen's piety. I have no such fear as regards
essential principles; but a certain indifference to her religious
duties and careless talk on such important matters are bad habits
contracted in the company of people who have imbibed the errors
of the century, and I regret to see her exposed to this danger.'
The Abbé was so distressed that he had sent her a long memorandum, and he had asked leave to resign his post since his services
were useless. The Ambassador had learned from various
sources that she had been impressed both by the memorandum
and the letter, but she had avoided the topic while showing
herself particularly gracious. 'The Queen is fully aware that
she could not replace this good and faithful servant, but she
believes she can keep him by a few kind words, as has happened
on three occasions. Yet I have never seen him so unhappy, and
I am alarmed. I have secured his promise to take no action till
after the return from Fontainebleau.'

The Ambassador then passes to the painful topic of the Queen's extravagance. Even when the lies and exaggerations were discounted, there were many regrettable items. The public was beginning to complain. The King's gift of the Petit Trianon had been generally approved, but the extension of the gardens, the balls, and the theatricals were very costly. The appointment of the Lamballe to the sinecure post of Superintendent had caused division in the Queen's household and was a waste of money. In addition to the pensions and grants, of which everyone heard, the critics produced a long list of small allowances given at her instance which added up to a considerable sum. Rarely did she refuse a request or even ask for reasons. And finally there were her debts. 'She has bought a lot of diamonds and she now plays for high stakes. The ladies and courtiers are frightened at the losses they incur in paying court to her. The King disapproves high stakes, and as far as possible he is kept in the dark.' Most of the Abbé's reports to Mercy were oral, but an undated note of a conversation with the Queen at this period shows how freely he spoke his mind. She was becoming very indulgent in regard to the reputation of her friends, he complained. She had dropped some women of good character, and a bad character was now a qualification for her circle. She listened with a smile, merely remarking that the Lamballe had a good name. The *liaison* of the Polignac with the Comte de Vaudreuil, to which Mercy and the Abbé made indirect allusion, was notorious. A further bulletin of November 15 described the systematic attempts of the Polignac circle to destroy the credit of the Lamballe. The latter was a better woman, but her circle was equally undesirable. With the gambling habit at its height, and a first-class quarrel raging between the old and the new favourite, the Court was not a happy place.

Mercy's last bulletin of 1776, dated December 18, records the rapid decline of the Lamballe. On the pretext of making certain changes in her apartments, she did not propose to give any parties during the winter. When, however, it was represented to the Queen that her Superintendent could not shirk her duty while costing the State nearly 100,000 crowns a year, she was instructed to provide suppers whenever there was a ball. The Polignac, on the other hand, after an absence of several weeks with relatives, had returned in undiminished favour. The Queen was becoming indifferent to the Lamballe and would soon have had enough of her. Things drifted on through the winter, the partisans on each side working unashamedly for their own interest; the Polignac, ran the bulletin of March 18, 1777, had increased her lead. The Lamballe, after fruitless torments, was waking up to the assets of her rival. She sought compensation in asking and obtaining little favours which compromised the Queen, particularly in the military sphere. 'Generally speaking, one could not mention any persons in the Queen's *entourage* who by their qualities or genuine zeal strive to make themselves of use to her.' That no one at Versailles could help was clear enough, but there was still a trump card for Vienna to play. 'I have one consolation,' wrote the Empress to her frivolous daughter, 'that the Emperor is coming to France and that you will profit by his advice.'

VI. *Brother and Sister*

THE outstanding event of 1777 was the visit of Joseph II, a grave and childless widower of thirty-six, who combined the authority of the Queen's eldest brother with the dignity of Holy Roman Emperor and Co-Regent of the Hapsburg Dominions. Though his love of travel, of inquiry, of new experiences was notorious, his desire to see what was generally regarded as the most civilised country in the world was not the main cause of his journey. For three years the project had been discussed both in Vienna and Paris, but for one reason or other it was always postponed. By the opening of 1777 it could wait no longer, for issues of high significance were at stake. Louis XVI had to be encouraged to do his duty, not only for the sake of the dynasty, but for the buttressing of the alliance. What was the use of a Hapsburg princess if she were not enabled to provide an heir? But there was a second and scarcely less cogent motive. The prestige of the Bourbon monarchy, Vienna's only ally, was compromised by the indiscretions of the Queen which the Austrian Ambassador reported in almost every bulletin. The military fame of France had been dimmed since the stricken field of Rossbach, and the economic foundations of the country were beginning to quake.

Turgot had been evicted from the Treasury after two years of gallant endeavour, and Necker, his successor, was not a fighter. The blameless King was a cipher, and the extravagant Queen had become the talk of Europe. If anyone could persuade Louis XVI and Marie Antoinette to change their respective ways it was the austere Emperor, who preached and practised the strenuous life. Mother and son differed sharply on many issues of foreign and domestic policy, but in this matter they were at one: things in France could not be allowed to drift.

The visit lasted from April 18 to May 31. On its conclusion the Ambassador despatched a copy of his journal filling thirty pages of print. On the morning after his arrival 'Count Falkenstein' drove to Versailles where, as arranged, he was met by Abbé Vermond, who conducted him unseen by private staircase to the Queen's apartments. The meeting was touching, brother and sister engaging in a long and silent embrace. For two hours they talked heart to heart, the Queen greatly worked up and the Emperor obviously pleased with her. If she were not his sister, he declared, he would like to marry such a charming woman. If she became a childless widow, he added, he wished her to return to Vienna and live with the Empress and himself. He had instantly won her confidence, and she proceeded to discuss her anomalous matrimonial position. He then spoke of her habits, her dissipations, her love of gambling and her favourites, though on the latter with some reserve. Though he had intended to keep his advice for a subsequent meeting, he seized the opportunity thus provided, but with such consideration and gentleness as to increase her confidence. He was then introduced to the King, whom he promptly put at his ease, to the princes and their wives, and to the chief Ministers. On his return to Paris in the evening he narrated the doings of a happy and eventful day to the Ambassador. After a second visit two days later he reported that he found the King fairly well informed and desiring to do right. That night he slept in a Versailles hotel. Next day he was shown the Petit Trianon, and while walking alone with his sister in the gardens spoke more freely than at the first meeting of the dissipations which would inevitably have terrible consequences. Her neglect of the King, her *entourage*, her distaste for serious occupations, and her passion for cards were passed in review, but with such moderation that she did not take offence. She admitted his charges, adding that the time would come when she would follow his good advice.   When he expressed his dislike of the Lamballe she frankly confessed that she had been mistaken in her and regretted her choice.   The more the Emperor saw of Versailles the less he liked it.   One evening he accompanied his sister at her wish to the apartments of the Princess de Guéménée and was horrified at the air of licence among the guests.   He watched them playing faro and heard whispers that the hostess was cheating.   Though he observed sharply to the Queen that it was a regular gaming-house, she tried to palliate it and returned there after midnight.   The kindly Ambassador reminded the Emperor that a sudden improvement could not be expected and that patience was needed.   On his next visit she recognised the justice of his criticism on the society of the Guéménée; but when she sang the praises of the Polignac he rejoined that she was too young and too dominated by her set to be a good influence.

When the traveller arrived in Paris he found the Ambassador ill in bed, and it was a fortnight before the latter could visit the Queen.   On the previous day there had been a rather stormy scene when Joseph had once more complained of the circle of the Guéménée, but it left no scars.   She spoke with emotion of his friendship and useful advice.   'I saw clearly,' reported Mercy, 'that she had been impressed by his language and was taking it to heart.'   When she expressed surprise at her brother's intimate knowledge of her situation the Ambassador diplomatically rejoined that so shrewd an observer could see things for himself. The Emperor was not very confident as to the result of his counsels, but Mercy, as usual, replied that with patience, kindness and tact he would secure something at once and much more in the future.   'When I analysed the complexities of her character, he confessed to surprise that she possessed so much sagacity and brains.'   There was occasional friction in their conversations, but it always ended happily.   In explaining the administrative system of France, the King surprised him by his intelligence. The two rulers spent hours in intimate conversation and parted with regret.   When the time came to say good-bye, late on May 30, the Queen could hardly control her feelings, and on the following day she completely broke down.

Mercy's voluminous journal closed on a cheerful note, for his forecast of the visit had been confirmed. By his enlightened and prudent conduct, he assured the Empress, the Emperor had captured Versailles—not an easy task. All the Ministers were pleased. He had hit the happy mean without causing jealousies or suspicions. 'I am certain he has made a real impression on the Queen on several essential points; the time was too short to observe the effect, but I am confident it will bear fruit. The King's character is too undeveloped and undecided to entertain profound esteem or strong friendship; these sentiments require more will and reflection than he possesses, but he has felt for the Emperor all the attraction of which he is capable.' A private letter added that the King had spoken of his regret that he had no children, had explained the physical reasons, and had asked for advice. 'I firmly believe that his counsels will produce an improvement in the conduct of the Queen. Already she has decided gradually to cease frequenting the Princess de Guéménée, to refrain from high stakes, to spend some hours each day in her apartments, and above all to be more with the King.' Mercy had had many disappointments, but he never lost hope.

The Emperor's memorandum, written in his own hand and presented to his sister on the eve of his departure on May 29, fills twenty pages of manuscript and fourteen of print. It opens with her special duties as the wife of a king. 'What are you doing here in France, what title to honour and respect have you, except as his consort? What place do you hold in his heart and above all in his esteem? Ask yourself whether you do your utmost to please him. Do you make yourself essential to him? Do you persuade him that no one loves him more sincerely and that no one has his glory and happiness more at heart? Are you always absolutely discreet about his failings and weaknesses? Are you tender with him? Do not you occasionally appear bored? If so, how can you expect such a cold man to love you? This requires your particular attention, and everything you do to secure this great object will bring you happiness. Encourage his hope that he can still have children; see that he never despairs; avoid separate rooms. Your strength is in your charms and in your friendship. Your influence should be felt, but never seen. Only the King should act and you should not appear in anything.

Do you sufficiently study his character? If he dislikes any of your friends you must make the sacrifice. Never identify yourself so strongly with a project that its failure would make you feel dishonoured; do not solemnly commit yourself in advance.' Passing to her duties as Queen, Joseph reminds his sister of the importance of respect for the Court. 'Think of the Empress and her high standards. Have you calculated the result of the visits to your ladies where all sorts of people are found who do not inspire esteem? Have you reflected on the effect that your friendships with persons whose character is not beyond reproach must have on the public, since you will seem to share in and authorise vice? Have you weighed the fearful consequences of the games of chance, the company they attract, the tone they exhibit, the confusion they produce in the fortunes and morals of a whole nation? Do you not know that all the sensible part of Europe would hold you responsible for the ruin of the young people, the shabby tricks they play, the abominations which result, if you patronise these games, and still more if you join in them? This is so important and so dangerous that I leave it to you to add the rest. Remember what has passed before your eyes. Then reflect that the King does not play and that it is scandalous that you alone of the family support it. Make a noble effort and the whole world will applaud.'

Passing to the balls at the Opera and the adventures of which she had told him, the Emperor stressed the resultant danger to her reputation. Her incognito was easily penetrated. That the Comte de Provence went with her meant nothing. It was a place of evil repute. 'Why, then, these adventures, these turpitudes, why do you mix with this mob of libertines, prostitutes, strangers, listening to their talk and perhaps joining in it? How unseemly! I must tell you that it is this which has most shocked all who love you. The King, left alone all night at Versailles, and you mixing with all the *canaille* of Paris!' Her love of riding, he continued, had led people to believe that for that reason she had no children. As a substitute for several so-called amusements he ventured to suggest one which was worth them all— reading. 'Please recognise its importance and choose books which make you think and instruct you. It will be a lifelong resource, even if you only devote two hours a day. But not

alone; try to read with some sensible and trusted man so that
you talk it over.   You will get to like it, and will not need to
chase after dissipation or to kill time by frequenting circles which
are dangerous, and which you yourself despise.   I stress this
piece of advice.   If I witness its adoption I should feel that the
happiness of your life was almost assured.   At the present
moment I am trembling, for things cannot go on as they are,
and the revolution will be cruel if you take no steps.   Reading
and suitable society—there is the happiness of life and for you
it is essential.   Allow me to say that the tone in society and
above all in the Royal Family is horrible.   Be careful about
gossip; it is very entertaining, but do not listen to stories about
people.   If you hear them, and even if everyone is relating them,
avoid comment.   Decent people are estranged and it looks as if
virtue does not count.   I implore you not to want to know
everything, for exaggeration is easy; often one is only told lies,
for there is a regular conspiracy.'

The next theme was patronage.   'Be careful about your
recommendations.   It is a delicate point.   You can do cruel
injustice without knowing it.   You disgust ten honest people
and scandalise the rest of the world.   So they seek devious
methods to reach their goal, and true merit, which always runs
straight, is forgotten.   Keep your credit for great occasions.
In other cases resist the solicitations courageously; do not take
up anyone's case hotly, but have the affair examined.   Do not
intervene in private affairs, above all in the quarrels and secrets of
the household, still less in the gallantries.   It would be horrible
that your curiosity should make you seem to know, approve,
protect or even foster vice, scandals, indecency.   It would be
abominable if you were discovered in the gaming-houses and in
intrigues, and if people could shelter themselves behind your
name.   Then—good-bye to your reputation for ever!   Such
things are beyond repair.'   More reserve was desirable.   Courtesy
and affability had limits and were only of value if rationed.   She
was too inclined to familiarity with young people and foreigners.
'A lot of English and other folk come here whom no one would
receive; you mix with them and single them out.   This produces
the worst effect abroad, where these people, to the general
astonishment, boast of your favours and convey a strange

impression of you and your tasks. This familiarity is often assigned to a coquetry which wants to please everybody and seeks the applause of the crowd. Is your behaviour in church what onlookers expect? For your own sake, think seriously about this point. Do not allow some accursed fashion to prevent you seeming to be—even if unfortunately you were not in fact—a devout member of the Church. There, I must say, you are at fault. Even the most impious should be so for tactical reasons. God keep you from that. You would lose the only true consolation in all the affairs of life, your tranquillity, and you would be an object of pity in this life; of the other I do not speak, but your conscience will tell you. Listen to it. That is the tenderest, surest, truest, most important of my counsels. It concerns your soul which I love so much, and your whole life will depend on it. Let the reading of evil books, calculated to tempt even the strongest souls, be banished from your home. The obscenities are so flagrant and they often occur in talk in the belief that it is the fashion. Detest the people who speak to you in this manner or make you doubt about your religion and its observances.'

After these vigorous exhortations the Emperor concludes on a gentle and loving note. 'There are my observations. You are made to be happy, virtuous and perfect, but it is time—and more than time—to reflect, to make a system and follow it. You have no longer the excuse of youth. What will happen to you if you delay longer? An unhappy woman and even more unhappy princess, you will break the heart of one who loves you most in the world. I shall never reconcile myself to not seeing you happy. I embrace you. Read me, believe me, and you will love me more when you feel the fruits. Remove the bandage which prevents you from seeing your duty and your true happiness. Become what you could be and earn the reputation which your virtues, your attractions, your character deserve. Constancy and firmness! Oppose all tempters with courage and strength.' A brief postscript, added at the last moment, urged her to keep order in her household and to avoid needless expense. 'Do not be ashamed to reduce your largesse, your fancies, your games in order to avoid running into debt. And take care what you write, even to your friends.' This sustained appeal to her better nature should have come from her husband. But the shyest of men could only teach by the example of a blameless life, and for a self-willed woman that was not enough.

From Brest, where he visited the dockyard after leaving Paris, Joseph despatched to Leopold a final summary of his impressions. 'I left Paris without much regret, though they treated me wonderfully. I had seen almost everything. It was harder to leave Versailles, for I was truly attached to my sister, and her grief at our parting increased my own. She is an amiable and honourable woman, rather young and unreflecting, but she has a core of honour and virtue which in her position deserves respect, in addition to an intelligence and penetration which has often surprised me. Her first reaction is always right; if she stuck to it, reflected a little more, and paid less heed to people who whisper into her ears—there are armies of them—she would be perfect. The urge to amuse herself is very strong, and as this is known to everyone they play on her weakness, and those who provide her with most pleasure receive attention and consideration. Her relations with the King are singular, for she forces him to do things he does not like. He is rather weak, but not imbecile. He has ideas and judgment, but he is apathetic in body and mind. The *fiat lux* has not occurred—the matter is still in the round. Such is the situation. Add to this that the Government under an octogenarian Minister lumbers along; no real system, no courage, no firmness, just plodding forward without looking right or left. Petty dealings are their stock in trade. Have they not spent an enormous sum on their fleet? Here there are fourteen vessels, but they are afraid of sending them out for fear of starting a war which they dread. Yet they are constantly sending officers and munitions to the Americans.'

The Queen's impressions of the visit were recorded in two letters to her mother. 'His departure leaves a void which cannot be filled. I was so happy during that short time that it all seems like a dream. His good advice is graven for ever on my heart. He gave me something I asked him for and with which I am greatly pleased: his advice in writing. Just now it is my chief reading. If ever, which I do not expect, I could forget what he said to me, I should always have this paper before me which would soon recall me to my duty. The King, too, felt his departure, for he is genuinely attached to him. When I was almost in despair at the moment of his leaving, the tenderness of the King was such as I shall never forget. My brother must have been pleased with the country, for he must have seen that, despite its levity, people in general have excellent hearts and are anxious to do right. It is only a question of good leadership, as in the navy with which he was very pleased.' Two days later she added that the Comtesse d'Artois was believed to be pregnant again. 'That is a disagreeable prospect for me after more than seven years of marriage, but it would be unjust to show resentment. I am not without hope. My brother will be able to tell you about it. The King discussed this matter with him in sincerity and confidence.'

In thanking her daughter for her letters the Empress expressed her satisfaction at the success of the visit with unusual warmth. 'I was a little afraid that his rigid philosophy and austerity would displease and that he would not like the nation, and it is a comfort to find I was mistaken. That is all I could have wished, so I am content, above all that he and the King made friends. God grant that it may endure throughout their reign, for the good of our states and families which I have long regarded as identical. You can do most for this happy beginning by following his counsels, and what you say about his written advice touched me to tears. Here are his words about you. 'I was sorry to leave Versailles, being truly attached to my sister. I found a sort of sweetness of life which I believed I had left behind me, but the taste for which I discover is still with me. She is amiable and charming; I spent many hours with her without noticing how quickly they passed. Her emotion at my departure was great, and I had to summon all my strength to rise and leave.' Imagine how this consoles a mother who so tenderly loves her children. I anticipate the happiest results, including your marriage about which I am encouraged to hope. The Emperor was very pleased with the nation, and that increases my satisfaction. He has shed several of the prejudices which he had been led to imbibe. He was very sorry to leave you and is happy in the friendship and confidence of the King. All you tell me about the latter's tenderness to you on this occasion fills your cup and, as you say, you will never forget it. Continue to follow the counsels of your friend

and brother; you will soon see the result and your happiness
will ensue. I embrace you tenderly.' For once the Empress
abandoned her rôle of Recording Angel and allowed her heart
to speak. At his next visit to Versailles the Ambassador found
the Queen moved to happy tears by her mother's loving words.

VII. *Motherhood at Last*

WHEN the Emperor was gone, Mercy had several reassuring
interviews with the Queen. During June, he reported, she had
only gone to the theatre at Paris thrice; she had accompanied
the King on several of his hunts; there had been no gaming at
other people's parties; the Princess de Guéménée was being
dropped, and was trying to make mischief in the family; the
Queen had spent an hour almost daily in reading. Without
being less affable, she was more dignified, especially with people
of age and rank. The change had made an excellent impression
in Paris. Yet the Ambassador knew her too well to feel quite
happy. 'Before we count on the solidity of these happy developments, we must see whether they stand up to the temptations
which never cease. While things go well I shall say little, as the
Queen likes to feel that she acts on her own initiative. She has
been deeply impressed by her brother's counsels, but she will
never admit that they have shaped her course.' The bulletin of
August 15 reported that the Queen showed more dignity and
more care in the choice of her society, but unfortunately there
was much too much gambling. She saw through Artois, but
did not fully realise the disadvantages of his company. For a
month she had kept to some of her good resolutions: her quiet
hours of reading, her increased consideration for the King, fewer
noisy dissipations. 'Yet one of the most dangerous remains
—gaming, for which she has a passion, though she has often
admitted its drawbacks to Abbé Vermond and myself. She
seemed to feel that she had broken her promise by going one
evening to play with the Princess de Guéménée the only time for
six weeks. Moreover, high play has steadily increased in her
own apartments; recently she has gained, but the luck has turned

and her present losses embarrass her. The debts contracted for the purchase of diamonds pay badly; there is no money for charities; the worst of it all is the bad example, the King's regret, the evil effect on public opinion.' On receiving this distressing news, the Empress made a further appeal. 'No more separate rooms nor late parties, above all no more play! My dear daughter, I beseech you, drop all these things; they involve bad company and talk. The Emperor said all that needs saying. You lose money which the King and you could employ to better purpose. A generous effort on your part, banishing it from Court, would do you great honour and fill me with consolation. Since no one expects it, people would see it was due to you alone. What a triumph! Your example influences your brothers-in-law; the King and the state have to pay everything and you are the cause. I cannot keep silence on this important matter on which your happiness and still more your glory depend.'

On the same day that the Empress despatched her rebuke the Queen announced joyful news.[1] If the Emperor had failed with the Queen, he had succeeded with the King, whom he had persuaded at long last to submit to the needed operation. Even now there was a delay of three months, and it was not till the end of August that Lassone, the Court doctor, removed the barrier which had frustrated the life of his wife for seven years, and was the main excuse for her frivolities. 'This is a happy occasion for me,' she wrote to her mother on August 30. 'I am in luck in a matter of supreme importance for my whole life. Over a week ago my marriage was perfectly consummated, and yesterday again even more satisfactorily! First I thought of sending a courier to my dear Maman, but I was afraid it would make people talk, and I wished to be quite sure. I do not think I am pregnant, but I hope I may be at any minute. I receive so many marks of affection from my dear Maman, and what happiness this will be to her! That delights me as much as my own.' Her next letter on September 10 added that she had had a moment of hope; 'it is gone, but I am quite confident it will soon return.' The friendship and tenderness of the King, she added, increased from day to day. The delighted Empress asked for a monthly memo-

---

[1] The letter, omitted by Arneth, is published in *Correspondance entre Marie-Thérèse et Marie Antoinette*, pp. 212–213.

randum from Lassone, and offered motherly advice. She might go for short rides, but must not get hot; she would have to be careful about jolts and accidents in driving. 'My dear daughter is so sensitive that she is moved to tears at the slightest hurt to the humblest of her attendants. A first pregnancy is always very important for all the rest; if one starts with a miscarriage, it is all up. With your constitution I do not expect it, but once accustomed to it there is no remedy.'

On arriving at Fontainebleau for the usual autumn visit, the Queen thanked her mother for the letter which she had read again and again. 'All the summer I have gone out very little, partly for my health, partly because I am learning to occupy myself a little better in my apartments. I read, I work, I have two music teachers for singing and the harp. I have taken up drawing again. The time of residence at Fontainebleau is always that of the greatest dissipation, but I can assure my dear Maman that it will mean very little change in my usual life. As for gaming, for the last two months I have only played in my own rooms, where it is absolutely necessary once or twice a week. If my dear mother saw things for herself she would realise it could not be otherwise. Otherwise I play nowhere, and if I go out I only play billiards. I very rarely ride, and at certain times I do not even go for a drive.' Unfortunately this was not the whole story, as the Empress learned from her Ambassador.

No one rejoiced more heartily at the lifting of the matrimonial blockade than the faithful Mercy, who had always attributed the Queen's failings in the main to her *entourage*. This event, he wrote to the Empress directly he heard the news, would give her a new and most auspicious position. 'The expectation of a speedy pregnancy opens the prospect of a favourable change in her moral ideas and system of life. This moment has been for so long the object of all my hopes, and I am now so certain of their fulfilment that I feel I must briefly mention some unsatisfactory details of the last month. The passion for play, which claims her more than ever, has given rise to several inconveniences. The gaming parties have become sometimes tumultuous and unseemly, and some ladies of the Court have cheated. This naturally makes people talk. The Queen realises the embarrassment and tries to prevent it in some measure by occasionally going to the Princess de Guéménée to play. Moreover, the losses increase, her finances are exhausted, the old debts are unpaid, and there is never money for charities. A new and unsuitable amusement, which happily would cease with the end of summer, was to station bands of the French and Swiss Guards on the great terrace about 10 P.M. The public was admitted, and the Royal Family move about without attendants and almost in disguise. Sometimes the Queen and the princesses were together, sometimes separately, taking the arm of one of their ladies. The King joined her once or twice. But these promenades can involve great disadvantages, especially for the Queen; in this nation, where youth is so giddy, one cannot be too careful to avoid misunderstanding. The Comte d'Artois is one of the chief promoters of this kind of unfitting amusement. Since his return [1] he has started gaming again at Versailles with more vigour, and, despite all the representations to the Queen, she lets herself go with a sort of regret which is, however, not strong enough to hold her back. There are still, however, some quiet times of reading. She is getting on with Hume's *History of England*, and often discusses it with me.' Mercy utilised the prospect of motherhood to renew his solemn warnings, but, as usual, it was uphill work.

When the Emperor read Mercy's despatches, he wrote to his sister complaining bitterly of the neglect of his counsels.[2] His letter is lost, but we learn its contents from Mercy's reports and the Queen's reply. The English, declared Joseph, compared Fontainebleau to Spa as a gambling resort. The letter ended by saying that he would no longer tax his eyes by writing to her about this matter, just as he had fruitlessly exercised his lungs in talking to her. The Queen replied that she was deeply pained. 'You turn against me the fruits of my sincerity and confidence in you. I was really astonished at certain gossip in Paris about the journey to Fontainebleau, and as most of it is without foundation it stopped soon after the return of eyewitnesses. It is very hard on me not to have the same backing in my own country and above all in you, my dear brother. People here would be astonished to see the Duc de Chartres mentioned as a cheat, for

---

[1] From a tour in the South of France with his brother.
[2] *Lettres de Marie Antoinette*, i, pp. 154–155.

he did not once play in my apartments during that time.   As for
the Comte d'Artois, I know what is attributed to him.   They are
so absurd that he is the first to laugh at them.   Of women's
cheating I have seen and heard nothing.   As for the bad company,
there has always been a little of it in the gaming at Court when
there is play at the round table, since it is the custom in France to
let everyone in.   I have seen it all these eight years, especially at
Fontainebleau, where there are far more people.   I quite hoped
to announce my pregnancy.   My hopes are deferred, but I am
confident not for long, especially since my return.   I enclose
a letter from the King.   For my part, I cherish more ardent
wishes for you than for anyone.   I desire above all that you
restore to me your esteem which I feel has somewhat diminished.   You have given me so many proofs of your friendship
—and I am equally attached to you—that I could never be happy
if it waned.   Adieu, my dear brother, I embrace you with all my
heart.'

The main purpose of the Emperor's visit in 1777 had been the
consolidation of the alliance, and at the opening of 1778 its
vitality was put to the test.   The death of the childless Elector
of Bavaria was hailed by him with delight as a golden opportunity
to secure compensation for the loss of Silesia.   The Empress, on
the other hand, weary of battles and longing to end her days in
peace, shuddered at the prospect of another war.   Her correspondence with Mercy during the first half of 1778 is full of the
Bavarian problem, for however much she disliked the policy,
she realised the importance of the attitude of France if it was
to succeed.   Only firm language from Versailles, she believed,
would stay the hand of 'the wicked man' in Berlin.   Hitherto
she had deprecated the Queen's intervention in political affairs on
the ground that they were outside her sphere.   Now it was a
very different story: it was her duty and her privilege to save
the alliance from collapse.

The first letter to the Ambassador in 1778 revealed her alarm.
'The Elector of Bavaria has died, a fatal event I always hoped I
should not live to see.   The King of Prussia will certainly oppose
our plans of aggrandisement and will try to detach France, where
he has a number of friends and where he is busy stirring up
suspicions against us.   I should be inconsolable if our relations

with France were to crumble away.' To her daughter she wrote in the same excited strain. 'I am greatly upset. Mercy will tell you all about it and I beg you to listen with attention. It concerns the peace of Europe and the friendship of the King, which is doubly precious owing to the tender tie which connects our political interests and which ought to be for ever indissoluble.' The Queen replied that at first she felt anxiety, but it quickly passed: the mere idea of a quarrel between Vienna and Versailles would make her miserable.

The Ambassador's report on the first reactions of French opinion was not encouraging. The event provoked at first a general cry of war. However ridiculous such talk, the Queen seemed impressed by it and, to relieve her anxieties, wrote to the Polignac that she feared her brother was playing for his own hand. He had urged her to be careful; if such expressions reached the French Ministers they would conclude that, far from supporting the views of her house, she disapproved them. Now she had been warned, he felt sure she would follow the wishes of her family. 'I have constant proof that, at the bottom of her heart, she is deeply attached to the interests of her august house, and desires to co-operate; but she does not always correlate this desire with the means of giving it effect, and, owing to inattention or to the influence of her *entourage*, she sometimes acts against her own feelings.' When she asked Mercy's advice how to answer her mother's letter he suggested an expression of her interest in the matter at issue. The Austrian measures, he frankly admitted to the Empress, were not altogether approved.

'The maintenance of the present system occupies my thoughts more than ever,' wrote the agitated Empress on January 31, 'and I should be inconsolable if the succession question were to interrupt my partnership with France. I beg you to employ all your brains, all your activity, all your credit to sustain it.' At the moment, however, it was to the Queen rather than to the Ambassador that she looked for help, telling her that she needed all her friendship for her mother, her house and her country. She added that a breakdown of the alliance would kill her and that the King of Prussia's only anxiety was the Queen. Mercy explained to his sovereign that the Queen's interest was due mainly to filial affection. When she came to the passage in her mother's letter declaring that a rift in the alliance would kill her, Mercy saw her grow pale. She was furious with the King of Prussia but she lacked the patience to study the problem in detail. When she had spoken to the King about the danger of weakening the alliance, she had received a rebuff.

THE KING. The ambition of your relatives is upsetting everything. They began in Poland, and now Bavaria is the second volume. I am worried about your position.

THE QUEEN. But you cannot deny that you were informed and agreed.

THE KING. So little am I in agreement that orders are going out to our representatives abroad that the dismemberment of Bavaria has taken place contrary to our wishes and that we disapprove.

The Empress, more alarmed than ever, expressed the hope that the King, when fully informed, would resist the seductions of evil men; she counted on his sense of justice and his affection for his *chère petite femme*. Never perhaps had there been a more urgent occasion to hold together; the whole system depended on it. 'The interest of our two Houses, but above all those of our states and indeed of Europe, are involved. Do not rush matters. Try to gain time to prevent a war which, once begun, might be a long one and involve grave consequences for us all.' To Mercy she wrote in growing distress. The alliance was weakened by the insidious assurances of the King of Prussia and by Austria's actions in Bavaria. 'Its destruction would be the climax of my unfortunate career. My chief anxiety is the situation of my daughter. I do not doubt her attachment to her family and her desire to give proofs of it so far as her levity allows her to take things seriously; but she must proceed with great prudence and skill so as not to importune the King and arouse his suspicions. Some of the French Ministers, if they ever sensed it, would try to weaken her credit.'

Marie Antoinette threw herself into the fight and was coached by the Ambassador for her political interviews, but the counter-attractions of carnival time were strong and Mercy thought she could have done more. She informed her mother that she was pleased with the King, who sincerely wished to maintain the tie with Vienna. She had seen Maurepas and Vergennes, who appeared genuinely attached to the alliance; but they were so afraid of a struggle that, when she asked what they would do if the King of Prussia began hostilities, she could obtain no clear reply. One reason was the deplorable state of the finances. She had explained that France was merely asked to keep her engagements. But what were they? France had no interest in the aggrandisement of her ally and was resolved to avoid entanglement in a new conflict while she had a naval struggle with England on her hands. A despatch dated March 30 flatly rejected the Hapsburg contention that the *casus fœderis* was involved and dismissed the appeal to the Treaty of Westphalia as irrelevant. The Empress complained to her daughter of the French representatives at the German courts, whose lukewarm words suggested that their sovereign cared little for the alliance. 'I quite realise,' she wrote to Mercy on April 2, 'that at the moment we cannot count on the support of France.' Armed intervention she had never demanded, merely steady diplomatic and moral support, as Prussia received from her Russian ally. Over and over again she declared that the two Powers could only live in safety if firmly united.

The Emperor, whose whole heart was in the Bavarian gamble, was incensed by the chilly attitude of his ally but did not hold his sister responsible. 'Since you do not wish to prevent war,' he wrote, 'we shall put up a good fight, and in all the circumstances you will not have to blush for a brother who will always deserve your esteem.' Mercy strove hard for the policy of his sovereigns and denounced Vergennes' despatch of March 30 as '*indécente*'; he and Maurepas were rascals who ignored the obligations of the alliance. After discussing with the Ambassador the evil state of affairs, the Queen reported to the Empress that she had summoned Maurepas and Vergennes. 'I talked to them pretty strongly and I made an impression, particularly on the latter. I was not altogether pleased with these gentlemen, who try to get at the King. It is cruel in a matter of such importance to have to deal with people who are not sincere.' Mercy believed that the more conciliatory tone of a second despatch of April 26 was partly due to the intervention of the Queen. One important assurance was secured: France would not permit the King of Prussia to attack the Austrian Netherlands.

The Empress expressed her gratitude for her daughter's zeal, but she had no use for the French Ministers and her denunciation of the King of Prussia was almost hysterical. 'No prince in Europe has escaped from his perfidies,' she wrote to the Queen, 'and this is the man who proposes to set himself up as dictator and protector of all Germany. And the great princes fail to combine to avert such a misfortune which sooner or later will fall on them all. For thirty-seven years he has been the scourge of Europe by his despotism and violence. In rejecting all recognised principles of sincerity and truth he laughs at treaties and alliances. We occupy the most exposed position, but no one comes to our aid. Perhaps we shall get through once again, but I do not speak for Austria alone; it is the cause of every prince. The future is dark. I shall not be here; but my dear children and grandchildren, our holy religion, our good peoples, will have to face it. I would give my life to make my children happier and more tranquil than ourselves.' The Queen replied that she would gladly shed her blood to bring her mother the happiness and peace she deserved.

Prussia's invasion of Bohemia at the beginning of July ended the six months of futile negotiation and plunged the Empress into even deeper gloom. The Saxons had joined the Prussians and she had two beloved sons at the front. 'So we are at war,' she wrote to Mercy. 'And what a war! There is nothing to gain and everything to lose. France has injured us by her mysterious dealings with the King of Prussia. We have also sinned against her, but nothing so bad as her shocking indifference. I am overwhelmed.' To the Queen she wrote with even less attempt at self-control. 'I do not know if I exist. Religion alone supports me, but I cannot bear up for long.' Never in the darkest hours of the three Silesian wars had she given way to such despair. Her daughter replied with soothing words. 'I know what you must be suffering. If only I could fly to you and mingle my tears with yours! Yet I am full of hope. No, God will not permit the triumph of so unjust a man. My dear Maman knows I have never attributed what has occurred to the King's heart but to his extreme weakness and lack of self-confidence. To-day he came to me and found me so sad and anxious that he was moved to tears. I was so pleased; it proves the extent of his affection and I hope he will at least take his own line and behave like a good ally.' This was merely wishful thinking, for on July 17 Mercy reported that the King was completely dominated by Maurepas. The best antidote would be for the Queen to win over the vain and timid old Minister by showing him favour and confidence, but of this he had no great hopes. 'When she has spoken to the King on some matter, when she has persuaded him, and when the Ministers seem won over to her views, she thinks that no more is needed and that everything will go as arranged. Thus it happens that the Ministers, convinced that she forgets what happened on the previous day, follow their own course.' Neither mother nor daughter could now influence events. Moreover, as summer melted into autumn, Marie Antoinette had something to think about of far greater significance in her life.

Despite the distant thunder of the War of the Bavarian Succession, the main event of 1778 was the fulfilment of her heart's desire. Since the operation on the King she had lived in the thought of motherhood. Vienna was as eager as Versailles, for issues of high politics were at stake. 'The idea that a courier may bring me news of a pregnancy,' wrote the Empress on January 5, 'excites me, comforts me, fills me with impatience. At sixty there is not much time to lose, and my affection for you and the King makes me dote. How I dread lest this eternal carnival should interfere with plans! Ought I not to declare war on all these continual dissipations which lead to so much damaging talk? Balls in your own apartments are well enough, but not at the Opera. You saw the drawbacks last year, and to me they were a terrible anxiety. But this year, when we have such hopes of your pregnancy at any moment, it would be unpardonable to expose yourself, to go out at night at this season to Paris, where no Queen of France has ever been seen, leaving the King alone at Versailles. Your health would suffer, and you must preserve it for us and for the state. My dear daughter, I beseech you, relieve me of this anxiety and look after yourself. My love deserves some consideration and consolation.'

Unfortunately Mercy's letters at the opening of 1778 brought little evidence of a break with the past. Play continued as usual twice or thrice a week in the Queen's apartments, at other times in those of Princess de Guéménée or Princess de Lamballe. There was more decorum, particularly when the Queen was hostess, but her plan of reducing the stakes had not materialised. 'Indeed in this respect things are worse owing to her own example since she finds this moderation unexciting. Now she plays for higher stakes than before: one evening at the close of December she lost 300 louis. The King paid it next day, as he very often does when she cannot face her debts. Sometimes, however, she wins four or five hundred louis, as happened a few days ago. Nevertheless, this ruinous amusement so upsets her finances that she has to refuse the charities which her good heart and natural generosity dictate. And this leads to undesirable public comment.' She was giving a little more time to music, not with the old zest, but rather to occupy her time. Reading was utterly neglected. On the credit side were the long daily talks with Abbé Vermond, and her excellent relations with the King. When the dreaded carnival arrived in February, she flung herself into the festivities, staying up all night at the balls at home, at the Opera, and at the Palais Royal several times a week.

At last, on April 10, 1778, after eight years of marriage, the Queen despatched joyful tidings to Vienna. 'My first instinct a week ago was to tell you my hopes, but I was afraid to disappoint you. Even now I am not quite sure, but next month I shall know for certain. Meanwhile I have grounds for confidence. I am wonderfully well, and my appetite and sleep have improved.' A letter from Mercy by the same courier reported that she was taking great care of herself, and had dropped drives and billiards; her amusements were music and conversation; games of chance were now very infrequent. 'You tell me great news,' replied the Empress. 'God be praised and may my dearest Antoinette be fortified in her brilliant situation by giving heirs to France. No precaution is superfluous; I am delighted you have given up the evening visits to Paris and even billiards. I note you are sacrificing your less dangerous amusements. Follow blindly the counsels of Lassone, who possesses my full confidence. I hope he will have the choice of an accoucheur, who should be both an expert and a Christian. If you could only see the joy in Vienna! Paris cannot be more pleased. They are better at demonstrations than our good Germans, but with us it goes deeper.' To Mercy she wrote that she hardly dared believe it till the baby was born. The joyful expectant mother begged the King for money as a thankoffering to be sent to the poor of Paris and Versailles. 'That was a way of doing a charity at the same time that I announced my condition. I know my dear Maman's heart too well to fear her disapproval.' The King wrote to the Empress that there was no more doubt, and that in December he hoped to announce the birth of a dauphin. The first movement of the child on July 31 was reported with pride; the King of Spain would be godfather, and the Empress was asked to be godmother.

In his bulletin of July 17, intended for the Empress alone, the Ambassador reported that the Queen, sobered by a new responsibility, had made her general confession to him. She spoke frankly of her amusements, her circle, and all the details of her private life, requesting him to say what he thought about every person and every point. Using the authorisation to the fullest extent, he declaimed against gambling, analysed the conduct of her favourites, male and female, and reviewed the intrigues of the Court. Not a single item was omitted, the Queen listening with extraordinary graciousness, and declaring once again that she realised the necessity of decisions. In the first warm glow of resolution, added the Ambassador in his report, there was danger of the pendulum swinging too far, since a certain amount of festivity was essential for her health. Unfortunately, the latest resolutions soon went the way of the old. In November, only a few weeks before her accouchement, Mercy wrote that during the residence of the Court at Marly gaming had been resumed at high pressure. The *salon* was open to everyone, rascals included. One of them was caught after giving a banker counters instead of louis—an incident which naturally found its way into the papers. The Queen lost 1,000 louis, but won 400 on the last evening. Mesdames, coming for the day from Bellevue, expressed their disapproval of the mixed society in forcible terms, which were sharply resented by the hostess. After returning to Versailles things had improved.

When the long-expected event occurred on December 20, 1778, the Ambassador sent a few lines in haste by the French official courier, who was just starting with despatches for Vienna.

That the Queen had shown great courage he could testify, for he had been present in the crowded bedroom all the time.   There were a few moments of anxiety after the birth, for her struggle to control herself caused a nervous crisis which was quickly overcome by an incision in the foot.   She was as well as possible, and the infant was large and strong.   There was no need for the Empress to be anxious.   The mother had not yet learned that it was a daughter.   Four days later, on Christmas Eve, he reported that there was not the slightest ground for anxiety, that the Princess looked the picture of health, and that the happy father was seen at his best.   In his private letter of the same day Mercy described the details of the accouchement, which by the barbarous custom of the country he had been officially compelled to witness. The shock of the Queen's convulsion had upset him more than he could say, but the fact that she had been in danger was being concealed from her.   It had been due firstly to the crowd in the stuffy room, secondly to her effort to stifle her cries, thirdly because the child's silence made her think it was dead, fourthly because when it cried there was an overwhelming revulsion from grief to joy.   The King and most other people had left the room with the baby before the crisis, but the danger was over in four minutes after the patient had been bled in the foot.   Next morning she had asked for him and hoped to write a line in pencil to assure her mother that all was well.   She added that she would send a portrait of herself with the child in her arms directly she was on the sofa.   Fearing that she would overtax her strength, Mercy persuaded the King to close her room to everyone except the Royal Family, the *dames d'honneur* and *d'atours*, the Superintendent (the Lamballe), the Polignac, the doctors, and Abbé Vermond.   The latter spent hours with her in light reading. During the confinement people had flocked to church, and they sympathised that it was not a dauphin.   The Queen herself showed no sign of distress at the sex of the child.   The Royal Family had behaved admirably, and even Artois had given no sign of satisfaction that it was not a prince.   In the last bulletin of 1778, on December 29, Mercy reported that mother and child were flourishing.   After the first quiet week she had received all who were entitled to pay their respects.   In a two hours' talk with the Ambassador she explained her plans for the education of the infant, and the courier bore a joint letter to the Empress from the happy parents.

During the first week of his wife's convalescence, the King, despite his imperious need for exercise, never left the palace, and rarely the bedside. The Lamballe and the Polignac, though rivals, were assiduous in their attendance, and the favour of the latter steadily increased. Faro was played in the royal bedroom, though she contented herself with very small stakes. In his private letter of January 25, 1779, Mercy reported that, to mark the occasion, the King had given her 100,000 livres, a most welcome windfall, since her finances were in confusion, and she owed over 3,000 louis. Since she kept a record of her gains and losses, Mercy suggested that a balance-sheet should be drawn up. Abbé Vermond undertook the task, and found that during 1778 she had lost 14,000 louis, and won nearly half that sum. She was impressed by the figures, and assured Mercy and the Abbé that she had resolved to put on the brake. 'I cannot express how during these quiet moments she gave us marks of her confidence by opening her heart to us. Her remarks on her circle showed judgment; in regard to the Polignac alone does she cherish illusions, and only time can open her eyes. Her esteem and friendship for the King were greater than ever, and she was deeply touched by his loving care. She seems to realise more fully the necessity and the practicability of winning his entire confidence.' Her confinement, Mercy assured the Empress, had made a great impression on all classes, and when she was believed to be in danger the public displayed genuine attachment. The petty criticisms had ceased, and now was the time to establish her credit on a solid foundation. For that only certain slight reforms were required—in regard to gaming, in her favouritism, more money for charity, more interest in serious and useful objects. She seemed more than ever inclined to do so, and she was hoping for another pregnancy as soon as possible.

The first jarring note was struck in a despatch of February 16, describing the customary thanksgiving service in Notre Dame. The official report, which was always read by the Emperor and Kaunitz, declared that the crowds displayed many marks of affection and delight: alms were distributed to the poor and debtors were released. The private letter, on the other hand,

regretfully admitted that the public reactions were disappointing.
'There were some cries of *Vive le roi et la reine* in certain parts;
in others there was complete silence, and one felt there was more
curiosity than affection. This coolness was due to certain
accidental causes, among them the rising price of food. Though
the Queen had nothing to do with it, the discontent made people
more critical. The idea of dissipation and extravagance and the
appearance of an immoderate desire for amusement in a time of
calamities and war estranges opinion and needs to be kept in view.'
It was doubtless owing to his advice, continued Mercy, that the
Queen had abandoned her plan of paying several visits to Paris
during the carnival; the only exception was a ball at the Opera,
whither she was accompanied by the King. It was a consolation
for Abbé Vermond and himself that she reposed more entire
confidence in them than in her most intimate friends. 'True, this
confidence consists more in revealing to us all her thoughts than
in following our advice, for in that respect the Comtesse de
Polignac has far more influence; yet it is always a precious
advantage to be able to tell the unadorned truth. It is to her
good intelligence and character that we must look for the effects
of this oft-repeated truth-telling, and meanwhile we must try
to diminish the disadvantages as opportunity affords.' How
many times had Mercy despatched precisely similar bulletins to
Vienna, and how little there was to show for his pains! If
anyone could sympathise with Sisyphus it was the devoted
Austrian Ambassador.

VIII. *Journey's End*

THE last two years of the life of the great Empress were full of
trouble and anxiety. She detested the War of the Bavarian
Succession unleashed by her temperamental son, and frowned on
his attempt at a *rapprochement* with the dissolute Tsarina. Little
comfort could be found in Mercy's bulletins, though the faithful
Ambassador always strove to spare his sovereign's feelings. Any
hope she might have entertained that motherhood would teach
her daughter wisdom was disappointed, for the young Queen
cared nothing for appearances. Her popularity was gone, and

even respect was forfeited by her thoughtless ways. A visit to a ball at the Opera, as usual without the King, led to an incident. The dilapidated cab in which, to preserve her incognito, the Queen was driving through Paris, broke down, and she had to wait in a shop till another was found. More serious at a time when France clamoured for a Dauphin was the resumption of riding. Mercy's news was that gaming was less frequent and on a more modest scale: Artois enjoyed less influence. Monsieur was treated with greater consideration. Only the Polignac possessed unlimited credit; that was the chief source of anxiety. The comments of the Empress were brief and chilly. 'I should rejoice more than ever to see my daughter adopting a more regular mode of life, but I have no great expectations, and I am always thinking about this Polignac favourite.' In her letters to her daughter she was less censorious than of old, and her main theme was the need of a Dauphin. 'I confess I am insatiable,' she wrote on April 1. 'Your dear child needs a companion and ought not to wait too long for one. My dear daughter, omit no precautions and above all moderate your riding, which is absolutely contrary to our wishes and to those of every good Frenchman and Austrian.'

The Empress was unpleasantly surprised to learn that, while the Queen was laid up with measles at the Petit Trianon in April, four of her men friends—Baron de Besenval, Count Esterhazy, the Duc de Coigny, and the Duc de Guines—were permitted to spend the whole day in her bedroom, which they only left for meals. Though it was authorised and indeed suggested by her indulgent husband as a method of combating her chronic ennui, the privilege accorded to them contrasted with the exclusion of several members of her household, and excited a good deal of criticism. The courtiers inquired ironically which four ladies would be chosen to look after the King if he were ill. When the four gentlemen audaciously proposed to watch over her at night as well, Mercy begged the Court doctor to intervene. Finally, with the aid of Abbé Vermond, it was decided that they should leave the bedroom at 11 P.M. Still worse was their poisonous talk, and that of Artois. Desiring to save the King from infection, she had given orders not to admit him, and he was blamed for submitting to this ukase. On the tenth day of the

illness Mercy and the Abbé persuaded her to write to her husband
that she had suffered much, but that her greatest distress was to
be deprived of the pleasure of embracing him.   The King, unused
to such tenderness, replied at once, and the correspondence
continued almost daily.   An excellent effect was produced in the
Court circles, and the gossip died away.   'Thank heaven,' wrote
Mercy, 'this deplorable period has ended with much less damage
than I feared.'   Before her illness he had had some lengthy
audiences, and she had appeared resolved on several essential
points of conduct which he had stressed; now he saw himself
baffled in several directions.   When he told her so she naïvely
replied that illness often affected morale.

A brief letter to her mother stated that it had been a bad
attack, that she was not seeing the King for three weeks as he had
never had measles, and that they corresponded every day.   She
was too weak to write more.   To Mercy the Empress replied
that her daughter's choice of the four gentlemen had distressed
her, not merely owing to the gossip it evoked, but even more
owing to the talk of these *mauvais sujets*.   Her first letter to the
Queen after her illness ignores the topic, and she confined herself
to the familiar complaint about riding.   'You owe it to the King,
to your people, and a little for my consolation, longing as I do for
a Dauphin.   I have not much time left, so you must hurry up.'
The young mother replied that she was taking every care of
herself, eating very little and keeping early hours; since her
illness she had not had a ride and would do so very little.   Mercy
reported that she went to bed at midnight or soon after.   Faro,
however, continued, and stakes were sometimes much too high.
The Ambassador's private letters during the summer of 1779
strike a new and sinister note.   The separation of the Royal pair
on account of the Queen's illness was used by mischief-makers
to try to lead the King astray.   'Though by his physical and moral
disposition he seems very disinclined to gallantry, I have never
lost sight of this possible danger and have kept it before the
Queen's mind.   For a long time it was no easy task, for I regretfully noted that her feeling of security on that score rendered
her too indifferent about studying her husband.   That has now
changed; but though she is more aware of public gossip, she is
no more resolved to play her part in counterworking it.   This

14

has formed the theme of several of our talks, and I feel I have won a good deal of ground. During her residence at Trianon I observed attempts to drive the King into gallantry, though I have not discovered how it was done. It was not very alarming, but the Queen was rather upset. Accordingly I made two suggestions to her; firstly to be with the King as much as possible, show him affection, bring him into her circle, and help him to enjoy it. That has been a success. She has brought him into contact with the Comtesse de Polignac, which, though it has some drawbacks, is on balance a gain. My second suggestion was that she should try to find the unworthy persons who were striving to pervert the King and, if her search is successful, to cover them with disgrace. She applauded the idea, which I regard as essential to counterwork the perverse intriguers who are so dangerous and so numerous at this Court.' She proceeded to tell Mercy of a recent conversation in which the King assured her that he loved her with all his heart and could swear to her that he had never felt the slightest attraction towards any other woman. This little incident seemed to indicate his awareness that she might have learned of the project of giving him a mistress. An unusually long letter in August assured her mother that she felt the necessity of having children too keenly to run any risks. 'If in old days I made mistakes it was owing to my youth and levity, but now I have much more sense. Besides, I owe it to the King for his tenderness, and, I think I may say, his growing confidence in me.' Mercy's bulletins throughout the summer and autumn were read with pleasure at Vienna—scarcely any visits to Paris, very little gaming, the autumn sojourn at Fontainebleau cancelled on account of the expensive American war. Best of all was the perfect union with the King.

The substitution of Marly for Fontainebleau for the autumn sojourn of the Court proved to be less beneficial than was expected. Bad weather interfered with walks and sport, and performances were cancelled for reasons of economy. In the absence of other pastimes gaming resumed its sway and was worse than ever. It was no longer due to the Queen, for the card-parties began with some of the ladies of the Court. The Lamballe permitted such enormous stakes that one evening the Duc de Chartres lost 8,000 louis. Though the Queen showed disapproval of her Superintendent, faro was resumed in her own *salon*. For once the King, without any prompting, took part and at the end of the fortnight at Marly he had lost 1,800 louis. The Queen lost nearly 1,200, but in the last evenings won it nearly all back. Artois and Chartres had plunged most deeply, the latter losing 11,000 louis. The Empress was grieved, but her letters to her daughter ignored the painful topic. Remonstrances, she had come to realise, were useless.

In his last bulletin of 1779 Mercy commented on certain changes at Court. Since many officers were in the war, and many of the nobility were spending more time on their estates, the vast palace seemed remarkably empty. For long there had been no fixed days for the Queen's circle, and in consequence the Parisiennes had almost ceased to come. As a remedy, she announced that they could pay court to her three days a week during her dinner, and in the evening while at play. When this brought no response, she discussed the matter with Mercy. The Ambassador recalled his warnings that her exclusive society would inevitably keep away those who felt they might be unwelcome. His observations appeared to make an impression. The suppers and weekly balls, he was informed, would be resumed at once. During the approaching carnival she did not propose to attend the Opera balls. She rarely visited Paris; during December she only went once to see a new ballet, and had been acclaimed by the audience. In compensation she proposed to make frequent visits to the masked balls held every winter in the theatre of the town of Versailles, which could be reached by a covered passage. The company, however, was very mixed, and Mercy hoped she might soon tire of them. She was worrying about the health of the Polignac, whose absence from Versailles left a void for several hours a day which no one could fill. The Lamballe appeared a little more frequently, but was not well received: the Duc de Guines had lost favour, which Count Esterhazy still enjoyed. The Queen's relations with her aunts and all the Royal Family were excellent. The little Princess was a great resource. The high stakes had almost ceased after the return of the Court to Versailles, though the improvement might not last. The Comte d'Artois, who had often been the ringleader of the card table, was for the moment more moderate. 'Moreover, it is certain that the Queen never really loved high stakes, and that when she gave way to it, it was owing to pressure rather than to taste.'

The least satisfactory feature in Mercy's picture of Versailles during the last two years of his sovereign's life was the position of the Polignac, who had entirely supplanted the Lamballe and now ruled without a rival. It was bad enough that she should press the claims of her relatives, but it was even more deplorable that she fought for her lover. 'She has just made a shocking misuse of her favour on behalf of the Comte de Vaudreuil, her relations with whom are too intimate and too notorious,' reported Mercy on October 16, 1779. 'Since his whole fortune is in the French Indies, whence he can receive nothing in time of war, he finds himself in difficulties. She could think of no other way of relieving him than by securing for him 30,000 livres a year from the Treasury, and the King, with his usual complaisance, made no objection. It was arranged that this most unseemly grant should remain a profound secret; if it leaked out there would be an outcry. She agreed with everything the Abbé and I have said, but when the desires of the favourite are placed in the scales remonstrances are in vain.' The only hope was that the Polignac, like the Lamballe, would overplay her hand. Perhaps because she was alarmed about her health, reported the Ambassador at the close of 1779, she had recently striven to secure a magnificent fortune for her family—nothing less than a royal domain worth 100,000 livres a year. Her circle fixed their gaze on the County of Bitsch, an appanage of the Duchy of Lorraine, which had come into the possession of France in 1737. Since the favourite felt unable to take the initiative in such an exorbitant demand without the grave risk of being found out, the services of Artois were requisitioned, and formidable pressure was applied to the Queen. For once she was a little alarmed, but as usual she gave way and proceeded to discuss ways and means. These were not easy to find, all the more because during the four previous years the Polignac family, without rendering any services to the State, was estimated to have received in various ways nearly half a million livres of annual revenue. 'All the most deserving families protest against such an unfair dispensation of favours, and if they now witness yet another grant on the largest possible scale, the

outcry and disgust would reach its height.   There is even some
risk of offending the King by such unprecedented demands, and
the Queen, who cannot shut her eyes to these truths, is terribly
upset.   As she broached the subject to Abbé Vermond and myself,
we told her exactly what we felt.   In consequence the matter
remains in suspense, and the King has not been approached.   I
dare not flatter myself that this is the end of the story, but instead
of a considerable domain the favourite will obtain a large sum of
money.   Count Maurepas seems to have been won over, but
Necker, despite his desire to please the Queen, has given her very
wise advice.   She has taken it in good part, without, however,
yielding on the main object, and merely consenting to a less
sensational method of assisting the Polignac family.'   The acid
comment of the Empress was that if the Polignac fell from grace
another favourite would doubtless emerge who might be better,
or might be worse.   The rôle of Artois in the latest incident
confirmed her conviction that he was the most dangerous influence
to which she was exposed.

1780, the last year of Maria Theresa's eventful life, opened with
the expression of an ardent longing for a Dauphin within the next
twelve months.   The hope was not to be realised, and the
correspondence is filled by the customary complaints from the
Ambassador and his sovereign, and the familiar denials or
excuses from the Queen.   On January 17 Mercy reported why
her effort to revive the faded glories of the Court had failed.
'Many people are afraid of being drawn into gaming risks which
they cannot afford.   This is undoubtedly one of the causes which
has kept them away, and now the Queen has grasped the fact it
looks as if the system will be reformed.'   Her plan of abstaining
from the masked balls at the Opera, he feared, would not be
carried out, for she was bored by the balls in the town theatre of
Versailles.   Passing to the depressing topic of the Polignac, he
had important news.   Nobody could conceive the importunity
with which her claim had been pressed.   After a series of
manœuvres, it had been decided that she should renounce her
claim to the County of Bitsch; she should, however, receive
400,000 livres to pay her debts, 800,000 livres in cash as a
dowry for her daughter, and the prospect of an estate worth
35,000 livres a year at some later date.   These exorbitant dona-

tions could hardly remain a secret, and the Queen was greatly concerned. 'She confessed to me that she now regretted not to have offered more resistance. She added that the Countess had entirely changed and was no longer the same person.' The experienced Mercy did not conclude from this remark that her fall was imminent, but a germ of disgust had been planted in the Queen's heart.

The Ambassador proceeded to draft a sentence for the Empress to incorporate in her next letter to Versailles if she thought fit, and accordingly it contained the following carefully phrased passage: 'It is said that the Polignac, simply owing to your favour, has asked for the County of Bitsch. The public has been astonished at a request which indicates more cupidity than attachment. It is also said that you wish to make her a gift of millions. I pay no attention to these rumours, and think them improbable, but I feel it necessary and useful that you should hear of them, especially at a time when the state has so many burdens to bear.' Mercy had explained that reference could thus be made to the County of Bitsch since it had been spoken of in Paris and Brussels; on the other hand, to mention the details of the money grants would be to reveal the source of information.

The Queen's reply contained no indication that the greedy favourite was losing ground. She was too accustomed to inventions and exaggerations to be surprised at the talk about Mme de Polignac. It was customary for the King of France to contribute to the dowry of persons of the Court and of good family who were not rich. Her friend had thought of the County of Bitsch, but only for a moment, and directly she learned its value she dropped the idea. As for the money, the King would certainly provide a dowry for *la petite Polignac*, and rumour would perhaps make it more louis than there would be crowns. 'It is a great joy for me to see how he spares me all solicitation for my friend, knowing her character and sentiments as he does. He will be charmed to do her a good turn for her own sake, but I am not less grateful for this mark of friendship to myself.' The King, she added, had just issued an edict inaugurating reforms in his household and her own. 'If it comes off it will be a great boon, not only for the state, but for the satisfaction of public opinion. We must await results before counting on it, for it was unsuccessfully attempted in the two last reigns. He possesses the power and the good will; but in this country there is so much red tape that unless care is taken new snags may arise as in the past.' The edict of January 29, 1780, was the first of a series by which Necker, with the full assent of the King and Queen, abolished hundreds of sinecures in return for compensation; but such well-meant efforts were on too limited a scale to count.

The Empress returned to the attack on April 1. 'You have not replied about the large donations I mention and which are listed in all the papers—that the King had given the Countess Polignac a dowry for her daughter of 800,000 livres, besides an estate of two million in addition to paying her debts. There is even a story, which I cannot believe, that a certain Comte de Vaudreuil, who is believed to be the lover of the Countess, has obtained through her a pension of 30,000 livres and a domain of the Comte d'Artois, and that by your intervention. I must warn you that this makes a rather bad impression among the public and abroad, especially when necessary reforms are being under-taken at Court. Such excessive liberality makes the restrictions on others seem more onerous. I could not keep silence on these tales, which so closely concern your glory, and in regard to which your goodness of heart submits to the cupidity of these pretended friends. If I did not warn you, who would have the courage? Your silence convinces me that it is not mere gossip. That is the proof of my affection.' Once again the indictment provoked a spirited reply. The Comte de Vaudreuil had served his country and had never asked for favours. He possessed large estates in the West Indies, but was receiving nothing from them owing to the war. 'The King has given him 30,000 livres, not as a pension, but merely till the return of peace. This favour he has renounced since the Comte d'Artois presented him with a domain. I had nothing to do with this benevolence: everyone here knows that Vaudreuil is sufficiently a friend of my brother-in-law to need no protection from him. I could say the same of Mme de Polignac in relation to the King. He is very fond of her, and though I am most grateful for his gifts to her, I have no need to ask him for them. The writers in the Press know more than I do. I have never heard talk of the estate of two millions or any other; if I did, I would tell my dear Maman, whose questions I shall always be ready to answer.' She had not told her mother the whole truth, for Vaudreuil had renounced the King's gift owing to the public outcry, and his *liaison* with the favourite was tacitly admitted in ignoring the charge. Mercy's spring bulletins reported that she was stronger than ever, and that her prestige was beyond imagination. It was expected that she would shortly become a Duchess; that was harmless enough, but there was also a project of purchasing for her an enormous estate. Necker opposed it, but Maurepas might talk the King round and the public would put it down to the Queen. The comment of the Empress was that the reigning favourite was at any rate much better than the Guéménée.

Maria Theresa had almost ceased to scold her daughter, and her last letter, dated November 3, 1780, was lit up by pale autumn sunshine. 'All yesterday (the birthday of Marie Antoinette) I was more in France than in Austria. My thoughts went back to the happy days of the past; memories are my consolation.' Mercy's last bulletin, dated November 18, reiterated his oft-expressed conviction that the Queen was far less to blame than her *entourage*. 'She is now more inclined to take interest in affairs of State. That, however, will not redound to her glory or to the public welfare while she is so strongly influenced by her friends. That is the chief source of my apprehensions, since I do not know how to counterwork them. It is not very difficult to enlighten her and to deflect her from harmful projects; the Abbé and I have often done it. Unhappily, surprises are sprung upon her and there is no time to offer advice.' This bulletin reached Vienna too late to be read by his revered sovereign, who died after a short illness on November 29, 1780. When the news reached Versailles, the Queen poured out her heart to the Emperor, the only relative to whom she was deeply attached. 'Overwhelmed by the most terrible grief, I write to you in tears. Oh! my brother, Oh! my friend, you alone are left in a land which I shall always love. Take care of yourself; you owe it to us all. It only remains to commend my sisters to you; they have lost even more than I. Adieu! I cannot see what I am writing. Remember we are your friends. Love me. I embrace you.'

When the great Empress was laid to rest, Mercy continued to report on public events and the life of the Court to the Emperor and Kaunitz. But an atmospheric change is perceptible in the fourth and fifth volumes of his correspondence. He continued to supply advice to the Queen, but he no longer spoke with the same authority. How often had he appealed to her love for her mother in reinforcing an argument and sounding a warning! How often had he suggested not merely the nature but the actual phrasing of maternal exhortations and reproofs! She never ceased to esteem him as a diplomatist and a man, but his influence inevitably waned. Marie Antoinette was now twenty-five and had in large measure put away childish things. A year after her mother's death the birth of a son strengthened her authority, and to some extent revitalised the Austrian alliance. The intimate details which had filled the Ambassador's private letters to her mother without a break for a decade were neither expected nor desired by a brother immersed in his work, his unceasing travels, and his wars. Had the Empress been spared a few months longer she would have rejoiced at the birth of a Dauphin, and would have found little to blame in the conduct of the devoted mother of four children. Yet who can wish the proud and sensitive ruler to have witnessed the grim spectre of the Diamond Necklace, still less, like the faithful Mercy, to have learned of the declaration of war against Austria, the abolition of the Monarchy, the execution of the King; above all, the crowning horror of Marie Antoinette mounting the steps to the guillotine?

Bibliographical Note.—The primary source for the first decade of Marie Antoinette's life in France is in the *Correspondance Secrète du Comte Mercy Argenteau avec l'Impératrice Marie Thérèse*, edited by Arneth and Geffroy. The three large volumes contain all that survives of the correspondence of mother and daughter and the far fuller exchanges between the Empress and her trusted Ambassador. Joseph's reports on his French tour in 1777 are in *Maria Theresia und Joseph II. Ihre Korrespondenz samt Briefen Josephs an seinen Bruder Leopold.* The most popular of the many biographies is by Stefan Zweig, a brilliant amateur. The fullest account is in La Rocheterie, 2 vols., the most balanced in the lectures delivered by the Comte de Ségur during the First World War. The four volumes of Pierre de Nolhac, Curator of the Château of Versailles, are indispensable.   The most important of the many memoirs of the period, so far as the Queen is concerned, are those of Mme Campan and the Duchesse de Tourzel.   The political history of the first half of the reign of Louis XVI is best summarised in the co-operative *Histoire de France*, edited by Lavisse, vol. ix, and in Comte de Ségur, *Au Couchant de la Monarchie*, 2 vols.   Arneth's exposure of the forged letters of Marie Antoinette is described in his *Aus meinem Leben*, ii, 154–162.

3

MODERN HISTORIOGRAPHY

The Age of Confessional Strife. The collapse of the mediæval system under the impact of the Renaissance and the Reformation, the invention of printing, and the discovery of the new world prepared the way for far-reaching changes in the writing of history. Two generations doubled the realm of space and the horizon of learning. Interest in man and his achievements succeeded the brooding asceticism of mediæval ideals. The process described by Lecky as the secularisation of thought began. The Middle Ages, which had opened with Augustine, were buried by Machiavelli and Rabelais, Erasmus and Copernicus. Tradition began to appear as an incubus rather than a command. Lorenzo Valla's exposure of the *Donation of Constantine* inaugurated the critical treatment of sources, and the taste for humanistic studies, originating in Italy, quickly crossed the Alps. The group of scholars at the Court of the Emperor Maximilian called attention to Germanic history and heroes. During the closing decades of the fifteenth and the opening decades of the sixteenth century a cool breeze blew over western Europe. Something of the intellectualism of Greece and Rome had come again.

Modern historiography begins in Florence, where Machiavelli and Guicciardini related it to the throbbing life of the Italian states. If *The Prince* inaugurates modern political thinking, the *History of Florence*, published in 1525, narrates the fortunes of the author's native city in a similar spirit of disillusioned observation. Broader in scope, larger in bulk, and more widely read was Guicciardini's *History of Italy* from the French invasion of 1494 to 1534. Though Ranke was to reveal its manifold short-

comings three centuries later, its flair for politics kept it alive.
Part of the same ground was covered in Sleidan's ponderous
survey of the reign of Charles V with its wealth of original
documents.

Though the transition from the theological authoritarianism
of the Middle Ages to the empiricism of the Renaissance produced
a marvellous flowering of the human spirit, the reign of humanism
was brief.   The demand for the reform of the Church, stronger
in Germany than anywhere else, and the emergence of Luther as
its leading spokesman, transformed the intellectual landscape
once again and secular studies became engulfed in the whirlpool
of confessional strife.   The monk of Wittenberg, himself
profoundly uninterested in secular learning, was a child of the
Middle Ages to whom humanism made no appeal.   Yet the
controversial fever contained within itself the germ of its cure.
The Schoolmen of the Middle Ages appealed to reason, their
successors to history.   When Luther and Melanchthon, Zwingli
and Calvin had fought their battles in the theological arena,
historians carried on the struggle with other weapons.   Protestants
strove to prove that the Church of the Medici Popes was not the
Church of the early Christians and to show by what stages the
degeneration had taken place.   Catholics attempted to confound
their enemies with heavy artillery from the Vatican archives.   In
the fierce tournament victory, not truth, was the aim; yet precious
material was brought to light.   Flacius and his collaborators in
the *Magdeburg Centuries* (1559–74), with the encouragement of the
Lutheran princes, compiled a volume on each of the thirteen
centuries of the Christian Church, a veritable broadside against
the Papacy.   The reply was entrusted to Baronius, whose
Ecclesiastical Annals were based on the treasures of the Vatican.
When he died in 1605 he had completed twelve massive volumes
of a work which, with its continuations, was eagerly bought up
throughout the Catholic world, and the publication of which
was one of the outstanding events of the Counter-Reformation.
While the Centuriators had painted a picture of continuous
decline, the Neapolitan Cardinal contended that the Church had
retained its primitive purity.   The rival gladiators were equally
credulous, for legends and forgeries were accepted without
suspicion if deemed useful for the campaign.   That the Catholic

champion had feet of clay was proved by a succession of Protestant scholars with Casaubon at their head.

The battle of the books was not waged solely between Catholics and Protestants, for Paolo Sarpi's *History of the Council of Trent*, published in London in 1619, was a far more formidable indictment of the Papacy than any missile hurled from the Protestant camp. The Venetian friar, who detested papal autocracy, the Jesuits and religious intolerance, collected material from actors in the drama, from the Venetian archives, and from private correspondence placed at his disposal. The whole work was a slashing attack on a gathering which, in his opinion, rendered the gulf between the churches unbridgeable. The rejoinder, published in Rome in 1650, was entrusted to Pallavicino, a Jesuit Cardinal who, like Baronius, was munitioned from the Vatican archives. Neither Sarpi nor Pallavicino attempted to tell the whole truth. Both books are equally polemical, equally one-sided, and equally indispensable, but that of Sarpi possessed literary qualities which kept it alive. To the same category of propaganda belong d'Aubigné's glorification of Henri IV, John Knox's *History of the Reformation in Scotland*, George Buchanan's *History of Scotland*, above all Foxe's *Book of Martyrs*, a dramatic tale of suffering and courage from the origins of Christianity to the fires of Smithfield. During the century of religious strife which culminated in the Thirty Years War and closed with the Treaty of Westphalia in 1648, almost every scholar had an axe to grind. Even Bacon's brilliant sketch of Henry VII had a dynastic purpose. Such purely academic treatises as Scaliger's *Thesaurus Temporum*, the first attempt at scientific chronology, were very rare.

The Age of Erudition. If the sixteenth and the first half of the seventeenth century were above all the age of religious controversy, the second half of the latter and the early decades of the eighteenth deserve the title of the age of erudition. Belgian Jesuits under the guidance of Bolland began a collection of lives of the saints on so vast a scale that it is still incomplete. Even greater were the services rendered by France. Tillemont compiled monumental works on the early Church and the Roman Empire which helped Gibbon to rear his stately edifice, and the Benedictines of St. Maur, in their Paris monastery of St. Germain des Près, poured forth the noble series of works which illuminated almost every aspect of ecclesiastical history. The leader was Mabillon, the historian of his Order, whose masterpiece, *De Re Diplomatica*, published in 1681, founded the science of Latin palæography by the comparative study of the manuscripts, the paper, the ink, the style of writing, the abbreviations, the seals, the system of chronology, as well as the contents and the language, thereby enabling experts to detect forgeries, to date authentic documents, and to guess where they were drawn up. A similar service was rendered to Greek palæography by Montfaucon. Of no less importance to the scholar's trade were the dictionaries of mediæval Latin and Greek of Du Cange, who was also the founder of Byzantine studies by his editions of Byzantine historians.

Next to France in order of merit stood England, though British scholars never worked in teams. The serious study of history was inaugurated by Camden's *Britannia*, the first scholarly survey of the background and evolution of the nation's life arranged under counties. Stow's *Survey of London* founded the study of municipal life. Coke and Selden investigated the evolution of law. Dugdale collected materials on the monasteries. Rymer's *Fœdera* assembled a vast array of official documents from the Normans to his own times. Antony Wood's writings on Oxford University illustrated every aspect of national life. Madox inaugurated the study of administration by his *History and Antiquities of the Exchequer*. The last and greatest figure of the age of erudition was Muratori, editor of the *Rerum Italicarum Scriptores* from the sixth to the fifteenth centuries, each item being furnished with an introduction and notes. Only less important were his *Antiquitates Italicæ medii ævi*, a vast compendium of documents enriched by dissertations, and the *Annali d'Italia*, which related the fortunes of Italy from Augustus to his own time in annalistic form. In Germany, Conring traced the development of German law, and Leibniz, turning aside from philosophy and mathematics, compiled the annals of the House of Brunswick which he so loyally served. The mighty scholars who adorned the university of Leyden in the golden age of Dutch culture devoted their talents mainly to the ancient world.

The accumulation of materials was the main preoccupation, and

for more than a hundred years little progress was made in their
critical use.   At the height of the French wars of religion Bodin,
the father of the doctrine of sovereignty, discussed the principles
and methods of historical study.   In language which anticipates
Montesquieu he pointed out the influence of geographical factors,
climate and soil, on the character and fortunes of nations, while on
the other hand he called attention to the influence of personal
motives, patriotic and religious bias, and the opportunities of
knowledge on the views and value of writers.   In the field of
criticism Spinoza declared that the Old Testament must be treated
like any other historical work, and Père Simon incurred the wrath
of Bossuet by the tentative application of critical methods to the
Jewish scriptures.   Launoi earned the name of *le dénicheur de
saints* by his rough handling of the records of the martyrs.
Bentley, the greatest of British classicists, exposed the spurious
epistles of Phalaris.   In the first half of the eighteenth century
Astruc discovered the composite nature of Genesis, Reimarus and
Semler inaugurated the critical discussion of the Gospels, Vico
challenged the unity of the Homeric poems, and members of the
French Academy of Inscriptions quarrelled over Livy's tales of
early Rome.

The seventeenth century produced some memorable works
which rank almost as primary authorities.   The series opens with
the histories of the French wars of religion by Davila, an Italian
soldier of fortune, and de Thou, a leading member of the *politiques*
or moderate Catholics who strove to cool the temperature in an
intolerant age.   Clarendon employed his first exile in describing
the origin and course of the Civil War and his second in compiling
an autobiography.   Only less important and influential was
Burnet's *History of my Time,* in which the Whig bishop wove his
exciting experiences into a denunciation of the later Stuarts, a
glorification of the Revolution of 1688, and a tribute to the
services of William of Orange.   In Holland, Hooft, proudly
proclaimed by his countrymen as the Dutch Tacitus, described
the revolt of the Netherlands in a work which has coloured
national sentiment for three centuries.   Less popular, though
not less essential to the student, was Pufendorf's large-scale
narrative of the reign of the Great Elector, commissioned by the
Prussian government and enriched by official documents.

The Age of Reason. The eighteenth century, often described as the age of reason, witnessed a new phase in the study of the past, and by the middle the sun of the *Aufklärung* stood high in the heavens. Bossuet's *Histoire Universelle*, composed for the instruction of the Dauphin, the son of Louis XIV, had presented the empires of the ancient world as stages in the pre-ordained march of mankind towards the portals of the Roman Church, but it was the last serious effort of the kind. Such theological interpretations went out of fashion when Bayle's *Dictionnaire Historique et Critique*, followed half a century later by the *Encyclopédie* of Diderot and d'Alembert, challenged the authority of tradition and assailed inherited beliefs. The atmospheric change was due above all to Voltaire, who combined considerable erudition with the sharpest pen in the Republic of Letters. He claims a place among the influences which prepared the world for historical science by allowing his keen intelligence to play freely over vast ranges hitherto untouched by the critical spirit. Though his most popular historical work was a life of Charles XII, Sweden's warrior king, his main interest was in the progress of society. His *Siècle de Louis XIV* painted the first picture of the multiform life of a civilised state. A few years later his *Essai sur les Mœurs* portrayed the moral, social, economic, artistic and literary evolution of mankind from Charlemagne to Louis XIII. His subject, he declared, was the history of the human mind, the advance of society from the barbarism of the Middle Ages to the civilisation of his own time, the march of reason and the arts of peace. The sparkling style and novel treatment enlarged the horizon of historical study by the creation of a new genre subsequently known as *Kulturgeschichte*. Despite its superficiality and complacent rationalism the historiography of the *Aufklärung* ended the era of mere compilation, cleared away a mass of rubbish, and passed beyond a record of events to a survey of civilisation.

If France claimed first prize in the campaign against the dead hand of tradition, eighteenth-century England boasted a trio of narrative historians which no other country could match. Though primarily a philosopher, Hume composed the first detailed *History of England* from Anglo-Saxon days, which was read all over the world and held its own for a century. More solidly constructed and only a little less popular were the writings of Robertson on

the history of Scotland and the reign of Charles V. Above all,
Gibbon, author of the most celebrated historical work since
Thucydides, constructed a bridge from the old world to the new.
The Decline and Fall of the Roman Empire survives by its magnificent
architecture and its incomparable style. The chapters on Constantine and Julian, Justinian and Mohammed belong to literature
as well as to scholarship. The second half of the book is markedly
inferior in value, for the polished sceptic had little interest in the
mediæval Church and shared the prevailing contempt for the
Byzantine Empire. It was his immortal achievement to show
how the Roman Empire lived on; of the new Christian world in
which it was merged he understood as little as other men of his
time. Useful manuals were produced by Heeren and other
professors at the university of Göttingen, founded by George II
in his capacity of Elector of Hanover, to which candidates for
the civil service flocked from many German lands. The only
narrative work produced in Germany before the nineteenth
century which still deserves to be read is the *Histoire de mon
Temps* by Frederick the Great, which possesses the value attaching
to an original authority.

The eighteenth century witnessed a bold advance towards the
philosophic interpretation of the past, for the idea of continuity
took root. In discussing the laws of change in his *Scienza Nuova*,
Vico argued that the process was cyclic. Turgot's pregnant
discourse at the Sorbonne on the successive advances of the
human mind defined history as the life of humanity, ever flowing
on through decay and revival. Progress denoted the gradual
evolution and elevation of man's nature, a co-ordinated advance
in material well-being, mental enlightenment and virtue. Cousin
has called Turgot the father of the philosophy of history, but
several of his contemporaries were thinking on the same lines.
His friend and biographer Condorcet consoled himself while
waiting for the guillotine by writing his optimistic *Esquisse du
Progrès de l'Esprit Humain*. In *The Education of the Human Race*
Lessing described religion as a progressive revelation, religions
as the school-books of humanity, each of them helpful at a
certain stage, none of them final. The most detailed analysis
of the conditions and nature of progress was attempted by
Herder, an evolutionist before Darwin, whose *Ideas on the History*

of Humanity emphasised the creative activity of the folk-mind and the concept of natural growth. In his *Esprit des Lois* Montesquieu founded the comparative study of institutions, explaining that they must be judged not by abstract principles but by their suitability for the time and place. Adam Smith related the rise and fall of states to their economic resources and policy. Though most of the men of 1789 turned their backs on the past and set out to construct a new world with the aid of pure reason, the ideas of relativity and organic growth, most eloquently proclaimed in Burke's *Reflections on the French Revolution*, were beginning to take root. What was lacking in the eighteenth century was the critical assessment of the materials with which the historian has to work, and the imaginative insight into the life and thought of eras widely different from our own.

The Nineteenth Century in Germany. The foundation of the University of Berlin in 1810 was Prussia's spiritual response to her overthrow by Napoleon. Under the inspiring guidance of Wilhelm von Humboldt the new institution quickly won its place as the Mecca of academic studies in Europe. Niebuhr lectured on Roman history, Boeckh wrote the first scientific treatise on the social life and administrative system of ancient Athens, Eichhorn undertook the first comprehensive survey of the growth of German law, and Savigny introduced into the study of law the fruitful concept of organic evolution.

The first commanding figure in modern historiography was Niebuhr, whose lectures grew into a book which appeared in 1811–12, and which, though almost entirely rewritten in later years, inaugurated the systematic study of ancient Rome. The subject had fascinated publicists from Machiavelli to Montesquieu, but his administrative experience as a Danish and Prussian official enabled him to approach the problem with an insight which no previous historian had possessed: only a statesman, he declared, could write the history of Rome. He had grasped the truth that the early history of every nation must be rather of institutions than events, of classes than individuals, of custom than law. Building the story round the struggle of patricians and plebeians, which originated in the tribal differences of conquerors and conquered, and investigating the agrarian problem for the first time, he made the Roman republic as vital and intelligible as a modern state.

Niebuhr's second achievement was the critical analysis of the sources of early Roman history. He was equally certain that the traditional narrative could not be true and that it was not wholly false. He had been impressed by Wolf's *Prolegomena to Homer*, published in 1795, which argued that the poems were composed long before they could be written down and were worked up probably in the sixth century. It was largely from Wolf that he derived his conviction that the history of early Rome had been enshrined and transmitted in poems. Knowledge, he believed, had been handed down in songs, funeral panegyrics, and annals kept by the *pontifex maximus*; some of the songs were separate compositions, others formed a cycle. Threading his way through the regal period he pronounces certain events mythical, some partially true, others definitely historical. 'Between the purely poetical and the completely historical age there is in all nations a mythico-historical era.' His hypothetical ballads suggested Macaulay's *Lays of Ancient Rome*. Though contemporaries thought him an iconoclast, later critics agree that we know even less of early Rome than he believed.

While Niebuhr only lectured for three years at Berlin, Boeckh adorned the new university for half a century and trained generations of scholars. His *Public Economy of Athens*, published in 1817, is the only important German historical work before Ranke which has not been superseded. Dedicated to Niebuhr, it achieved for Athens the partial resurrection which the latter had accomplished for Rome. It first made known the daily life of a state of the ancient world: the whole economic organisation stood revealed, and a realistic view of Greek civilisation became possible. One of the most valuable sources of information was the inscriptions of which he persuaded the Prussian Academy to undertake a *corpus*. This enterprise remained the chief preoccupation of his long life and inspired similar collections in other fields of antiquity. His favourite pupil, Otfried Müller, composed his first important work on Greek history in his book on the Dorians, and his death in Greece from sunstroke at the age of forty-three was the greatest loss suffered by Greek studies during the nineteenth century. Unlike his master Boeckh and his pupil Ernst Curtius, author of the first large-scale history of Greece, he possessed a touch of genius.

While Niebuhr and Boeckh were breathing life into the classical world, Eichhorn was founding the historical school of jurisprudence. Useful pioneering work had been done by the Göttingen professor, Hugo, who first proclaimed that the law of a people could be understood only through the national life of which it was the expression. This fruitful conception inspired Eichhorn's *History of German Law and Institutions*, the first volume of which appeared in 1808. The rich material had never been critically examined or fused into a coherent whole, and law was at last presented as the product of all the factors which influenced the life of society. By tracing the connexion between legal ideas and institutions he revealed the continuity of evolution. Hitherto regarded as the creation of rulers, law now took its honoured place not as a manufactured article but an organic growth.

If Eichhorn provided the first consummate example of the historical treatment of law, it is to Savigny that we owe the most brilliant exposition of the evolutionary creed itself. *The Vocation of our Time for Legislation*, published in 1814, one of the most influential books of the nineteenth century, was inspired by a demand for the codification of the law which grew out of the new consciousness of nationality generated by the war of liberation. In advocating legal reform, Thibaut, a Heidelberg professor, argued that a code was urgently needed on the ground that the fatherland was a mosaic of little states, that Roman law was a foreign element, that the old law-books were full of anomalies. A simple code, he added, constructed by statesmen and scholars in a German spirit, would render it easy both for judges and ordinary citizens to master the subject and would unify the inhabitants of the different states. While respecting his patriotism, Savigny rejected the plan so convincingly that it was deferred till the unification of Germany in 1870 rendered it imperative. Law, he explained, was the child of custom, popular sentiment, national experience, silently operating forces, not the arbitrary will of a lawgiver. A code would paralyse the study of the past and inspire no reverence. Existing law should be improved by legislation, for law is subject to the same development as every other expression of the life of the people. Savigny was right in his view that the time for codification had not come, but wrong in his argument that it would never arrive, and the shackles he laid on his countrymen required to be broken by Ihering. Yet, despite his exaggeration of the evils of codes and the difficulty of making them, he served historical studies by explaining how law had come into being. The greatest jurist of the nineteenth century was also the author of one of the most illuminating historical investigations ever made. *The History of Roman Law in the Middle Ages*, which began to appear in 1815, traced its survival in every part of what had once been the Roman Empire, in municipal institutions, local customs, canon law, and the universities. The nearest German equivalent of Gibbon initiated a fruitful contest between 'Romanists' and 'Germanists' which was continued almost to our own time.

In the same wonderful decade which witnessed the earliest works of Niebuhr and Boeckh, Eichhorn and Savigny, Jacob Grimm founded the science of Teutonic origins. The study of national antiquities was uncongenial not only to the *Aufklärung* but to Goethe and Schiller. A new epoch opened with Herder, who paved the way for the historical study of literature by his conception of native poetry, of the folk-soul, of language as a treasure-house to which every generation made its contribution. His interest in the childhood of the world inspired the Romantic Movement, though its leaders were artists and poets, not philologists or historians. It was the glory of Jacob Grimm that he added the critical scholarship which they lacked. From his master Savigny he learned the reverence for the past which illumines all his works. The *Fairy Tales*, published in 1812, in which he was aided by his brother Wilhelm, made the name of Grimm a household word throughout the world. The romanticists had grasped the cardinal truth that the historian, in addition to describing institutions and recording events, must reconstruct the life and thought of the community. Conscious creation was reckoned inferior to unconscious, the work of the individual to the collective activities of the *Volk*.

Grimm's mission was to breathe the atmosphere and to discover the mind of early man. From fairy tales he passed to language. The *German Grammar* sought for its laws in a comparison of all Teutonic tongues and dialects, and concluded that all the families

of German speech were related.   The book, which extended to
four volumes and introduced the comparative method into
Teutonic philology, was in truth a history of Teutonic languages.
His third contribution to the study of German origins, *Legal
Antiquities*, collected and analysed the customs, actions and forms
of an unlettered age.   A fourth aspect of the remote past was
explored in the *German Mythology*, in which written evidence of
the pre-Christian world was supplemented by oral tradition.
The *German Dictionary*, the last of his major enterprises, in which
he was aided by his brother, was designed to include all words in
use from Luther to Goethe.   'All my works,' he wrote in one of
his latest essays, 'relate to the fatherland, from whose soil they
derive their strength.'

The intensive study of German history was the result of the
fiery ordeal of the Napoleonic Wars, and the chief civilian
architect of liberation turned to a new task of national service.
Meeting with no encouragement from official circles for his
project of a collection of German sources, Stein founded a society
for the exploration of early German history.   He selected the
title *Monumenta Germaniæ Historica*, and the motto *Sanctus amor
patriæ dat animum* expressed the spirit of the enterprise.   Pertz,
a young Hanoverian archivist, was appointed editor in 1820, and
in 1824 the plan was announced.   It was to consist of five parts
—writers, laws, imperial acts, letters, antiquities—of which only
the first two were taken in hand.   Beginning with the Carolin-
gians, Pertz produced the first instalment in 1826.   The volume
marks an epoch in historical study, for it was the first time that
German writers had been edited on the same critical principles
as the classics.   Some manuscripts were credited with too much,
others with too little authority, and the criticism was rather
textual than historical; yet it was a not unworthy prelude to the
greatest co-operative historical undertaking of the nineteenth
century.   The second volume of the Carolingian *Scriptores*
appeared in 1829, and in 1835 the first volume of the *Leges*.
When Pertz resigned his editorship, after half a century, he could
look round on twenty-five stately folios, almost all enriched by
his own labours.   'Without your great work,' declared Ranke,
'I could never have attracted a circle of young men to these
studies.'

The publication in 1824 of Ranke's first book, *Histories of the Romance and Teutonic Peoples* (1494–1514), is usually described as the starting-point of modern historical scholarship, for his critical analysis of the chief authorities revealed how little most of them deserved their reputation. In Guicciardini's voluminous *History of Italy*, for instance, much of the material was lifted from other books, much was false, much was doubtful, speeches were invented, treaties were altered, important facts were misrepresented. There was nothing new in the maxims that the nearest witness to an event was the best, that the letters of the actors and the minutes of meetings were of greater value than the entertaining gossip of the chronicler, that all credentials must be scrutinised with the utmost care. The significance of Ranke's achievement lay in the fact that he applied these axioms for sixty years with incomparable skill and taught generations of scholars that a house could not be built on shifting sands.

Scarcely less important than the critical study of sources was the declaration in the same book that his aim was 'merely to show how things actually were'. Ranke came nearer to this ideal of objectivity than any of his contemporaries. *The History of the Popes* (1834–36) exhibited the Papacy of the Counter-Reformation primarily as an historic institution. No one, he declared, could truthfully maintain that it was written for or against the Roman Church. Believing in the fundamental unity of all Christian churches, he looked with tolerant eyes on external and even dogmatic differences. The tone was too cool for some of his Protestant readers, but he atoned by his *German History in the Reformation Era*, an encyclopædic survey of the structure of the Empire, the activities of the princes, the manifold attempts at political and religious reform. Here, as in all his works, the historian keeps the whole life of western Europe continually in view. Though he hails the Reformation as the greatest achievement of the German spirit, he does full justice to Charles V and awards the highest praise to the moderates in both camps, whether rulers or theologians, who strove for confessional peace. The three imposing works of the next twenty years—on the emergence of Prussia as a Great Power, France under the absolute monarchy, and England during the constitutional struggles of the seventeenth century—reverted to the tranquil detachment manifested in the *History of the Popes*. All of them, like the later monographs on Wallenstein, the Fürstenbund, and Hardenberg, were based on new material. At the age of seventy the Nestor of German historians began to revise and in some cases enlarged his works for a collected edition in fifty-two volumes, which did not include the gigantic *Weltgeschichte*, left unfinished at his death in his ninety-first year. The chief glory of the greatest historical scholar of modern times is to have rendered the history of Western Europe since the Middle Ages intelligible, to have established its essential unity, and to have portrayed most of its leading actors.

Ranke's services were not confined to his writings or his lectures at Berlin. The famous school by which historical method was revolutionised was founded in his own study. He was not the first professor to hold a *Seminar* but the first to train an army of specialists. Though his own studies lay mainly in the modern field, he directed the members of his *Seminar*, which started in 1833, to the less trodden paths of the Middle Ages. His earliest pupils suggested that they should undertake some co-operative task, and the annals of the Saxon Emperors, which began to appear in 1837, inaugurated the critical study of mediæval Germany.

The oldest and most academically eminent of his pupils was Waitz, whose *German Constitutional History*, dedicated to his teacher, began to appear in 1844. The eight volumes, bringing the story to the twelfth century, rendered possible the reconstruction of institutional life. Unlike Stubbs, he lacked the gift of style. Like his venerated master he was less impressive in the lecture-room than in his *Seminar*, many of whose members aided him in his lifelong labours on the *Monumenta*. Mediævalists from many lands learned their trade in his study at Göttingen.

The second pupil to win fame was Giesebrecht, whose *History of the Mediæval Empire* began to appear in 1855. When he died, in 1889, he had reached Barbarossa, but the massive work was not a page too long for the eager generation which witnessed the revival of the *Reich*. The picture is aglow with colour and national pride, for the author was an artist no less than a patriot. It was received with equal delight by Catholics and Protestants,

by north and south, and its faultless scholarship earned the respect
of his fellow-experts.   The only discordant note was struck by
Sybel, who complained that the merits of the Empire were
exaggerated.   The Emperors, he argued, injured the German
nation by their universalism, since their first duty was to build
up a compact and vigorous national life.   *Qui trop embrasse, mal
étreint.*   The reply came, not from Giesebrecht himself, who
disliked controversy, but from the leading Austrian authority
on the mediæval Empire.   The realm of the Ottos, declared
Ficker, was neither a world monarchy nor a national state, but
grew naturally out of the time: without the Empire Germany
would have gone to pieces even sooner.   Sybel rejoined that he
tested politics by their compatibility with German interests, and
that the shrinkage of the Empire in the thirteenth century was a
blessing for the nation.

Sybel, like Giesebrecht, was trained in Ranke's *Seminar* and
made his name by a critical analysis of the authorities for the First
Crusade.   He soon turned to modern times, threw himself into
Prussian politics, and rejected his master's ideal of standing above
the battle as incompatible with the historian's duty of upholding
moral standards.   The *Era of the French Revolution*, the first of
his two major works, surveyed European diplomacy as a whole
and explained that the statesmen of Vienna and Berlin were
thinking as much of Poland as of France.   His dislike of Austria
reappeared in his more important work, *The Foundation of the
German Empire*, which utilised the Prussian archives, made
Bismarck the hero of the story, and defended Prussian policy
through thick and thin.

Ranke's detachment, serenity, and mildness of judgment were
anathema to the Prussian school to which Sybel transferred his
allegiance in middle life.   To Ranke, born a Saxon, Germany
always meant more than Prussia.   To Droysen, born in Prussia,
she was the predestined maker and leader of a united nation, for
she alone had been faithful to German interests as a whole.   In
the stagnant years after 1848 she seemed to have forgotten her
mission, and it was the object of his *History of Prussian Policy* to
remind her.   The book was a pæan to the Great Elector,
Frederick William I, and Frederick the Great, who felt the
national call and gave the Germans the leadership they lacked.

Fourteen volumes, based exclusively on the Prussian archives, had carried the story to the eve of the Seven Years War when the fiery patriot died at the age of seventy-eight in 1886. He depicts the early Hohenzollerns as working for the reform of the Empire till they saw that the first need was the reform of the Church. With the Reformation Protestanism became part of the national idea, and Austria ceased to share the growing intellectual life of Germany. He in no way exaggerated the impotence of Austria to create a nation-state, but his interpretation of Prussian policy down the centuries in terms of German nationalism was rejected even by Koser, the greatest of his pupils.

While Droysen's ponderous work, almost entirely confined to diplomacy, was read only by scholars, Treitschke's *German History in the 19th Century*, the Continental equivalent of Macaulay, was a best-seller. The youngest, greatest, and last of the Prussian school was the most eloquent of preachers and the most passionate of partisans, embodying most completely the blending of scholarship and patriotism which it was the aim of the school to achieve. Though a Saxon by birth he had no use for small states, and indeed he was more Prussian than Bismarck himself, for he wished Prussia not only to dominate but to annex the rest of Germany. In his belief she had done all that was really great in Germany since 1648 and was herself the supreme achievement of the German people. But though Prussia is naturally the back-bone of the *German History*, it deals with all the states which went to the making of the Deutscher Bund. No such panorama of the national life from the reign of Frederick the Great had ever been attempted, and no one but Treitschke could have made the drab years of the Restoration live again. The first volume, published in 1879, surveyed the revolutionary period and the wars of liberation, and closed with the Congress of Vienna. It was enjoyed even by those who disapproved its militant Prussianism, its contempt for the minor states, and its unfairness to Austria and other Powers. It rivals Mommsen in the magic of style, and the throbbing vitality left all other German historians far behind. Yet Treitschke is more than a superb literary artist, for the work rested on solid research; the chapters on culture are as masterly as those on political movements and events. His death in 1896 at the age of sixty-two, when the fifth volume had

reached 1847, deprived the world of the picture of the year of
revolution to which his readers were eagerly looking forward.
'The Bismarck of the Chair', who wrote history less to record
than to preach, had many admirers but no pupils.   The stream of
historical studies, temporarily deflected by the powerful magnet
of the Prussian school, returned to the channel which Ranke had
marked out for it.

To the post-Ranke generation belong such admirable achievements as Gierke's studies of mediæval corporations, Davidsohn's
gigantic history of early Florence, Brunner's record of the
evolution of German law, Andreas' panorama of Germany on
the eve of the Reformation, Brandi's judicial estimate of Charles V,
Moriz Ritter's balanced narrative of the Counter-Reformation,
Michael's *England in the 18th Century*, Koser's monumental study
of Frederick the Great, Meinecke's sketch of the transition from
the cosmopolitanism of the eighteenth century to the nationalism
of the nineteenth, Gerhard Ritter's life of Stein, Veit Valentin's
story of the Revolution of 1848–49, Stern's ten volumes on
European history, 1815–70, Schnabel's picture of Germany in
the first half of the nineteenth century, and the assessments of the
Bismarckian era by Oncken and Brandenburg, Erich Marcks and
A. O. Meyer.   In Austria the fine tradition of Arneth, the
historian of Maria Theresa, was carried on by Srbik, the biographer of Metternich and the interpreter of Austro-German
relations in the nineteenth century.   No other scholar, Austrian
or Prussian, has approached so closely to the ideal of holding the
scales level between the rivals for the hegemony of Central
Europe.

The Nineteenth Century in France.   In France historical
studies remained longer in the hands of amateurs.   During the
first half of the nineteenth century the Romantic Movement,
craving for colour rather than critical scholarship, inspired the
brilliant narratives of the Norman Conquest and the Merovingian
kings by Augustin Thierry, who acknowledged his debt to
Chateaubriand and Scott.   Sismondi provided the first detailed
history of France till the eve of the Revolution, but its solid merits
were obscured by its carping radicalism and its uninviting style.
It was the achievement of Michelet, the Victor Hugo of historical

studies, to compose a picture of mediæval France in a spirit of sympathetic insight which restored a vanished world to life. The first six volumes of his *History of France* were written when his genius had reached full development and before his imagination became diseased. The *Tableau de France* in the second volume emphasised the significance of the geographical factor and sketched the provinces in turn, their features, their climate, their inhabitants, their contribution to the national life. Resting on a generous recognition of the complex elements of which his country was composed, the book is of all the larger French histories the least dynastic and the most truly national. The narrative is rather a series of *tableaux* than a record of events. Hurrying across large tracts of territory, he lingers over individuals and occurrences which strike his imagination, such as the fall of the Templars and the epic of the Maid. His story of Joan of Arc, one of the glories of French literature, was read with equal pleasure in the palace and the school. His hero is the people, but he is not yet the enemy of kings, and the treatment of the Church sometimes recalls the warm tints of Chateaubriand's *Génie du Christianisme*. When he reached the close of the Middle Ages he turned aside to the French Revolution, details of which he had learned from his father and other eyewitnesses. Here again his hero is the people. Through the smoke and flames he perceives the growth of a new France, a new Europe. In the sunlit dawn the whole people were the actors; in the grim phase of cruelty only a few individuals were concerned. Despite the Terror it was the greatest event in the life of France since Joan of Arc. The *Histoire de la Révolution*, with its unique evocation of atmosphere, is the epic of democracy and the most eloquent defence of the ideals of 1789 ever written. When after a decade he resumed his *History of France*, his right hand had lost its cunning. He was a changed man, and a new spite against the Monarchy and the Church throws the picture out of focus.

While the romantic school was floodlighting the historic life of the French people, a more analytical approach was made by Guizot in his lectures at the Sorbonne. His *History of Civilisation in Europe* provided the first concise and convincing interpretation in any language of the story of 2,000 years. Rome bequeathed the municipal system, written law, and the conception of imperial rule. The Christian Church contributed lofty doctrines and a world-wide organisation. The Germanic tribes brought personal liberty and the habit of voluntary association. These diverse elements needed a prolonged period for their amalgamation, and the Middle Ages were the battleground of their claims. The main organ and symbol of progress was to be found in the gradual emergence of a class midway between the aristocracy and the peasants, since its existence involved in the long run the invention of representative government. The Reformation encouraged the critical spirit, and the Puritan revolution marked the triumph of self-government in England and the beginning of its conquest of the civilised world. The lectures ended on the eve of the French Revolution, which the growth of the *tiers état* in numbers, intelligence and wealth rendered inevitable.

Guizot's bird's-eye view of Europe was followed by a detailed examination of the origins of civilisation in France. He begins with the social, intellectual, civil and religious conditions of Gaul before the German invasion, the character and institutions of the Germans beyond the Rhine, the invasion itself, and the inter-action of the barbarian and romanised societies. A study of the barbarian codes, the organisation of the Church, and the dawn of intellectual life is followed by a full account of the work and influence of Charlemagne. A second series, on the feudal period beginning with Hugh Capet, was interrupted by the Revolution of 1830 which launched the historian on the troubled sea of politics. Fragmentary though it is, the *History of Civilisation in France* ranks among the major achievements of nineteenth-century scholarship. Guizot was the first historian to dissect a society. The lectures proved the possibility of applying scientific methods to history, though Sainte-Beuve and other critics complained that he ignored the chapter of accidents and that his pattern was too neat to be true to life.

Scarcely less influential a member of the analytical school was Mignet, who won fame by his *Précis of the French Revolution* published in 1824. Having learned a good deal from Talleyrand and other surviving actors, he presented it as an organic whole to a generation which thought of it rather as a nightmare or a battle-cry. It was not an accidental convulsion, he argued, but the logical result of French history and the mother of a new society.   Like most Frenchmen he approved the work of 1789 and condemned the Terror.   None of his later writings, including the masterly edition of the documents relating to the Spanish succession, approached the popularity or influence of his first attempt.   His lifelong friend Thiers, covering the same ground in his early *History of the French Revolution* and the later and far more important narrative of the Consulate and the Empire, found as many readers; but he lacked the patience of the scholar and won more enduring fame in the political field.

While brilliant amateurs were awakening interest in mediæval France, critical studies began with the foundation of the École des Chartes in 1821.   From this famous seminary of learning, the first of its kind, came Quicherat, who edited the *dossier* on the trial of Joan of Arc, Léopold Delisle, the master of palæography, and generations of scholars who carried forward the Benedictine *Histoire Littéraire de la France*.   The most conspicuous, though not the soundest, of mediævalists was Fustel de Coulanges, whose *History of the Institutions of Ancient France* raised issues of more than academic interest.   While Frenchmen were smarting under defeat they were informed in 1872 by an eminent scholar in the *Revue des Deux Mondes* that the German invasions of the fifth century had no direct influence on the history, religion, customs, government, or structure of French society; that the barbarians had brought nothing but confusion; and that their arrival merely fostered the feudalism already existing in germ.   Stimulated by critics of this gigantic paradox, he proceeded to defend it in erudite studies of Roman Gaul, the German invasions, Merovingian institutions, and land tenures.   The fifth and sixth volumes, left unfinished at his death and edited by Camille Jullian, the most distinguished of his pupils, dealt with vassalage and the Carolingian institutions.   The academic conflict between Romanists and Germanists was as old as Savigny, but never had the former possessed so brilliant a champion.   The Franks, he declared, brought nothing of their own, for they had nothing to bring; the invasion was not a conquest but a pacific settlement of romanised Germans.   The wealth of learning, the logical structure and the literary skill made a deep impression, but the book was praised beyond its deserts.   Though he had diligently studied the sources he often misunderstood them; he was weak in law; he was sometimes deceived by forged charters; and his rejection of Germanic factors in the making of France was far too absolute. Less brilliant but more satisfying surveys of the evolution of French institutions came from Paul Viollet, Ferdinand Lot, Flach and Luchaire. All previous narratives were superseded by the co-operative *Histoire de France* edited by Lavisse.

Though the *Ancien Régime* was a more controversial subject than the Middle Ages, the later decades of the century brought a more judicial spirit. Hanotaux's story of the early phases of Richelieu, Chéruel's volumes on Mazarin, Lavisse's balanced survey of the reign of Louis XIV, the Duc d'Aumale's history of the Condé princes, de Boislisle's superb edition of Saint-Simon, the Duc de Broglie's monographs on the foreign policy of Louis XV, Ségur's studies of Turgot, Necker and Marie Antoinette, revealed French scholarship at its best. The *Manuel Historique de la Politique Etrangère* of Émile Bourgeois provided an authoritative text-book for University students, and the *Recueil des Instructions données aux Ambassadeurs de la France* furnished a key to policy of which no other country can boast.

Less progress has been made towards an agreed verdict on the French Revolution. The first scientific approach was made in Tocqueville's *L'Ancien Régime et la Révolution*, published in 1855, based on researches in provincial archives. Where others had seen a radical contradiction between the absolute monarchy and the Revolution, he found a logical continuation. The *Ancien Régime* was strongly centralised; the Revolution centralised administration still further. The former destroyed the greater part of feudalism; the latter destroyed the rest. The driving principle of the Revolution was equality; it was equality before the law which the Monarchy had sought in its long struggle with feudalism.

A similar continuity in the field of foreign affairs was proclaimed in Sorel's *L'Europe et la Révolution Française*, perhaps the greatest historical work produced in modern France. His object was to exhibit the Revolution—which appeared to some the subversion, to others the regeneration, of the old world—as the natural result of the history of France and Europe. Tocqueville had found the model of the internal policy of the Revolution in the reigns of Louis XIV and Louis XV. Sorel

proclaimed that in their foreign policy the revolutionists were
the heirs of the Monarchy, since the slogan of *les frontières
naturelles*—the Rhine, the Alps, the Pyrenees—was common to
both.   Of equal importance was his analysis of the interaction
of foreign and domestic affairs.   He does justice to the better
side of the revolutionists and never forgets their difficulties.   He
respects the Declaration of the Rights of Man, but questions its
utility.   He distinguishes between the earlier *émigrés*, who tried
to arm Europe against their country, and the later, who were
the victims of persecution.   He censures the policy of the Court,
but comprehends its feelings.   He charges the Girondins with
direct responsibility for the war, though the explosive forces of
the Revolution and the old instinct for aggrandisement prepared
the way.   Yet his sympathies are with his country in the long
fight, since the integrity of the national territory and the maintenance of the priceless achievements of the Revolution were at
stake.   Compared with the sobriety and insight of Tocqueville
and Sorel, Taine's attack on the Revolution and all its works is
the explosion of a gifted amateur.

Organised documentary study began in the last quarter of the
nineteenth century.   The leader of the team was Aulard, the first
holder of a Chair of the History of the French Revolution,
founded for him at the Sorbonne in 1886 by the Municipal Council
of Paris.   He and his pupils produced a series of large-scale
publications relating to the history of the capital, the Jacobin
Club, and the Committee of Public Safety.   Some results of these
researches were embodied in his successive volumes entitled
Lectures and Studies on the Revolution and in his largest work,
Political History of the French Revolution, published in 1902.   The
subtitle, *Origin and Development of Democracy and the Republic*,
indicates that it is a monograph, not a comprehensive survey of
the period.   He merely glances at the events of the first three
years, which he had already mapped in his chapters contributed
to the *Histoire Générale* edited by Lavisse and Rambaud.   His
theme is the evolution and application of the two governing
principles of the Revolution, the sovereignty of the people and
the doctrine of equality.   He shows how small a part was played
by abstract formulas, how late was the origin of the republican
idea.   The Terror, he argued, was due, not to 'Jacobin psycho-

logy', as Taine had proclaimed, but to the necessity of repelling the invader and safeguarding reforms. Without defending the September Massacres he explains the state of mind from which they arose—the whole achievement of the Revolution at stake, the allied armies marching on Paris, the boasts of royalist prisoners that their triumph was at hand. His favourite is 'the great and good Danton', but the real hero of the drama is the people. His greatest pupil, Mathiez, soon became his rival, for the two experts quarrelled over a cardinal issue. While the henchman of Danton despised Robespierre, Mathiez denounced Danton as a bad man and a bad patriot, and exalted Robespierre as the unselfish friend of the Fourth Estate. The most useful work of Mathiez, a convinced socialist, was in the field of social and economic history, in which Jaurès, whose large-scale *Histoire Socialiste de la Révolution Française* he edited, was a pioneer. The one-volume narrative of the whole drama, written in his closing years, is indispensable, but it is less balanced than the earlier masterpiece of Madelin, the most satisfying summary since Mignet. When Aulard and Mathiez were gone the leadership passed to Georges Lefebvre.

The intensive study of Napoleon began with the publication of his voluminous correspondence under the auspices of his nephew, Napoleon III. No one has done so much to reveal the man as Frédéric Masson, the friend and literary counsellor of the Bonapartes, who had access to the family papers. Though his admiration knew no limits, he holds nothing back. His largest work, *Napoléon et sa Famille*, is at once a ruthless exposure of the greedy throng and a demonstration that the family system was a mistake. Josephine fares no better than the brothers and sisters, but he finds little to blame in Marie Louise. Vandal's masterpieces are of higher literary quality. *Napoléon et Alexandre*, which appeared when Frenchmen were rejoicing over the Russian alliance, instantly became a favourite. The brief and uneasy partnership is presented as an episode in the titanic duel with England, the only means of leaving the Emperor free to compel her to recognise his conquests. Though the Tsar proved a disloyal ally, Vandal admits that the ultimate responsibility for the failure of the alliance rests on Napoleon, who frittered away his strength in Spain. His even more popular *L'Avènement de*

Bonaparte is a story not of folly and failure, but of inspired statesmanship and merited success. Brumaire—interpreted not as the destruction of liberty but as the restoration of order and prosperity—executed the judgment of the people on the discredited Directory. Equally successful were the volumes of Henri Houssaye on the campaigns of 1814 and 1815, glowing with enthusiasm for the Emperor and the soldiers he led. The work of these specialists has been worthily continued by Madelin in his life of Fouché, his history of France during the Consulate and Empire (in the same series as his volume on the Revolution), and in the vast biography of Napoleon which he alone was competent to write. For the nineteenth century we possess three elaborate works of the highest importance—Thureau-Dangin on the reign of Louis Philippe, La Gorce on the Second Empire, and Hanotaux on the first decade of the Third Republic. The latest researches are utilised in the ten-volume co-operative history of France since 1789 edited by Lavisse. No French historical work of the last half-century exceeds in importance Élie Halévy's unfinished *Histoire du Peuple Anglais au dix-neuvième Siècle*, a triumph of sympathetic interpretation.

The Nineteenth Century in Britain and America. The second quarter of the nineteenth century witnessed the dethronement of Hume, for the contemptuous indifference to the Middle Ages ended with Scott's novels, and the Tory interpretation of the Stuart era dissatisfied the contemporaries of the Reform Bill. The outlines of Anglo-Saxon England began to emerge in the works of Palgrave and Kemble, and the Whig interpretation of modern history was forcefully presented by Hallam and Macaulay. The former's *Constitutional History, 1485-1760*, published in 1827, is a sustained attack on the Tudor and Stuart despotism and a glorification of the Revolution of 1688. The effect of the work, which became canonical in the universities and from which Queen Victoria and the Prince Consort learned the limits of the royal prerogative, was enhanced by the studied moderation of tone. No English historian had so successfully donned the mantle of a judge, and he speaks throughout as a lawyer to whom the majesty of the law means more than party. He applauds the resistance of the lawyers and the country gentlemen to the encroachments of Charles I, but condemns his execution and that of Strafford and Laud. He recognises Cromwell's achievement in making England once again a Great Power, but depicts him as a selfish despot. On the other hand he delights in the conservative Revolution of 1688, carried through without bloodshed and with the consent of the two great parties. Though he belonged to the extreme right of the Whig camp, no one was more profoundly convinced of the right and duty of a people to preserve its liberties against a despotic executive.

Hallam's relative leniency in dealing with the Stuart era was deplored by Macaulay in one of the earliest and most brilliant of his contributions to the *Edinburgh Review*. Succeeding essays on the seventeenth and eighteenth centuries made him by far the most popular of English historians, for the sparkling style and boundless self-assurance carried most of his readers away. Though they differ greatly in merit, they did even more than Hallam's *Constitutional History* to enthrone the Whig interpretation of the critical centuries. Convinced that Whig principles were the essence of political wisdom, he measured men and movements with the yardstick of 1832. Of much higher value is the *History of England*, the first two volumes of which appeared in 1848. There is far more learning and thoroughness than in the essays, and the tone is less rhetorical. Though only a fragment of a large design—his death at the age of fifty-nine interrupted his story of the reign of William III—it is none the less the greatest historical work in the language since Gibbon. The famous third chapter on the condition of England in 1685 supplies a background for the detailed narrative which begins with the accession of James II. The core of the book is the Revolution of 1688, the hero William of Orange, the most arresting portrait he ever painted. If its colours are a little too bright, the portrait of James is too dark, and his Marlborough is a caricature. Though he is more successful in narrative than in analysis of character, though his use of authorities is often uncritical, and though he is weak in foreign affairs, the *History of England* retains its place as a literary classic.

During the middle decades of the nineteenth century no one except Macaulay gave such an impetus to historical studies as Carlyle. While the English Whig employed history to justify his political convictions, the Scottish Calvinist used it to illustrate his ethical creed. His lectures on *Heroes and Hero-Worship* stressed the need of the born leader—Mahomet, Luther, Cromwell, Knox—whom it was the duty and privilege of the common herd to follow and obey. In the *History of the French Revolution*, published in 1837, we hear a prophet calling sinners to repentance; injustice, inefficiency, immorality, corruption, bring their own punishment. His knowledge was superficial and his use of authorities uncritical; his conception of the Revolution as merely a huge bonfire of rubbish and abuses ignored its creative work; and his neglect of events beyond the frontier left the Terror unexplained. His supreme merit is that he brought the whole drama to life. More important for historical students was the collection of Cromwell's letters and speeches. Through allowing him to tell his story in his own words Carlyle destroyed the royalist legend of a hypocritical fanatic and restored to England one of her greatest sons. Yet his scorn for democracy led him astray. He believed that the history of the Commonwealth proved the incapacity of a popular assembly to govern, whereas it established the impossibility of personal government in modern England. Of his three historical works *Frederick the Great*, the only one resting on serious study, is the most important. 'The last of the kings' was almost unknown to British readers when he portrayed the superman at work, overcoming obstacles, getting things done, the first servant of the state. Like Cromwell he is overpraised, but the man, the ruler, the warrior comes to life. Among the best portions of the book are the descriptions of the campaigns. The battle of Torgau is a masterpiece.

Carlyle found a friend, disciple and biographer in Froude who, like his master, combined shining merits with serious defects. The twelve volumes on Tudor England, from the fall of Wolsey, where Brewer laid down his pen, to the defeat of the Armada, were the fruit of prolonged research, and the style was scarcely less brilliant than that of Macaulay. The revelation of gross carelessness in the transcription of documents damaged his authority, but a graver weakness was his strident partisanship. Deeply convinced that the Roman Church had always been the enslaver of mind and soul, he expressed heartfelt gratitude to the men who broke its bonds. The Reformation, in his opinion, was the outstanding event in English history, the beginning of the greatness of the country, a ringing blow for human freedom. Engaged in a life-and-death struggle, Henry VIII was bound to use every weapon of offence and defence, and the people applauded his vigorous strokes. Mary's fires at Smithfield reminded England what Catholicism meant and completed the country's conversion. The later and larger half of the work is devoted to Elizabeth, and is enriched by the priceless archives of Simancas, which he was the first English historian to explore. He denies her outstanding ability and denounces her stinginess. The hero of the story is Burleigh, 'the solitary author of Elizabeth's and England's greatness', who used his forty years of power to establish Protestantism on an impregnable foundation. In the Scottish chapters we witness the conflict of good and evil in Knox and Mary Stuart. His later work, *The English in Ireland in the Eighteenth Century*, continues the feud with the Roman Church and may be described as an Orange manifesto. No leading English historian has made less effort to stand above the battle, and the modern student of the Tudors prefers the skilled guidance of Pollard, Neale and Rowse.

The third quarter of the nineteenth century witnessed the coming of the experts. Stubbs, who had made his name as the editor of mediæval chronicles, was appointed Professor of Modern History at Oxford in 1866, and published the first volume of his *Constitutional History of England* in 1874. Though primarily a study of institutions, it is virtually a history of the country from the end of the Roman occupation to the coming of the Tudors. There is little about diplomacy, but it embraces church and state, law and justice, administration and finance. The first volume, extending to the Norman Conquest, was the least successful, for the materials were scanty and difficult of interpretation. Convinced that England rested on a Teutonic foundation, he failed to realise the complexity of society. In the second and third he is on firmer ground, and the panorama at the close of the Middle Ages is superb. The fairness of his judgment is as notable as the accuracy of his scholarship.

Freeman, his friend and successor in the Oxford chair, who ranged over a far wider field in time and place, is weakest where Stubbs is strongest, namely in the study of institutions, but the *History of the Norman Conquest*, followed by *The Reign of William*

Rufus, is a spirited political narrative. He cared little about law, economic conditions and culture, had no taste for manuscripts and no knowledge of palæography. The chapter on Domesday Book is superficial, Godwin and Harold are over-praised, and his pages breathe a strident Teutonism. If Stubbs is a greater Waitz, Freeman is a lesser Giesebrecht. More popular though less erudite than either of them was Green, the third and youngest member of the Oxford School, whose *Short History of the English People*, published in 1874, presented the English-speaking world with the first coherent and readable summary of its past. The hero of the book, as the title implies, was the people; only thus could English history be conceived and presented as a whole. No less admirable than the design was the execution. By skilful grouping of periods, the omission of burdensome detail, a vivid style, and sympathy with every aspect of life, he reconstructed the growth of the nation within the compass of a single volume. Emphasis was transferred from dynasties and wars to internal development, above all the growth of political and religious liberty.

In the field of mediæval studies the mantle of Stubbs fell on a lawyer of genius. The *History of English Law* by Pollock and Maitland, published in 1895, was mainly the work of the latter. Anglo-Saxon law was pronounced to be almost purely Germanic: whatever was Roman in the early documents was ecclesiastical. Not till the Norman Conquest did Roman elements in any quantity filter in, and even then the Germanic foundation remained. The greater part of the two massive volumes is devoted to Angevin law, and the survey ends with Edward I, since whom legal life has been continuous. *Domesday Book and Beyond* confirmed Vinogradoff's view of the complexity of pre-Norman society, equidistant from the older conception of the free village community dear to Germanist historians and from the Romanist interpretation impressively presented in Seebohm's *English Village Community*. A second monograph, *Township and Borough*, revealed the wide variety of origin and privileges. In a third he argued from his study of a manual by Lyndwood, an official of the Archbishop of Canterbury, completed in 1433, that England was as much subject to Canon Law as any other country. The explanation of the working of mediæval institutions was

continued in the publications of the Selden Society, founded
by Maitland in 1887, in Tout's comprehensive analysis of the
administrative machinery of the state, and in Tait's studies of the
early phases of town government.   No works written in the first
half of the twentieth century on mediæval England surpass in
importance Stenton's survey of the Anglo-Saxon centuries and
Powicke's volumes on the reign of Henry III.   For the later
centuries we gratefully resort to Holdsworth's monumental
History of English Law.

While Stubbs was inaugurating the serious study of the
Middle Ages, Gardiner narrated the most controversial period of
English history with unruffled serenity.   Forty years of research
in public and private archives went to his seventeen volumes on
the years 1603–56, when death interrupted the work almost
within sight of his goal at the Restoration.   Though he never
doubted that the policy of James I and Charles I deserved to fail,
he is gentler to these rulers than his Whig predecessors, who
forgot that both sides could appeal to tradition.   The chief error
of the first two Stuarts and Strafford was their failure to recognise
that England's middle class was rapidly growing up and that
the system of personal government which had satisfied Tudor
England was out of date.   Moreover, if James was tactless,
Charles was impossible, and his duplicity hurried him towards the
abyss.   Cromwell's character, lofty ideals and relative moderation receive higher praise than his statesmanship.   Gardiner's
task of reconstructing the history of the seventeenth century
was continued in the same impartial spirit and with the same
encyclopædic knowledge by Firth.

While Gardiner's main interest was in domestic affairs, Seeley, a
miniature Ranke, surveyed the European system as a whole.
His largest work, *Life and Times of Stein*, applauded the gallant
struggle of Prussian nationalism against the universal state.   The
Cambridge lectures on *The Expansion of England* presented the
British Empire as a by-product of the age-long struggle with
France.   The unfinished *Growth of British Policy* analysed the
achievement of Elizabeth, Cromwell and William III who made
England a Great Power.   More interested in diplomacy than in
institutions, individuals, or party strife, he believed that the
destiny of a state depended mainly on its place in the world.

The story of the eighteenth century was authoritatively told for the first time by the fifth Earl Stanhope, who utilised his family archives at Chevening and compiled the first adequate record of the younger Pitt. Lecky's *History of England in the Eighteenth Century*, a less pedestrian performance, provides little more than a sketch till the accession of George III and ends with the outbreak of the great war in 1793. The narrative of the conflict with the American colonies is a triumph of impartiality. In a later edition the Irish chapters, the most valuable portion of the whole work, were disentangled from the English. Himself an Irish Unionist, Lecky is proud of the healthy nationalism of the Grattan Parliament, which, though a Protestant body, was friendly to the Catholics and loyal to the English crown. Though convinced that the rebellion of 1798 rendered union inevitable, he condemns the methods by which it was engineered. The same high standard is attained in Keith Feiling's record of the early Tories, Winston Churchill's spirited eulogy of his famous ancestor, Trevelyan's panoramic survey of the age of Anne, Basil Williams' studies of Stanhope and Carteret, Newcastle and Chatham, Lord Ilchester's biography of Henry Fox, Namier's analysis of the political system of George III, Fitzmaurice's defence of his unpopular ancestor Shelburne, Thompson's volumes on the French Revolution, and the biographies of Pitt and Napoleon by Holland Rose. The political history of the nineteenth century, conveniently summarised by Spencer Walpole, is best studied in the official biographies of the Prime Ministers, in which England is particularly rich, and in such monographs as those of Webster on Castlereagh, Temperley on Canning, and Seton-Watson on later Victorian diplomacy. The results of a century of research have been presented in the *Cambridge Modern History*, the *Cambridge History of British Foreign Policy* and in the co-operative *Oxford History of England*. Fortescue's immense work on the British Army and Oman's detailed narrative of the Peninsula War are of more than merely military value.

For half a century American readers learned their lessons from Bancroft's *History of the United States*, which appeared in 1834-74, and contained new material from American and foreign archives. The robust Jeffersonian democrat rejoices in the triumphs of political and religious liberty achieved by his countrymen under inspired leadership. The larger portion is devoted to the quarrel with England, who is charged with making war on human freedom. At the age of eighty-two he added two volumes on the making of the constitution. His picture of a colonial golden age was challenged by Hildreth and in a later generation by Osgood, Andrews, Beer and James Truslow Adams. The most valuable work on the early presidencies is the elaborate study of Jefferson and Madison by Henry Adams. Lincoln's story was first told in detail in the vast compilation by his secretaries, Nicolay and John Hay, and the slavery struggle was described at length by James Ford Rhodes. Bancroft has been superseded by Channing, and S. E. Morison's shorter *History of the United States* illustrates the welcome diminution of the national complacency and traditional anglophobia in the text-books.

American scholars have also played their part in exploring the fortunes of other lands. Washington Irving aroused widespread interest in Spain and prepared the way for the solid works of Prescott and, in our own time, of Merriman on the spacious days of Ferdinand and Isabella, Charles V and Philip II. Motley's pæan to the Dutch patriots who threw off the hated yoke of Spain is marred by his interpretation of a national uprising as primarily a Protestant revolt, and much of his work has had to be done again. Less exciting but of more enduring value was Parkman's narrative of the colonisation of Canada by the French and its conquest by England in the Seven Years War. Admiral Mahan's *Influence of Sea Power on History, 1660–1783*, published in 1889, set all the world thinking and encouraged William II to build a formidable fleet. His subsequent volumes on the revolutionary and Napoleonic wars and on Nelson presented the gigantic drama as primarily a struggle for the control of the sea. A fourth work on the Anglo-American war of 1812 describes a by-product of the conflict with Napoleon. A fifth, a biography of Farragut, emphasised the importance of naval power in the American civil war. Though not the earliest student of naval history, Mahan was the first to emphasise its wider bearings. Among the achievements of scholars in the smaller countries may be noted Kluchevsky's *History of Russia*, the writings of Fruin and Geyl on Dutch history, the brilliant *Histoire de Belgique* by Henri

Pirenne, Heckscher's elaborate study of Mercantilism, and Villayi's contributions to the history of Florence.

The Revelation of the Ancient World. Among the sensational events of the nineteenth century was the resurrection of the ancient East. We now realise that classical Greece and Rome, far from standing near the beginning of recorded history, were the heirs of mature civilisations. The ancient world has ceased to be merely the vestibule to Christian Europe. The discovery of the Rosetta Stone, with an inscription in three languages, enabled Champollion to decipher Egyptian hiero-glyphics. His interpretation was confirmed by Lepsius, who was sent to Egypt in 1842 by the Prussian government and whose sumptuous *Monuments of Egypt and Ethiopia* enshrined the results of the mission. His subsequent *Chronology of the Egyptians* laid the foundations for an intelligible history of the valley of the Nile. A third pioneer was Mariette, the most successful of diggers and the first in the field. A fourth was Maspero, excavator, philo-logist, historian. A fifth was Flinders Petrie, founder of the Egyptian Exploration Fund, who devoted his long life to excavation. The results of a century of work were summarised by Eduard Meyer in his comprehensive *History of Antiquity*, by the American Breasted, by Erman, the successor of Lepsius at Berlin, and, most recently, by Dr. Margaret Murray in *The Splendour that was Egypt*. The first glimpses of pre-dynastic Egypt came from de Morgan's examination of primitive cemeteries. No single event in the annals of Egyptology since the finding of the Rosetta Stone compares in importance with the discovery of the dazzling treasures in Tutankhamen's tomb.

No less sensational was the discovery of Babylonian civilisation. The riddle of cuneiform was guessed by Rawlinson from a proclamation by Darius cut on the side of a precipitous rock 300 feet above the plain at Behistun. Imposing monuments of Assyrian civilisation were brought to light by Botta, a French consul, who discovered the palace of Sargon at Khorsabad, near Mosul, and by Layard, who unearthed Koujunik, the ancient Nineveh. The revelation of the earlier civilisation of Babylonia began a little later when de Sarzec, French vice-consul at Basrah, uncovered Tello, the ancient Lagash, and proved that a large part of Babylonian culture, including the art of writing, was inherited from the Sumerians. The most arresting discovery ever made in Babylonia is the elaborate code of Hammurabi, unearthed by de Morgan at Susa in 1901. Still later came the recovery of an advanced civilisation in Crete in the second and third millennia B.C. by Arthur Evans, who purchased the site at Knossus, started excavations in 1900, and described the results in his superbly illustrated volumes, *The Palace of Minos*. The discovery of early graves at Ur in Southern Mesopotamia, and the exploration of the Hittite capitals at Boghazkeui and Carchemish and of the Canaanite city of Ugarit, filled gaps in our knowledge of the Ancient East. The Minoan script, like Hittite and Etruscan, still baffles philologists.

During the last quarter of the nineteenth century the discoveries of Schliemann at Troy, Mycenæ and Tiryns revolutionised the approach to the early history of Greece. The enthusiastic amateur confused the different historical strata at Troy, and experts smiled at his identifications of the objects and buildings mentioned in the *Iliad*; but when he died in 1890 he had revealed Mycenæan civilisation. He possessed both the zeal and the limitations of the pioneer, and much of his work had to be done again by Dörpfeld. The German excavations at Olympia brought the matchless Hermes of Praxiteles to light, and Aristotle's treatise, *The Constitution of Athens*, was published by Kenyon in 1891. The exploration of sites, the recovery of numberless objects of art, the growing mass of inscriptions and papyri, and the reconstruction of the civilisations of the ancient East encouraged fresh attempts to write the history of Greece. Grote's vigorous defence of Athenian democracy was out of date, and Curtius was less interested in politics than in culture. Scholarly surveys of Greek civilisation were supplied by Holm and Bury. Beloch, following the lead of Droysen, rendered full justice to the Hellenistic era, and Tarn sympathetically expounded the ideology of Alexander the Great. Eduard Meyer's volumes on Greece, which form the latter portion of his *History of Antiquity*, illustrate its connexion with other Mediterranean peoples. Freeman's last work described the flourishing Greek colonies in Sicily. Various aspects of Greek life and thought

have been illuminated by generations of scholars from Zeller and
Rohde to Wilamowitz and Werner Jaeger, Gilbert Murray,
Farnell and Cook.   Zimmern's *The Greek Commonwealth* depicts
Athens at the height of her power and fame.

The history of Roman studies since Niebuhr is largely the
record of a single man.   After prolonged wanderings in Italy,
Mommsen produced a history of the Roman Republic which,
like Ranke's *History of the Popes*, took the world by storm; its
impeccable scholarship appealed to the expert and its throbbing
vitality to the general reader.   No portion is so thrilling as the
struggle of Cæsar with his enemies, but none aroused so much
criticism.   Pompey, Cicero and Cato are castigated, while Cæsar
dominates the stage, radiant, peerless, the saviour of society.
The overthrow of the republic is applauded on the ground that
it deserved to die.   Mommsen never repeated his early success,
but his most valuable writings were still to come.   In 1853 the
Prussian Academy commissioned him to edit a *corpus* of Latin
inscriptions, twenty volumes of which—nearly half his own work
—appeared during his life.   No enterprise has been so fruitful
for Roman studies, for it illuminated every department of public
and private affairs.   Solid treatises on chronology, the coinage,
criminal law, and the provinces followed, but the *Staatsrecht* was
justly regarded by the author as his crowning achievement.   The
most original portion is the analysis of the Principate, which, he
argued, was neither empire nor monarchy but a dyarchy, a skilful
compromise between the old oligarchy and the absolutism of
Cæsar.   Augustus, its architect, divided power between the
princeps, who was not hereditary, and the senate: not till
Diocletian and Constantine did unqualified absolutism prevail.
Rome before Mommsen was like modern Europe before Ranke:
he found it of brick and left it of marble.   No work on the
Empire comparable to his survey of the republic exists, but
Gardhausen's *Augustus*, Bury's picture of the later centuries,
Camille Jullian's monumental history of Roman Gaul, and
Haverfield's writings on Roman Britain are of outstanding merit.
Gaetano de Sanctis' great *Storia dei Romani* has renewed the
discussion on the credibility of early Roman history.   Ferrero's
Greatness and Decline of Rome envisaged the critical period of
Roman history as a struggle of economic forces rather than of

party chiefs. The rich harvest of modern research has been garnered in the *Cambridge Ancient History*.

The story of the Byzantine Empire, so ignorantly undervalued by Gibbon, may be regarded both as an epilogue to the Græco-Roman world and as a chapter of mediæval history. Its rehabilitation began with Finlay and was continued by Krumbacher, Bréhier, Bury, Diehl, Vasiliev, Schlumberger, Ernst Stein, Norman Baynes, Steven Runciman, and other pundits of the *Byzantinische Zeitschrift*. Its services to the preservation of European culture are now fully recognised. Just as in its early days it kept Arabs out of eastern Europe, so in later times it barred the road to the Turks. Though it finally succumbed to their onslaught, it held the fort until emissaries carrying Greek learning migrated to Italy and planted the seeds of the Renaissance. The fruits of a century of Byzantine studies are summarised in the fourth volume of the *Cambridge Mediæval History*.

The Jews and the Christian Church. The recovery of the civilisations of the Ancient East stimulated the critical study of the Jewish scriptures. The composite character of the Pentateuch had been recognised in the eighteenth century, but the first comprehensive narrative of the Jewish people was furnished by Ewald in the middle of the nineteenth century. A generation later Wellhausen argued—as Vatke and Graf, Reuss and Kuenen had guessed—that the priestly code was composed after the Exile and that the Mosaic law was the starting-point, not of the history of ancient Israel, but of Judaism. His interpretation was confirmed by Robertson Smith, Professor of Arabic at Cambridge, who related Hebrew religion to the beliefs and practices of other branches of the Semitic family. Renan initiated a *corpus* of Semitic inscriptions, and discoveries in the valleys of the Tigris and the Nile supplemented the historical books of the Old Testament. We can now trace Palestine far back into the third millennium and observe the cave-dwellers being gradually dispossessed by Semite invaders. Though tradition is no longer treated as sacrosanct, and the Jewish scriptures are now studied like any other book, the uniqueness of the Prophets as the founders of monotheism remains unchallenged.

The critical approach to church history proved more difficult.

Mosheim, professor at Göttingen in the middle of the eighteenth century, wrote the first survey which belongs to the modern world, envisaging the Christian Church primarily as a great institution. A deeper note was struck by Neander, a converted Jew who loved the Fathers and the saints, in his *History of the Christian Church* which began to appear in 1825. As a disciple of Schleiermacher he was less interested in dogma or institutions than in the Christian life. Less edifying but far more influential were the writings and lectures of Baur, whose appointment to the Chair of Historical Theology at Tübingen in 1826 inaugurated the brief reign of the Tübingen school. As a disciple of Hegel he introduced the conception of growth into the sphere of dogma; his business was less with men, institutions and events than with the evolution of thought. The idea of the Resurrection, he declared, was the 'basis of the Christian faith'; whether it occurred was a question beyond the scope of history. Early Christianity, in his view, was dominated by the opposition between the universalism of Paul and the Judaism of Peter. His arbitrary dating of the canonical books in the light of this conflict, relegating the gospels to the second century and challenging the Pauline authorship of all the epistles except the *Romans*, the *Galatians* and the *Corinthians*, has long been rejected.

While Baur devoted his main attention to the apostolic age, his most celebrated pupil attempted to separate the legendary from the historical elements in the gospels and denied the divinity of Christ. The challenge of Strauss led to the more critical examination of the sources which is still in progress. It is agreed that Mark is the earliest of the synoptics, that Matthew and Luke used a common source, that the fourth gospel, which is difficult to date, is rather philosophy than history. Ritschl reduced the antagonism between Peter and Paul to modest dimensions. Experts now accept more of the Pauline epistles than Baur, and place the first three gospels and the Acts in the later decades of the first century. The necessity of studying the soil out of which Christianity grew has been recognised, and Schürer, Hausrath and Pfleiderer reconstructed the world into which Christ was born. The debt of the Early Church to Greece was brilliantly assessed by Hatch; Weizsäcker's masterpiece, *The Apostolic Age*, visualised the life and ideas of the early communities; Lightfoot's edition of the Early Fathers analysed Christian organisation in the second century; the treasures of the Roman catacombs were explored by de Rossi; Harnack won fame by his *History of Dogma*, his *Expansion of Christianity*, and his survey of early Christian literature. Renan's brilliant *Origines du Christianisme* enjoyed more popularity than authority. Three Catholic scholars of the first rank deserve mention: Döllinger, the leading antagonist of the ultramontanism which culminated in the Vatican decrees of 1870; Hefele, who devoted his life to the church councils; and Duchesne, whose *History of the Early Church* was placed on the Index. Caspar's torso on the early Papacy and Inge's *Philosophy of Plotinus* are acknowledged masterpieces.

Milman's *History of Latin Christianity* relieved England of Newman's reproach that she possessed no ecclesiastical historian except Gibbon. More interested in action than in thought or feeling, the Dean of St. Paul's portrayed the Church rather as an institution than an influence on the individual life. Yet he recognised the greatness of certain popes and the immense contribution of monasticism and the Mediæval Church to Western civilisation. Such detachment is rare either in Catholic or Protestant circles. There is a gulf between such works of edification as Montalembert's *Monks of the West* and the darker tints of Coulton and Henry Charles Lea, whose learned histories of the Inquisition and sacerdotal celibacy make repulsive reading. The opening of most of the treasures of the Vatican archives by Leo XIII in 1881 supplied mediævalists with material for numberless monographs. No other country can boast of such a national monument as Hauck's survey of the German mediæval Church. Gregorovius' large-scale *History of the City of Rome in the Middle Ages*, Carlyle's six volumes on mediæval political theory, and Bryce's *Holy Roman Empire* link up the ancient and the modern world. The story of the Crusades has been explored by Röhricht and more recently by René Grousset and Steven Runciman.

It is natural that Protestants and Catholics should clash over the Reformation, though a few scholars have tried to stand above the battle. The serene neutrality of Bishop Creighton's story of the fifteenth century and Renaissance Popes stirred Acton, a stern Catholic moralist, to indignation. Luther remains the most controversial figure in church history. Every available missile has been hurled at him by Janssen, Grisar and Denifle, and no Catholic approach to the Reformation is so dispassionate as that of the Protestant Kawerau. No single work on the sixteenth century has added so much to our knowledge as Pastor's gigantic *History of the Popes*, based on the Vatican archives. The Reformation in England as described from an Anglican standpoint by Dixon, Gairdner and Maynard Smith is a very different story from the older Protestant eulogies of Burnet and Froude; but Cardinal Gasquet's indictment of the Dissolution of the Monasteries swings too far in the opposite direction. Among works of major importance on the religious history of the seventeenth, eighteenth and nineteenth centuries may be mentioned Sainte-Beuve's classical study of Port-Royal, Abbé Brémond's unfinished *Histoire Religieuse de la France*, Ritschl's *History of Pietism*, Reusch's *Index of Forbidden Books*, Dean Church's eye-witness record of the Oxford Movement, and Wilfrid Ward's biographies of Wiseman, Newman and W. G. Ward.

The History of Civilisation. The conception of history has widened till it includes every aspect of life. The influence of nature, geographical exploration, the pressure of economic factors, the origin and transformation of ideas, the contribution of science and art, religion and philosophy, literature and law, the fortunes of the masses, claim our attention no less than the rise and fall of nations, the exploits of supermen, the shaping of institutions, and the quarrels of parties. The first outstanding achievement of *Kulturgeschichte* was Voltaire's *Essai sur les Mœurs*, the second Winckelmann's glowing survey of Greek art. Not till the second half of the nineteenth century, however—owing to the revolutions of 1848, the influence of Marx, the growth of national self-consciousness, the opening of public and private archives, and other causes—was *Kulturgeschichte* systematically pursued. Gustav Freytag's *Pictures from the German Past* was the first best-seller of the type of which Rambaud's *Histoire de la Civilisation Française* and Trevelyan's *English Social History* are familiar examples. The life and thought of the Roman Republic was brilliantly interpreted in Fustel de Coulanges' *La Cité Antique*, of the Empire in the comprehensive surveys of Friedländer, Otto Seeck, and Samuel Dill.

No work in the sphere of *Kulturgeschichte* was so influential and so profound as Burckhardt's *Civilisation of the Renaissance*, published in 1860. His first effort, *The Time of Constantine the Great*, which revealed his capacity for seizing the character of an epoch, impressed the experts, but the second was read all over the world. In the Middle Ages, he declares, man was a member of a class, a corporation, family; society was a hierarchy, tradition supreme. With the Renaissance man discovered himself and became an individual. The fetters of a thousand years were broken and self-realisation became the goal. The complete man, *l'uomo universale*, emerged, combining action, learning and art. These wonderful human plants grew in the soil of the Italian city-states, and the great ladies developed a brilliancy never attained by women before or since. Though Burckhardt recognises the savagery and bestiality by which the age was disfigured, he, like his English counterpart Symonds, hails the Renaissance, brief though it was, as the springtime of the modern world. The chief work of his later years, *History of Greek Civilisation*, based on his lectures at Basle, appeared after his death. If he incurred the charge of being dazzled by Italy's supermen, the greatest of Swiss historians was never carried away by Greece. His fame has risen steadily and his place in the first rank of scholars is secure.

Among other outstanding achievements in *Kulturgeschichte* may be mentioned Lecky's studies of European morals in the early Middle Ages and of the spirit of rationalism in modern times, Vossler's dissertations on Dante, Rashdall's survey of mediæval universities, the interpretation of mediæval political ideas by the Carlyle brothers, Troeltsch's analysis of the social teachings of the Christian churches, Leslie Stephen's *English Thought in the Eighteenth Century*, Dilthey's penetrating monographs on German thought from the Reformation to Schleiermacher and Hegel, Meinecke's *Die Entstehung des Historismus*, and Menendez y Pelayo's learned treatises on Spanish religion and literature. We have begun to explore the dim world of primitive man out of which civilisation grew. The name of Tylor, the founder of anthropology, cannot be omitted from any survey of historical work, for the distinction between history and prehistory is purely arbitrary. To the massive treatises of Frazer—*The Golden Bough, Totemism, Folk-Lore in the Old Testament, Belief in Immortality*, the editions of Pausanias' travels in

17

Greece and Ovid's *Fasti*—we owe more of our understanding of primitive life and thought than to the writings of any other man.

The philosophy of history, so popular in the days of Hegel, Comte and Buckle, has gone out of fashion. The more we learn, the less dogmatic we become. The purpose of history, if such there be, is guesswork. To quote Trevelyan, 'philosophy must be brought to history, it cannot be extracted from it'. Yet discussion of the factors which shape its course never flags. Spengler's *Decline of the West*, so widely read after the First World War, revived the old theory of cycles, each civilisation passing through spring, summer, autumn and winter. More illuminating and more impressive is Toynbee's panorama of the rise and fall of civilisations, *A Study of History*, in which every kind of determinism is rejected and the master-key is sought in the formula of challenge and response. Croce interprets the story of mankind as above all an instinctive striving for liberty. More popular, if not more convincing, is the glib Marxian interpretation which finds the answer to the riddle in the satisfaction of material needs and the fierce struggle of classes resulting from the inequality of possessions. Despite the crudities of the doctrine, history has profited by the ever-increasing attention to economic questions, for the central figure in the human drama is the common man who, though he does not live by bread alone, cannot live without it. No country has more to show in this field than England, with Thorold Rogers, Cunningham and Ashley as the pioneers, the Webbs and the Hammonds, Clapham, George Unwin, Tawney and Eileen Power carrying on the torch. In Germany, Roscher founded the historical school of economics of which Schmoller became the high priest, and Max Weber's lectures at Heidelberg inspired generations of students. Russian scholars, among them Rostovtseff with his masterpieces on the economic life of the classical world, and Kovalevsky with his survey of recent centuries, have done their share. Beyond the Atlantic, Charles Beard has related the growth of American civilisation to the exploration and organisation of an empty continent. If the purpose of history remains a riddle, the duty of every scholar is clear enough: it is to make some modest contribution to the task of recovering, recording and interpreting the life of the human race.

4

THE STUDY OF THE FRENCH REVOLUTION.

THE French Revolution is the most important event in the life of modern Europe. Herder compared it to the Reformation and the rise of Christianity, and it deserves to be ranked with those two great movements in history. Like them, it destroyed many landmarks of the world in which generations of men had passed their lives; like them it was a religion, with its doctrines, its apostles, and its martyrs. It brought on the stage of human affairs forces which have moulded the actions of men ever since and have taken a permanent place among the formative influences of civilisation. As Christianity taught that man was a spiritual being, and the Reformation proclaimed that every soul must find its own way to God, so the French Revolution asserted the equality of men, and declared each one of them, regardless of birth, colour, or creed, to be possessed of inalienable rights.

The universal significance of the event was recognised both by those who took part in it and by those who watched it from afar. The orators on the Seine were fully conscious that the eyes of the world were upon them. 'Your laws will be the laws of Europe if you are worthy of them,' declared Mirabeau to the Constituent Assembly; 'the Revolution will make the round of the globe.' 'Whoever regards this Revolution as exclusively French,' echoed Mallet du Pan, 'is incapable of pronouncing judgment upon it.' 'The French Revolution,' wrote Gentz in 1794, 'is one of those events which belong to the whole human race. It is of such dimensions that it is hardly permissible to occupy oneself with any subordinate interest, of such magnitude that posterity will eagerly inquire how contemporaries of every country thought and felt about it, how they argued and how they acted.' Friends and foes of the 'principles of '89' were at one in emphasising the

power of its appeal.   Men like Burke and Tom Paine, Kant and
Joseph de Maistre, who agreed in nothing else, were convinced
that the problems it raised concerned humanity as a whole.[1]

I

Historians of every school have sought its roots in the generations and, indeed, the centuries which preceded it.   Louis Blanc
declared that no man could date its beginning, since all nations
had contributed to produce it.   'All the revolts of the past
unite and lose themselves in it, like rivers in the sea.   It is the
glory of France to have performed the work of the human race
at the price of her own blood.'   The socialist historian commences
his long-winded narrative with Hus, but this is to pile a needless
burden on our backs.   We must, however, at the outset form a
clear conception of the life of the French people and the methods
of government under the monarchical system elaborated by
Richelieu and Louis XIV.   This should be obtained from the
later volumes of Lavisse's co-operative *Histoire de France*.

The structure of the *Ancien Régime* in the last century of its
existence was analysed for the first time by Tocqueville's *L'Ancien
Régime et la Révolution*, published in 1855.   The author described
his work as a study, not a history, but it threw more light on the
coming of the Revolution than any of the histories that had
appeared and inaugurated the era of documentary research.   The
Revolution itself had exerted such fascination that it had occurred
to no one to ascertain its relation to the régime which it superseded.
Realising the necessity of exploring the provincial archives,
Tocqueville made a prolonged stay at Tours, where he found a
complete collection of the records and correspondence of the
Intendants.   He pursued his researches in his native Normandy
and in Languedoc, studying the decrees of the Provincial
Parlements and the registers of the parishes, and thus gradually

---

[1] Brief bibliographical surveys are provided in an appendix to Lord Acton's
Lectures on the French Revolution; chapter thirteen of *History and Historians in the
Nineteenth Century* by G. P. Gooch; the Introduction to Thompson's *Life of Robe-
spierre*, vol. i; Crane Brinton's *A Decade of Revolution*; and Cobban, *The Causes of
the French Revolution: A Course of Reading* (Historical Association, 1946).   *Some
Historians of Modern Europe*, edited by Bernadotte E. Schmitt, contains studies of
Aulard, Mathiez and Sée.

acquired a clear conception of the classes of society, the nature and extent of feudal rights, the central and local administration. His results were as unexpected as they were irrefutable. 'As I advanced I was surprised to find at every moment traits which meet us in France to-day. I discovered a mass of sentiments and habits which I had thought were the offspring of the Revolution.'

The centralised administration of the nineteenth century proved to be an inheritance from the *Ancien Régime*. France had been subject to three governments: the King and his ministers, working through the Intendants; the feudal powers and jurisdictions; and finally the provincial institutions. Of these the first were by far the strongest; the feudal powers were weak, and the provincial institutions were ghosts of their former selves except in Brittany and Languedoc. Feudalism as a political system, aristocracy as a political force, had disappeared; the feudal privileges which remained appeared all the more odious because the system of which they formed a part was dead. 'Some good people have endeavoured to rehabilitate the *Ancien Régime*. I judge it by the sentiments it inspired in those who lived under it and destroyed it. I see that all through the Revolution, cruel as it was, hatred of the old régime outweighed all other hates, and that during the perilous vicissitudes of the last sixty years the fear of its return has outweighed all other fears. That is enough for me.' The verdict is the more impressive since the writer was neither a radical nor a socialist but a liberal conservative.

Tocqueville, declared Scherer, accomplished for the Revolution what Lyell had done for the history of our planet: he destroyed the cataclysmic theory and substituted the slow action of secular causes. Where men had seen a radical contradiction between the Monarchy and the Revolution, he saw a logical continuation. The *Ancien Régime* was strongly centralised: the Revolution still further centralised the administration. The *Ancien Régime* had destroyed the greater part of feudalism: the Revolution destroyed the rest. The driving force of the Revolution was equality of rights: it was equality before the law which the Monarchy had been striving to establish in its long struggle with feudalism. The fruitful researches of Tocqueville inspired generations of students, Russians included, to reconstruct the administrative machinery, the system of land tenure, and the social pattern of eighteenth-century France. Of special importance are the writings of Albert Babeau on the province, the town and the village. Arthur Young's invaluable *Travels in France in 1787-1789*, should be read in the excellent editions of Constantia Maxwell or Henri Sée. No French scholar since Tocqueville has thrown so much light on feudal burdens and rural conditions under the *Ancien Régime* as the latter, who summarised his conclusions in a valuable little book *La France Economique et Sociale au XVIII Siècle*, published in 1925. Conditions, he declares, were never good, but they varied greatly in different districts and also within each of the main classes of society.

The Revolution was due to the union of concrete grievances, which were actually worse in many other parts of the Continent, with an intellectual ferment which made the France of Louis XV and XVI the leader of European thought. John Morley's studies of Voltaire, Rousseau, Diderot and the Encyclopædists provided English readers with a vivid picture of the group of men who encouraged the French bourgeoisie to think, to criticise, and to rebel. Sorel's little volume on Montesquieu and Higgs' study of the Physiocrats, the dominant school of economists, are equally indispensable. Rocquain's *L'Esprit Révolutionnaire avant la Révolution*, Kingsley Martin's *French Liberal Thought in the Eighteenth Century*, and Roustan's *Pioneers of the French Revolution*, which exaggerates the political influence of the *Philosophes*, are useful. The long chapter entitled 'Causes of the French Revolution' in the sixth volume of Lecky's *History of England in the Eighteenth Century* should not be overlooked. The most satisfying account of the attempts to avert a catastrophe by financial reform is provided in Ségur's *Au Couchant de la Monarchie*, one of the classics of French historical literature. The first volume deals with Turgot, whose noble aims during two years' tenure of office are gratefully recognised but whose hasty methods are condemned. The second portrays the five years' rule of his successor, Necker, who aimed at less sweeping changes, but whose endeavours to render France solvent were shipwrecked on the demands of the American war. The commanding figure of Turgot was revealed to English readers by John Morley, whose essay in the second volume of his *Miscellanies* still retains its appeal. All—and perhaps more than all—that can be fairly said for the *Ancien Régime* in its later phases may be found in Funck-Brentano's *L'Ancien Régime en France*, which presents a people pulsing with energy, rapidly increasing in numbers, 'that vigorous, magnificent nation which will make the Revolution and supply the victorious volunteers reared in the strong and healthy habits of the eighteenth century.' The Revolution—brutal, terrible, splendid—destroyed much that was good as well as much that deserved to die. Local groups, traditions, franchises and institutions gave place to a centralised bureaucratic state. The author minimises the sufferings and frustrations of the people and stresses the popular character of the Monarchy, but he rightly reminds us that thought was free and criticism unrestrained. Lady Blennerhassett's full-length study of Mme de Staël connects the last phase of the *Ancien Régime* with the Revolution and the Empire.

II

Mignet's concise and lucid narrative, published in 1824, was the first book to present the Revolution as the story of a connected series of events, organically related to the periods which preceded and followed it. Instead of closing with Thermidor, or the establishment of the Directory, or Brumaire, as most historians have done, he brings the narrative down to the fall of Napoleon, thus presenting the story of twenty-five years as a single drama of disturbance. The printed material at his disposal was very limited and he made no attempt at research, but many of the actors were still alive and he made good use of what he was told. Though in general sympathy with the Revolution, he was the least emotional of men, and his cool narrative, translated into many languages, was a boon to readers for a couple of generations. The prolix narrative of his lifelong friend Thiers is of much less analytical value, but it contains material derived from surviving eyewitnesses. Both books were missiles in the campaign of the Constitutional Royalists against the ultra-royalism of the restored Bourbon Monarchy and were heralds of the Revolution of 1830.

Carlyle's immortal work, published in 1837, which should be read in C. R. Fletcher's or Holland Rose's edition, revealed the greatest event in modern history to the English-speaking world. By a supreme effort of creative imagination he succeeded in rendering the vision as real to his readers as it was to himself. If Mignet's book may be compared to an academic lecture, that of Carlyle is at once a dramatic performance and a sermon. The storming of the Bastille, the oath in the Tennis Court, the women's raid on Versailles, the Fête of the Federation, the flight to Varennes, the trial and death of the King, the Girondins and Danton, the moving tragedy of Charlotte Corday, the fall of Robespierre—these pageants we carry with us through life. No writer except Michelet has approached him in the power of rendering the atmosphere of hope and horror, of tense passion and animal fury. No less remarkable is his insight into the character of the leading actors. Though misconceiving the Girondins, like most other writers before Biré, he drew portraits of Louis and Marie Antoinette, Mirabeau and Lafayette, Danton, Robespierre, and Marat, which require little correction. The deficiencies of his epic are as conspicuous as its merits. His knowledge of the period was far more limited than that of Croker, whose hard-hitting Tory *Essays on the Early Period of the French Revolution*, reprinted from the *Quarterly Review* in 1857, utilised his priceless collection of 48,000 pamphlets which have found a home in the British Museum. Carlyle took the memoirs of the actors at their face-value. The relations of France with Europe are neglected. The provinces are forgotten. The Revolution is conceived as the Day of Judgment, a huge bonfire of feudal lumber and of institutions which had outlived their time. That it inherited many principles and tendencies of the *Ancien Régime*, that constructive work of a permanent character was accomplished, that its two main watchwords, equality and the sovereignty of the people, were to mould the thought and action of the nineteenth century, was beyond his grasp. His literary triumph frightened British scholars off the field, and it was not till half a century later that Morse Stephens summarised the researches of French scholars. The chief novelty of his book, which breathes an ardent sympathy with the revolutionists, was that he traced the course of the Revolution in the provinces and presented it as a nation-wide experience; but after bringing his story down to 1793 he migrated to the United States, and the expected third volume never appeared.

The two middle decades of the century contributed little of importance except the forty volumes of the *Histoire Parlementaire de la Révolution Française, ou Journal des Assemblées Nationales, 1789-1815*, edited by Buchez and Roux, which contained material not easily accessible elsewhere. Lamartine's rhapsodical *Histoire des Girondins*, the most eloquent and the most worthless of the large-scale works on the period, depicted them, without the slightest justification, as high-souled idealists who went down before the brutal assault of the men of blood and iron. The twelve-volume narrative of Louis Blanc, though embodying a good deal of research, was the work of a publicist who employed history to illustrate his socialist and republican convictions. The seven volumes of Michelet, the Victor Hugo of the historical world, were superior to anything written in France since Mignet, and may still be read with profit. They embodied material which perished when the Hôtel de Ville was burned by the Communists in 1871, and he had learned much from his father who had lived through it all; but they formed part of the campaign waged by an emotional genius against the *Ancien Régime* and the Church to which he devoted the second half of his life. Like Carlyle he pities the masses, but, unlike Carlyle, he glorifies their instinctive goodness and wisdom, and acquits them of complicity in the organisation of the September Massacres. No famous historian has possessed less of the judicial temper.

During the Second Empire it was natural that attention should be focused on Napoleon, and it was not till the establishment of the Third Republic that the Revolution became the most favoured field of French historical research. The most resounding attack since the days of Burke was delivered by Taine. While his volume on the *Ancien Régime*, published in 1878, won wide approval for its literary brilliance and its relatively balanced attitude, its three successors aroused enthusiasm in royalist and Catholic circles and indignation among radical Republicans. That there was desperate need for reform is admitted, but it was carried out in the wrong spirit. Taine, like Burke, was a believer in continuity and evolution, an enemy of *l'esprit classique*. In

politics England, the land of compromise and moderation, was
his spiritual home.   He brushes aside the traditional distinction
between the principles of 1789 and the principles of 1793.   When
Malouet was asked when the Terror began, he replied, 'On
July 14, 1789.'   Taine shared his opinion.   The 'Golden Dawn'
never existed;   moderate men were never at the helm;   sound
principles never prevailed;   bloodshed and rapine started at once.
It was more than a revolution: it was a dissolution.   The
Revolution was in essence a transfer of property.   'That is its
permanent force, its primary motive, its historical meaning.'
He discovered a good deal of evidence in the archives on the
burning of châteaux in the summer of 1789, but his picture of
France rushing headlong into anarchy is a gross exaggeration.
The *Ancien Régime* collapsed in thousands of villages without
disturbance or regret.

No less unconvincing were the second and third volumes,
devoted to the Jacobins, whom he depicts as half-crazy
doctrinaires, the slaves of abstract theory, thirsting for blood and
revelling in destruction.   Taine's Jacobins are the nightmare of
a sensitive philosopher who had lived through the Commune
and never recovered from the shock.   He charges them with
blindness to the facts around them, but he himself seems blind
to influences which shaped their course.   He depicts them as the
ill-favoured children of Rousseau and the *Philosophes*, nurtured
on the flatulent doctrines of natural rights, learning nothing and
forgetting nothing, whereas they were all monarchists in the early
years of the Revolution.   The *Émigrés* on the Rhine, the ceaseless
intrigues of the Court with foreign Powers, the flight to Varennes,
the hostile armies massed on the frontier a few days' march from
the capital, the savage threats of the Brunswick Manifesto, the
rebellion in the Vendée—these tremendous factors, without which
the Terror is unintelligible, are left virtually unnoticed.   Many
of the acts of the Constituent, the Legislative, and the Convention
were hideously cruel and tragically unwise, but reasons can be
assigned for them independently of any philosophy.   We should
bear continually in mind the warning of Acton: 'The Revolution
will never be intelligibly known to us till we discover its conformity to the common law, and recognise that it is not utterly
singular and exceptional, that other scenes have been as horrible

as these, and many men as bad.' Taine's slipshod methods of research have been sharply criticised, above all his arbitrary selection of evidence from different periods to prove a thesis and his reliance on memoirs sometimes compiled long after the event. In his *Taine, historien de la Révolution Française*, Aulard argued that the book is virtually worthless for the purposes of history, but this is an exaggeration. Augustin Cochin, a Catholic writer, in *La Crise de l'Histoire révolutionnaire*, replied to the attack and reiterated the thesis that the Jacobins were indeed fanatical doctrinaires who planned the Terror and trampled underfoot the traditional values of Western Christendom. Taine, the founder of the anti-revolutionary school, may still be consulted by advanced students as an antidote to the hardly less uncritical pæans which the great upheaval continues to inspire; but as a guide for the uninitiated he is as dangerous as Michelet himself.

Taine's volumes were missiles hurled against the theory and practice of radical democracy. The work of his friend Albert Sorel, on the other hand, which was begun a few years later, is as dispassionate as any history of the Revolution by a Frenchman can be. *L'Europe et la Révolution Française* presents a panorama of the conflict between the new France and the old Europe from 1789 to 1815, but the three volumes devoted to Napoleon are far less satisfactory than the first five. His object was to exhibit the Revolution, which appeared to some as the subversion and to others as the regeneration of the world, as the natural result of the history of France and of Europe. While Tocqueville had found the model of its internal policy in the reigns of Louis XIV and Louis XV, Sorel argued that in their foreign policy the revolutionists were equally the direct heirs of the Monarchy. In his monumental *Geschichte der Revolutionszeit 1789–1800* Sybel had been the first to connect the Revolution with the main stream of European history, and to elucidate the Polish and other factors which coloured the self-seeking policy of Prussia, Austria and Russia during its course. Sorel, writing a generation later, enjoyed the advantage of access to a mass of new material, and his book was a far more revealing and far more readable study of the Revolution in its international bearings.

After devoting an admirable preliminary volume to the political methods and ideas of the eighteenth century in various countries and to the decrepitude of France and of feudal Europe, Sorel traces the atmospheric change from the noble principles with which the leaders set out.   He does not scoff at the Declaration of the Rights of Man, but he contests its practical value.   He is fair to the *Émigrés*, distinguishing the early intransigents, who in their blind hatred endeavoured to arm Europe against their fatherland, from the later victims of persecution who fled for their lives.   He comprehends the sentiments of the Court while censuring its policy.   Like Sybel, he ascribes the immediate responsibility for the war to the chauvinism of the Girondins, though the explosive forces of the Revolution and the old instinct for 'the natural frontiers' of the Rhine and the Alps pointed the way.   Yet his sympathies are always with his countrymen, since the integrity of the national territory and the maintenance of the priceless achievements of the Revolution were at stake.   He recognises the intimate connexion between the danger on the frontier and the worst excesses in Paris, but makes no attempt to palliate them.   Rejecting Taine's wholesale indictment, he returns to the sensible tradition of supporting the principles of 1789 and condemning the Terror.   The lights and shadows are evenly distributed.   'Taine,' wrote Hanotaux, who was the friend of both, 'only sees blood dripping from the scaffold; Sorel sees it spread over the battlefield to save the country and to fertilise Europe.'   Though his pages often throw light on the fate of individuals and the struggles of parties, his real theme is France as a Great Power.   'Instead of investigating the human interior,' writes Acton, 'he is on the lookout across the Alps and beyond the Rhine, writing, as it were, from the point of view of the Foreign Office.   He is at his best when his pawns are diplomatists.   In the process of home politics and the development of political ideas he does not surpass those who went before him.'   Mathiez complains that he never understood democracy.   He began his career as an official at the Quai d'Orsay; but even in the field of foreign affairs he does not always tread with equal sureness, and his dealings with British policy fall below his high standard.

  During the interval which separated the earlier and the later portions of Sorel's *magnum opus* the first critical and comprehensive survey of the Revolution was presented in the eighth volume of the *Histoire Générale* edited by Lavisse and Rambaud.

In accordance with the scheme of the work it is the whole revolutionary era which forms its theme; but France occupies as of right the centre of the stage, and the chapters in which Aulard outlines the history of the critical years form its most valuable feature. Though he was to work for decades at his subject, and to publish a vast number of monographs, he never again attempted a narrative of the opening years. His contribution was the first authoritative summary by a scholar who derived much of his knowledge directly from the archives.

While Sorel was calling attention to the international aspects of the great upheaval, two men of rare ability were busy on the history of parties and ideas. The *Histoire Socialiste, 1789-1900*, a co-operative illustrated history of modern France in eleven volumes from the socialist point of view, began to appear in 1901. The first four volumes were contributed by the editor Jaurès—philosopher, statesman, orator, historian—who found time in his crowded life to obtain a singularly wide knowledge of the printed materials and the Press of the revolutionary era. Though its bias is as unblushing as that of Taine, it is a landmark as the first large-scale attempt to understand the economic and social aspects of the mighty struggle and to champion the cause of the Fourth Estate. It should be read in the eight-volume edition of 1922-24, revised by Mathiez, who did little more than correct mistakes and misprints. 'Tout ce qu'a écrit cet évocateur prodigieux est sacré,' writes his admiring friend, who explains that the author as an actor on the public stage was peculiarly fitted to revive the emotions of the revolutionaries. He adds that all previous histories were political, and therefore inadequate. 'The bourgeoisie had tried to make people believe that it was only a political revolution. The proletariat will now know that it was a revolution of property, a social revolution.' Here he agrees with Taine, though one comes to curse, the other to bless.

The note of the work is struck in the Introduction and reverberates through its three thousand pages. 'The key to the French Revolution is the passage from the bourgeois oligarchy to social democracy.' Jaurès begins with a vivid picture of the country in 1789, making full use of the *Cahiers*, and devotes three volumes to the Constituent and Legislative Assemblies; but he is less interested in the fall of the *Ancien Régime* than in the rise of the

Fourth Estate. Socialism is part of democracy, he argues, since it desires to organise the sovereignty of the whole community in the economic as well as in the political sphere; and socialism flows from the Revolution, as he notes 'with passionate joy'. Jaurès was a humane man, and he deplores the violence which accompanied the change, but his heart overflows with gratitude as he contemplates the epic of emancipation. His journey ends at Thermidor, and in taking leave of the actors he gratefully summarises their achievements. 'They affirmed the idea of democracy in all its amplitude. They displayed to the world the first example of a great country governing itself and saving itself with the strength of a whole people. And they gave to France and the world such a prodigious urge towards liberty that, despite reaction and eclipse, it has come to stay.' The student who reaches Jaurès after a long course of political histories will be surprised to find how much his conception of the Revolution is deepened and enlarged by the work of this gifted amateur. If Jaurès is too big a mouthful to swallow, a briefer socialist rendering of the drama may be found in Prince Kropotkin's volume *The Great French Revolution*, in which the instinctive wisdom and virtue of the Fourth Estate are exalted at the expense of the selfish bourgeoisie.

No one has done so much to reveal and expound the history of the Revolution as Aulard. 'In order to understand it,' he declared, 'it is necessary to love it.' A Chair of the History of the French Revolution was founded for him in 1885 by the Municipal Council of Paris, and he held it till his retirement in 1922. He edited the journal, *La Révolution Française*, founded in 1881, from 1887 till his death in 1927, and contributed numberless articles which were reprinted in successive volumes entitled *Études et Leçons sur la Révolution Française*. His chief narrative work, *The Political History of the French Revolution*, published in 1902,[1] bears the subtitle, *Origins and Development of Democracy and the Republic*, and makes no pretence to offer a history of France between 1789 and 1795. He merely glances at the events of the first three years which he had described in the *Histoire Générale*, edited by Lavisse and Rambaud, and has little to say of the Court, finance, economic conditions, diplomacy

---

[1] English translation in four volumes.

and war.   His theme is the evolution and application of the two governing principles of the Revolution—equality and the sovereignty of the people.   The most arresting novelty is the demonstration of the relative conservatism of the men of 1789 and of the late emergence of the republican idea.   No one of note except Brissot and Condorcet clamoured for a republic till the autumn of 1790, and the Legislative Assembly was as monarchical as the Constituent.   The Monarchy was overthrown not by republicans but by the blunders and intrigues of its champions.   The turning-point was the flight to Varennes.

Aulard's second and more controversial thesis is that the Terror was due not to the sway of abstract ideas, but to the necessity of repelling the invaders and of safeguarding the precious reforms already achieved.   The men who believed in the principles of 1789 and were determined to uphold them acted as might have been expected.   The Jacobins were realists, not *idéologues*.   They were the custodians of the Revolution and of the national territory, and against their savagery must be set the supreme achievement that they saved their country both from the return of the *Ancien Régime* and from conquest and spoliation by foreign armies.   Here, however, he presses his argument too far, for by the end of 1793 the worst of the danger on the eastern frontier was over and the Terror raged most fiercely in the spring and summer of 1794.   'I am a respectful and grateful son of the Revolution which has emancipated humanity and science,' writes the historian, who stands for the militant radicalism and the anti-clericalism characteristic of France at the turn of the century. He finds a hero in Danton, the man of iron will and swift decision, yet the real guide of the Revolution was the people itself.   After the decisive constitutional victories of 1789 a rift began between the bourgeoisie and the masses; it was owing to the latter that the Revolution did not stop short with political changes but undertook the championship of the peasant and the artisan. Aulard's book is written with a mastery of the sources that no historian had ever approached, and he renders the evolution of the drama intelligible; but he lacks literary charm and is a frank partisan.   In glorifying the Revolution he is championing the Third Republic.   His dislike of monarchy, feudalism and the Church is only equalled by his gratitude to their destroyers.

His praises have been sung by Georges Belloni in *Aulard,
Historien de la Révolution Française*, published in 1949. Two
years after the appearance of Aulard's epoch-making work the
eighth volume of the *Cambridge Modern History* presented the
first critical and comprehensive survey of the revolutionary
era in the English language. Among the most useful chapters
are those on finance by Henry Higgs and on law by Paul Viollet.

Lord Acton's *Lectures on the French Revolution*, delivered at
Cambridge at the close of the nineteenth century but not published
till 1910, offered a luminous survey of the derivation and significance of the ideas by which it was inspired. The opening lecture
on 'The Heralds of Revolution' is remarkable for the prominence
assigned to Fénelon, 'the first man who saw through the majestic
hypocrisy of the Court and knew that France was on the road to
ruin'. The second, on 'The Influence of America,' is the most
novel and valuable in the book. Acton proceeds to ascribe the
failure of the moderate reformers mainly to the intrigues of the
Court with foreign Powers; for, though the King began as a
friend of reform, he was surrounded by evil advisers, the worst of
whom was the Queen. Of the Declaration of the Rights of Man
he speaks with the enthusiasm of a Liberal idealist. 'It is the
triumphant proclamation of the doctrine that human obligations
are not all assignable to contract or to interest or to force. This
single page of print outweighs libraries and is stronger than all
the armies of Napoleon.' It had, however, one cardinal fault;
it sacrificed liberty to equality, and the theoretical absolutism
of the King was succeeded by the practical absolutism of the
Assembly. The attack on the Church, represented by the Civil
Constitution of the Clergy, was a fatal blunder and turned the
conscientious monarch as well as the majority of the minor clergy
into enemies of the Revolution. The Constituent Assembly was
better than the Legislative, the Legislative superior to the Convention. The reign of violence began when the danger on the
frontier became acute and ended after it was removed. A
despotic executive was inevitable, and the Girondins went down
before the Jacobins, who were worse men and cared still less for
liberty, yet who knew how to defend the fatherland against the
intrigues of the Court with foreign rulers. Despite its horrors
and its crimes, the Revolution was a great effort towards the

emancipation of the common man. Acton was chiefly influenced by Tocqueville, Sorel and Aulard, and no eminent Catholic scholar has found so much to approve in the most exciting drama in modern history.

If Acton's lectures were the most stimulating survey of the course and meaning of the movement attempted in England during the nineteenth century, Madelin's *La Révolution*, published in 1911 as a volume in Funck-Brentano's *Histoire de France racontée à tous*, provided the best introduction for the student which existed at that time in any language. To study the level pages of Madelin—who gratefully describes himself as a pupil of Sorel—after reading the fulminations of Carlyle or Michelet or Taine is to measure the advance that has taken place in our knowledge and interpretation of forces, persons and events. Written in a spirit of almost chilly detachment, distinguished by the usual French clarity of arrangement and furnished with useful bibliographies, the work is as useful to the advanced student as to the apprentice. He approached his theme, he tells us, without any preconceived idea, and he claims that he has rendered justice to all. He realises the strength and justification of the demand for a Constitution in 1789, and he applauds the opening attack on feudal privileges; but he has no enthusiasm for democracy and he vastly prefers the firm hand of his hero Napoleon to the era of domestic strife. He quotes with warm approval the protest of Vandal against a view of the Revolution enshrined in a celebrated phrase of Clemenceau: 'Loin d'être un bloc, la Révolution est peut-être le phénomène le plus complexe qui ait existé. C'est un phénomène le plus essentiellement multiple dans ses causes, dans ses éléments, dans ses mouvements, dans ses conséquences.' A later volume, of which the translation bears the title *The Revolutionaries*, provides a fascinating portrait gallery of the leading actors in the drama, and may be regarded as an appendix to the earlier work.

The lofty standard set by Madelin was followed in the co-operative *Histoire de France contemporaine*, edited by Lavisse in continuation of the *Histoire de France* which brought the story to 1789. The first volume, covering the three opening years of the Revolution, was written by Sagnac, long distinguished as one of the leading authorities on the period, who succeeded

18

Aulard in the Chair of the History of the French Revolution. There are none of the thrills that fascinated our fathers and grandfathers, and indeed there is more analysis than narrative in these tranquil pages. He calmly assesses the strength and weakness of the Declaration of the Rights of Man, which was full of dangers and omissions yet none the less embodied a new religion. The march to Versailles left the King popular, and, given skill and courage, the game was not yet lost. The Constituent Assembly is credited not only with 'an infinite love of the public good' but with a mass of useful reforms. The war of 1792 was inevitable sooner or later, for Europe could hardly tolerate a proselytising France. The author's general sympathy with the Revolution does not prevent him from denouncing the horrors which dishonoured the people, from the taking of the Bastille to the September Massacres and the Terror. In the second volume, continuing the record to Brumaire, Pariset attempts to do justice both to Danton and Robespierre who, though they personified different policies, were both patriots. After the fall of the Girondins in the summer of 1793, he declares, two policies were possible, represented respectively by the two chief Jacobin leaders. Danton desired to reconstitute patriotic unity: despite his failings, his vision was lofty and humane, and he had no wish to identify the Revolution with a few of the elect. Robespierre, on the other hand, believed that reconciliation with Royalists and Moderates would compromise not only the Revolution but the safety of France. No one could make the Directory interesting, but Pariset does his best. The illustrations form an important feature in these handsome quartos, and the bibliographical notes are beyond praise.

The three little volumes in a popular series summarising the history of the Revolution published by Mathiez in 1922, 1924 and 1927, and gathered into a single stout volume in the English translation, differ in several respects from the works of Madelin, Sagnac and Pariset. In the first place the curtain falls on Thermidor. In the second, there are no bibliographies and scarcely any notes, since the book, as the Preface explains, is intended for the general reader. He adds, however, that it is based on many authorities, some of them unpublished; and indeed nobody would challenge the erudition of the scholar who after the death of Aulard was unquestionably the chief French authority on the Revolution. But the most striking difference from his immediate predecessors was the fact that he had a new hero. Aulard's admiration for Danton was known to all the world and readily understood, but the partiality of Mathiez for Robespierre was more paradoxical. The two experts resemble one another in their contempt for the comfortable bourgeoisie; but while the one was a radical, the other was a socialist, and their paths diverged widely when they came to weigh the merits of the rival Jacobin chiefs.

Danton, declares Mathiez disdainfully, was the hired agent of the Royalists; morality, private and public, was his weak point. Robespierre, on the other hand, as Louis Blanc had argued long before, was not only a man of unselfish character but the champion of the weak and the unfortunate, who strove not merely for political liberty but for social justice. He desired to abolish primogeniture and to impose restrictions on inheritance, but he was never a communist. His ideal was not to abolish property but to prevent its abuse. The Girondins were chained to the bourgeois mentality, regarding the populace as unfit for power and the rights of property as sacrosanct. The Jacobins, though no less bourgeois by birth, represented the humbler classes; but the venial Danton lived in style, while his incorruptible rival had no thought but the interest of the Revolution. A great democrat and a great patriot, he raised the Republic from the abyss. The Jacobins were indeed a minority, but a dictatorship was inevitable and so was the Terror. 'They slew that they might not be slain.' France accepted the Terror as the condition of victory, and the victory was won. While other historians of different schools, sickened by the fumes of blood, greet Thermidor with a cheer, Mathiez wrings his hands over the disappearance of the man who struck boldly at the selfish rule of wealth. 'The levelling Republic of his dreams, without rich or poor, received its death-blow. In the person of Robespierre they had slain the democratic Republic for a century.' While Aulard spoke for the Tiers État which made the Revolution of 1789, Mathiez, the Marxist son of a peasant, championed the cause of the manual worker and hailed Robespierre as a pioneer of socialism. Whatever we may think of his Leftish ideology, there can be no question as to the enduring significance of this remarkable book by the founder of the *Société des Études Robespierristes* and the first editor of its organ, *Annales Historiques de la Révolution Française.*

One more synthetic work calls for favourable mention before we pass to the monographs. *La Révolution Française* by Lefebvre, Guyot and Sagnac, published in 1930, forms the thirteenth volume of the *Histoire Générale* edited by Halphen and Sagnac. Like the *Cambridge Modern History* and the *Histoire Générale*, it deals with the life of Europe as a whole as well as with France. Lefebvre, since the death of Mathiez the leading French authority on the Revolution, covers the years 1789–95; Guyot returns to his familiar theme of the Directory, devoting more attention to foreign policy than to domestic events; and Sagnac adds two thoughtful chapters on the constructive work of the Revolution and its influence on European civilisation. All three admire it as a powerful and enduring impulse to the construction of a better social order based on equal rights. In the unending dispute between the partisans of Danton and Robespierre, Lefebvre occupies a middle position, recognising the venality of the one and the comparative disinterestedness of the other, though without sharing the uncritical enthusiasms of Aulard and Mathiez for their respective champions. The men of 1789 were driven further than they intended by the resistance of the aristocracy and the King, for the danger of counter-revolution was real. The bibliographical notes are of special value to advanced students of the revolutionary era in Europe. The best brief popular surveys in English are in Miss Bradby's *A Short History of the French Revolution* and Clare Brinton's *A Decade of Revolution 1789–1799.* A much fuller and equally balanced narrative is provided in Dr. M. Thompson's *The French Revolution* published in 1943. If an English-speaking student had now to limit himself to a single work, this admirable book would be the one to choose. His *Leaders of the French Revolution* conveys many of his conclusions in more popular form.

III

Most of the best work on the Revolution is stored in a vast array of monographs and biographies. In *La France d'après les Cahiers de 1789* Champion summarises the astonishingly moderate demands for reform put forward in the first half of 1789 by the people of France, who hated what was left of feudalism but remained monarchist in sentiment and were largely unaffected by the spread of radical ideas. To visualise the atmosphere of the spring and summer of 1789 we should first master Georges Lefebvre's popular but authoritative *Quatre-vingt-neuf*, published in 1939 under the auspices of a committee to celebrate the 150th anniversary. An English translation, entitled *The Coming of the French Revolution*, appeared at Princeton in 1947. Taking up a position midway between Aulard's mainly political approach and Mathiez's predominantly economic interpretation, he analyses the aspirations of the various social classes and, unlike most historians of these eventful months, includes the provinces in his survey. The Revolution, he is convinced, was inevitable since the Government was incapable of undertaking the necessary measures of reform. The overthrow of absolute monarchy and the establishment of equality before the law fulfilled the desires of the nation, which were worthily summarised in the Declaration of the Rights of Man. The first phase, which is all that he covers, extends to the march of women to Versailles on October 5, and is presented as a drama in four acts: (i) The futile Assembly of Notables. (ii) The meeting of the States-General and the establishment of bourgeois domination. (iii) The Fall of the Bastille and the assumption of power by the working classes of the capital. (iv) The land hunger of the peasants in the countryside.

Lefebvre's monograph *La Grande Peur de 1789* may be regarded as an elaborate appendix to his popular narrative of the opening phase of the drama. Utilising a mass of material from the archives of Paris and the provinces, he paints a sorry picture of the condition of the manual workers in many parts of France. For the great majority, he declares, the main enemy on the eve of the meeting of the States-General was hunger. The miserable condition both of town and country was incontestable, and the chronic distress was aggravated by the bad harvest of 1788. The population was increasing rapidly, and there were two million more mouths to feed in 1789 than in 1770. Hunger produced begging, for there was no machinery of relief and the ranks of unemployed were reinforced by professional mendicants. Here was the raw material of brigandage and of the revolts in the spring and summer of 1789 which figure so prominently in the pages of Taine. To the fear of famine and brigandage a new cause of panic was added when the fate of the Revolution seemed to be trembling in the balance. The air was thick with rumours that 'the aristocrats' were plotting the restoration of the *Ancien Régime* and the employment of armed brigands for their evil purpose. It was largely owing to 'la grande peur' that the seigneurial system fell with a crash on August 4. If Taine may be described as Extreme Right, Madelin as Right Centre, Jaurès and Mathiez as Extreme Left, Lefebvre, like Aulard, is Left Centre. No living French expert inspires such confidence in his judgment.

A lively controversy has arisen as to the derivation of the Declaration of the Rights of Man, the articles of which, with an elaborate commentary, are printed by Eugène Blum in *La Déclaration des droits de l'homme et du citoyen*. The Heidelberg jurist Jellinek argued in his booklet, *Die Erklärung der Menschenrechte*, of which French and American translations exist, that the Declaration would not have been drawn up but for the example of America, and pointed out that many phrases were borrowed from the constitutions of the separate States. Émile Boutmy replied in an article in *Les Annales de l'École Libre des sciences politiques* (reprinted in his *Études politiques*) that the resemblances were mainly external, and that the Declaration arose from the needs and traditions of France and the atmosphere of the *Aufklärung*. The subject is exhaustively discussed in Wilhelm Rees' *Die Erklärung der Menschen-und Bürgerrechte von 1789*, which leans rather to Boutmy than to Jellinek. The 'ideas of 1789' are analysed at length by Redslob in *Die Staatstheorien der Französischen Nationalversammlung von 1789*, and by Karl Löwenstein in *Volk und Parlament nach der Staatstheorie der französischen Nationalversammlung von 1789*. Champion's *J. J. Rousseau et la République Française* discusses the relation of his teaching to the different phases of the movement, and warmly defends him from the charge of being the spiritual father of the Terrorists. Hedwig Hintze's *Staatseinheit und Föderalismus im alten Frankreich und in der Revolution* traces the progressive triumph of centralised bureaucracy over provincialism and federal theory in a survey which extends from the *Ancien Régime* to the fall of the Girondins. Sydney Herbert, *The Fall of Feudalism in France*, summarises the researches of half a century.

The two years of the Constituent Assembly should be studied with the aid of Wickham Legg's *Select Documents illustrating the History of the French Revolution*, Thompson's *French Revolution Documents*, Morse Stephens' *The Principal Speeches of the Statesmen and Orators of the French Revolution*, and Aulard's *Les Orateurs de la Constituante*. For the stormy career of its dominating figure we must turn to the rich material in Loménie's five volumes *Les Mirabeau*, and to the two-volume German biography by Alfred Stern. The best brief lives are by Willert in the Foreign Statesmen Series and by Barthou, himself a distinguished orator and statesman. We come closer to him than through any of the biographies in the *Correspondance entre le Comte de Mirabeau et le Comte de la Marck*, edited by de Bacourt in two volumes in 1851, which revealed his relations with the Court in his own impressive memoranda and in his letters to his closest friend. The high-souled Belgian nobleman, whose memoirs fill half the first volume, had long been a *persona grata* at Versailles and as such was the obvious channel of communication between the great tribune and the distracted sovereigns. That Mirabeau needed and received large sums for his debts and his extravagances is true enough, but it is equally true that the programme of constitutional monarchy he recommended was precisely the same before and after he established contact with the Government. Far from attempting to conceal his financial and personal relations with the Court he was proud of his attempts to combine loyalty to the 'ideas of 1789' with the maintenance of monarchy on the English model which the modest and kindly King, if not the Queen, was willing to accept. It was for the purpose of vindicating his memory that on the approach of death he entrusted the most important collection of his papers to his admiring friend.

The gigantic figure of Mirabeau dwarfs the minor performers on the stage, few of whom have attracted competent biographers. Clapham's *Life of the Abbé Sieyès* portrays the cold-blooded publicist who was mainly responsible for the Declaration of the Rights of Man. Lanzac de Laborie's *Mounier* narrates the fruitless efforts of the moderate reformers at the outset to secure the adoption of something like the British Constitution. Miss Bradby's two-volume *Life of Barnave*, the most valuable contribution to the history of the Revolution made by a British scholar during the generation between Morse Stephens and Dr Thompson, not only revives the attractive figure of the young provincial lawyer who gave advice to the Queen after the flight to Varennes but describes the activities of his little group of moderates and analyses in detail the political, ecclesiastical, and colonial problems they had to face. The most valuable of the biographies of the vain and ineffectual Lafayette is by Louis Gottschalk, of which the first four volumes bring us to 1789. In *La Révolution Française et le régime féodal* Aulard describes the feudal regime as it survived under Louis XVI, and traces the successive stages in the liquidation of feudal rights. The tragic episode of the flight to Varennes may be studied in Lenotre's *Le Drame de Varennes*.

'It had only one fault left to commit,' declared Taine in concluding his account of the Constituent Assembly, 'and this it committed by resolving that none of its members should find a place in its successor.' The Constitution of 1791, which it had taken the Constituent two years to elaborate and which Louis XVI was compelled to accept, retained a shadow king and entrusted power to an Assembly of new and untried men. The Legislative Assembly was inferior in ability and character to its predecessor, and it was dominated by the Girondins. The eloquence of Vergniaud, the fascination of Madame Roland, and the butchery of the leaders captivated the historians of the first half of the nineteenth century. In his pungent work *La Légende des Girondins* Biré reminded his readers that they were for the most part as prone to violent courses as the Jacobins, that they desired a war which Robespierre and other Jacobin leaders were anxious to avoid, and that the majority for the execution of the King was secured by their votes. Sybel and Sorel emphasised their responsibility for the declaration of war in the spring of 1792, and Aulard argued that nothing but the rigid centralisation which they opposed enabled the Jacobins to keep the invaders at bay and to frustrate the counter-revolution. The partisan character of the Memoirs of Madame Roland, once so popular, is now recognised, and her correspondence clearly reveals her faults of mind and temper. Brissot, the leader of the party at the height of their power, has found a competent American interpreter in Miss Ellery, and the rather shadowy figure of the eloquent Vergniaud comes to life in the biography of Lintilhac. Cahen's *Condorcet et la Révolution Française* depicts the boldest thinker of his party and his time in France. On the political philosophy of the Girondins there is a sharp division between Aulard and Mathiez, the former maintaining that they merely differed from the Jacobins in their championship of the provinces against the domination of the capital, the latter arguing that they represented the well-to-do bourgeoisie while the Jacobins stood for the working classes. It is refreshing to exchange this heated atmosphere for the cooler temperature of Brinton's *The Jacobins* which reconstructs the transformation of moderates into extremists. A concise discussion of the origins of the struggle between France and the old Europe is given in Clapham's *Causes of the War of 1792*, and Ranke's balanced *Ursprung und Beginn der Revolutionskriege* retains its value. Frédéric Masson's *Le Département des Affaires Étrangères, 1787–1804*, is a mine of information on the conduct of foreign affairs. Important speeches are given in Aulard, *Les Orateurs de la Législative et de la Convention*.

The Legislative Assembly, like the Constituent, was monarchical in sentiment, but during the first half of 1792 republicanism made rapid advances. Brunswick's invasion and Manifesto overturned the throne, provoked the September Massacres, brought Danton to power, and substituted the radical Convention, elected on a wide franchise, for the exhausted Legislative Assembly; but the flight to Varennes had doomed both the monarchy and the monarch. The fall of the throne may be studied in Mathiez's little book *Le Dix Août*. For the next two years domestic politics were dominated by the war, which took a favourable turn with the cannonade at Valmy and the retreat of Brunswick, passed through a highly critical phase in 1793, and in 1794 scored victories in Belgium and on the Rhine which removed every shred of excuse for the guillotine. The story of the titanic efforts of the young Republic to vanquish a world in arms is told in the eleven small volumes of Chuquet's *Guerres de la Révolution*, based on the archives of the War Office.

For the Terror we must continue to consult three massive monographs of the pre-Aulard era, all based on arduous research. The earliest, Campardon's *Le Tribunal Révolutionnaire de Paris*, two substantial volumes published in 1866, described for the first time from the official records the organisation and activities of the dreadful instrument of mass extermination presided over by Fouquier-Tinville and summarised the trials of its most celebrated victims. The ground was covered for a second time in greater detail in the six volumes of Wallon's *Histoire du Tribunal Révolutionnaire de Paris avec le journal de ses actes*, published in 1880–82, which connected its activities with the general movement of the Revolution. We are thrilled by the story of the famous trials ending with those of the bloodstained monsters of the tribunal itself, but its most horrible feature was the punishment of the young and the obscure for trifling or unproved offences. There were a few acquittals, but in the later stages there were too many cases to leave time for questions. In the famous words of Camille Desmoulins, the gods were athirst. The creation of the Tribunal, declares Wallon, was both the crime and the error of the Revolution; for the system was the condemnation of the regime. Many priests and nobles were executed merely on account of their status, 'and so many men of all sorts, so many women, so many young girls. And why? For a letter written or received, a reported conversation, a drunken remark. How many poor drunks perished without even recalling the words which had sealed their fate! It is in the minor cases—if we can speak of minor cases where death is involved—that we must see it at work. Here, more than in the major cases, we witness the monstrous disproportion between the crime and the punishment.' Many of the victims, of course, deserved the fate they had meted out to others. Philippe Égalité confessed to a priest that he merited death for his vote in the trial of the King. 'Why should these things be described? To prevent their occurrence. The Commune brought us very near the Terror and added new crimes—the burning of palaces, libraries, Hôtel de Ville, archives, churches. We thought the Terror could not revive; it did, and it may do so again.' The Tribunal, he declares at the close of the sixth volume, destroyed the Revolution and ruined its principles. He had done his best to erect a barrier to its revival.

The longest and most important of the three large documented monographs on the Terror retains its place as one of the indispensable books on the Revolution. In the eight volumes of his unfinished *Histoire de la Terreur*, written during the later years of the Second Empire, Mortimer-Ternaux narrated the sickening story for the first time from the registers of the Paris Sections and reports to the Commune, selections from which fill about two hundred pages in each volume. The reports or debates in the *Moniteur*, which historians had accepted without question, are shown to be very incomplete and tendentious. The Introduction explains the standpoint of the author who expresses his horror at the bloody drama he describes. France, he declares, was saved, not by the Terror, but in spite of it. Though he was a man of the Centre and Michelet a man of the Left, their verdict on responsibilities is very similar. In 1792, he declares, the French nation was virtuous, liberty-loving, and patriotic. The Terror was the work of a vile minority. 'The executioners were not the soldiers.' It was the author's hope that his narrative would open the eyes of the uncritical worshippers of Robespierre and Danton. The Terror, he declares, began with the invasion of the Tuileries on June 20, 1792, of which he claimed to provide the first authoritative account. In 1789 power passed from the Crown to the Assembly, in 1792 from the Assembly to 'la rue'. Pétion, the Mayor of Paris, knew of the coming revolt but took no steps to avert it. Many members of the crowd were harmless enough, but others were out for murder. The King's courage was admirable. Of even greater value is the detailed account in the third volume of the September massacres, which proves that they were neither the instinctive reaction of patriotic citizens maddened by foreign threats nor the will of the relatively moderate Legislative Assembly, but the work of 'a few hundred wretches, French only in name and human only in form. Here is my verdict: Before God and man the population of Paris was not guilty.' Marat was the first preacher of massacre, but it was Danton who proclaimed that they must frighten the Royalists. 'We find his hand everywhere. He marked the names of the victims on the lists which were brought to him.' Robespierre was indirectly guilty since he made no attempt to stop the bloodshed. The actual murderers were mainly thieves and rogues.

The victims numbered about 1,400.   The fifth volume is devoted to the trial of the King who in his last weeks and hours revealed a sublimity and dignity which he had never displayed on the throne.   The work was planned on too large a scale, for the author only lived to bring his narrative down to the death of Marat.

After listening to the shrill debate about Danton between Aulard and Mathiez, we turn with relief to Madelin's biography, a model of psychological insight.   Here is a coarse, full-blooded creature, born for action, venal yet not wholly degraded, who overthrew the Monarchy and approved the September Massacres but who deplored the Terror as a system of government.   Danton, he declares, was an opportunist in the best sense of the word, and therefore ten times more of a statesman than Robespierre the inflexible doctrinaire.   In 1792 he was the man of the moment despite his atrocious faults, and it is his glory that he saved his country.   Of Robespierre no satisfactory French biography exists, for Hamel's three enormous volumes, published during the Second Empire, are merely a quarry.   No student dare ignore the monographs in which Mathiez has striven to rescue the reputation and exalt the statesmanship of his hero—the *Études Robespierristes, Autour de Robespierre, Robespierre Terroriste, Autour de Danton, Danton et la Paix*, and *Girondins et Montagnards.* Like Lamartine and Louis Blanc before him, he presents to us 'not an imaginary Robespierre, but the real man, a just and clear-sighted statesman who lived but for the good of his country.' His private character, we are told, was stainless.   Though he supported the Terror as a means to the attainment of social justice and was inexorable towards enemies of his country, he was a moderating influence and saved—or tried to save—some innocent lives.   He was never a Dictator, and Fouquier-Tinville was not his obedient tool.   Danton was liquidated, not because he was a rival, but because he was a traitor to France and to the Revolution—a bad man and a bad Frenchman.   Robespierre was one of the greatest orators who ever lived, ranking with Pericles, Demosthenes and Cicero, and towering above Danton and Gambetta.   'There was a time when Robespierre and democracy were synonymous.   It will return.'   Meanwhile 'la légende Dantonienne,' created by Michelet, Robinet and Aulard, must be demolished by the exposure of his utter selfishness, his shameless venality, his defeatism, and his shady friends. The reader soon wearies of these polemics, but he is grateful for the mass of new material which every work of Mathiez provides. *Robespierre's Rise and Fall*, by Lenotre, paints a vivid picture of the personal life of the arch Terrorist and of the Duplay family who gave him a happy home.

Here for once an English scholar has beaten the French at their own game. Dr. Thompson's two-volume biography of Robespierre allows the most celebrated and the most detested of the leaders of the Revolution to present his case in his speeches, leading articles and letters. We are introduced to a cultivated, plodding, abstemious, cat-like doctrinaire, a sincere, clean-living fanatic, genuinely sympathising with the common man but lacking personality, dynamism and human warmth, forever dreaming of the Republic of Virtue, recognising the existence of *l'être suprême*, with himself, immaculately costumed, permanently at the helm. Unlike Mirabeau and Danton, the spiritual child of Jean-Jacques was a publicist, not a leader of men. 'The greatest spokesman of the Revolution, he could put its thoughts into words but never its words into action. He could never let himself go, could never be natural, could never trust himself to life. He had virtues and vices as neatly catalogued as a confessor's manual. He saw all life like a chessboard, in black and white squares, and no neutral colours.' Few actors on the world stage have won an immortality of fame with less pretensions to greatness than Carlyle's 'sea-green incorruptible' who succeeded Mirabeau as the central figure of the Revolutionary era.

There is no wholly satisfactory life of Marat, but the American scholar Gottschalk, a disciple of Mathiez, has given a careful and not wholly unsympathetic sketch. Special attention is devoted to the political ideas of the man who declared in ominous words 'I am the anger of the people', and who laboured more effectively than any of his contemporaries to render the proletariat class-conscious. The best brief account of his murderess, Charlotte Corday, 'the angel of assassination' as Lamartine called her, is in J. B. Morton, *The Bastille Falls, and other Studies of the French Revolution*, who has also written a biography of St.

Just, the youngest and most bloodthirsty of Robespierre's body-guard. Camille Desmoulins, the most powerful of Jacobin journalists after Marat, found a competent biographer in Jules Clarétie. The second volume of Moncure Conway's *Life of Thomas Paine* describes the activities of the only Anglo-Saxon member of the Convention, who owed his election to *The Rights of Man*, the most popular and effective of the replies to Burke. The last days of the King and Queen are eloquently described in Belloc's *Life of Marie Antoinette*, and with deeper learning in the great biography by La Rocheterie. No student should miss the poignant Memoirs of Duchesse de Tourzel, Gouvernante des Enfants du Roi, so much more reliable and so much less known than those of Madame Campan. A flood of light is thrown on the activities of the Convention in Paris and the provinces and on the revolution of Thermidor by the first volume of Madelin's *Fouché*, the one outstanding French biography of the revolutionary era. The story of national defence is illustrated by Levy-Schneider's *Jean-Bon Saint-André*. Nesta Webster's *Chevalier de Boufflers* is among the most attractive of the numberless books which describe the life of the upper class victims before and during the tornado.

While only the expert will need to digest the twenty-six volumes of Aulard's *Recueil des actes du Comité du Salut Public*, it aids us to visualise the methods by which France was governed during the Convention if we open its pages at random, watch its members at work in Paris, and read a few reports from St. Just and other zealous Representatives on Mission in the provinces. Of smaller bulk but of no less importance are the six volumes, entitled *La Société des Jacobins*, commenced by Aulard simultaneously with the *Recueil*, and covering the five years from the foundation of the Jacobin Club in 1789 till its existence was terminated after Thermidor by Fouché simply locking the door. With the record of the debates before us we learn that the famous Paris club, far from being from the first the haunt of wild men, began with a monarchist atmosphere, and reflected rather than caused the change as public opinion drifted towards republicanism. During the Convention the debates in the club were often of greater importance than those in the Assembly, as the rival leaders rehearsed their parts and tested their strength before the decisive struggle and the operative vote. A third documentary source of the utmost value is the great collection *Les Actes de la Commune de Paris pendant la Révolution*, edited by Lacroix. A brief but useful account of that influential body is given in Alger's *Paris in 1789–1794*, Chapter III. The registers of the wards have been utilised in Mellié's *Les Sections de Paris pendant la Révolution Française*, and are summarised in Alger's *Paris*, Chapter IV. As a result of these publications we dare no longer confine ourselves to the main stream of history in the three Assemblies, but must follow the tributaries that flow in from the political clubs and the Municipality. It is in such contemporary records, not in the tendentious reminiscences written in many cases long after the events described, that the changing phases of the drama are most faithfully mirrored. The prestige of autobiographies and apologias is diminished, though they retain a certain value for those who are aware of their limitations.

The last year of the Convention after the crisis of Thermidor, and the four years of the Directory which succeeded it, have never appealed very strongly to the experts. The best brief introduction to the period of anticlimax is in Lefebvre's admirable *Les Thermidoriens*. Most of them, he declares, were decent folk, but wise and inspiring leadership was lacking. Their outstanding achievement was the enthronement of the bourgeoisie after the hectic *intermezzo* of radical and mob rule. A much darker picture is painted in Madelin's lectures *La France du Directoire* which lead up to the same conclusion as that of his revered master Vandal—that Brumaire was a merciful deliverance, not a usurpation. The Directory is compendiously described by Madelin as the Reign of Barras, a renegade Vicomte destitute of all public and private virtues, caring only for power, money and women. Few epochs were so lamentable, for France became the prey of a band of charlatans and of filibusters because better men lacked the necessary energy to combine and suppress them. That they found France sick is no excuse for garrotting and plundering a nation, neither Jacobin nor Royalist, which craved for constitutional liberty and the reign of law. Rapine in high places was accompanied by the orgy of frivolity, immorality and corruption in the capital under the presiding genius of 'Notre Dame de Thermidor', the Queen of the Directory, Theresa

Cabarrus, the flashy mistress of Barras, Tallien and other lesser men. Of the other Directors Madelin has little flattering to say. Rewbell was out for money, Larévellière-Lépeaux, the founder of a fantastic system of *Théophilanthropie*, was a fanatical anti-clerical. Sieyès, who had more head than heart, realised that the system was doomed and began to look round for 'a sword'. The silent Carnot alone receives praise for his solid and disinterested patriotism as the organiser of victory. Happily for France, while the *nouveaux riches* feathered their nests at home, the brave armies of the Revolution kept the frontiers inviolate and Bonaparte awaited his call.

Mathiez's *La Réaction Thermidorienne*, which denounces with equal severity the shady adventurers who overthrew his hero Robespierre, is indispensable for the dying Convention whose leaders, according to him, made politics their trade. The approach, as is usual with this scholar, is both sociological and socialistic, the deciding factors always being found in the economic field. The fever of the Revolution has abated, and interest begins to shift from Paris to Bonaparte and his campaigns. Neither Barras nor Carnot has tempted a competent biographer, but the *début* of Talleyrand, the Bishop *malgré lui* turned diplomatist, may be studied in Duff Cooper's sparkling narrative and in the first volume of the larger biography by Lacour-Gayet. Sciout's comprehensive work, *Le Directoire*, which first utilised the documents in the National Archives, is now partly out of date. Foreign relations are surveyed in Sorel's fifth volume and more recently in Guyot's enormous monograph, *Le Directoire et la paix de l'Europe*, which finds more to praise in its work than Sorel would admit. A grim picture of the political, economic and social anarchy under the Directory, perhaps a little exaggerated, is painted in the first volume of Vandal's masterpiece *L'Avènement de Bonaparte*. For the early life of the superman we turn to the standard biographies of Holland Rose and Fournier, for more detail to Chuquet's *La Jeunesse de Napoléon*, Masson's *Napoléon Inconnu*, and the opening volumes of Madelin's colossal biography. The *Recueil des Actes du Directoire Executif*, edited by Debidour, and Aulard's vast collection of material, *Paris pendant la Réaction Thermidorienne et sous le Directoire*, are indispensable to the advanced student.

To understand the course and the scope of the Revolution we must extend our vision beyond the sphere of politics and personalities. A useful collection of essays entitled *L'Œuvre sociale de la Révolution*, edited by Émile Faguet, summarises the problems of the army, education, the clergy, socialism, and the land. Legislation is admirably surveyed in Sagnac's *La Législation civile de la Révolution Française 1789-1804: Essai d'histoire sociale*, and in Cahen et Guyot, *L'Œuvre législative de la Révolution*. The vital problem of finance was fully analysed for the first time in Stourm's *Les Finances de l'ancien régime et de la Révolution*, and has been explored more recently in Gomel's *Histoire financière de l'Assemblee Constituante*, and *Histoire financière de la Legislative et de la Convention*. In *La vie chère et le mouvement social sous la Terreur*, one of the most valuable of his books, Mathiez explored price fixing, inflation, monopolies, taxation, requisitions and restrictions. Economic offenders were among the victims of the guillotine.

Religious life during the decade of upheaval has attracted authors of different schools. The best summary in English is in Jervis, *The Gallican Church and the Revolution*. La Gorce, the eminent historian of the Second Empire, has provided a monumental *Histoire religeuse de la Révolution Française* from the standpoint of Catholic Royalism, which carries the story down to the Concordat in five volumes. *La Revue de la Révolution*, created in 1883 to receive the contributions of Catholic Royalists, only survived for six years. In his *Études sur l'histoire religieuse de la Révolution Française* Gazier shows, with the aid of Bishop Grégoire's papers, that the churches were only shut from the end of 1793 to the beginning of 1795, when Notre-Dame was reopened for worship and the dying Convention retreated from the extreme anticlericalism of its prime. Though France was ripe for a Concordat in 1795, the Directory renewed the persecution. Aulard's instructive little book *Le Christianisme et la Révolution Française*, published in 1925, records the author's discovery—contrary to his earlier impression—that there was not much more faith in the villages than in the towns. The lower clergy approved the beginnings of the Revolution and no one dreamed in 1789 of attacking religion, which the *Constitution Civile* left intact. If, however, the Terror and its anticlerical policy had continued very much longer, Aulard believes that

Catholicism and even Christianity might have been completely uprooted, a consummation which he would have witnessed with equanimity. He described part of the conflict in more detail in *La Révolution Française et les Congrégations* and in *Le Culte de la raison et le culte de l'Être suprême*. Mathiez defended the Civil Constitution of the Clergy in his important work *Rome et le clergé français sous la Constituante*, and explored the curious movement associated with the name of Larévellière-Lépeaux in *La Théophilanthropie et le culte décadaire 1796–1801*. He discussed other aspects of the religious history of the years 1789–1802 in *Les Origines des Cultes Révolutionnaires*, and in the two volumes of essays entitled *Contributions a l'histoire religieuse de la Révolution Française* and *La Révolution et l'Église*, which sympathetically records the efforts to 'nationalise Catholicism'. Aulard and Mathiez, though divided on many other matters, were at one in their dislike of the Church.

The literature of the end of the eighteenth century is most conveniently approached in the great co-operative *Histoire littéraire de la France*, edited by Petit de Julleville. A vivid picture of social life, derived from newspapers and brochures, fly-sheets and caricatures, is painted in the volumes of Edmond and Jules de Goncourt, *Histoire de la société française pendant la Révolution et le Directoire*, which may be supplemented by Adolf Schmidt's *Tableaux de la Révolution Française*, based on the police reports to the Minister of the Interior, E. F. Henderson's *Symbol and Satire in the French Revolution*, and Alger's *Paris in 1789–1794*. Lenotre's essays collected in the six volumes of *Vieilles Maisons, Vieux Papiers*, and his many monographs, among them *Paris in the Revolution, The Guillotine and its Servants, The Tribunal of the Terror*, are as scholarly as they are readable. Approaches to socialism—the residuary legatee of the equalitarian ideology of 1789—are described in André Lichtenberger's *Le Socialisme et la Révolution Française*, and in David Thomson's admirable study, *The Babeuf Plot*. That ardent publicist, he reminds us, was not the first crusader to preach Communism, but he was the first to plan its enthronement through the forcible overthrow of a government. His strength lay not in the number of his doctrinal converts but in his championship of the discontented and in his gospel of the welfare state.

An outstanding feature of recent research has been the study of social and economic conditions, the early stages of which were described in Boissonade's booklet, *Les Études relatives a l'histoire économique de la Révolution Française*, published in 1906. An Economic Commission, created by the State in 1904 at the instigation of Jaurès, undertook the publication of the *Cahiers*. The six volumes printed at the end of the Second Empire neglected the documents of the villages, which are more valuable than the ambitious efforts of the three Estates, often drawn up by lawyers and in many cases copied from models with a few local additions. The *Collection de documents inédits sur l'histoire économique de la Révolution Française* already runs to scores of volumes. The publication of the proceedings of the Committees of the Assemblies on agriculture and commerce, feudal rights, mendicity, and food supply, unlocks an aspect of the time of which the political historians knew practically nothing. Students who desire to consult the French archives should consult Pierre Caron's *Manuel pratique pour l'étude de la Révolution Française*. The Revolution in the provinces and the cities has a literature of its own so vast that it is impossible even to glance at it in a brief survey.

IV

In a triple sense the French Revolution belongs to European history. It grew out of conditions which were in large measure common to other countries; its course closely affected and was continuously modified by the policy of almost every state in Europe; and its influence on the institutions and ideas of the Old World was deep and enduring. The intrepid student must travel beyond the meridian of Paris and view its repercussions on the life and thought of other members of the European family. It was the merit of Sybel and Sorel to establish the vital connexion of the internal and external policy of France with that of the rulers and ambitions of the great European states. The Émigrés, for instance, belong as much to European as to French history, as we learn from Ernest Daudet's classical *Histoire de l'Émigration*, Lady Blennerhassett's volumes on Madame de

Staël, Bernard Mallet's life of his grandfather Mallet du Pan, and Baldensperger's *Le Mouvement des Idées dans l'Émigration Française*. The gradual crumbling of feudalism on the Continent is traced through half a century in Doniol's *La Révolution Française et la Féodalité*.

The countries most interested in and most affected by the eruption of the French volcano were Great Britain and Germany, in both of which the opening scenes of the drama were welcomed with general enthusiasm. The best introduction to its political effects on the former is P. A. Brown's *The French Revolution in English History*, which describes the Radical movements and societies with the help of new material. The same theme is instructively discussed by Laprade, *England and the French Revolution, 1789–1798*; Hall, *British Radicalism, 1791–1797*; Veitch, *The Genesis of Parliamentary Reform*; Kent, *The English Radicals*; Brinton, *The English Jacobins*; and Meikle, *Scotland and the French Revolution*. *The Debate on the French Revolution, 1789–1799*, edited by Cobban (in the series *The British Political Tradition*), illustrates the party strife. The later volumes of Lecky's *Ireland in the Eighteenth Century*, Litton Falkiner's masterly *Studies in Irish History and Biography*, and Guillon, *La France et l'Irlande pendant la Révolution*, supply the Irish side of the drama. John Morley's classical biography of Burke should be followed by the intensive study of the *Reflections on the Revolution in France* and the *Letters on a Regicide Peace* in the excellent edition of E. J. Payne. Lord Rosebery's *Pitt* should be digested before approaching Holland Rose's standard biography. André Lebon's *L'Angleterre et l'émigration française, 1794–1801*, describes the futile negotiations with the Émigrés. Alger's *Englishmen in the French Revolution* and Thompson's *English Witnesses of the French Revolution* follow the footsteps of many British visitors to Paris. The fertilising influence on letters may be studied in Dowden's delightful lectures *The French Revolution and English Literature*; Cestre's *La Révolution Française et les poètes anglais*; Brailsford's *Shelley, Godwin and their Circle*; and Legouis's *La Jeunesse de Wordsworth*, which utilises the new material relating to the poet's French romance.

The effect of the Revolution on the mind and institutions of Germany was far greater than on England. While in the latter the reform movement was thrown back by a generation, in the former the ideas of 1789 and the onset of the French armies swept away the worst abuses of feudalism, and overthrew the decrepit Holy Roman Empire.   A full account of the repercussion of the Revolution on the mind of Germany, the institutions of the Empire, and the individual German states, is given in Gooch's *Germany and the French Revolution*.   Certain aspects of the same subject are treated in Wenck's scholarly volumes *Deutschland vor Hundert Jahren*.   Alfred Stern's *Der Einfluss der französischen Revolution auf das deutsche Geistesleben* includes German Switzerland in its scope.   German enthusiasts figure largely in Mathiez' *La Révolution et les Étrangers*.   The political history of the revolutionary era is related with admirable impartiality in Heigel's massive *Deutsche Geschichte, 1786–1806*, which supersedes Häusser's narrative of the same period and supplements Sybel.   A colourful sketch of Germany before and during the Revolution is provided in the first half of the first volume of Treitschke's *History of Germany in the Nineteenth Century*.   Martin Philippson's *Geschichte des preussischen Staatswesens vom Tode Friedrichs des Grossen,* covering the reign of Frederick William II, though faulty in scholarship, is of value for its new material.   Ernst von Meier's *Preussen und die franzosische Revolution* analyses the influence of French ideas on the reformers of Prussia, contesting their importance in the case of Stein, in opposition to his biographer Max Lehmann, and admitting it in the case of Hardenberg.   The latest and fairest discussion of Stein's ideology is in Gerhard Ritter's two-volume biography.   The significance of the ideas of the Revolution for Prussia is stoutly maintained in Cavaignac's *La Formation de la Prusse contemporaine*.   Rambaud's *Les Français sur le Rhin* and Sagnac's *Le Rhin français pendant la Révolution et l'Empire* describe the conquest of the Left Bank and the reforms introduced during the twenty years of French occupation.   Some interesting utterances are collected in Raif's *Die Urteile der Deutschen über die französische Nationalität im Zeitalter der Revolution ünd der deutschen Erhebung.*

The political history of the revolutionary era in Italy is most authoritatively related in Franchetti's *Storia d'Italia, 1789–1799.* Hazard's learned monograph, *La Révolution Française et les lettres italiennes, 1789–1815,* describes the effect on literature and thought.

Giglioli's *Naples in 1799* reconstructs the tragic episode of the short-lived Neapolitan Republic, modelled on that of France. For Spain we may consult Baumgarten's *Geschichte Spaniens während der französischen Revolution*; for Belgium, Lanzac de Laborie's *La Belgique sous la domination française* and Engerand's *L'Opinion publique dans les Provinces Rhénanes et en Belgique, 1789–1815*; for Russia, Larivière's *Catherine II et la Révolution Française*, mainly based on extracts from the correspondence of the Empress, with a valuable Introduction by Rambaud. Bernard Fay's *L'Ésprit Révolutionnaire en France et aux États Unis*, a study of the relations of thinkers and reformers on both sides of the Atlantic between 1770 and 1800, based largely on a survey of the Press, was, in the author's words, 'a story of love.' Hazen's *American Opinion on the French Revolution* sketches the attitude of Jefferson, Gouverneur Morris, the observant American Minister to France, and Monroe; the brief and fruitless mission of the French Minister Genet in 1793 to drag the United States into war; the democratic societies; and the evidence of contemporary literature.

V

The Revolution has coloured the whole subsequent history of France. Some typical judgments by distinguished men have been collected in Janet's *La Philosophie de la Révolution Française*. In the early years of the nineteenth century French thought was divided into the schools of the counter-revolution and the supporters of 'the ideas of 1789.' The most powerful opponent of the Revolution who used the French language was Joseph de Maistre. The Savoyard nobleman, who summoned the survivors from the revolutionary flood to rally round the principle of authority embodied in the Pope, may be approached in John Morley's essay in his *Miscellanies* and in Cogordan's volume in the *Grands Ecrivains Français*. The moderate Liberals, who admired the principle of 'the separation of powers' enshrined in the British Constitution, were known as *Les Doctrinaires*. Both schools of thought are included in the first volume of Faguet's incomparable *Politiques et moralistes du dix-neuvième siècle*, which dissects the ideas of de Maistre and de Bonald, Madame de Staël and Benjamin Constant, Royer-Collard and Guizot. The most comprehensive and illuminating survey of French political thought since the Revolution is to be found in the fine work of Henri Michel, *L'Idée de l'État: essai sur l'histoire des théories sociales et politiques en France depuis la Révolution*.

The extension of the principle of equality of rights, which was the central message of the Revolution and the mainspring of its energies, proceeded in ever-widening circles throughout the nineteenth century, like a huge stone thrown into a stagnant pond. The novel conception of common citizenship rendered it impossible to maintain the disabilities of the Jews or to tolerate slavery, nor was it logical any longer to evade the demand for equal rights and equal opportunities for the sexes. Above all, the principle of equality gave an incalculable impetus to socialism. The nationalisation of the land makes frequent appearance in the pamphlets of the revolutionary era, and with the conspiracy of Babeuf socialism became a political programme. The wholesale transfer of land, and the circumstances under which it took place, undermined the idea of the sacredness of property; and when the promised equality of political rights failed to secure the welfare and happiness of the masses, the elastic principle of equality was naturally stretched to embrace the economic sphere. The Tiers État having extracted from the Revolution most of the benefits that it could provide, it is in the socialist movement that the operation of its governing principle is most clearly traceable in the twentieth century.

If equality of rights and opportunity was the central tenet of the revolutionary faith, the sovereignty of the people was its necessary corollary. When the doctrine of hereditary privilege was abandoned, power could only reside in the mass or the majority of citizens. The third watchword of the Revolution, nationality, was foreign to the cosmopolitan teaching on which its leaders were nourished, nor did it make its appearance till Europe began to threaten interference; but it arose naturally enough from the conception of popular sovereignty. Before 1792 men had thought of states as territorial entities subject to a certain authority rather than as communities bound together by ties of blood, religion, language, common traditions and common aspirations. The French Revolution astonished mankind by the spectacle of a nation thinking and acting independently of its Government. The conception of nationality was ignored at Vienna; but the idea had taken root, and the arrangements of the Congress in which the principle was violated were those which were most speedily upset.

The doctrine of nationality was no more invented by the Revolution than the doctrines of equality and popular sovereignty; but their adoption by France opened a new chapter in the life of humanity, and their proclamation by the revolutionary trumpet carried the gospel of democracy to the uttermost parts of the earth. 'France did more than conquer Europe,' writes Sorel in an eloquent passage; 'she converted her. Victorious even in their defeat, the French won over to their ideas the very nations which revolted from their domination. The princes most eagerly bent on penning in the Revolution saw it, on returning from their crusade, sprouting in the soil of their own estates which had been fertilised by the blood of French soldiers. The French Revolution only ceased to be a source of strife between France and Europe to inaugurate a political and social revolution which in less than half a century had changed the face of the European world.'

5

THE CAMBRIDGE CHAIR OF MODERN HISTORY

A CENTURY before the foundation of the Regius Professorship of Modern History a gallant attempt to provide historical instruction in the University of Cambridge was made by Fulke Greville, first Lord Brooke, the friend of Philip Sidney and Spenser, of Bacon and Giordano Bruno, the counsellor of James I, the patron of Camden and Speed.[1] The regulations which he drew up in 1627 for 'A Publique Lecture of Historie' prescribed the conditions of appointment and the duties of the lecturer in great detail. No clergyman nor married man was to be eligible, nor anyone whose occupation would distract him from his studies. A mastery of Latin, Greek, geography and chronology was essential. 'Such as have travelled beyond the seas and so have added to their learning knowledge of modern tongues and experience in foreign parts, and likewise such as have been brought up and exercised in public affairs, shall be accounted most eligible.' The lecturer should be at liberty to choose any province of secular or ecclesiastical history. Lectures were to be delivered twice a week, and on a third day he was to discuss points with his class. The appointment was for five years, the salary to be £100 a year. Lord Brooke's design that the presentation should remain for ever in his family was altered after his death, and the patronage was vested in the University.

In his anxiety to obtain the best available scholarship, the founder wisely inserted a clause authorising the appointment of distinguished foreigners. Finding no suitable candidate in England he invited Gerard Vossius to fill the new Chair, but the great Dutch scholar was unwilling to leave Leyden. A less

---

[1] See Mullinger, *History of the University of Cambridge*, iii, 81–90 and 674–677, and Cooper, *Annals of Cambridge*, ii, 201–202, and v, 370–371.

distinguished son of the same university, Isaac Dorislaus, who
had for some time resided in England and was married to an
English wife, accepted the offer. Dorislaus began his lectures
at the end of 1627, but the course was destined to be brief.
Selecting the *Annals* of Tacitus as his text-book, his reflections on
kingship, moderate as they were, scandalised the Anglican divines
who dominated the University. The Vice-Chancellor forbade
the continuance of his course, and the prohibition was confirmed
by royal injunction at the instigation of Laud. Many years
later the unfortunate scholar was assassinated by royalist refugees,
while representing the Commonwealth at The Hague, in revenge
for his share in the trial of Charles I. After this ill-starred
commencement the story of the Chair is involved in obscurity,
and the office was probably a sinecure. The names of two
subsequent Readers have been disinterred, but there is no evidence
that they delivered lectures, and the endowment appears to have
lapsed.

In 1724, a century after Lord Brooke's scheme had been
wrecked by royalist intolerance, George I founded twin chairs
of Modern History and Languages at the two great English
universities. In his masterly biography of Edmund Gibson
Professor Norman Sykes [1] has shown how the project was
initiated and carried through by the learned Bishop of London,
himself an Oxford man, and has thrown a flood of light on the
purposes and the nature of the enterprise. The ambitious
prelate never realised his dream of the Primacy, but he was for
many years the ecclesiastical adviser of the Whigs, and his
practical mind realised ths importance of converting the Universities to the Hanoverian régime. He reminded Townshend
that it was the intention of the Universities to train persons for
the service of God in the State as well as the Church, and that
a supply of men with a knowledge of foreign languages was
necessary for the effective functioning of our diplomacy. The
lack of such linguists, he pointed out, led to the employment of
foreigners by British Embassies and the engagement of foreign

[1] *Edmund Gibson*, 94–107. Cp. Firth, 'Modern History at Oxford, 1724–1841,'
in *English Historical Review*, 1917; Firth, *Modern Languages at Oxford, 1724–1920*,
chapter 1; Oscar Browning, *Cambridge Review*, November 25 and December 9,
1897; J. W. Clark, *Endowments of the University of Cambridge*, 183–192; and
Winstanley, *Unreformed Cambridge*, 154–162.

tutors by the nobility and gentry to accompany their sons on their travels.   Moreover, the honour of the Universities demanded that they should be the seat of universal learning.   His plan was to appoint two professors proficient in modern languages to be 'the chief directors' of the study of modern languages and history, who would instruct, both in speaking and writing, twenty Bachelors of Arts nominated by the Crown.   Each professor was to have qualified assistants in his task.

The scheme worked out by Gibson and Townshend was announced by the King in a letter of May 16, 1724, countersigned by Townshend, to the Vice-Chancellors of the two Universities. 'We, being greatly desirous to favour and encourage our two Universities, and to enable them more effectually to answer the trend of their institution by sending forth constant supplies of learned and able men to serve the public both in Church and State, and having observed that no encouragement or provision has hitherto been made for the study of Modern History and Modern Languages, and having seriously weighed the prejudice from this respect, persons of foreign nations being often employed in the education and tuition of youth both at home and in their travels, and great numbers of the young nobility and gentry being either sent abroad directly from school and taken away from the universities before their studies are completed, and opportunities frequently lost to the Crown of employing and encouraging members of universities by conferring on them such employment, both at home and abroad, as requires a competent skill in writing and speaking the modern languages.   In order therefore to remedy these inconveniences, we have determined to appoint two persons of sober conversation and prudent conduct, skilled in Modern History and in the knowledge of Modern Languages, to be Professors of Modern History, who shall be obliged to read lectures in the Public Schools.   They shall have a stipend of £400 per annum, and out of the said stipends shall be obliged to maintain with sufficient salary two persons at least well qualified to instruct in history and speaking the said languages, which said teachers shall be under the direction of the Professors and shall be obliged to instruct *gratis* in the Modern Languages twenty scholars of each University, to be nominated by us, and each scholar so nominated shall be obliged to learn two at least of the said languages. Professors and teachers shall be obliged once every year to transmit an attested account of the progress made by each scholar to our principal Secretary of State to be laid before us, that we may encourage the diligence of such amongst them as shall have qualified themselves for our service by giving them suitable employments, either at home or abroad, as occasions shall offer.'

The response of Cambridge was as grateful as that of Jacobite Oxford was grudging. The Royal Letter, wrote the Vice-Chancellor on May 10, had been read in the Senate, 'intimating Your Majesty's gracious and princely intentions of establishing a new Professorship, with an appointment so ample as wellnigh to equal the stipend of all our other Professors put together. We are firmly persuaded that when Your Majesty's noble design shall have taken effect, there shall be a sufficient number of academical persons well versed in the knowledge of foreign courts and well instructed in their respective languages; when a familiarity with the living tongues shall be superadded to that of the dead ones; when the solid learning of antiquity shall be adorned and set off with a skilful habit of conversing in the languages that now flourish, and will be accompanied with English probity, our nobility and gentry will be under no temptation of sending for persons from foreign countries to be entrusted with the education of their children; that the appearance of an English gentleman in the courts of Europe, with a governor of his own nation, will not be so rare as hitherto, and that your Universities, thus refined and made more completely serviceable to the education of youth, will be able to furnish you with a constant supply of persons every way qualified for the management of such weighty affairs and negotiations as Your Majesty's occasions may require.' In September the Royal Letters Patent were despatched to both Universities, setting forth among other regulations that the professors were to be appointed for one year only, with a right to apply for renewal — a precaution suggested by the frowns of Oxford and the desire of the Government to retain control of a foundation which was political rather than academic in character.

The first of a long line of Cambridge professors was Samuel Harris, Fellow of Peterhouse, Doctor of Divinity and Fellow of the Royal Society. He delivered his inaugural lecture in 1725, and the *Oratio Inauguralis* was published at Cambridge in the same year.[1] In ponderous Latin he laments the moral dangers incurred by young men who have to repair abroad to learn languages, and congratulates his hearers that the necessity is at an end. Turning to the other aspect of the foundation he credits the King with the hope that the knowledge of the achievements of their ancestors in peace and war would fire the imagination and mould the character of the students, some of whom might perhaps rise to the highest posts in the state. The discourse, which in its emphasis on the practical aim of historical studies is a curious anticipation of Seeley, closes with a fulsome panegyric on the royal founder. Harris never lectured again, and no other lecture was delivered from the Chair for nearly half a century.

Though the Professor took his duties lightly, a French and an Italian instructor were appointed, and twenty scholars were duly chosen. In 1726 Harris reported their progress. In one or two instances he wrote 'perfect' against the names, and he dutifully added that the effects of the new foundation were already visible in the University in the increase of loyalty and useful learning. A second report, drawn up in April 1727, announced that two Trinity men had become secretaries to the British envoys at Turin and Ratisbon, and that one or two were learning German and Spanish. During the same month some more scholars were selected. When the enterprise had been auspiciously launched, the indefatigable Bishop of London left its supervision to the Secretary of State; but the Government soon lost interest, and the ensuing vacancies were left unfilled. In 1728 George II confirmed his father's foundations and ordered that the professors should retain their chairs, but with the disappearance of their scholars the posts became sinecures. 'The late Royal Institution for the study of History,' wrote Warburton hopefully in 1727, 'must produce the master-builders to give us that promising body of English history so long wanted and till now despaired of.' It was, however, a false dawn. No builders, still less master-builders, came forward in the Cambridge of the eighteenth century to erect the temple of historical learning. Harris died in 1733, and two years later *A Commentary on the Fifty-third*

[1] A copy is in the British Museum.

Chapter of Isaiah was published in London,[1] dedicated by his widow to Queen Caroline. A preface of fifty pages reveals the author's knowledge of classical literature, his interest in Hebrew philology and the ancient world, and his impeccable orthodoxy. These qualities, however estimable in themselves, do not explain his appointment to a Chair of Modern History, and the clue is doubtless to be found in his strident loyalty to the Hanoverian dynasty. 'I am very sure that under the most auspicious and happy reign of his present Majesty King George, the glorious guardian of our religious as well as civil liberties, force will never be made use of to compel men in matters of religion, except it be such a force as arises from his own illustrious example.'

After the death of Harris the Chair remained vacant for over a year. On the appointment of his successor, Shallett Turner, Fellow and Junior Dean of Peterhouse and a student of law, the Government woke up for a moment and asked for information. The new Professor replied that it was over seven years since the last list of King's scholars was made, and that all the places were consequently vacant. He added that the documents and nomination forms would doubtless be found in the office of the Secretary of State. No further steps were taken, and the long tenure of the second Professor, who never delivered a lecture, is a blank. At the end of the summer term of 1737 Gray wrote ironically to Horace Walpole: 'Not to tire you with my travels, you must know that Mr. Turner is come down. His list is vastly near being full, notwithstanding which, and the cares and duties of his office, he says he thinks to go to Paris every year.'[2] An anonymous pamphlet, *Free Thoughts upon University Education*, published in 1751,[3] asserted that if the Professor of History would reside at Cambridge, with his proper assistants, a numerous audience would regularly attend his lectures or classes; but this confident prediction was never put to the test.

As the Professor advanced in years the question of his successor began to be eagerly discussed, and among the aspirants to the coveted sinecure was the greatest English poet of his age, a

[1] A finely bound quarto, bearing the arms of George III, is in the British Museum.
[2] *The Correspondence of Gray, Walpole, West and Ashton* (1734–71), ed. Paget Toynbee, 1915, i, 151–152.
[3] Cp. T. A. Walker, *Peterhouse*, chapter 7. A copy is in the Library of Trinity College. See Wordsworth, *Scholae Academicae*, 150.

Peterhouse man who had recently migrated to Pembroke. 'Old Turner is very declining', wrote Gray to a friend in 1759, 'and I was sounded by Dr. —— about my designs (so I understood it). I assured him that I should not *ask* for it, not choosing to be refused. He told me two people had applied already. *N.B.* All this is secret.' [1] 'Old Turner' lingered on for three years more, and when the end came Gray attempted to mobilise his friends.

To John Chute (*undated*)

My dear Sir,—I was yesterday told that Turner (the Professor of Modern History here) was dead in London. If it be true, I conclude it is now too late to begin asking for it. But we had (if you remember) some conversation on that head at Twickenham,[2] and as you have probably found some opportunity to mention it to Mr. W. since, I would gladly know his thoughts about it. What he can do, he only can tell us: what he will do, if he can, is with me no question. If he could find a proper channel, I certainly might ask it with as much or more propriety than any one in this place. If anything were done it should be as private as possible, for if the people who have any sway here could prevent it, I think they would most zealously.

The result of the application was announced to Warton in the course of a long letter dated December 4, 1762, describing a country tour.[3] 'When I arrived here (London) I found Professor Turner had been dead above a fortnight, and being cockered and spirited up by some friends (though it was rather of the latest) I got my name suggested to Ld. B. You may easily imagine who undertook it, and indeed he did it with zeal. I received my answer very soon, which was what you may easily imagine, but joined with great professions of his desire to serve me on any future occasion.'

The coveted prize fell to Laurence Brockett, a Fellow of Trinity, the least reputable holder of his chair, but possessing the qualification of having been tutor to the son-in-law of Lord Bute, in whose hands the appointment lay. We catch a glimpse of him in 1757, when Gray wrote to ask him, 'when he has occasion to go into Trinity Library,' to be good enough to inquire for some old

---

[1] *Gray's Letters*, ed. Tovey, ii, 262.
[2] Horace Walpole's house, Strawberry Hill.
[3] *Gray's Letters*, ed. Tovey, ii, 268.

English books.[1] The new Professor was more interested in University politics than in academic studies, and his shadowy figure assumes flesh and blood for the first and last time in the fierce contest for the post of High Steward left vacant by the death of Lord Hardwicke in 1763.[2] After months of conflict the second Lord Hardwicke succeeded his father, and the assault on the authority of the Duke of Newcastle, the Chancellor of the University, was repulsed; for the defeated candidate was the unsavoury Lord Sandwich, the boon companion of Wilkes. Despite his unenviable notoriety, Sandwich was supported by the Court and Ministry, and among his champions in the University none was more active than Brockett, who was reported to Newcastle as 'most violent in his counsels.'[3] When the Master of Trinity died early in 1768, Brockett was mentioned as a competitor for the post.[4] Six months later, returning from a visit to Lord Sandwich at Hinchinbroke, he fell off his horse —'drunk, I believe,' commented Gray—and died three days later.

Gray's hour had come at last. Disheartened by his previous rebuff he refused to renew his application, but his friend Stonhewer, Fellow of Peterhouse and Secretary to the Prime Minister, the Duke of Grafton, was ready for action.[5] The appointment took place without delay, and the joyful news was communicated to Mary Antrobus on July 29.

Dear Mary,—I thank you for all your intelligence (and the first news I had of poor Brockett's death was from you) and to reward you in part for it I now shall tell you that this day, hot as it is, I kissed the King's hand; that my warrant was signed by him last night, that on Wednesday I received a very honourable letter from the D. of Grafton, acquainting me that His Majesty had ordered him to offer me this Professorship, and much more which does me too much credit by half for me to mention it. The Duke adds that from private as well as public considerations he takes the warmest part in approving this measure of the King's. These are his own words. You see there are princes (or Ministers) left in the world that know how to do things

---

[1] Gray's Letters, ed. Tovey, ii, 1.
[2] The full story is told in Winstanley, The University of Cambridge in the Eighteenth Century, chapter 2.
[3] Winstanley, 117.
[4] Gray's Letters, ed. Tovey, February 3, 1768, iii, 180.
[5] In 1769 Gray described him as his best friend, and he left him £500 in his will.

handsomely; for I profess I never asked for it, nor have I seen his Grace before or after the event.[1]

The new Professor expressed his gratitude to his benefactor in a graceful letter of which the draft is dated Cambridge, July 1768.[2]

My Lord,—Your Grace has dealt nobly with me; and the same delicacy of mind that induced you to confer this favour on me, unsolicited and unexpected, may perhaps make you averse to receive my sincerest thanks and grateful acknowledgements. Yet your Grace must excuse me, they will have their way. They are indeed but words; yet I know and feel they come from my heart, and therefore are not wholly unworthy of your Grace's acceptance. I even flatter myself (such is my pride) that you have some little satisfaction in your own work. If I did not deceive myself in this, it would complete the happiness of, my Lord, your Grace's most obliged and devoted servant.

A letter of August 3 to the Rev. Norton Nicholls added one or two details.[3] 'You are to say that I owe my nomination to the whole Cabinet Council, and my success to the King's particular knowledge of me. This last he told me himself, though the day was so hot and the ceremony so embarrassing to me that I hardly know what he said.' The Professor's satisfaction continued to bubble over in letters to his friends. 'It is the best thing the Crown has to bestow (on a layman) here,' he wrote to James Beattie on October 31, 1768[4]; 'the salary is £400 per annum, but what enhances the value of it to me is that it was bestowed without being asked. Instances of a benefit so nobly conferred, I believe, are rare; and therefore I tell you of it as a thing that does honour not only to me but to the Minister.' The debt was partially repaid by the 'Ode for Music' written on the Duke's installation as Chancellor a few months later. None of his friends was more delighted or surprised than Horace Walpole. 'Yes, it is my Gray, Gray the poet,' he wrote on August 9, 'who is made Professor of Modern History, and I believe it is worth five hundred a year. I knew nothing of it till I saw it in

[1] *Gray's Letters*, ed. Tovey, iii, 199–200. A shorter account was sent to Warton on August 1, iii, 202–203.
[2] *Ib.*, iii, 198.
[3] *Ib.*, iii, 205.
[4] *Ib.*, iii.

the papers, but believe it was Stonhewer that obtained it for him.' [1]

'It is only to tell you,' wrote the new Professor to Mason on August 1, 1768,[2] 'that I profess Modern History and Languages in a little shop of mine at Cambridge, if you will recommend me any customers.' That this was no more meaningless phrase is suggested by an undated document in Gray's handwriting published in 1926.[3] The scheme may have been drawn up when he was hoping to succeed Turner in 1762; but it more probably dates from the fulfilment of his hopes in 1768, when, as Mason tells us,[4] he laid before the Duke of Grafton three different schemes of choosing his pupils, one of which found so much favour that it was sent to Oxford for the benefit of the new Regius Professor in the sister University.

1. That the Professor shall apply to the several Heads of Colleges: and desire them to recommend one or more young Gentlemen, who shall be instructed without expense in some of the modern languages, and attend such lectures as he shall give. The number (if each smaller College send one and the larger two) will amount in the University of Cambridge to nineteen.

2. That the Professor shall nominate and pay two Præceptors, qualified to instruct these Scholars in the French and Italian tongues.

3. That He shall reside the half of every Term at least in the University (wch. half-terms at Cambridge make about a hundred and ten days, almost one-third of the year) and shall read publickly once at least in every Term a lecture on modern History to his Scholars, and to any others that shall be present.

4. That He shall besides at short and regular intervals give private lectures to his Scholars on the same subject, prescribe a method of study, direct them in their choice of Authors, and from time to time enquire into the progress they have made in the Italian and French tongues.

5. That if he neglect these duties, he shall be subject to the

---

[1] To Hon. H. S. Conway, *Letters of Horace Walpole*, ed. Toynbee, vii, 211–212; cp. the letter of September 20 to Warton, vii, 227–228.

[2] *Gray's Letters*, ed. Tovey, iii, 203–204.

[3] In a letter of Dr. Paget Toynbee in the *Times Literary Supplement*, March 4, 1926.

[4] *Memoirs of the Life and Writings of Thomas Gray*, first edition (1775), 397.

same pecuniary mulcts that other Professors are according to statute.

We learn from Mason [1] that immediately after his appointment Gray sketched out an Inaugural Lecture in Latin. 'He also wrote the exordium of this thesis, not indeed in a manner correct enough to be here given but so spirited in point of sentiment as leaves it much to be lamented that he did not proceed to its completion.' He engaged and paid teachers of French and Italian, and he fretted that no 'customers' came to his shop. 'Notwithstanding his ill-health,' writes Mason, 'he constantly intended to read lectures, and I remember the last time he visited me at Acton in the summer of the year 1770 he expressed much chagrin on this subject and even declared it to be his steadfast resolution to resign his Professorship if he found himself unable to do real service in it. What I said to dissuade him from this had so little weight with him that I am almost persuaded he would very soon have put this intention into execution. But death prevented the trial.' The prickings of conscience continued till the end. On May 24, 1771, he wrote to Warton of his cough and of his idea of a visit to the Continent in the summer. 'My own employment so sticks in my stomach and troubles my conscience, and yet travel I must or cease to exist.' Two months later he was dead. 'I know that till he did accept the Professorship from the Duke of Grafton,' wrote Horace Walpole to Mason,[2] 'it was my constant belief that he would scorn any place.' A tribute from the same lifelong friend [3] fittingly commemorates the only immortal among the occupants of the Cambridge Chair. 'The loss of him was a great blow to me and ought to be so to the world, as Mr. Mason tells me he has left behind him nothing finished, which might have compensated his death to them, though not to his friends. He was a genius of the first rank, and will always be allowed so by men of taste. You, sir, will be honoured by them for having done justice to his merit; and as he was so averse to receiving favours, it will be a great proof that he did justice to yours in consenting to be obliged to you.'

---

[1] *Memoirs*, 395–399.
[2] March 2, 1773. *Letters*, viii, 247.
[3] Published by Paget Toynbee in *The Times*. The letter is dated September 16, 1771, and was probably addressed to Stonhewer.

To Gray's successor, John Symonds, Fellow of Peterhouse and a man of wide learning and liberal views, belongs the merit of being the first occupant of the Chair to discharge his duties. The most interesting of his writings, *Remarks upon an Essay intituled the History of the colonisation of free states of antiquity applied to the present contest between Great Britain and her American colonies*, published in 1778, boldly attacked the argument that, as the free states of antiquity taxed their colonies, Great Britain had a right to tax hers. A survey of ancient colonisation, based on classical sources and modern French and English commentators, leads to the conclusion that the human race has advanced and that the American colonies are in the right. 'We live not under the Commonwealth of a Carthage, an Athens or a Rome; but (thanks be to the virtue of our ancestors) we live under a monarchy where the meanest subject may assert his rights, consistently with the duty which he owes his sovereign; and yet nothing is wanting to a necessary authority any more than a rational liberty. This is a short answer to a thousand precedents of antiquity; but every good Englishman will think it a satisfactory one.' His later works on the revision of the New Testament contain one or two passages of personal interest. The *Observations upon the expediency of revising the present English version of the four Gospels and the Acts*, published at Cambridge in 1789, is dedicated to the Duke of Grafton, Chancellor of the University, who was not quite so bad as Junius urged his readers to believe. 'By your recommendation, unsolicited and even unasked, I have for many years had the honour of enjoying a distinguished appointment in this University, and you have ever since ranked me in the number of your particular friends.' He adds that the Duke in repeated conversations has shown his interest in a subject so near to the author's heart. 'The more frequently I reflect upon the important truths of Christianity, the more ardently I wish to see our version revised by proper authority.'

The *Observations on the Epistles*, which followed in 1794, contains a preface replying to an attack on the earlier work. Among the charges was that of speaking well of Priestley, whose political and theological views were not in favour with traditionalists; but Symonds has no apology to offer. 'Ever since his *Lectures upon History* were published I have constantly recom-

mended them to the students in our University as the best book
in its kind which has fallen within my observation.' An allusion
to 'my excellent friend Bishop Watson' confirms the impression
that the Professor was a man of the left centre; and it is a feather
in his cap that Arthur Young [1] refers to 'the admirable essays of
my valuable friend Professor Symonds upon Italian agriculture,'
which appeared in the *Annals of Agriculture*.

When Symonds succeeded Gray in 1771 he lost no time in
getting to work, and the set of rules which he proposed was
accepted in 1773.[2] The fees of the noblemen, fellow-commoners
and their attendant private tutors was to be devoted to remunerat-
ing the teachers of languages and the purchase of books and maps.
He collected and bequeathed nearly a thousand volumes for the
use of his pupils, each bearing the title *Scholae Historicae Canta-
bridgiensis Liber*, thus founding the Historical Library to which his
successor was to make large additions.[3] Some printed notices
survive of the commencement of his courses, which included
hints on text-books and the study of history. In his survey
of European civilisation since the Roman Empire we are not
surprised to learn that he reprobated 'intolerance in religion and
civil government'.

Symonds had done his best, but his classes were very small.
He was succeeded in 1807 by William Smyth, the fifth Peterhouse
occupant of the Chair, and the first of the professors to make a
serious study of history. An Irishman, educated at Eton and
King's, and later a Fellow of Peterhouse,[4] he became tutor to
Sheridan's son. As a *persona grata* in Whig circles, he obtained
the Cambridge post through the influence of the youthful Lord
Henry Petty, Chancellor of the Exchequer during the brief
Grenville Ministry which followed the death of Pitt, and Member
for the University. In her obituary of the third Marquis of
Lansdowne, written nearly half a century later,[5] Harriet
Martineau speaks with some severity of the appointment.

[1] *Travels in France*, ed. C. Maxwell, i.
[2] C. Wordsworth, *Scholae Academicae*, 1877, 147–151.
[3] See J. W. Clark, *Endowments of the University of Cambridge*, 184–185. A MS.
volume of his lectures, 640 pages, quarto, boards, undated, bearing the names at the
end Panting, Coll. John Cant, 1790, recently appeared in a catalogue priced 21*s*.
[4] Two windows in Peterhouse Chapel perpetuate his memory. Walker's
Peterhouse, 31, note.
[5] *Biographical Sketches*, ed. 1885, 94–95.

Cambridge, she declares tartly, would have no more of the young Liberal; but he indulged himself in a last act of patronage in securing the appointment of Smyth, whom his friends called the amiable and accomplished. 'It was, like most of Lord Lansdowne's appointments, an act of kindness to the individual, but scarcely so to the public. There is no saying what benefit might have accrued to British statesmanship if a man of more vigour, philosophy and comprehensiveness of mind had been appointed to so important a chair.'

Harriet Martineau had a sharp tongue, and her censure seems a little excessive. It is true that in 1810 Gillray depicted Smyth lecturing to a few slumbering students.[1] Modern history was then regarded as a subject of little importance, and it is improbable that British statesmanship would have profited by a different appointment. No one at any rate could deny that Smyth was a man of active mind. In his leisure hours he composed lyrics, which passed through five editions and earned the praise of the *Edinburgh Review*, and a work on the Evidences of Christianity. His first historical publication, *A List of Books recommended and referred to in the Lectures on Modern History by Professor Smyth*, appeared in 1817. The brochure of twenty-one pages suggested, even for the shortest course of reading, selected chapters of Gibbon, Hume, Robertson, Coxe, Voltaire, with parts of Clarendon, Burnet and other memoirs. But the pupil was encouraged to throw his net wide. 'Adam Smith should also be studied, and the late work of Mr. Malthus, with the best works in morals and metaphysics.' The bibliographical guide reveals a wide knowledge of the English and French works then available, and in reprinting it in 1819 with his *Lectures* he called attention to Hallam, Lingard, Sismondi and other bright lights in the new firmament.

If Symonds was the first Professor to lecture, Smyth was the first to publish his lectures, and the volumes which appeared in 1840 enable us to test his quality. The first two, entitled *Lectures on Modern History*, were dedicated to his benefactor Lord Lansdowne. 'It has always been a source of pride to me to have owed my Professorship to your Lordship's favourable opinion.' The survey of the centuries from the fall of Rome to the Reforma-

---

[1] *Caricatures of James Gillray*, ed. by T. Wright, 360.

tion is very brief, and the continual comments on modern historians impede the flow of his tale. The course ends with a full treatment of the American War of Independence which reveals the orthodox Whig. 'I know not how any friend to his species, much less any Englishman,' he concludes, 'can cease to wish with the most earnest anxiety for the success of the great experiment. What efforts can be made for the government of mankind so reasonable as these—a limited monarchy and a limited republic? Give civil and religious liberty and you give everything; deny them and you deny everything.' Three volumes of *Lectures on the French Revolution*, the first delivered in 1826–27, carry the story to the fall of Robespierre, examine the state of opinion in England, and sketch the teaching of Burke, Godwin and other gladiators. The work concludes with half a dozen supplementary discourses of later date. During the crisis of the Reform Bill he declared that he never intended in his lectures to mix himself up in the politics of the day, but added that the lesson he had always endeavoured to enforce was the duty of moderation. In a lecture of 1832 he warned his hearers against Robert Owen and other revolutionists. He never wearied of drawing lessons from the French Revolution, which revealed 'what man becomes when he attempts to be wiser than the God that made him.' Smyth's utterances, without being in any way distinguished, mark a considerable advance on anything that had been heard in the realm of historical teaching in either University. They found a place in many an early Victorian home, and received the honour of a reprint in Bohn's Library. In 1837 Whewell, Master of Trinity, described his lectures as 'eloquent and thoughtful disquisitions which had long enjoyed great popularity'.

On the death of Smyth in 1849 the Prince Consort as Chancellor of the University was anxious to secure a scholar of real eminence, and the most famous historian of the age was invited to fill the vacancy. 'To the Palace,' wrote Macaulay in his diary on July 1, 1849.[1] 'The Prince, to my extreme astonishment, offered me the Professorship, and very earnestly, and with many flattering expressions, pressed me to accept it. I gratefully and respectfully declined. It would be strange if, having sacrificed for liberty a seat in the Cabinet and £2,500 a year, I should now

---

[1] Trevelyan, *Life and Letters of Macaulay*, ii, 261.

sacrifice liberty for a chair at Cambridge and £400 a year. Besides, I never could do two things at once. If I lectured well, my History must be given up; and to give up my History would be to give up much more than the emoluments of the Professorship.' It was a wise decision, though it is tempting to reflect on the crowds who would have flocked to hear the most eloquent voice of his time.

A fortnight after Macaulay's refusal Lord John Russell recommended Sir James Stephen. 'It seems to me,' wrote the scholarly Prime Minister to the Prince Consort on July 20, 'that experience in the practical business of life is a good foundation for an historian. Xenophon, Tacitus, Davila, Guicciardini were all men engaged in political or military affairs.' [1] At the Prince's request Stephen explained his view of the duties of the office in a Memorandum which found entire satisfaction, and a personal interview was followed by the appointment. 'Sir James Stephen has after all become Professor of History in Cambridge,' wrote the Prince to the faithful Stockmar. 'We have had him here, and I was able to have much conversation with him. Never have I seen an Englishman with a mind more open and free from prejudice. I understand now why he was unpopular, for he hits hard at the weak points of his countrymen.'

The father of the new Professor had been a prominent member of Wilberforce's evangelical circle, and had taken an active part in the struggle against the slave-trade. His mother was a daughter of John Venn, a leading member of the Clapham Sect.[2] Sir James himself, after studying at Cambridge, spent his early years at the Bar, but in 1834 he became Under-Secretary in the Colonial Office.[3] During the next decade his strong hand and powerful brain were felt in every detail of legislation and administration, above all in the abolition of slavery and the grant of responsible government in Canada; and Sir Henry Taylor, his colleague in the Colonial Office, declared that he literally ruled the

[1] *Life of the Prince Consort*, ii, 203.
[2] See Leslie Stephen, *Life of Sir J. F. Stephen*, chapter 1. L. S. Wood, *Selected Epigraphs* (published for the Historical Association in 1930, Leaflet No. 80), discusses the Inaugural Lectures of the Regius Professors of Modern History at Oxford and Cambridge since 1841.
[3] See *The First Sir James Stephen*. Letters with biographical notes by his daughter C. E. Stephen. Printed for private circulation, 1906. Cp. the brief biography by his son James in the fourth edition of the *Essays in Ecclesiastical Biography*.

Colonial Empire.   The commanding personality of the greatest civil servant of his time is suggested, perhaps a little unkindly, in the titles King Stephen, Mr. Over-Secretary Stephen, Mr. Mother-Country Stephen (the latter attributed to Charles Buller), by which he was familiarly known.   Though his work was continuous and exacting, he stole time from sleep and relaxation to write articles for the *Edinburgh Review* which, when collected and revised in 1849 under the title of *Essays in Ecclesiastical Biography*, enjoyed a popularity second to those of Macaulay alone.   The vigour of his style, his wide knowledge and broad sympathy with leading figures of different churches—Hildebrand and St. Francis, Luther and Loyola, the French Benedictines and the Port-Royalists —won innumerable friends, and the book may still be read with pleasure and profit.[1]

The new Professor was hardly in the saddle before he was exposed to a virulent attack for the views on eternal punishment which he had expressed in an Epilogue to the *Essays*.   The danger of daring to say what most educated men had already begun to think was to be proved four years later when the saintly Maurice lost his chair in London; but Maurice was a Professor of Theology and his case was complicated by extraneous factors.[2] An anonymous pamphlet [3] entitled *The Government Scheme of Education in the University of Cambridge* argued that religious errors in the Professor would vitiate his teaching of Modern History. 'It is the clear duty of the members of the Senate,' declared the author, 'to prove to the country at large that they are watching with godly jealousy over the faith and morals of the youth committed to their charge.'   The attempt to secure an inquiry by the Senate was frustrated by a modest and wholly admirable letter to the Vice-Chancellor.[4]   Stephen protested his orthodoxy, recalled the fact that he had subscribed to the Thirty-nine Articles only a few weeks before, and resented the insinuation that he would use the Chair to attack the doctrines of the Church which he loved.   He was indeed a deeply though unobtrusively religious man, and he

---

[1] A reprint in the Silver Library in 1907 secured new readers in the post-Victorian world.
[2] See Hearnshaw, *History of King's College, London*, 206–216.
[3] A copy is in the British Museum.
[4] This letter is printed and the Cambridge years are described in *The First Sir James Stephen*, chapters 5–8.

made his public reply to his critics in the Inaugural *On certain so-called Philosophies of History*, rejecting the fatalist and positivist attitudes and acclaiming the theory of Providence.

Stephen had long been a celebrity, and his first impressions were favourable. 'Conyers Middleton was certainly mistaken,' he wrote to Henry Taylor, 'in thinking that there has been an end of all miracles since the time of the Apostles. My own lectures prove it. Gownsmen and gownswomen, filling room or college hall, the female students of history occupying the gallery, while I at the other end address my audience in a sonorous voice and with an assurance which the most intrepid of your Downing Street bores might envy.' Two years later he expressed his pleasure in resuming his gown at Cambridge and writing lectures on history, believing that 'though there were many men much more conversant with the events of former times, there was no candidate for the office who could in any degree claim equality with myself in that kind of historical knowledge which is derived from a long and intimate connexion with the actual government of mankind'.

Stephen chose for his first courses the history of France, after consulting John Austin, who advised him to explain the institutions of the old French monarchy, and Macaulay, who emphasised the claims of the wars of religion.[1] He had retired from the Colonial Office owing to ill-health in 1847, and he never regained his strength, though his intellectual energy was unabated. After delivering his first series in 1850 he fell dangerously ill, and completed the second series in Paris during the winter of 1851. The two solid volumes covering the internal history of France from Roman Gaul to the eve of the Revolution received a warm welcome, and a third edition, with large additions, appeared in 1857. 'I claim no place among historians,' he writes in a modest preface; 'I have written only as a commentator.' No apology was needed, for the lectures reveal the same sterling qualities as the *Essays*. His survey is singularly lucid, comprehensive and well arranged. Among its most valuable features are the addresses on the rise of the municipalities and the results of the Crusades, the administration of justice and the collection of

---

[1] See the dedicatory letter to Whewell in volume one of the first edition of the *Lectures on the History of France*, 1851.

revenue, and the full narrative of the meetings of the States-General. The three lectures on the Power of the Pen contain attractive portraits of thinkers and scholars, saints and sinners, from Abelard and St. Bernard to Rabelais and Descartes. Leslie Stephen was justified in pronouncing his father's lectures to reflect his experience of administrative work and to reveal an unusual appreciation of the constitutional side of French history. In his study of the *Ancien Régime* he anticipated some of the results of Tocqueville, who expressed cordial appreciation of his work.

The interest in the new Professor soon flagged, and he reported that his audience had dwindled. In 1855 he became Professor of Modern History and Political Economy at the East India College at Haileybury, holding the two chairs at the same time, and writing out lectures on the history of India which were never published. He found the new audience more satisfactory than the old. 'The difference is that here the boys listen with anxiety to get up the subject for their exams. At Cambridge they listen or not as it happens to interest them.' Stephen was growing old and weary, and in 1858 decided that he would resign in the following year. He died in 1859 at the age of seventy. His successor paid public tribute to his 'large-hearted humanity', and his decade of office notably enhanced the prestige of the Chair.

The vacant post was offered by Palmerston to Charles Kingsley. 'He accepted it,' records his wife, 'but with extreme diffidence.'[1] 'I cannot bear to think of my own unworthiness,' he confessed to his wife. His hesitation was intelligible. He was a popular preacher and lecturer, a moralist, a poet, a pamphleteer, a country parson and Chaplain to the Queen. Though he was the author of *Hypatia* and *Westward Ho!* he had never made any systematic study of history. 'It is with a feeling of awe, almost of fear,' he declared in his Inaugural,[2] 'that I find myself in this place upon this errand.' He cut the knot by delivering a sermon. To understand history we must understand men. Biography and autobiography were essential. Human welfare was founded not on mind but on morals. 'As the fruit of righteousness is

---

[1] *Charles Kingsley: Letters and Memories of his Life.* Edited by his wife, vol. ii, chapter 20.
[2] Printed separately and reprinted in *The Roman and the Teuton.*

wealth and peace, strength and honour, the fruit of unrighteous-
ness is poverty and anarchy, weakness and shame.   For not upon
mind, gentlemen, not upon mind, but upon morals is human
welfare founded.   So far from morals depending upon thought,
thought, I believe, depends upon morals.'   Thus prosperity was
the correlative of morality.   In a word, history was the record
of God's education of man.   It was the same message which
Thomas Arnold had brought to his Oxford hearers in his
Inaugural in 1841.

   The seed sown in Kingsley's Inaugural ripened in his first
and most celebrated course, *The Roman and the Teuton*.   The
rejuvenation of Europe by the unspoiled races from the north
was a theme after his own heart.   From the paralysis of the
ancient world we pass to the swarming barbarians, who are
speedily civilised by the joint influence of Christianity and Rome.
Huns, Goths and Lombards sweep across the stage.   The closing
lecture bears the characteristic title, 'The Strategy of Providence'.
The conquest of Rome by the Teutons, he declares, was directed
by God.   'Was this vast campaign fought without a General?
No! the hosts of our forefathers were the hosts of God.'   There
are passages of genuine eloquence and skilful dramatisation, but
there is little learning and the reflections are commonplace.   His
brother-in-law and admiring friend, Max Müller, admits that he
would have done better to write an historical novel or drama on
Theodoric.[1]   'History,' he adds, 'was but his text; his chief aim
was that of a teacher and preacher.'   The Professor's peculiar
gifts were well understood by his audience.   'He preached,'
writes a pupil, 'without seeming to do so.   Men all over the
world have thanked God for the lessons of manliness, charity
and godliness they learned in his lecture-room.'   The lecturer
would have valued such a testimonial far more than any tribute
to his scholarship.

   Kingsley's second course, on the *History of America*, suggested
by the outbreak of the Civil War, ended with the words, 'If I have
convinced you that well-doing and ill-doing are rewarded and
punished in this world as well as in the world to come, I shall
have done you more good than if I had crammed your mind with
many dates and facts.'   It was utterances of this sort which

---

[1] *Chips from a German Workshop*, vol. ii.

moved Lord Morley to declare that Kingsley had less of the historic sense than any other professor who ever sat in a Chair of History.   Though he attracted one of the largest audiences in Cambridge, and held it enthralled, his lectures did not lead to serious study.   His quick sympathy, fervent emotions and robust personality made him the idol of young men, and he was chosen by the Prince Consort to teach history privately to the Prince of Wales during his residence at Cambridge; but he knew that he was unfitted for an academic career.   *The Roman and the Teuton* was sharply criticised, and his later courses were never published.   He was not much in residence, and was happiest in his rectory at Eversley.   A newspaper attack in 1868 turned his thoughts to resignation, and in 1869 he withdrew from the post which he ought never to have accepted.   'My brains as well as my purse,' he explained, 'rendered the step necessary.'

Gladstone's choice fell on Seeley, who had won fame as the author of *Ecce Homo*, and had been for some years Professor of Latin at University College, London.[1]   In his Inaugural he recalled Stephen's lectures, which he had attended as an undergraduate.   'The recollection is discouraging.   I do not hope to give better lectures than Sir James Stephen.   It was—and I think the Professor felt it—a painful waste of power.   There was teaching of the highest kind, and no demand for it.   The causes which were at work to depress the study of modern history have not quite ceased to operate, though they may operate less powerfully, and it is in no sanguine spirit that I commence my labours.'   His theme was the Teaching of Politics.   Why should history be studied? he asked.   Because it is the school of statesmanship, came the reply.   'Our University is and must be a great seminary of politicians.   Without at least a little knowledge of history no man can take a rational interest in politics, and no man can form a rational judgment about them without a good deal.'   That this truth was so little recognised was due to the common error that history dealt with the remote past.   It was to modern history that he invited the attention of the young men 'from whom the legislators and statesmen of the next age must be taken'.   'As the indispensable thing for a lawyer is a knowledge of law and for

[1] See Gooch, *History and Historians in the Nineteenth Century*, 369–374, and Rein, *Seeley, Eine Studie über den Historiker*, 1912.

a clergyman of divinity, so the indispensable thing for a politician is a knowledge of political economy and history.'

The new Professor found time to write several books of outstanding significance. The earliest and the largest, *The Life and Times of Stein*, the first important historical work written by a holder of the Cambridge Chair, approached the history of Napoleon from a new angle. It contained no revelations, for he consulted no manuscripts, but he mastered the whole mass of printed authorities. Though hero-worship was no temptation to his austere temperament, and biographical detail had no attraction for him, he does not conceal his admiration for the strong, silent man whom he ranks with Turgot among leading political architects. If the work has a fault it is its portrait of the Emperor. His *Short History of Napoleon*, written some years later, once more revealed his inability to measure the greatness of a genius whose character and policy he abhorred.

If the *Life of Stein* met with less than its legitimate success, his next work brought generous compensation. *The Expansion of England* occupies a place in our political history, for it appeared at a moment when the nation was becoming interested in the Colonies and the Empire. The two courses dealt with the conquest of Canada and India, explaining with crystal clearness the relation between the foundation of the British Empire and the conflict with France. His thesis was less original than he believed, but he was the first to work it out. He produced his effects by focusing a brilliant light on the principal factors, and exhibiting the connexion between a number of apparently isolated phenomena. He loved large surveys, international problems, comprehensive generalisations. The book was read throughout the British Empire, and quickened the sense of the magnitude as well as the responsibility of our heritage. He rejects the notion that its vastness proves either our invincible heroism or our genius for government, and his pages stimulate reflection rather than exaltation.

The last ten years of Seeley's life were devoted to the composition of a work on British foreign policy. Like Ranke, to whom he owed most, he regarded history as mainly concerned with the fortunes and relations of states. Intending at first to begin with 1688, he pushed his starting-point ever further back.

Finally, he commenced his survey with Elizabeth, and was over-taken by death when he had reached William III.   *The Growth of British Policy*, though but a fragment in two volumes, is his most mature and most valuable work.   His power of marshalling facts was unrivalled, and no one but Ranke has been more successful in making the reader sense the diplomatic unity of Europe.   He believed that the destiny of a state depended less on its institutions than on its place in the world.   If he occasionally traced results too exclusively to diplomatic factors, and was blind to the full significance of internal development, his mastery of foreign relations often placed domestic occurrences in a new light.   His tenure of the Chair will ever remain memorable.   He was the first scholar of the front rank to hold the post, and the first to realise the significance of German scholarship.   He had a horror of lazy thinking and careless work, and he scorned such pictu-resque writers as Macaulay and Carlyle.   No one has more ardently proclaimed the capacity of history to guide the footsteps of the statesman and the citizen.   When a separate Historical Tripos was established in 1873 [1] he claimed a leading place in it for political science.   Politics, he declared, were vulgar when they were not liberalised by history, and history faded into mere literature when it lost sight of its relation to practical politics. The attempt to build up a science of politics was pursued in the Conversation Classes held at his own house to which Cambridge men, myself among them, look back with gratitude.   Despite the limitations of his method, his twenty-five years at Cambridge raised the whole level of historical study and production in the University.

Lord Acton's appointment by Lord Rosebery in 1895 aroused unusual interest.[2]   Though his name was unknown in the market-place, he had been a conspicuous figure for nearly forty years in the republic of learning.   He had taken a leading part in opposing the Ultramontane movement which culminated in the Vatican decrees, he was familiar with the statesmen no less than the scholars of the Continent, and he was perhaps the most erudite Englishman of his time.   Half a German by birth and

---

[1] The Law and History Tripos had begun in 1870. See J. O. McLachlan, ' The Origin and Early Development of the Cambridge Historical Tripos,' *Cambridge Historical Journal*, vol. ix, No. 1, 1947.

[2] See Gooch, *History and Historians in the Nineteenth Century*, chapter 20.

training, he brought an international atmosphere into the University. Though he had never written a book, his articles and reviews in the Catholic journals which he had edited, in the *Quarterly Review* and the *Nineteenth Century*, and more recently in the *English Historical Review*, were appreciated throughout Europe. A Catholic Professor of History was a novelty; but the choice was justified, not only as a fitting tribute to a scholar of world-wide reputation, but from the narrower standpoint of the Cambridge historical school. Though not the greatest historian, he was the most commanding personality who has held the Chair of Modern History. The University has never possessed a teacher more capable of inspiring his students to research and reflection or one more ready to enter into their interests. For himself it was an Indian summer after a life of controversy and disappointment. 'Cambridge is really a haven of delight,' he wrote to Gladstone at the opening of 1896, 'and I am grateful to them all round for the way they tolerate and even accept me.' [1]

The Inaugural Lecture on the 'Teaching of History' sounded a note which had never been heard at either University. In his opening paragraphs he struck off the fetters in which Seeley had attempted to bind his pupils. 'Politics and history,' he declared in those deep, strong tones which his hearers will never forget, 'are interwoven but not commensurate. Ours is the domain that reaches further than affairs of State. It is our function to keep in view and to command the movement of ideas, which are not the effect but the cause of public events.' The first of human concerns was religion, the second liberty, and their fortunes were intertwined. Passing from the scope of the science to the spirit which should govern its study he emphasised the sanctity of the moral code. 'I exhort you never to debase the moral currency, but to try others by the final maxim that governs your own lives, and to suffer no man and no cause to escape the undying penalty which history has power to inflict on wrong. If in our uncertainty we must often err, it may be sometimes better to risk excess in rigour than in indulgence.' The fear that he would shield his own Church disappeared when it was realised that the

[1] Lord Acton's *Correspondence*, i, 157, and John Pollock, 'Lord Acton at Cambridge,' in *Independent Review*, October 1904.

severest sentences were passed where religion should have taught men better. In judging men and things, he declared, ethics go before dogma, politics and nationality. He practised what he preached, and he never wrote a word as Regius Professor which revealed him as member of a particular church.

The message that history embraced the whole life of man and the whole process of civilisation came like a breath of spring after the rather wintry rule of Seeley, but his passionate exhortation to moral severity provoked lively opposition. In his Presidential address to the American Historical Association, on 'Ethical Values in History,' Henry Charles Lea, the historian of the Inquisition, joined direct issue. The new gospel, he declared, presupposed a fixed and unalterable standard of morality, together with the comfortable assurance that we have attained to that absolute knowledge of right and wrong which enables us to pass final judgment on the men of the past. Every age has similarly flattered itself, and presumably every succeeding one will continue to cherish the same illusion. We must judge men, declared the Nestor of American historians, by their time. To transport ethical ideas into bygone centuries was to introduce subjectivity into what should be purely objective. Philip II, for example, conscientiously believed that in his mortal struggle with heretics he was rendering the highest service to God and man. To censure him was unjust, for the real culprit was the age. Even Acton's most devoted admirers must admit the substantial justice of this measured criticism.

The Professor delivered two courses of lectures, which were published after his death. 'My tendency to read everything I can get that relates to my subject,' he wrote to Gladstone, 'proves a drawback and a vice when I have to lecture, and I am always a little late and hurried.'[1] The course on Modern History covered the centuries from the Renaissance to the French Revolution. Designed for students reading for an examination, it naturally contains a great deal of familiar information, but we catch his personality in the judgments and reflections. His dominant theme is the advance of man towards ordered freedom. In a striking phrase he pronounces the emancipation of conscience from authority the main content of modern history. He is at his

---

[1] Lord Acton's *Correspondence*, i, 157.

best in the sixteenth century, and the lecture on Luther is a triumph of impartial interpretation. It is piquant to hear a Catholic agree with the Protestant Ranke that the Reformer was 'a profound conservative and a reluctant innovator', though he adds on a later page that, 'with all the intensity of his passion for authority, he did more than any single man to make modern history the development of revolution'. He understands as fully as any Protestant historian why the Reformation occurred, and he admits the debt of his Church to her enemies. 'Rome, with a contested authority and a contracted sphere, developed greater energy, resource and power than when it exercised undivided sway over Christendom in the West.' Next in interest to the judgment on Luther is that suggested by the fate of Strafford, Laud and Charles I. 'It is certain that they were put to death illegally and therefore unjustly. But we have no thread through the enormous intricacy and complexity of modern politics except the idea of progress towards more perfect and assured freedom and the divine right of free men. Judged by that test the three culprits must be condemned.'

More significant and personal is the course on the French Revolution, which Acton once described to me as the greatest subject in history. The volume is equally distinguished by its erudition and its sanity, its eloquence and its strength. 'The Revolution,' he declared, 'will never be intelligently known till we recognise that it is not utterly singular and exceptional, that other scenes have been as horrible and many men as bad.' In contrast to Taine's lurid picture of the actors, he declares them to have been for the most part average men, with a large number above the common standard, while Mirabeau and Sieyès possessed some claim to genius. Of the Declaration of the Rights of Man he speaks with enthusiasm. 'It is the triumphant proclamation of the doctrine that human obligations are not all assignable to contract or to interest or to force. This single page of print outweighs libraries and is stronger than all the armies of Napoleon.' Yet it had one great fault. It sacrificed liberty to equality, and the absolutism of the King was succeeded by the absolutism of the Assembly. Like Aulard he attributes the main responsibility for the degradation of the reform movement to the Court. The well-meaning King was surrounded by evil

counsellors, and the worst of them was the Queen; yet the
Revolution, despite its horrors, was a great effort at emancipation.
'The best things that are loved and sought by men are religion and
liberty, not pleasure or prosperity, not knowledge or power.
Yet the paths of both are stained with infinite blood.'

A few months after his appointment Acton received an
invitation from the University Press to edit a comprehensive
history of the modern world.[1] 'We shall avoid the needless
utterance of opinion or service of a cause. Ultimate history we
cannot have in this generation, but we can dispose of conventional
history.' He looked forward with special pleasure to the later
volumes, which could be enriched with secrets not learned from
books. He drew up a list of specialists and secured the acceptance of the greater number; but in 1901 he was struck down by
illness and died in 1902, a few months before the appearance of
the first volume. The introductory chapter in which he intended
to assess the legacy of the Middle Ages, and the survey of the
later Gladstonian era which he thirsted to undertake, were never
written. The work was carried out with admirable loyalty to
his plan and will always be connected with his name.

On Acton's death the Prime Minister, Arthur Balfour, proposed
as his successor Admiral Mahan, whose writings on sea-power
had been as diligently studied by rulers and statesmen as in the
universities of the Old and the New World.[2] Believing that the
appointment even of such a distinguished foreigner would be
unpopular, Edward VII suggested John Morley, the biographer
of Cromwell and Walpole, Cobden and Gladstone. When
Balfour argued that he was too little of an historian and
too much of a Parliamentarian to qualify, the King expressed
his willingness to appoint Lecky or any other competent British
subject. Finally, another ornament of Trinity College, Dublin,
was selected. Bury won European reputation by his histories
of Greece, Rome, and the early Eastern Empire and by his
incomparable edition of Gibbon; and he may be described as
the greatest historian who has ever held the Cambridge Chair.
His Inaugural Lecture, entitled 'The Science of History,' revealed

[1] See *The Cambridge Modern History: An Account of its Origin, Authorship and
Production,* 1907.
[2] Sidney Lee, *King Edward VII,* ii, 53–54.

an attitude in sharp contrast to those of his three predecessors.[1]
To Kingsley history was theology, to Seeley politics, to Acton
morals, to the new Professor science. History, he declared, was
a science, no less and no more. This famous aphorism, which
lends itself to misunderstanding if quoted *in vacuo*, is fully explained
in the course of the lecture. 'The transformation which historical
studies are undergoing is a great event in the history of the world.
A revolution is slowly and silently progressing. Erudition has
been supplemented by scientific method. History has been
enthroned among the sciences.' We owed the beneficent
transformation to Germany, where it was inaugurated by Wolf,
Niebuhr and Ranke. Nationalism has encouraged research, but
the twentieth-century historian must emancipate himself from its
yoke. The doctrine of development, enunciated by Leibniz, was
necessary for the understanding of history, but the historian *qua*
historian had no business with philosophical or teleological
interpretations. 'Though she may supply material for literary
art and philosophical speculation, she is herself a science, no
less and no more.'

Old as is the human race, Bury reminds us, we are still at the
beginning of the story, and our experience is much too short for
confident generalisations. 'We must see our petty periods *sub
specie perennitatis*,' and approach their study without presuppositions. Ranke's gospel—*Ich will bloss zeigen wie es eigentlich gewesen
ist*—was still the watchword. For the first time in a pronouncement from the Cambridge Chair we sense the full impact of
scientific discovery on the thought and perspective of the
historian. Freeman had proclaimed the unity of history, but
he had lived in a very limited world. History, as envisaged by
Bury, embraced human life in all its length and breadth. Its
theme was 'the material and spiritual development of man'. If
the lecture seems on cursory reading to lack colour and warmth,
it was from no tepid devotion of the new Professor to his calling.
'In prosecuting historical research,' he concludes, 'we are not
indulging in a luxury but doing a thoroughly practical work and
performing a duty to posterity.' In a sentence which revealed an

---

[1] Bury's writings on the nature of history are collected in his *Selected Essays*,
edited by Professor Temperley. Cp. the Memoir by Norman Baynes, and R. H.
Murray's Introduction to the Lectures on the *History of the Papacy in the Nineteenth
Century*.

aspect of his mind of which more was to be known later, he added that history would become 'a more and more powerful force for stripping the bandages of error from the eyes of men, for shaping public opinion, and advancing the cause of intellectual and political liberty'.

The ideas scattered by the Inaugural in rich profusion were developed in Bury's later utterances. 'The place of Modern History in the Perspective of Knowledge,' an address delivered at St. Louis in 1904, renewed the solemn warning against taking short views. Philosophies of history, such as that of Hegel, are splendid failures, for they are all imposed from without. In whatever period he lives, the historian is under the spell of the present, and in our day it is tempting to believe that Christianity, Democracy and other familiar landmarks are the last word. 'Historical relativity triumphs over the Procrustean principle. Our syntheses and interpretations can only have a relative value.' This absence of finality in no way diminishes the interest and importance of particular eras, and the scholar who gave most of his life to antiquity and the early Middle Ages stresses the special importance of modern history. For full knowledge—including knowledge of the mind and feeling of the time—is necessary for full understanding; and it is less difficult to know and therefore to understand the modern world than more distant and different epochs.

Five years later, in 1909, Bury contributed a paper on 'Darwinism and History' to a centenary volume entitled *Darwinism and Modern Science*, which reiterates the leading ideas of the Inaugural. 'The growth of historical study in the nineteenth century has been determined and characterised by the same general principle which has underlain the simultaneous developments of the study of nature, namely, the genetic idea. The conception of history as a continuous, genetic, causal process has revolutionised historical research and made it scientific. History is the reconstruction of the genetic process.' The meaning of genetic history was not fully realised till the first quarter of the nineteenth century, and its implications had not yet become axioms. 'History cannot become a science until it is conceived as lying entirely within a sphere in which the law of cause and effect has unreserved and unrestricted dominion.' Darwinism emphasised continuity, and 'the perspective of history is merged in the larger perspective of development.'

Though the human process is depicted as part of the genetic process, Bury points out that general laws were insufficient to explain historical development; for the part played by coincidence and individuals rendered it impossible to deduce the past or predict the future. This, however, was also the case in organic development. The element of contingency is analysed in the essay 'Cleopatra's Nose', published in 1916. Among his illustrations of apparently fortuitous synchronism of men and events are such outstanding occurrences as the invasion of Silesia by Frederick the Great, the loss of the American colonies by George III, and the conversion of Constantine to Christianity. With the advance of democracy and science, he concludes, contingencies will become less important in human evolution. The idea of contingency haunted him and prompted his oft-quoted confession: 'On days when I am a determinist I look on history in one way, and on days when I am an indeterminist in quite another.' It is significant that in dealing with the fall of the Roman Empire in the later edition of his greatest work he pronounces general causes alone insufficient to explain the catastrophe.

The substantial volume, *The Idea of Progress*, published in 1920, boldly grapples with the doctrine which Bury describes as the animating and controlling idea of Western civilisation. Its practical utility is frankly recognised, for it carries with it the elevating conception of duty to posterity; but this consideration is irrelevant to the question of its truth. 'The progress of humanity belongs to the same order of ideas as Providence or personal immortality. It is true or it is false, and like them it cannot be proved either true or false. Belief in it is an act of faith.' The idea involved a belief not only in advance during the past but in an indefinite advance in the future. The classical world and the Middle Ages knew nothing of it, and its principal sponsors were sons of France. Evolution was a purely neutral conception, compatible either with optimism or pessimism, and he labels believers in progress the optimists. He ends on a note which reveals the core of his thought. The idea of progress, he reminds us, had to overcome the illusion of finality, and in so doing it had rendered a most valuable service, but there was no finality in the notion itself. 'A day will come, in the revolution of centuries, when a new idea will usurp its place. And it too will have its successors.' This ever-present sense of the immense duration of the drama and the vastness of the stage partly accounts for the fact that he was less interested in individuals than in institutions, movements and ideas.

No survey of Bury's academic activities could omit a reference to the *History of Freedom of Thought*, contributed in 1913 to the Home University Library. We might be listening to Buckle or other mid-Victorian rationalists as we read his narrative of the struggles of the European mind to break the fetters of dogma, superstition and ecclesiastical authority. For the first time the grave professor left his desk for the market-place and laid about him with a big stick. To a mind anchored in the doctrine of relativity such notions as a chosen people, a final revelation and an infallible church were anathema. We find the same mixture of exasperation and contempt in his lectures on the Papacy in the nineteenth century, which, despite their interest, betray a curious lack of understanding of the varieties of religious experience.

The appointment of George Macaulay Trevelyan to succeed Bury in 1927 restored to Cambridge the best-known English historian of our time. His early works on the fourteenth and seventeenth centuries had won him readers outside professional circles, but it was from the Venetian colouring of the Garibaldi saga that we learned that the spirit of his great-uncle had returned to earth. His conception of the functions of the historian was first stated in the challenging manifesto entitled *Clio: a Muse*, published in 1913. Two generations earlier, he declared, history was a part of our national literature, but its popular influence had diminished as the expert displaced the amateur. If there was a gain in academic circles, there was a loss in its wider national life. The modern German idea of history as a science is unfavourably contrasted with the older English ideal of conveying the results of learning to a wide public in attractive form. Carlyle combined warm human sympathy with the highest imaginative powers, and his interpretations of the French Revolution and Cromwell were still alive. Historical sources could never tell us all we wanted to know, and imagination was essential to discover the causes of human action. 'To recover some of our ancestors' real thoughts and feelings is the hardest, subtlest and most educative function that the historian can perform.' The historian has three tasks — the scientific, the imaginative and the literary. To Seeley, who attacked story-telling and told his students, 'Ask yourself questions, set yourself problems,' he rejoins that the principal craft of the historian is the art of narrative. History is a tale, not a science. The historian should write for the nation, not merely for his fellow-students; for 'the ultimate value of history is not scientific but educational'.

The Professor's Inaugural Lecture many years later, entitled 'The Present Position of History', renewed the plea for 'the true English tradition', but in a less provocative tone.[1] His *History of England* had displayed a serene impartiality which made it welcome to every school of thought, and his official declaration of 1927 breathes the maturity of middle age. Though he spoke with greater respect for research, he once again argued that literature and learning should go hand in hand. While Bury wrote primarily for scholars and envisaged history first and foremost as intellectual enlightenment, his successor stresses its value for the enrichment of character and life. 'The truth about the past, if taught or read with broad human sympathy, can give a noble education to the mind of the student, not only in politics but in all kinds of civic and social relationship, and even in the domain of personal, religious and ethical ideals.' The appeal of history, he concludes, is in the last analysis poetic, for the historian is consumed with the longing 'to know what really happened in that land of mystery which we call the past'. Some of us possess this urge to peer into the magic mirror in a greater degree than others, but it exists in us all. History is too wonderful and too inspiring to be the monopoly of the professional, for the past 'gathers round it all the unscrutable mystery of life and death and time'. 'Let the science and research of the historian find the fact, and let his imagination and art make clear its significance.' That Dr. Trevelyan can realise his own lofty ideal, that he inherits

[1] The 1930 edition of *Clio: a Muse*, contains the Inaugural as well as the essay of 1913.

the artistry of Macaulay without his partisanship, he showed once again in his panorama of the age of Anne and in his *English Social History*.

Twenty years later Dr. Trevelyan returned to the old problems in a Presidental Address to the Historical Association entitled 'Bias in History'.[1] Defining it as 'any personal interpretation of historical events which is not acceptable to the whole human race'—in other words, as individual feeling and opinion—he regards it as inevitable and not intrinsically either good or bad. 'The ideal history, never yet written by any man, would so tell the tale of the Civil War that the reader would not only grasp with his mind but would warmly feel in his heart what Cavaliers and Roundheads respectively felt and would also understand what they, none of them, understood. The ideal history requires indeed a more vigorous combination of qualities of heart and head, of science and of art, than any other study undertaken by man. No wonder there has never yet been the perfect historian. His functions have to be put into commission. There have to be various kinds of history.' For instance he himself had once written three volumes on Garibaldi. 'They are reeking with bias. Without bias I should never have written them at all. For I was moved to write them by poetical sympathy with the passions of the Italian patriots of that period which I retrospectively shared. Such merit as the work has, largely derives from that. And some of its demerits also derive from the same cause. Even I can now see that I was not quite fair to the French, or to the Papalist, or to the Italian Conservative points of view. If I had to write it again I should alter this somewhat, though not enough to satisfy everyone. But in fact I could not possibly write the book again. What is good in it derived from the passions and powers of my youth, now irrevocable. *Si jeunesse savait, si vieillesse pouvait!*' However emotional and intellectual maturity may lessen creative artistry, it should at least bring us deeper insight, wider sympathies, more disinterested determination to understand the life and thought of the past.

That deeper insight is possible but full understanding beyond our grasp was proclaimed anew by Dr. Trevelyan in recent addresses

[1] Published in *History*, January 1948, and reprinted in *Autobiography and Other Essays*, 1949.

on 'History and the Reader' and 'Stray Thoughts on History'.[1] History, we are told, is the cement which holds together all the studies relating to the nature and achievement of man, but it supplies no final answer to our deepest questionings. 'As a great poem, an epic without beginning or end, I read History and never tire. But I can find in it no "philosophy of history". Philosophy must be brought to history, it cannot be extracted from it. And I have no philosophy of my own to bring beyond a love of things good and a hatred of things evil.' Toynbee is suggestive, but no one can supply a complete explanation. 'History can record the facts, but neither philosophy nor science can tell us why they occurred, nor why Cæsar, Mahomet and Shakespeare were born in their appropriate times.' Though history is more than a chapter of accidents, the unpredictable plays far too great a part in human experience to be ignored. Few generalisations and few formulas can stand up to searching criticism.

In his Inaugural Lecture delivered in 1944 Professor G. N. Clark, the successor of George Trevelyan, similarly cautioned his students against setting their target too high and claiming more wisdom than they possessed. He knew of no master-key which would unlock all doors, no formula such as the belief in progress or the doctrine of cycles which would light up the whole horizon and give meaning to the chequered story of mankind. Moreover, why should we even assume that there is a secret, a plan, a purpose to be discovered? 'I do not believe that any future consummation could make sense of all the irrationalities of the preceding ages. If it could not explain, still less could it justify. The crimes and sufferings of countless millions of beings were facts as real as anything that can occur in the future in the same historical process. The future cannot undo them, and any one of them by itself frustrates the search for rationality in the world of time. To me therefore it seems that no historical investigation can provide either a philosophy or a religion, or a substitute for a religion, or even an adequate excuse for doing without a religion. We work with limited aims. We try to find the truth about this or that, not about things in general.' The same note of caution is sounded in the Inaugural Lecture of Professor J. R. M. Butler delivered in 1949. 'History,' he declares, 'is concerned only with

[1] In *Autobiography and Other Essays*.

happenings in the world of space and time.   With the mightier movement, with the things that are eternal, she is not equipped to deal, though she can guess at their existence and their power. She sees the bending corn, but the wind she cannot see; she hears the sound thereof, but she cannot tell whence it cometh nor whither it goeth.'   Philosophies of history, so much in fashion at Cambridge and elsewhere when men knew less of the past than they know to-day, are the concern of philosophers.   And even philosophers can only guess at the riddles of the sphinx.

6

LORD ACTON: APOSTLE OF LIBERTY

LORD ACTON may be studied as a personality, an historian, a Roman Catholic, a moralist and a Liberal. As a personality he ranks among the most fascinating figures of the nineteenth century. Young and old agreed that there was no one like him. Lord Morley used to say that if he could summon one—and only one—of his friends from the grave it would be Acton. Gladstone, declares his biographer, could never have enough of his company, and the present writer preserves the memory of delightful talks fifty years ago. The reissue of some of his writings and Archbishop Mathew's recent study of his formative years suggest that interest in the man and his work tends to grow rather than to wane. The historian who never published a book has outlived most of his more productive contemporaries on the strength of two posthumous collections of essays and two courses of Cambridge lectures. His strenuous efforts to broaden the intellectual horizon of English Catholics and to combat the Ultramontanism which he abhorred have been described in Professor Noack's *Katholizität und Geistesfreiheit*, a book too little known outside Germany. His celebrity as a moralist is largely due to the fact that some of his maxims have become current coin. It was Acton's task to try men and movements, institutions and ideologies, by the acid test of Christian ethics, convinced as he was that since the coming of Christ there was no excuse for anyone to pretend that he did not know the difference between right and wrong. On his death-bed he confessed to his son that his judgments had occasionally been too harsh, but he would have reproached himself far more if he had ever failed to condemn wrongdoing in church and state.

It is with the fifth aspect of this many-sided man that this article is concerned, for it is above all as an apostle of liberty that his name and influence survive. His reputation grew steadily after his death with the publication of his writings and correspondence; and the revival of the detestable theory and practice of dictatorship after the First World War increased the authority of a teacher who ranks with Jefferson and Humboldt, Mill and Croce among the eminent Liberal thinkers of the modern world.[1] In a celebrated phrase Gladstone declared that the price of liberty is eternal vigilance, and a familiar couplet of Goethe proclaims that he alone merits liberty who conquers it afresh from day to day. A recent American biography by Lally, entitled *As Lord Acton Says*, stresses his unceasing struggle against political and intellectual coercion. If he returned to the world of to-day and was told, as we have been assured both from the Fascist and Marxist camp and by once popular oracles such as Spengler and Möller van den Bruck, that nineteenth-century liberalism was dead he would surely rejoin: So much the worse for the twentieth century! The *laissez-faire* economics which prevailed in his lifetime formed no essential portion of his gospel of liberty, which rests on the notion that we are neither slaves nor robots and that every man, however humble and weak, should have his place in the sun.

The first of human concerns, declared Acton is his famous Inaugural Lecture at Cambridge in 1895, was religion; the second was liberty, and their fortunes were intertwined. His conception was more fully expounded in the two lectures delivered in 1878 on *The History of Freedom*, which make us sadly aware what the world has lost by the failure even to commence what should have been the principal work of his life, and to which he always referred as the Madonna of the Future. 'By liberty I mean the assurance that every man shall be protected in doing what he believes his duty against the influence of authority and majorities, custom and opinion. The state is competent to assign duties and draw the line between good and evil only in its immediate sphere. Beyond the limits of things necessary for its well-being, it can only give indirect help to fight the battle of life by promoting the influences which prevail against temptation —religion, education, and the distribution of wealth. The most certain test by which we judge whether a country is really free

[1] See Ulrich Noack, *Politik als Sicherung der Freiheit*.

is the amount of security enjoyed by minorities.   Liberty is not
a means to a higher political end.   It is itself the highest political
end.   It is not for the sake of a good public administration that it
is required, but for security in the pursuit of civil society and of
private life.   A generous spirit prefers that his country should be
poor and weak and of no account, but free, rather than powerful,
prosperous and enslaved.   It is better to be the citizen of a
humble commonwealth in the Alps than a subject of the superb
autocracy that overshadows half of Asia and Europe.'   It is no
new doctrine that the quality of the citizen matters more than the
size, the wealth and the power of the state; but no one has held
the principles of the Periclean oration with deeper conviction
or proclaimed them with more fervent eloquence than this liberal
aristocrat who combined cosmopolitan culture with the Englishman's instinctive determination to stand firmly on his own legs.
There is always a ring in his voice when he speaks of liberty.

Every Liberal, it has been truly said, is something of an
optimist about human nature; the higher our estimate, the more
can citizens be encouraged and allowed to go their own way.
The worse we are—or are believed to be—the greater the need
for coercion and control in society and government.   As a
Christian individualist hating revolution no less than despotism,
Acton asked, not that we should follow every whim of the natural
man, but that we should have the opportunity to fulfil our lofty
destiny as the children of God.   'The end of civil society is the
establishment of liberty for the realisation of moral duties.'
Though one of the most learned men of his time was only too
familiar with the history of human temptation, he believed that
we are divinely endowed with the instruments of resistance and
that conscience is the mariner's compass in the stormy voyage of
life.   The way to secure the flowering of personality, to get the
best out of the citizen, to aid him to grow to his full spiritual
stature, is to make the highest claims on him, to give him the
maximum chance of self-realisation, to say to him: 'Freely ye have
received, freely give'.   The way to make men better, he declared
in an aphorism which is the pure milk of Liberalism, is to set them
free.   For machine-made and mass-produced citizens, as for the
systems which produced them, he had nothing but angry contempt.   He looked to the Puritans, to Locke, to Jefferson, to

Burke and Mill, not to Hobbes or Rousseau, Hegel or Joseph de Maistre, in whose systems the individual was pushed to the wall.

Since ordered liberty was the greatest prize of civilised mankind, and indeed the hall-mark of civilisation itself, its evolution appeared to Acton not only the most fascinating but the most significant theme in the whole range of historical studies. Hegel's *Philosophy of History* had proclaimed the same doctrine, but while the interest of the German thinker was concentrated on the might and majesty of the state, Acton's eyes were fixed on the individual. 'Twenty years ago,' writes Lord Bryce in a memorable passage, 'late at night in his library at Cannes, he expounded to me his views of how a history of liberty might be written and how it might be made the central thread of all history. He spoke for six or seven minutes only; but he spoke like a man inspired, as if from some mountain summit high in air he saw beneath him the far-winding path of human progress from dim Cimmerian shores of prehistoric shadow into the fuller yet broken light of the modern time. The eloquence was splendid; but greater than the eloquence was the penetrating vision which discerned throughout all events and in all ages the play of those moral forces, now creating, now destroying, always transmuting, which had moulded and remoulded human institutions, and had given to the human spirit its ceaselessly changing forms of energy. It was as if the whole landscape of history had been suddenly lit up by a burst of sunlight. I have never heard from any other lips any discourse like this, nor from his did I ever hear the like again.' Though the outlines were never filled in, we possess enough material to indicate his attitude to the main phases of the ascent of man. 'We have no thread through the enormous intricacy of modern politics,' he declared in his *Lectures on Modern History*, 'except the idea of progress towards more perfect and assured freedom and the divine right of free men.'

Dismissing the economic interpretation of history proclaimed by Marx as a childish over-simplification, Acton also rejected what may be described as a predominantly political approach. History, he declared, derived its best virtue from beyond the sphere of state. Institutional changes, transformations of society, the rise and fall of empires, have many causes, but at the back of everything is the conflict of ideas. There was little liberty in the

ancient world, for the individual was at the mercy of the state.
'It is the Stoics who emancipated mankind from its subjugation
to despotic rule, and whose enlightened and elevated views of life
bridged the chasm that separates the ancient from the Christian
state and led the way to freedom. They made it known that
there is a will superior to the collective will of man and a law that
overrules those of Solon and Lycurgus. That which we must
obey, that to which we are bound to reduce all civil authorities
and to sacrifice every earthly interest, is that immutable law which
is perfect and eternal as God Himself.' True freedom, declared
the most eloquent of the Stoics, consists in obeying God. These
doctrines were adopted and applied by the great jurists of the
Empire. Readers of the first volume of Carlyle's monumental
survey of mediæval political theory will discover how much the
Christian doctrine of the state took over from the sages of Greece
and Rome. The difference between the ancient and the Christian
world was not the difference between darkness and light. 'There
is hardly a truth in politics or in the system of the rights of man
that was not grasped by the wisest of the Gentiles and the Jews,
or that they did not declare with a refinement of thought and a
nobleness of utterance which later writers could never surpass.
But although the maxims of the great classic teachers, of Sophocles
and Plato and Seneca, and the glorious examples of public virtue,
were in the mouths of all men, there was no power in them to
avert the doom of that civilisation for which the blood of so many
patriots and the genius of such incomparable writers had been
wasted in vain. The liberties of the ancient nations were crushed
beneath a hopeless and inevitable despotism, and their vitality
was spent when the new power came forth from Galilee, giving
what was wanting to the efficacy of human knowledge to redeem
societies as well as men.'

If the recognition of 'the law of nature' was the first step
on the long and winding road from despotism to liberty, the
second was the proclamation of the spiritual independence of
every human being by the Christian Church. 'When Christ
said, "Render unto Cæsar the things that are Cæsar's, and unto
God the things that are God's," those words gave to the civil
power, under the protection of conscience, a sacredness it had
never enjoyed and bounds it had never acknowledged, and they

were the repudiation of absolutism and the inauguration of freedom. For our Lord not only delivered the precept but created the force to execute it. To reduce all political authority within defined limits ceased to be an aspiration of patient reasoners and was made the perpetual charge and care of the most energetic institution and the most universal association in the world.' That the Church often abused its power and betrayed its principles is true enough, but it was, above all, ecclesiastical resistance which prevented Europe from falling under the yoke of a Byzantine despotism. It was the first great organisation which dared to tell the state: 'Thus far and no further!' From the conflict of the secular and ecclesiastical authority arose civil liberty, for both were driven to acknowledge, at any rate in theory, the sovereignty of the people and to claim its support.

The third decisive advance was the invention of representative government. 'Neither an enlightened philosophy, nor all the political wisdom of Rome, nor even the faith and virtue of the Christians, availed against the incorrigible tradition of antiquity. Something was wanted beyond all the gifts of reflection and experience—a faculty of self-government and self-control, developed like its language in the fibre of a nation and growing with its growth. This vital element, which many centuries of warfare, of anarchy, of oppression had extinguished in the countries that were still draped in the pomp of ancient civilisation, was deposited on the soil of Christendom by the fertilising stream of migration that overthrew the Empire of the West.' In this pæan to our Teutonic ancestors, to 'the noble savage' of the poets, we might be listening to the voice of Freeman himself. While the main outcome of ancient politics was an absolute state resting on slavery, the Middle Ages witnessed the progressive restriction of the executive by the combined pressure of feudalism, cities and the Church. This process of the dispersion of power was challenged by Machiavelli and Protestant reformers, by Bodin and Hobbes, who revived the doctrine of the unfettered sovereignty of the State as the only method of dealing with the abuses of feudalism and particularism and the best way of preserving order. Once again, as in the ancient world, centralisation was carried too far in the absolute monarchies created in sixteenth-century Europe, Catholic no less than Protestant.

22

Fortunately for mankind, the cause of liberty was saved by England and America. Acton had always had a particularly warm place in his heart for the Puritans who, primarily for religious motives, stood up to the first two Stuart kings and were ready to pay any price for obeying the voice of conscience. Though Lilburne can hardly be classified as a Puritan in the stricter sense, he is hailed as one of the first writers to understand the need of democracy. Locke, the most typically English and therefore the most influential of our publicists, proclaimed the virtues of the *juste milieu*. Montesquieu emphasised the value of the 'separation of powers' as the strongest guarantee of free institutions. Acton the Liberal admired the Constitution of the United States as much as Maine the Conservative. Detesting the concentration of power above all things, he applauded a system which divided authority between the Executive, the Legislature, the Supreme Court, and the federal units, the whole structure of government being set forth in a maturely considered document, the provisions of which could only be altered by an elaborate ritual of national consultation. 'It was democracy in its highest perfection, armed and vigilant against its own weakness and excess.' Acton spoke with no less enthusiasm of the Declaration of Independence and of the decision of the American Colonies to fight, though the justification he presents is not quite in line with the older American interpretation. 'Their grievance was difficult to substantiate and trivial in extent. But if interest was on one side, there was manifest principle on the other—a principle so sacred and so clear as imperatively to demand the sacrifice of men's lives, of their families and their fortunes. They represented liberty as a thing so divine that the existence of society must be staked to prevent even the least infraction of its sovereign right.'

Of the contribution of France to the making of a free world, which forms the theme of his second course of Cambridge lectures, Acton speaks more critically. Despite the heavy artillery of Burke and Bentham, and the denunciation of the French Revolution by nine Catholic publicists out of ten, he acclaims the Declaration of the Rights of Man. 'It is the triumphant proclamation of the doctrine that human obligations are not all assignable to contract or to interest or to force.   This

single page of print outweighs libraries and is stronger than all
the armies of Napoleon.'   Yet it had one grave fault; it sacrificed
liberty to equality, and the absolutism of the King was succeeded
by the absolutism of the Assembly.   Rousseau, who finds no
favour in Acton's eyes, proclaimed the sovereignty of the people,
not the self-determination of the citizen.   France had been denied
the privilege of learning the art of constitutional government by
the method of trial and error, and the Revolution, despite its
horrors, was a great effort at human emancipation.   'The best
things that are loved and sought by men are religion and liberty,
not pleasure or prosperity, not knowledge or power.   Yet the
paths of both are stained with infinite blood.'

Having thus briefly explained Acton's conception of liberty,
and having under his guidance surveyed its slow advance through
the centuries, let us turn to its principal foes.   The first and the
oldest is autocracy, dynastic or otherwise—what we now call the
totalitarian state.

> 'Nature hath put this tincture in our blood,
> That each would be a tyrant if he could,'

wrote Defoe in the days of William III.   How easy it is for
ambitious adventurers when favoured by circumstances to overthrow free institutions is more obvious to the twentieth than to
the nineteenth century, when it was commonly assumed that
the main struggle was over.   Such was the case in the British
Commonwealth and the United States, but in the larger part of
Europe the enemies of mixed government have never laid down
their arms.   While the privileged Anglo-Saxon inherits freedom
'slowly broadening down from precedent to precedent', and
instinctively approaches the problems of political science from
the angle of citizens' rights, the Continental thinker and statesman
usually starts with the conception of the overriding authority of
the state.   Hobbes has always been the prophet without honour
in his own country, but the Great Leviathan has found plenty of
disciples abroad.   In Germany, the land of obedience, as Herder
described it, Kant and Humboldt, Stein and Dahlmann were
voices crying in the wilderness, Hegel had no use for the separation
of powers, Bismarck took care that the grant of adult male
suffrage for the Reichstag should leave the power of the executive

virtually unimpaired, and Treitschke thundered that the state
was power, not an academy of arts.   In this great argument
Acton, despite his partially Continental upbringing, was a
thorough Englishman.   He detested Carlyle and the whole
school of apologists for the Nietzchean superman.   He had no
love for Palmerston, but in his rough challenge to autocracies
the most celebrated of British Foreign Ministers spoke for his
countrymen.

Autocracy was an enemy fighting in open daylight, and
everyone could see its ugly face.   But there was another terrible
danger to liberty which it was Acton's unceasing endeavour to
expose.   To overthrow an autocracy by frontal attack was not
enough, for the foe might only too easily enter by the back door
in disguise.   He believed in the Rights of Man as much as Tom
Paine or Jefferson or the Abbé Sieyès, but his historical studies
convinced him that there was little prospect of obtaining them
from an omnipotent executive.   'All power tends to corrupt,'
runs the most familiar of his aphorisms, 'and absolute power
corrupts absolutely.   Great men are almost always bad men.'
The ultimate problem to be faced was less the form of government than the abuse of power.   *Étatisme* was the unpardonable
sin against the Holy Ghost.   'It is bad to be oppressed by a
minority, but it is worse to be oppressed by a majority.   For there
is a reserve of latent power in the masses which, if it is called into
play, the majority can seldom resist.   But from the absolute will
of an entire people there is no appeal, no redemption, no refuge
but treason.'   Rousseau's doctrine of the General Will could
be easily perverted into the ruthless tyranny of the majority—
'an evil of the same nature as unmixed monarchy, requiring, for
nearly the same reasons, institutions that shall protect it against
itself and shall uphold the permanent reign of law against arbitrary
revolutions of opinion'.

Acton abhorred the notion of government merely by counting
heads; yet the Liberal in him realised that the days of upper and
middle class rule were over, and he welcomed the extension of
the franchise to the manual worker.   Though he described
Burke's teaching as the noblest political philosophy in the world,
he never shared his conviction that power should rest in the
hands of those who, to use the ambiguous phrase, had a stake in

the country. 'The men who pay wages ought not to be the political masters of those who earn them,' he wrote to Mary Gladstone; 'for laws should be adapted to those who have the heaviest stake in the country, for whom misgovernment means not mortified pride or stinted luxury, but want and pain and degradation, and risk to their own lives and to their children's souls.'

Though he had little spiritual affinity with Bentham and his utilitarianism, Acton accepted the formula 'everybody to count for one and nobody for more than one'. That birth or wealth should bring special political privileges was an offence both to Liberal ideology and Christian ethics. 'The danger is not that a particular class is unfit to govern. Every class is unfit to govern. The law of liberty tends to abolish the reign of race over race, of faith over faith, of class over class. It is not the realisation of a political ideal; it is the discharge of a moral obligation.' He belonged to the Liberal party because in his opinion it was least dominated by class. 'The nature of Toryism is to be entangled in interests, traditions, necessities, difficulties, expedients, to manage as best one may, without creating artificial obstacles in the shape of dogma or superfluous barriers of general principle.' As an English Liberal, he wrote to Lady Blennerhassett in 1879, 'I judged that of the two parties—of the two doctrines—which have governed England for 200 years, that one was most fitted for the divine purpose which upheld civil and religious liberty.' 'The House of Lords represents one great interest—land. Except under very perceptible pressure it always resists measures aimed at doing good to the poor. It has been almost always in the wrong—sometimes from prejudice and fear and miscalculation, still oftener from instinct and self-preservation.' His beloved leader expressed the same view in his well-known formula that in the great political controversies of his lifetime the classes were usually wrong and the masses usually right.

The main task of government in a democratic community in Acton's view was to combine majority rule with the spiritual freedom of the individual which was dearer to him than life. Lecky grappled with the problem in his comprehensive *Democracy and Liberty*, which combined a good deal of sound argument with petulant attacks on the Liberal party. Acton's approach is

indicated in his lengthy and pregnant dissertation on Erskine
May's *Democracy in Europe* published in 1878 and in his letters to
Mary Gladstone.   Since all power tended to corrupt, it was plain
common sense—and indeed the healthy instinct of self-preservation—to limit the amount entrusted to any man or group.   The
first step was the reform of the franchise machinery on the lines
suggested by Hare and blessed by Mill.   'The one pervading
evil of democracy is the tyranny of the majority, or rather of that
party, not always the majority, that succeeds by force or fraud in
carrying elections.   To break off that point is to avoid the danger.
The common system of representation perpetuates the danger.
Unequal electorates afford no security to majorities.   Equal
electorates give none to minorities.   Thirty-five years ago it was
pointed out that the remedy is proportional representation.   It is
profoundly democratic, for it increases the influence of thousands
who would otherwise have no voice in the government; and it
brings men nearer an equality by contriving that no vote shall be
wasted and that every voter shall contribute to bring into Parliament a member of his own opinions.'   Acton spoke with special
sympathy of the class of citizens whom Bagehot described as
'between sizes', for during his six years in Parliament he lamented
that he agreed with nobody and nobody agreed with him.

A second and far more important device for preventing the
abuse of power was to divide the functions of government
between central and regional authorities.   The ardent admirer
of the American Constitution desired its central principle to be
applied as widely as possible.   'Of all checks on democracy
federalism has been the most efficacious and the most congenial.
The federal system limits and restrains the sovereign power by
dividing it and by assigning to Government only certain defined
rights.   It is the only method of curbing not only the majority
but the power of the whole people, and it affords the strongest
basis for a second chamber, which has been found the essential
security for freedom in every genuine democracy.'   Like Gladstone he sympathised with the South in the American Civil War,
not because he approved slavery, but because he believed in
upholding State Rights against the domination of the federal
executive.   Had he lived to read Lord Bryce's *Modern Democracies*
he would have approved his friend's verdict that Switzerland,

with her cantonal system and her plebiscites, came nearest to the ideal of decentralised self-determination. In countries with a long unitary tradition and a homogeneous population, federal institutions, which were natural in the United States, Canada and Australia, Mexico and Brazil, the German Empire and Switzerland, were impossible; but the principle of devolution could be applied in a limited degree in Great Britain without a written constitution. Acton was one of the earliest and strongest advocates of Home Rule for Ireland; Scotland has a Minister and could have a Parliament of her own if she wished; Ulster stands in federal relationship to Westminster and Whitehall; Wales can have a Minister whenever she desires. The plan of a federated Great Britain put forward after his death, with separate parliaments for England, Wales, Scotland, and Ireland, would at any rate have received his respectful consideration. Rejecting the cynical maxim of despots, *Divide et Impera*, he would have substituted the maxim: Divide in order that you do not rule too much. He was one of the earliest English admirers of Gierke, who, though a Prussian, emphasised the significance of voluntary associations for the healthy development of the state. Autocracy was almost as bad for the ruler as for the ruled.

No exposition of Actonian ideology would be complete if we confined our attention to the purely political sphere, for the liberty of the individual is threatened by various influences and institutions. The emancipation of conscience from authority, he declared, was the main content of modern history. Like other oracular utterances this must not be taken too literally, but it contains a valuable truth. For by authority he meant external authority, the attempt to place the mind and soul of man on the bed of Procrustes. Tolerance of error, as Mill had argued in the noblest of his writings, was requisite for freedom. Many of the worst offenders had been found in the Christian churches. An early essay on *The Protestant Theory of Persecution* condemned the Protestant leaders for advocating liberty of conscience when they were weak and forbidding it when they were strong. Luther's despotic nature, he declares, hated political and religious liberty, and he is described as the inventor of the theory of passive obedience. That Melanchthon shared his view was worse, for his blood was cooler. The Church was merged in the State.

Yet in the long run the Reformers, without intending it, contributed to the growth of political and religious liberty. 'Luther
gave to the individual conscience an independence which was
sure to lead to an incessant resistance.' The earliest and bravest
champions of liberty of conscience were to be found, not among
the dignitaries of the Protestant churches, but among the little
sects in England and Holland who insisted on worshipping God
in their own way. Here, far more than among the Barons at
Runnymede, were the true pioneers of liberty, fighting not for
their property or their privileges, but for the fundamental right
to call their soul their own.

Enemies of liberty were not found in the Protestant camp alone.
The same spiritual individualism which led Acton to salute the
Puritan conscience compelled him to combat the concentration
of ecclesiastical authority which culminated in the Infallibility
Decree. Having praised his Church in his early essays as the
guardian of liberty and conscience by its unceasing war against
the despotism of the state, he was shocked to witness the authoritarian drive during the pontificate of Pius IX. *Corruptio optimi
pessima.* The position of a highly critical individualist in a Church
claiming divine authority was difficult enough before 1870 and
even more uncomfortable afterwards. Even in 1869 the Pope
complained to an English visitor of certain people who were not
Catholics *di cuore*, of whom Acton was the type. He supported
Döllinger's campaign against Ultramontanism with passionate zeal.
The celebrated aphorism of Pius IX, 'I am tradition', filled him
with dismay. He objected to autocracy in his Church as much as
to an omnipotent secular ruler on the throne. He regarded the
failure of the Conciliar movement in the fifteenth century as a
tragedy, not only because the leadership of the reform movement fell into other hands, but because it paved the way to the
domination of the Vatican.

The keenest disappointments of Acton's life were the defeat
of the South in 1864 and the triumph of the Jesuits in 1870. In
both cases, as he saw it, the same issue was at stake—the diffusion
versus the concentration of power. Religious no less than civil
absolutism was anathema. How deeply he felt was revealed in
the *Letters of Quirinus*, in which Döllinger embodied his reports
from Rome during the Vatican Council. The Pope, he com-

plained, had been captured by the Jesuits; Romanism had triumphed over Catholicism. 'We have to meet an organised conspiracy to establish a power which would be the most formidable enemy of liberty as well as science throughout the world.' Acton, like the old Puritans, was not prepared to subordinate his conscience to any authority, secular or ecclesiastical, Council or Pope. The Church, he believed, was more than the Papacy, and the Christian conscience, God's choicest gift, was above them both. Holding such minority views it was not surprising that most of his closest friends were in the Protestant camp.

The defeat of his ideal of a tolerant and scholarly Catholicism threw a lasting shadow over Acton's later years. Not even the best or wisest of men—Pope or Emperor, President or Prime Minister—was good enough or wise enough to be entrusted with unlimited authority. The Papacy had shown itself unfit to possess absolute power, above all by the creation of Acton's *bête noire*. 'The Inquisition is peculiarly the weapon and peculiarly the work of the Popes. It is the principal thing with which the Papacy is identified and by which it must be judged.' He was probably the only Catholic who welcomed the publication of Henry Charles Lea's monumental *History of the Inquisition*. Hating all persecution, he particularly detested 'the regime of terror' in the sphere of religious convictions, regardless of whether or not they were his own. Heresy was merely an error, intolerance a sin. Though he expected to be excommunicated like Döllinger, the blow never fell, partly, no doubt, because he was a layman, partly because he discontinued the fight. Neither master nor pupil joined the Old Catholic Movement founded by some of their colleagues in the fray, and Acton's apprehensions were partially relieved by the fact that neither Pius IX nor Leo XIII used the power attributed to them by the Vatican Decrees. When Gladstone in a celebrated pamphlet denounced them as incompatible with civil allegiance, Acton replied in a series of letters to *The Times*. Without abandoning his conviction that the proclamation of Papal infallibility was a lamentable mistake, he asserted that the dangers of divided allegiance among English Catholics were theoretical and unlikely to materialise. Though he accepted his defeat in the struggle against Ultramontanism, he had no further contacts with the victors and became an increasingly lonely man.   More than ever he interpreted liberty as the privilege and the duty of the Christian citizen to obey his conscience.

During the distracting decades between the two World Wars and in the earlier phases of the second conflict Acton was dismissed as a voice crying in the wilderness.   Free institutions went down like ninepins in country after country in Europe, and the strident trumpeters of totalitarianism proclaimed that only the concentration of power could deliver the goods.   In the eyes of Hitler and Mussolini, Stalin and Franco, Pétain and his fellow-quislings, liberal democracy, the delicate child of Western civilisation, meant disunity and weakness.   Liberty, shouted the Duce, was a rotting corpse; discipline had taken its place.   For a brief period the strutting dictators could point to spectacular successes at home and abroad, and the masses, deprived of all means of expressing their opinions and intent on earning their daily bread, fed out of their hand.   With the defeat of the Axis and the growing realisation of the catastrophic consequences of absolute power, the wheel has come full circle.   While the historic Liberal parties have gone down in many countries before the combined onslaught of Right and Left, the proclamation of the Four Freedoms and the emergence of new parties in Western Europe, neither Fascist nor Communist, suggest that the spirit of Liberalism is not dead, and that it is capable of evoking support from outside the middle classes among whom it had its birth. 'To assert that liberty is dead,' declares Croce, the Nestor of European Liberalism, 'is to say that life is dead, that its mainspring is broken.   Ever in peril from the imperfections of human nature, it can never be wholly destroyed.'

Every member of the family of self-governing nations which took part in the greatest struggle in history will define in its own idiom the 'way of life' for which it fought and bled, for the loftiest ideals defy the dictionary.   Whatever formula we adopt we shall do well to bear in mind the truths which Acton never ceased to proclaim: that man does not live by bread alone; that the state was made for man, not man for the state; that every citizen counts; that the Christian conscience is his safest guide; that minorities should have their recognised place in the sun;

that liberty is not a mere political contrivance but a spiritual principle and a tonic for the soul; that ordered liberty is the highest prize of civilised society; that men and women, like flowers, need light and air to have their chance and produce their best; that, since all power tends to corrupt, the only way to prevent its abuse is to cut it up into little bits.

7

HAROLD TEMPERLEY

HAROLD WILLIAM VAZEILLE TEMPERLEY was born at Cambridge on April 20, 1879. His father, a Fellow and Tutor of Queens', belonged to a north country family and counted among his ancestors the Mrs. Vazeille who married John Wesley. He was a gifted mathematician of whom his contemporaries expected great things, but he died young. His wife was the daughter of Thomas Wildman, D.D., Episcopal Chaplain at Callander. There were four children, one of whom became Major-General Temperley. After his school years at Sherborne, Harold entered King's College, Cambridge, in 1898. He was awarded the Gladstone Memorial Prize for his work in Part II of the Historical Tripos, and the Prince Consort Prize for a dissertation on the growth of the office of Prime Minister. He tried for a Fellowship at King's. Without waiting to try again he accepted an offer from Peterhouse in 1905, and began a fruitful association which lasted till the end. His first post was at the University of Leeds.

His first work, the *Life of Canning*, published in 1905, was a spirited performance. Our greatest Foreign Minister, as Acton described him, became and remained his hero. The book made his name, but there was not very much research in it and there is a touch of youthful exuberance in these glowing pages. Canning, we are told, like Bentham and Adam Smith, was too completely successful in the sense that his ideas have come to be taken as a matter of course. His gospel that every nation had a right to manage its own internal affairs was so fully accepted in the century of nationalism that no one asked by whom it was framed. That some of his principles have become platitudes is no reason why honour should not be paid to the man who foresaw and promoted the growth of national liberty on the Continent.

'For Canning alone among English statesmen can we make the double claim that his own work has been permanent and indestructible, whilst his visions of the future have in some measure approached to reality. . . . The principles which he laid down, though their application may now be different, should still be the guide and polar star of our course.' The verdict on his private character is equally favourable. The whole volume is a pæan to a creative statesman, a dazzling orator, a great gentleman.

Returning to Cambridge as Lecturer and Assistant Tutor at Peterhouse after his brief sojourn at Leeds, Temperley was claimed by the *Cambridge Modern History*. The senior editor, Sir Adolphus Ward, who was also Master of the college, recognised his ability and yoked him to the team. Between 1907 and 1909 five chapters from his pen appeared in volumes v, vi, x, xi. That on 'The Revolution Settlement, 1687–1702,' describes the follies of James II, the Trimmer's triumph in 1688, and the solid achievements of William III. 'Party Government under Queen Anne' continues the story, and depicts Marlborough without adulation or invective. 'The Age of Walpole and the Pelhams,' which carries us to the glories of Chatham, is the longest of his contributions. The safe mediocrity of the first two Georges, he declared, was their salvation. In 'Great Britain in 1815–32' he was on familiar ground, and his enthusiasm for Canning lights up the narrative. So strongly, however, is he on the side of Parliamentary Reform that he pronounces the Prime Minister's death in 1827 not inopportune either for his country or his fame. The short chapter entitled 'The New Colonial Policy 1840–70' is a tribute to the Durham Report, the inspiration of which is traced back to Bentham and Fox. Volume xi, in which it appeared, owed more to Temperley than this brief section. Owing to the illness of one of the editors he was invited to help with its production, and the Preface pays tribute to his work. 'He has discharged the task which devolved upon him with conspicuous ability and devotion, and we desire to assure him of our cordial gratitude.'

Though none of his contributions to the *Cambridge Modern History* were directly concerned with international relations, Temperley's interests extended far beyond the bounds of the British Empire. Travel was a lifelong passion, and in 1905 he

paid the first of seventeen visits to Serbia. In 1907 he visited
Slovakia, at that time a backward and discontented province of
Hungary. 'Everywhere he went,' writes Professor Seton-
Watson, who had just returned from his first visit to the same
country, 'he told me he found surprise among the small group
of nationally-minded Slovaks. After thirty years, without anyone
from our country taking note of their existence, they suddenly
received two visitors within a few weeks of each other, and began
to draw the utterly false conclusion that they had been "discovered
by England" and that these were Government emissaries. In
Budapest fantastically comic tales were evolved to prove "Panslav
designs" behind this imaginary interest on the part of London
official circles. It was I who by a pure accident had just managed
to forestall Temperley, but we soon found ourselves in almost
complete agreement. The sole difference was that I rushed into
print about "Slovak wrongs," whereas he remained silent until
he had paid further visits to Hungary.'

An article on 'Racial Strife in Hungary', published in the
Westminster Review, January 1908, recorded some impressions of
his visit, and a spirited article in the *Contemporary Review*,
inspired by the death of Maurus Jokai, the Hungarian Scott, in
1904, shows how early his interest in Hungary had begun. The
novelist is hailed as the greatest romanticist of his time, too little
known in England, and is placed above Sienkiewicz. In a
memorial notice Dr. Joseph Balogh, editor of the *Hungarian
Quarterly*, declares that in the years immediately preceding the
First World War Hungarians had great hopes of Temperley.
He adds regretfully that he later transferred his affection to the
Little Entente, above all Jugoslavia, though shortly before his
death he turned towards Hungary again.

His chief service to that country was the Introductory Essay
of fifty pages prefixed to a translation of his friend Marczali's
classical work on Hungary in the eighteenth century. He
persuaded the Cambridge University Press in 1910 to undertake
the burden on the double ground that the book was of first-class
quality and that Hungarian history had been strangely neglected.
The distinguished Professor at the University of Budapest had
been invited by the Hungarian Academy of Science to write a
history of his country in the time of Joseph II and Leopold II.

He began by a sociological study of the problems with which they had to deal as searching as that of Tocqueville in regard to the *Ancien Régime*. While other writers had contented themselves with war, diplomacy, and the strife of parties, Marczali investigated the economic conditions, the stratification of society, the conception of nationality, the status of the Church, the machinery of administration.

It was a happy inspiration to supply the background of this elaborate picture of Hungary in the latter half of the eighteenth century, and Temperley's Introduction is worthy of the work. His impressions of travel help us to visualise the life of a community differing widely from any other people in Europe. 'Even to-day in Hungary there are still many relics of an immemorial past. Traces of the most primitive savagery still abound in the folk-lore, the songs and the customs of the peasants. In the Eastern Carpathians bears, lynxes and wolves are still to be found, buffaloes are still to be found in the marshes of Hungary, and in Transylvania men are still living who have seen horses tread out the corn in true Biblical style. Even to-day a hussar stands with drawn sword before the County Assembly hall, ready if necessary to resist the King and his soldiers in the true spirit of mediæval autonomy.' He goes on to describe the physical features of the country. 'The eye beholds an endless flat, now covered by reeds and marshes, at times completely inundated with water or now stretching away bare and sandy to a seemingly infinite distance. Nothing more monotonous or dismal can be conceived, though, as in the fens of England, there is a certain grandeur in its melancholy and a certain majesty in the endless sweep of its horizon. . . . Like Sparta such a land has no walls, and its strength could only lie in stout hearts and strong hands.' The aim of the Introductory Essay is to give a broad survey of the more striking facts in Hungarian history. Beginning with the arrival of the Magyars under Arpad, he passes to St. Stephen, Louis the Great, and Matthias Corvinus, 'one of those rulers of whom legend is never weary, and of whom a thousand traits are preserved in ballad and anecdote'. The Turkish victory at Mohacz brought part of the country under Hapsburg rule, and inaugurated a period of friction lasting till 1918. The Magyar loved the bigoted Hapsburgs of the seventeenth century no more than the Turks.   For a brief moment the misfortunes of Maria Theresa evoked a passionate loyalty such as no Hapsburg ruler, before or since, ever enjoyed.   With the accession of Joseph II, 'that gifted and hapless ruler whose wonderful energy and enthusiasm could not save him from becoming one of the most tragic failures of history', the two countries drifted apart again.

In the same year Temperley took part for the first and last time in a domestic political controversy.   The conflict over the Budget of 1909 raised the old question of the composition and powers of the House of Lords in an acute form.   *Senates and Upper Chambers*, published in the autumn of 1910, was based on lectures delivered at Cambridge and elsewhere.   The list of acknowledgements, which included prime ministers, ambassadors, and foreign professors, indicates how widely he cast his net.   In approaching 'this vast and complex subject' his object was to attempt a general survey of the Upper Chambers of the English-speaking world and the Continental states, to compare them with our own, and to discover their lessons.   His sentiments, he explains, inclined to Liberalism, though he could not approve of the resolutions of the Liberal Government.   Enriched by copious appendixes and a detailed bibliography, the book is still useful as a mine of information.   Looking back after forty years the reader may feel that the gravity of the crisis is exaggerated. England, he wrote, was ringing with the cry 'the Constitution in danger', yet Englishmen remained strangely calm.   'Were it the calm of strength it would be well, but it is the calm of in-dolence, impassivity, worst of all ignorance. . . . As our political system declines in credit, the popular lethargy seems to increase.' In the time of Canning, and two generations following the Reform Bill, our institutions were a byword for stability and strength.   In those days other countries had turned to us for guidance: now, 'in the present abasement of our institutions', we must turn to them.   'Heavy indeed is the responsibility of those who have turned English statesmen from teachers into pupils, and have cast shame on the Mother of Parliaments.'   The note is rather shrill, but the reader is in doubt whether the lash is intended to fall on Liberals for forcing the pace or on Conservatives for blocking the way.   Fortunately the position was not utterly desperate. 'Our political eminence may not, indeed, be wholly or permanently lost, so long as we reform ourselves aright and draw profit from the lessons of other countries.' In this matter we had confessedly failed, and certain other nations had admittedly succeeded. Reform was confessed by all to be a necessity, but to be permanent and final it must be based on agreement. Without such agreement we should be driven to Single Chamber Government, which is emphatically rejected on the ground that it endangers the rights of minorities. The survey of constitutions, which fills the larger part of the book, explains in each case the composition and powers of the Upper Chamber, and the methods of adjusting disputes with the Lower House. The author's ideal is a Senate with suspensory power sufficient to defend minorities without enabling them to impose its will.

It was a mark of Temperley's growing reputation that he received an invitation to lecture at Harvard during the first half of the academic year 1911–12. 'He gave a half course for graduates and undergraduates from 1688 to 1832,' writes Professor Merriman, 'and a seminar on topics in recent English history. At that stage of his development his interests were mainly in the eighteenth century, and especially in the War of Jenkins' Ear. There were quite a number of undergraduate jokes and cartoons about this. I have often wished that it had been possible for him to stay a full year. He was just beginning to make his mark on the place when he was called back to England. Everybody was very fond of him, and some of his more advanced students were given a start by him on their profession for which they will never cease to be grateful.' The War of Jenkins' Ear was the subject of an address to the Royal Historical Society, published in its Transactions for 1909. After exploring the dispatches from Spain in the Record Office he pronounces that the decision for war was intelligible but not inevitable. His interest in the seventeenth and eighteenth centuries was further illustrated between 1912 and 1914 in contributions to the *English Historical Review* on the Cabinet and Privy Council, to the *American Historical Review* on the repeal of the Stamp Act, to the *Quarterly Review* on Chatham, North, and America, with unpublished letters of Chatham, and in an address to the American Historical Association on the relations of England with Spanish America, 1720–44. Many years later he wrote a chapter on the

Peace of Paris (1763) for the first volume of the *Cambridge History of the British Empire*, in which he said all that can be said for Bute.

Though it was not published till 1914, *Frederick the Great and Kaiser Joseph* was mainly written in 1911. He owed his first interest in the Prussian King to Reddaway, the best of his English biographers, with whom he tramped the Silesian battlefields; but the occasion of the book was the discovery that unpublished dispatches from British diplomatists of the years 1776–79 were of interest and importance. Here is the story of the attempt of the Emperor to seize Bavaria on the death of the childless Elector Max Joseph at the end of 1777, and the portraits of the protagonists are so vivid that our interest is held to the end. 'Among the long gallery of faces, cynical or coarse, voluptuous or depraved, that confront us in the mid-eighteenth century, the womanly face of Maria Theresa exercises an indescribable fascination. The brow is broad and noble, the mouth firm yet sensitive and kind, the eyes direct, clear and true, the whole expression one of innocence, sincerity and strength.' Her son, Joseph II, with 'as warm a zeal for his people, as genuine a care of the poor and degraded and weak, and a heart as tender as ever beat in the breast of a sovereign', always fascinated Temperley. 'The history of his devoted efforts, of his pitiful failures, are written in those passionate eyes and upon those tremulous lips.' Frederick is less sympathetically portrayed, and the campaign showed that as a soldier he was past his prime. The appendixes contain extracts from dispatches, with an analysis of the temperaments and sources of their writers. The book was the more welcome since Carlyle had tired of his task, and to some extent of his hero, before reaching the only war in which no battles were fought.

Temperley's first visit to Serbia in 1905 was followed almost every year by a tour in the Near East. In 1908 he witnessed the Young Turk revolution, and in 1909 he was present at Abdul Hamid's last public appearance at the Selamlik after the failure of the counter-revolution. In 1910 he was in Albania during the revolt against Turkey, and was shot at by Albanian Comitajis. In 1911 he sampled Macedonia at the height of the troubles and was pursued by a Greek band. In 1912 he visited Dalmatia and Bosnia. In 1913 he paid his first visit to Montenegro. Of all the countries of south-eastern Europe Serbia attracted him most. He learned the language and wrote a history of the country which was nearly finished when war began in 1914. Completed during a period of convalescence, it was published in 1917.

The *History of Serbia*, described as the fruit of years of travel and study in the Near East, breathes a warm admiration for the Serbian race. Serbian history, he declares, is unintelligible without reference to the splendid and tragic past, since the battle of Kossovo and the reign of Stephen Dushan awaken far more living sentiments than Waterloo for ourselves. At the moment of publication the country was in foreign occupation, but the author was confident that the storm would pass, for the soul of the people was unconquerable. 'So long as the songs of Kossovo are sung and a Serbian exists in any land to sing them, so long will there always be a Serbia.' The conflict of Serbians with other Slav races was scarcely fiercer than that between the rival dynasties at Belgrade in the nineteenth and twentieth centuries. Yet Temperley never allowed the strife and horrors of the past to weaken his conviction that 'the rugged stock' of Serbia was both destined and worthy to play the part of Piedmont in the *Risorgimento* and to become the core of a Jugoslav federation. The ink on his manuscript was scarcely dry when the dream was fulfilled. The sketch of Serbian history is enlivened by the author's intimate knowledge of the Balkan peninsula. There are interesting chapters on the short-lived Empire of Dushan, on Serbian mediæval society, and on the catastrophe of Kossovo, celebrated in the cycle of heroic lays which Goethe compared to Homer. Despite his ardent sympathy for Serbian nationalism, he is fair to the Turks who held the country for centuries in their grip. On the whole, we are told, Turkish rule was not so oppressive as a Latin conqueror might have been. The Serbians were not forced to forsake their religion, and their local government was left almost intact. The worst grievance was the tribute of Christian children for the corps of Janissaries. 'The Turk persecutes Serbs, Bulgars, Greeks, or Armenians only when he believes that their religious beliefs lead them to political conspiracy against the Ottoman rule.' The story of Serbian liberation, which begins with the rugged figure of Kara George, is brought down to the eve of the Balkan war of 1912. Montenegro's part in the long struggle against the Turk is fully recognised, but arouses less admiration. 'Freedom Montenegro has, but it is primitive, savage, uncontrolled, and the stern spirit of many of her sons accords ill with modern ideas. Her task in history is really over, for she has achieved that for which she struggled, and has enabled the Serb race to be united.' His interest in Jugoslavia never failed. Professor Seton-Watson records that there were times when he spoke of a preference for being buried in Jugoslav soil. He counted King Alexander and the sculptor Mestrovich among his friends.

On the outbreak of war Temperley became First Lieutenant and later Captain in the Fife and Forfar Yeomanry. He went out to the Dardanelles, but was soon compelled by illness to return. He was appointed head of the Political Sub-Section of the Intelligence Division of the General Staff, where he helped to produce a number of memoranda subsequently issued as *General Staff Papers* for the Peace Conference. In 1918 he returned to active service as Assistant and Acting Military Attaché to the Serbian army at Salonica with the rank of Major. He was on the staff during the Salonica offensive, and slept in fifty-nine different beds within seventy-six days. After the Armistice he travelled through Jugoslavia and Hungary in order to stop the fighting, and was under fire on several occasions. The attempt to mediate between the rebels and the Government in Montenegro brought new perils, and one night in Old Serbia he was attacked in a block-house and had to defend himself with an axe. His official reports, testifies Professor Seton-Watson, were of very real value to the British Delegation, and his unique knowledge of actual conditions was utilised in the fixing of the new frontiers. During the Peace Conference he was a member of the Military Section of the British Delegation from April to July, and he took part in drawing the frontiers of Czechoslovakia. Both the Military Staff and the Foreign Office, testifies Professor Webster, were eminently pleased with his work. That he was present at the final scene in the Galerie des Glaces on June 28, 1919, he always reckoned as one of the memorable experiences of his life.

When the treaty was signed Temperley returned to the East as Acting Military Attaché to the Serbian army at Belgrade from July to October 1919, and again from August to December 1920.

In September he went to Montenegro to rescue Mr. Baerlein, a British subject imprisoned at Scutari. He was the first Allied officer to see the new Government of Albania, and he met Zog, the future King. His report on Montenegro was printed as a Parliamentary Paper. He was twice mentioned in dispatches 'for valuable services rendered in connexion with the war'. His decorations, apart from the 1914–15 star, the Allied and Victory Medals, were the Order of the British Empire, the Order of the Rumanian Crown, the Order of the Serbian White Eagle, the Order of Kara George, and the Order of Polonia Restituta. Unfortunately the war years left him not only a wealth of exciting memories but also a legacy of impaired health.

One of the happier results of the Peace Conference was the foundation of the Institute of International Affairs. The British and American experts summoned to Paris formed the nucleus of a permanent organisation whose first task was the compilation of an authoritative account of the Conference. A scheme was drawn up by George Louis Beer, the historian of the American Revolution, and Lord Eustace Percy. Temperley was appointed editor, and carried through the formidable enterprise with unflagging energy. That the work was planned on comprehensive lines and published in six sumptuous volumes was due to generous gifts by Mr. Thomas Lamont, the American financier, and Sir John Power. The Editor's Foreword to the first volume, dated June 1920, explained the nature of the enterprise. 'The object of this history is neither to criticise nor to defend the German or any other treaty, still less to defend or to criticise the policy of any government or nation taking part in the Conference. The aim is to produce a history at once independent and objective, to detail the facts and to sketch the opinions that prevailed at the Conference.' Against the lack of perspective must be set the advantage that the work was compiled by men with an intimate knowledge of the events they described.

The Introduction traces the origins of the struggle back to the end of the seventeenth century. 'The war was a conflict between the principles of freedom and of autocracy, between the principles of moral influence and of material force, of government by consent and government by compulsion. In one form or another the conflict is as old as mankind, but for our purpose it

began in 1688.   For it was then that the British system of self-
government or constitutionalism was established, and it was
about that time that a new and formidable type of government
arose, which was eventually to threaten not only Anglo-Saxon-
dom but democracy itself.'   After many vicissitudes, constitutionalism advanced rapidly during the nineteenth century till Bismarck
'set the pride and strength of a great nation against the rights,
interest or existence of small ones. . . . To these doctrines
there could ultimately be but one answer and one end'.   Constitutionalism endured the strain of the war, and all parties to the
Armistice agreed to substitute a League of Nations and a
covenanted peace for the old unstable and perilous Balance
of Power.   The general principle or guiding thread in the
volumes was the attempt to exhibit the Peace as a great constructive experiment.   'Guilty nations have been punished,
and war, which was previously regarded as justifiable, is hence-
forward looked on as a crime.   Disarmament has begun.   A
League has been created to enforce peace and to repair wrong or
injustice, if necessary to rewrite such parts of the treaty as seem
inconsistent with justice or expediency.'   Such were the ideals
and illusions of 1920.

To the first volume, which describes the preliminaries of peace,
the editor contributed a chapter on war aims, drawing a vital
distinction between the declarations of the two sides.   Secret
agreements, it is true, hampered those of the Entente, but
German statesmen made speeches entirely at variance with their
real objects.   The survey ends with a glowing tribute to Wilson.
The thesis that it was on the whole a Wilson peace is developed
in the editor's introduction to the second volume, whose theme
is the settlement with Germany.   Only one territorial decision,
in the writer's opinion, was open to criticism, namely the refusal
to permit Austria to join Germany.   The third volume contains
documents and an elaborate chronological table dealing not only
with events but with the opinions of the Press.   The fourth,
which describes the new or enlarged states erected on the ruins
of the Hapsburg Empire, is in a special sense the editor's own.   A
massive chapter of seventy pages, entitled 'The Treaty of
London', summarises the discussions which led to the delimitation of Italy's new frontiers.   In the hot dispute between Italy

and Jugoslavia his sympathies are with the latter. 'For Jugo-slavia Fiume was and is vital.' He was thoroughly dissatisfied with the post-War arrangement which gave the city to Italy and Susak, its suburb, to Jugoslavia. The closing pages trace the history of Albania from its emergence as a state in 1913 to its admission to the League in 1920. 'This decision not only gives great moral support to Albania, but in case of future attack by any Power it gives her the right to appeal to the League and such protection as is afforded by Article 10 of the Covenant.'

His second contribution is entitled 'The Making of the Treaties with Austria, Bulgaria and Hungary, and the Principles underlying them.' In one respect it was easier to deal with these problems on their merits than in the case of Germany, for there was less popular prejudice. On the other hand, obligations to Italy had been incurred under the Treaty of London which hampered the Supreme Council. South Tyrol, for instance, despite its solidly Teutonic population, was allotted to Italy. The veto on the union of Austria with Germany, except with the consent of the Council of the League, is attributed to the desire to safeguard the independence of Czechoslovakia in her early days, and to the belief that a plebiscite would have been influenced by desire for food and other temporary considerations. The Bulgarian treaty was no less severe, and the Bulgarian Delegation seemed surprised that no one offered to shake hands with them when they arrived in Paris; but Temperley was never particularly interested in Bulgaria and he shed no tears over her fate. The discussions leading to the Treaty of Trianon, including the historic speech of Count Apponyi, are described with equally little sympathy. The plight of Austria, on the other hand, arouses his genuine sympathy. 'When all is said, an appalling tragedy remains—the spectacle of a land bankrupt and starving, enduring more suffering to-day even than the devastated areas in war-time.'

The third and last contribution to the fourth volume concerns 'The New Hungary'. Of all the enemy states she had been the loudest in her outcries. Her attitude was the result of her long history of domination and of the recent deterioration of her statesmanship. 'The Magyar policy has always been the same since 1867. An able, small and fanatically Magyar oligarchy has dominated the parliament, the administration and the state by sheer force of character and achievement. Even before the war the burden of the subject races was becoming intolerable.' He is not greatly impressed by her territorial or other grievances. The arable land left to her was very rich and her agricultural wealth was largely indestructible. The old conservative régime was shattered in the war, and nationality problems no longer existed in any serious form. 'Hungary is to-day and for the first time really the Land of the Magyars, but it is, or at least it should be, the land of all the Magyars and not of the privileged few.'

The fifth volume, dealing with economics and the protection of minorities, contains a brief summary by the editor of the stages by which the new states came to be recognised by the Allies. The sixth, published in 1924, concerns the Turks and Arabs, Egypt and Persia, Poland and Russia, the British Dominions, the attitude of the American Senate to the Treaty of Versailles, the making of the Covenant with its subsidiary bodies, the International Labour Office and the Permanent Court of International Justice. It opens with a chapter by the editor on the four secret agreements concerning the Near and Middle East reached between 1915 and 1917, and revealed when the Bolshevists came into power—the Constantinople arrangement of March 1915, the Treaty of London of April 1915, the Sykes-Picot deal of May 1916, and the pact of St. Jean de Maurienne in April 1917, by which Italy was to obtain a slice of Asia Minor. Though well aware of the sharp criticism they evoked, the writer argues that these commitments must be seen in their proper setting—the gigantic struggle for national survival which requires the use of every expedient permissible in diplomacy and war. A shorter chapter on the Independence of Egypt comments on her status before the war, her transformation into a British Protectorate, the rise of Zaghlul, the Treaty of Sèvres, the Milner Mission of 1920, and the abolition of the Protectorate in 1922, combined with the announcement of a virtual Monroe Doctrine over Egypt.

A thoughtful epilogue admits certain mistakes of method and policy. The refusal of oral discussion with the Germans was unwise; the passionate eagerness to secure a general settlement at the earliest date led to hurried decisions; the conflict between Wilsonian doctrines and the secret treaties generated untenable compromises. That many high hopes were disappointed was not wholly the fault of the statesmen, for they were the spokesmen of their respective peoples. In 1926 Temperley contributed the article on the Peace Treaties to the new edition of the *Encyclopædia Britannica*, and he occasionally intervened in discussions of war-guilt as defined in the Treaty of Versailles. Contrary to the usual interpretation of Article 231 he denied that it contained that accusation, adding however that the charge was plainly stated elsewhere. An article in the *National Review*, December 1927, entitled 'Mr. Lloyd George as Historian of the Peace Treaties', contained a slashing attack on his inaccuracies.

The Second Year of the League, a study of the second Assembly of the League of Nations, published early in 1922, may be regarded as a postscript to the *History of the Peace Conference*. The story opens with snapshots of the principal delegates, among whom Lord Balfour receives the highest marks. The two principal themes are the Upper Silesian Award and the settlement of the Albanian question. The disagreement between England and France in regard to the former threatened the alliance, and the writer applauds the efforts of the peace-makers. 'The Supreme Council (Temperley was present at the last meeting, when Lloyd George referred the question to the League) had failed, and had failed lamentably. Yet where it failed, the League Council succeeded.' In regard to the second he speaks with special authority, for he had been on the Albanian Boundary Commission at Paris in the previous month, and he was an official adviser to the chief of the British Delegation. Here again it was a triumph of constructive work. 'At every stage of her origin and development since the war the League has been the friend and champion of Albania, and this work has been accomplished by purely moral force.'

After the manifold distractions of the war Temperley resumed his duties at Peterhouse, which he and Sir Adolphus Ward had helped to make a busy hive of historical studies. He was particularly successful in getting the best out of advanced students, whom he always encouraged to undertake research. Among his pupils were Lord Allen of Hurtwood, Professor Adair of McGill University, Mr. Loveday, Director of the Financial Section of the League of Nations, and Professor Butterfield,

author of the obituary in *The Times*.   His first wife, Gladys
Bradford, whom he married in 1913 and lost in 1923, was herself
a teacher of history and author of a scholarly work on Henry VII.
'In his early days at Peterhouse,' writes Professor Adair,
'Temperley achieved his success as a tutor rather than as a
lecturer.   As a lecturer he often found it difficult to cultivate a
fluency in wedding words to thought, but this very hesitation
was all in his favour as a tutor.   It inspired a feeling of friendliness; his students felt that he was weighing their views carefully,
striving to understand their difficulties.   And this was no mere
accidental trick of the voice, for it almost unconsciously was
expressing the real Temperley.   No student ever came to him
in vain, no trouble was too great for him to take in helping to
solve a student's intellectual problems; yet it was all done with a
kindliness and a diffidence that gave the student who really had
something to say every encouragement and opportunity to say it.
Being a tutor was to Temperley a real labour of love, and that
was no inconsiderable reason for his astonishing success.'

In 1919 he was appointed University Reader in Modern
History, a post which he occupied till he was chosen for the Chair
of Modern History, created in 1931.   In 1923 he founded the
Cambridge Historical Journal, of which he was editor till ill-health
compelled him in the year before his death to transfer the reins
to younger hands.   It grew out of the Cambridge Historical
Society, originated by Professor Clapham, and the Editorial
Board contained the names of several leading teachers of history
in the University.   Its main purpose was to encourage research
by publication of its results, and every number contained a
selection of hitherto unprinted documents.   His own contributions included articles on 'Lord Acton on the Origins of
the War of 1870' and on 'British Secret Diplomacy from Canning
to Grey'.

Temperley catered for a wider public in several directions.
He published an edition of the Treaty of Versailles with a brief
commentary.   He was joint editor of a series of booklets entitled
'Helps to Students of History', written in popular form and
published at a popular price.   From 1922 to 1928 he edited the
Annual Bulletin of Historical Literature, published by the Historical
Association, contributing the section on the latest age.   His

services to the Association also included a brochure on *Foreign Historical Novels* and a bibliography of modern European History in co-operation with Professor Lillian Penson. The former contained studies of Victor Hugo and Dumas, Jensen, Jokai, Sienkiewicz, Merejkowski, and Tolstoi. He developed the theme in a little book published in 1931, *Scenes from Modern History by Great Imaginative Writers.*

When the end of the *History of the Peace Conference* was in sight Temperley returned to his first love. It was natural that the editors of the *Cambridge History of British Foreign Policy, 1783–1919*, should invite him to cover the years 1822–27, and a massive chapter of seventy pages appeared in the second volume, published in 1923. It is interesting to compare the judgments of the youthful biographer of Canning with those of the middle-aged scholar. If the halo of romance is gone, respect and admiration remain. Canning, we are told, was not greatly influenced by sentiment. His attitude in the liberation of Greece, for instance, was often misunderstood. He was neither Turko-phobe nor Grecophil, and he once described the Greeks as a most rascally set. Frankly an opportunist, he was guided by events. If the suppression of the Greek revolt proved impossible, some new method would have to be tried. He did not believe in the modern doctrine of self-determination. In a word he was much less of a nationalist and a liberal than Palmerston.

Two years later, in 1925, Temperley published his masterpiece, *The Foreign Policy of Canning, 1822–1827*, a massive volume of 600 pages, which won him a place in the front rank of historians. He had studied the subject for twenty years, he declared in the preface, had read every dispatch of Canning in the Record Office, had consulted the archives of Paris and Vienna, and had been allowed to inspect a mass of private papers. 'If something of youthful enthusiasm is diminished by experience, there is nothing to suggest that Canning was not one of the greatest of our Foreign Ministers. It is certain that no greater intellect has been placed at the service of British diplomacy.' A more important difference is in regard to Castlereagh, who in the earlier work received less than his due. He accepts the verdict of Professor Webster and Professor Alison Phillips about the respective merits of Canning and Castlereagh. 'During the most crucial years of the nineteenth century these two men guided the destinies of England. If the one possessed constructive qualities, serene steadfastness and cosmopolitan detachment, the other had infinite resources, intellectual imagination and a hitherto unexampled power of national and popular appeal. Both men, though in different ways, rendered immortal services to their country.'

The volume opens with Castlereagh's resistance in 1820 to the doctrine of intervention preached and practised by Alexander and Metternich, and passes on to a preliminary analysis of Canning's political system. He was a philosophic Tory, a disciple of Burke, disliking equally despotism and democracy. The King grudgingly accepted his new Foreign Secretary, and some of his Cabinet colleagues ruefully remembered the sallies of his wit. Happily he had plenty of courage as he proceeded to show at the Congress of Verona, where Wellington was instructed to announce that England would take no part in the suppression of Spanish Constitutionalism. The second act was to limit the sway of autocracy and legitimacy by calling the new world into existence to redress the balance of the old. 'If the barrier of the Pyrenees could not be defended by a British army, the gates of the Atlantic could be held by a British fleet. If France could humble Spain on land, England could humble France on the sea.' No conflict was necessary, for the proclamation of the Monroe Doctrine confirmed the British veto on interference in South America. When Canning proceeded to strike a blow at the Neo-Holy Alliance by the recognition of the revolting colonies, he gave a lead which was bound to be followed by the Powers who angrily protested at the time. If, as we are reminded, the danger from France to the New World and the importance of South America in world politics were less than he believed, that in no way diminishes our admiration for the firmness, foresight, and skill of the man who went boldly forward despite the scruples of the King and the Cabinet. A further triumph in the same field was the restoration of British influence in Portugal and the recognition of Brazilian independence.

At this point, in 1825, when 'Canning's personality became supreme at home and powerful and triumphant abroad', the narrative is interrupted by a series of chapters entitled 'Canning and England'; for what Temperley calls the world-wide triumph of his policy and system was only rendered possible by his ascendancy at home. 'His full power was not felt abroad until he had dragged the wavering King and his reluctant colleagues with him by his influence over Parliament, the Press and the people.' The clever and perfidious monarch was a dangerous opponent, but he was conquered at last, and in 1826 he admitted that the Foreign Secretary had shown great talents. Canning was too much of a Liberal for Wellington and Eldon, and only the steady support of Liverpool, the Prime Minister, made his position reasonably secure. An instructive chapter entitled 'The Day's Work at the Foreign Office' summarises his numerous administrative reforms, and reviews his relations with British representatives abroad. A shorter chapter explains his ceaseless and successful efforts to interest and educate public opinion in foreign affairs.

The later portion of the volume describes his share in the liberation of Greece from the Turkish yoke, which 'puts the finishing touch to his policy and marks the culmination of his fame'. Canning, like most British statesmen of his time, had been pro-Turkish, but he realised that the attempt to suppress the rebels was more dangerous than the recognition of their independence. He admired the ancient more than the modern Greeks, and condemned 'the most disgusting barbarities' perpetrated by both sides. Moreover, he wished to preserve the Turkish Empire in order to keep Russia out of Constantinople. When, however, Alexander informed Canning that he was ready to break with Metternich and to co-operate with England in regard to Greece, the Neo-Holy Alliance collapsed. For the brief remainder of his life Canning, not Metternich, was the dominating figure in Europe. France was easily won over, and when, shortly after his death, the Turkish fleet was destroyed at Navarino, the freedom of Greece was in sight. The Hundred Days of Premiership, a period of bitter party strife, are described with deep sympathy. 'This malevolent meteor, this scourge of the world, a revolution in himself', as Metternich called him, had worn himself out at the age of fifty-seven. He had not lived in vain. 'Without Castlereagh the world might not have been saved, and without Canning it might not have been freed.' No reader of this fine work, which ranks in interest and im-

portance with Professor Webster's study of Castlereagh, can fail
to be impressed by its mastery of the materials, its insight into
a complicated personality, and its grasp of the diplomacy of
nineteenth-century Europe.

Among the unpublished sources utilised in the book was the
diary of Princess Lieven, wife of the Russian Ambassador in
London, the leader of society in England for twenty years, the
friend of George IV, Castlereagh, Canning, Wellington, Grey,
Aberdeen, the mistress of Metternich in early life, and the lover
of Guizot when her charms were waning. The publication of
her correspondence had increased the desire of historians for the
journal which she was known to have kept. In 1923 a transcript
covering the years 1825–30 came into Temperley's hands, and in
1925 he edited the *Diary of Princess Lieven* with some of her
political sketches and letters. He was justified in describing the
book as an important contribution to the social and diplomatic
history of the period. The career of 'the princess of diplomacy'
makes a fascinating story, though the heroine was too much of an
egotistical intriguer to capture our sympathy. The gem of the
journal is the story of the secret mission entrusted to her by
Alexander shortly before his death in 1825, the purpose of which
was to inform Canning of his resolve to break with Metternich
and to co-operate with England in the policy which was to lead
to the emancipation of Greece. Of scarcely less interest are
the vivid pictures of George IV and of Canning's struggle for
the Premiership. Other aspects of the career and the epoch
of his hero were discussed in contributions to the *English
Historical Review*, the *American Historical Review*, *The Cambridge
Historical Journal*, and the *Dublin Review*, before and after the
appearance of his book. He wrote an introduction to F. A.
Kirkpatrick's authoritative *History of the Argentine Republic*,
published in 1931.

Temperley collaborated with Professor A. J. Grant in a work
which reached a wider public than any of his other writings.
The elder scholar had been invited by Longmans to write a sketch
of European history from 1789 to 1914. He asked Temperley
to share the burden, and in particular to undertake the later
years. No indication is given as to the authorship of the different
portions of the book, but it may now be revealed that each wrote

about half. *Europe in the Nineteenth Century* (*1789–1914*) won immediate success, and went through three editions. Its title was changed to *Europe in the Nineteenth and Twentieth Centuries, 1789–1932*, when Temperley added supplementary chapters on the World War and the post-War years for the fourth edition. The fifth, bringing the story up to the Munich crisis, appeared in January 1939. The writers made no attempt to tell the story in full. 'At the most a sketch, a few outlines, some impressions can be given. . . . The authors offer this book as their conception of how the main threads of the period cross and interweave with one another, and of how the tapestry was composed. Their view is cosmopolitan rather than national; political and cultural rather than military or religious. Ideas rather than events are the stuff of this history.'

The chapters on the last years before the war of 1914 were written by Temperley. He recognises that when England abandoned isolation she automatically encouraged Japan, France, and Russia to pursue their respective ambitions. The verdict on the latter is severe. Her internal instability, her unscrupulous diplomacy, and the fears and ambitions of her General Staff rendered her a serious danger to peace. 'It is certainly true that she did not want war in 1914, because her generals knew her military weakness only too well. But it cannot be said that a Government so constituted really made ultimately for peace. It maintained and was increasing a great army, it built strategic railways menacing to Germany in Europe, it was destroying the integrity of Persia in Asia, and was perpetually intriguing in the Balkans and stretching out a greedy hand towards Constantinople.'

The volume in its original form concluded with a series of essays ranging over the whole period—the growth of nationality, the development of parliamentary institutions, the race of armaments, and the efforts to organise peace. The final paragraph welcomed the League of Nations as at once a natural development and a daring experiment. The supplements are of interest for his judgments on men and events. But for the United States, he declares, France might have been defeated and England could not have won. The chapter on the Peace Conference contains snapshots of the Big Four and an eyewitness account of the signing of the Treaty of Versailles. In the chapter entitled

'Nation-making in the New Europe' he says all that can be said for the Peace settlement.   He has high praise for Czechoslovakia, but he declares Poland's frontiers too advanced on the Russian side.   In the chapter on the Near and Middle East he denounces 'the sickening tragedy' of Armenia.   The closing chapter, 'Hitler's Drive to the East', pays homage to the moderation of Beneš throughout the Sudeten crisis.

Temperley returned to his favourite field of foreign affairs in his Inaugural Address at the Cambridge Local Lectures summer meeting in 1928 entitled *The Victorian Age in Politics, War and Diplomacy*, published by the University Press.   In politics he notes the revival of the prestige of the Crown, the coming of age of the Dominions, and the democratisation of Parliament.   No such significant changes took place in the defence forces, for the navy remained strong and the army weak.   Castlereagh and Canning are saluted as the greatest figures in modern British diplomacy, though Castlereagh's dream of an organised Europe was a splendid failure.   He ignored public opinion and failed, while Canning lived by it and succeeded.   Canning, it is added, was ready to take part in European Congresses on conditions which have been incorporated 'with almost literal exactness' into the Covenant of the League of Nations.   Palmerston kept a bust of Canning in his study, but there were important differences in method and aim.   'Palmerston believed in settling each question on its individual merits, Canning in a system based on real intellectual principles.'   While the master never bluffed, the disciple had to retreat when confronted with Bismarck's iron will. Salisbury's diplomacy is praised as firm and resolute, but in his later years he failed to visualise new tendencies.

In 1931 a Chair of Modern History was founded at Cambridge, and Temperley was chosen to fill it.   His Inaugural Lecture, *Research and Modern History*, was published by the University Press.   The increasing popular interest in history, began the new Professor, brought certain dangers.   People formerly demanded that it should be a kind of pseudo-science: now they asked for a kind of pseudo-art.   To such blandishments there could be only one reply.   The great historian impresses, not by the evidence he reveals, but by the vast hidden wells of knowledge on which he relies.   His most precious gift is not the abundance but the certainty of his information, and the best road to immortality is to produce work which need never be done again. Such models are Ranke, Mommsen, Stubbs, Gierke, Maitland, Bury, and Tout. Great historical artists, like Macaulay, Carlyle, and Froude, are untrustworthy guides. Even Vandal is placed among those who are too clear to be convincing and too certain to be credible. The aim of research is to find out how men and institutions work. For this purpose the lecturer stresses the importance of a knowledge of the countries and peoples about which we decide to write. 'It is quite impossible to understand Metternich without knowing something of Austria, or Kossuth without knowing something of Hungary. And the smaller and the more Oriental the country, the greater the difficulty of deducing anything without first-hand knowledge.' For instance, the Serajevo murders only become fully intelligible if one has known Serbian or Bosnian students or Comitajis, who are quite unlike the students or even the burglars of the West. Similarly the Turk before the World War had to be seen to be believed. The scholar should train himself by travel and the study of men as much as by the study of books. The historical novels of Jokai and Sienkiewicz are recommended for atmosphere. Imagination and the critical sense must work hand in hand. 'There is no reward like the scholar's when after long search he suddenly sees his way into the heart of a problem.'

The same gospel of disinterested research was preached in the introduction to a selection from Bury's essays published in the same year. Writing with personal knowledge as well as intellectual sympathy, Temperley explains the attitude and methods of the greatest British historical scholar of his time. Neither of them accepted or invented a 'philosophy of history'. When Acton's successor declared in a celebrated aphorism that history is a science, no less and no more, he meant that it must be released not only from the temptations of rhetoric but from patriotic, pragmatic, and philosophical obsessions. If he taught any definite lesson, it was the doctrine of relativity, the sway of contingency, the illusion of finality. Progress was a fact and a hope, not a law, and things might easily have gone another way. The fall of the Roman Empire, for instance, was due to a combination of coincidences. The highest duty of universities was

24

research, though imagination was essential to the interpretation of its results. Half the volume is devoted to Byzantine studies, in which Bury's supremacy was unchallenged; but its chief value is that his reflections on history, perhaps the most profound and suggestive in our language, are collected and rendered accessible.

In the summer of 1924 the present writer was invited by Ramsay MacDonald, who combined the offices of Prime Minister and Foreign Secretary, to edit the proposed series of *British Documents on the Origins of the War*. He consented on condition that a second editor should share the burden, and suggested that Temperley should be approached. The invitation was given and accepted, but before the arrangements were complete the Labour Government was defeated, and it was Austen Chamberlain, MacDonald's successor at the Foreign Office, who gave the final authorisation. The decision was announced in *The Times* of December 3, 1924, in an exchange of letters between Professor Seton-Watson and the new Foreign Secretary. While a great mass of documentary evidence, wrote the former, had been made available by the German and Austrian governments illustrating the course of events from the standpoint of the Central Powers, and the Bolshevists had also been busy, historians had no authentic first-hand material on the British side, and were in consequence gravely handicapped in dealing with the charges and insinuations directed against British policy in the period preceding the war. Sir Austen replied that Mr. MacDonald had already given instructions to this effect, and that it only remained to confirm them. 'As regards the publication of the official documents bearing on the general European situation out of which the war arose, a collection of documents will be edited by Mr. G. P. Gooch and Mr. H. W. V. Temperley, who will, I hope, be in a position to begin serious work at a very early date. The reputation of the editors offers the best guarantee of the historical accuracy and impartiality of the work.'

The last sentence was our charter. How could we be impartial unless we were permitted to publish whatever we wished? Nothing was said at this stage as to our having a free hand, but it was tacitly understood that there would be no obstruction from the Foreign Office. Subsequent interviews with the Foreign Secretary proved that he was as anxious as ourselves for the whole truth to be told. Our resolve to put all the cards on the table produced protests from several foreign governments, for the usual practice of submitting the relevant documents to foreign Powers before publication was followed except in regard to our enemies in the World War. In every case we carried our point, and on one occasion Sir Austen personally intervened in Paris to remove the veto on a particular document. After the first difficulties had arisen we inserted a warning in the preface to the third and all subsequent volumes. 'The Editors think it well to state, what was already implied in their preface to volume i, that they would feel compelled to resign if any attempt were made to insist on the omission of any document which is in their view vital or essential.' In maintaining this attitude to the end Temperley was a tower of strength.

It had been the intention of the Government to begin with 1904, when the treaty with France opened a new chapter in British diplomacy. We argued that a more satisfactory starting-point was 1898, when the growing perils of isolation began to alarm Joseph Chamberlain and other influential statesmen. It was finally decided to publish two introductory volumes on 1898–1904 before proceeding to cover the following decade in greater detail. We estimated that ten volumes would be required. For that reason the work on the outbreak of the War for which Sir James Headlam-Morley, the first and last Historical Adviser to the Foreign Office, had already begun to collect material was issued as volume xi, before any of the others appeared. We underestimated the magnitude of the undertaking, and in consequence volumes ix and x appeared in two parts. The work, in which we received the invaluable assistance of Professor Lillian Penson, contained many thousand large and closely printed pages. Following the precedent of *Die Grosse Politik* we arranged the material in chapters on particular subjects; and though the editors of the French, Austrian, and Russian documents adopted the chronological method, we never regretted our choice. On the other hand, whereas Thimme, the chief editor of the German documents, provided notes which were of great interest but often highly controversial, we expressed no opinions in our elucidations. Temperley possessed the flair for essential documents characteristic of the born researcher, and his unflagging energy was in large measure responsible for the successful accomplishment of a formidable task.

British Documents on the Origins of the War, 1898–1914, provided by far the fullest account of any period of British foreign policy. The work, which was translated into German, was enriched by copious extracts from the private correspondence presented to the Foreign Office by Grey and Nicolson on the conclusion of their official service, and Lord Hardinge kindly allowed us to utilise his papers. Of scarcely less importance was the publication of innumerable minutes which enabled the student to reconstruct the evolution of policies and to visualise the human beings who sponsored them. No feature of the work excited more general interest than the Germanophobe memoranda of Eyre Crowe. An appendix in the final volume summarising the chief revelations was from Temperley's pen. They included Salisbury's plan in 1898 of a delimitation of British and Russian spheres of influence in Asia, the text and date of the mysterious so-called 'Treaty of Windsor' in 1899, the English side of the secret Anglo-German alliance discussions in 1901, the making of the Japanese alliance in 1902, the reconciliation with France in 1904, the anxieties of the Tangier crisis in 1905 and the Algeciras Conference in 1906, the elaboration of the Anglo-Russian Convention in 1907, the conversation of Sir Charles Hardinge and Iswolsky at Reval in 1908, Grey's efforts to limit the repercussions of the Bosnian crisis, the fruitless attempts from 1908 to 1912 to reach a *détente* with Germany in regard to naval competition, the nerve-racking summer of *Agadir*, the disappointments of the Haldane Mission, the Mediterranean agreement of 1912, the successful Baghdad railway negotiations, the Balkan wars, the friction with Russia in Persia, and the plan of an Anglo-Russian agreement in 1914. There had been Blue Books and White Papers on atrocities in the Congo, on Macedonian reform, and on the struggles of Persian constitutionalism, but the full story of the greater crises and the major decisions was now told for the first time. After mastering the details of the picture it became possible to view it as a whole. With the conquest of the Sudan and the annexation of the Boer Republics the British Empire became a satiated state. Thus the whole story is one less of British initiatives than of reactions to the approaches and activities of other Powers. The decisive event of the period, so far as Great Britain was concerned, was the reconciliation with France.

When the *British Documents* were nearing completion Temperley embarked on the most ambitious of his enterprises. 'My plan,' he wrote in the preface to *England and the Near East: the Crimea*, published in 1936, 'is to narrate the history of England's relations with the Near East from the death of Canning until the day when Disraeli brought back "peace with honour" from Berlin. The period begins with the British fleet's destruction of Turkish sea-power at Navarino and ends with its protection of the Turkish fleet against Russia. The aim, however, is not a study of diplomatic or naval history, but a general narrative in which these special features are found side by side with a study of Oriental institutions and Balkan nationalities.' The real problem was whether the old Turkish Empire could survive or recover its strength. This in turn depended on three factors—the ability of the Turks to set their house in order, the willingness of their Christian subjects to acquiesce in the process, and the readiness of the Great Powers to help 'the sick man of Europe'. It is a complicated drama, in which the Powers, the Turkish governing class and the subject races play their part. 'The Eastern question can only be understood if we know how Orientals intrigue, how Western diplomatists negotiate, and what Balkan peasants think about.' The survey was to be made in three volumes of which only the first, bringing the story to the outbreak of the Crimean War, was completed and published in his lifetime. No European scholar was better fitted by knowledge of languages, travel and research to do justice to what our fathers called the Eastern Question. A wealth of fresh material from British and Continental archives was utilised, and his visits to the scene of historic events add colour to his tale.

The story opens with an arresting picture of Sultan Mahmud, the greatest Ottoman ruler for centuries, half savage and half statesman, who strove to modernise his backward realm. If anyone could have given it a new lease of life it was he; but his labours were in vain for he was succeeded by lesser men. Book II describes the rude challenge of Mehemet Ali, the founder of modern Egypt, who was only beaten off with British aid. Palmerston cared nothing for the Turks, but he had no desire to see their empire crushed between Russia on the north and the ruler of Egypt on the south. The fear of Russia was growing apace in the West, and her dark shadow falls across the landscape. In resisting the rebellious vassal he risked a war with France; but, while some of his colleagues shivered at the prospect, the Foreign Minister coolly played his hazardous game and won. 'He was the greatest personality in foreign policy between Canning and Disraeli, and was the disciple of the one and the model for the other. . . . He was too daring in uttering threats of war, too ready sometimes to abandon them, too fond of lecturing foreign Powers and of provoking applause from English audiences. Yet his incorrigible gaiety disguises the seriousness and solidity of his character.' The duel between the resourceful statesman and 'the barbarian of genius' makes a thrilling story.

Book III describes the uneasy years between the collapse of Mehemet Ali in 1841 and the approach of the Crimean War. Half-hearted attempts at reform were made at Constantinople, and the commanding figure of Stratford Canning advanced to the centre of the stage. In Book IV we return to more familiar ground, and it is interesting to note the historian's verdicts on the principal actors. Gladstone called Aberdeen the best public character with whom he had ever worked, but he was the worst possible Prime Minister when dark clouds gathered overhead. Convinced that he would never fight, the Tsar took greater risks than if Palmerston had been at the helm. Aberdeen was one of the men responsible for what is described as the tragic blunder of the Crimean War. Napoleon III was another. Stratford Canning's share, it is argued, was less than has been generally believed. The conflict was in no way inevitable. 'Had Nicholas been weak, Aberdeen strong or Mensikov tactful, there might have been no war.' Numerous studies preparing the way for his *magnum opus* appeared in English, American, and French reviews. Among them may be mentioned a series on Stratford Canning in the *English Historical Review*, two articles on the Treaty of Paris in the *Journal of Modern History*, and an address to the British Academy on the 'Bulgarian and Other Atrocities, 1875–78'.

In the summer of 1938 two handsome volumes were published by the Cambridge University Press. The larger and more

important, *Foundations of British Policy from Pitt (1792) to Salisbury
(1902)*, edited by Temperley and Professor Lillian Penson,
contained 200 documents and 86 introductory notes. It at once
took its place not merely as a source-book containing a good deal
of new material but as an authoritative guide to the principles
of statesmanship. The continuity of ideas in our diplomacy is
remarkable. Eyre Crowe's famous Memorandum in 1907
reproduces the teachings of Canning. 'The balance of power,
the sanctity of treaties, the danger of extending guarantees, the
value of non-intervention, the implications of what Castlereagh
called "a system of Government strongly popular and national
in its character" were understood by all. It is true that
Palmerston, in his robust vigour, was ready to interpret "non-
intervention" in a sense which would have surprised Castlereagh
and Canning; that Russell glorified the revolutions which
Disraeli disliked; that Salisbury hated publicity and parliamentary control; that Gladstone preferred the concert of Europe
to the balance of power. But these differences do not prevent us
from seeing that there is a great similarity between the views of all
these men, despite the illogicality of their methods. There are
times when Castlereagh is English, when Canning is European,
when Palmerston admits the superiority of moral ideas, when
Gladstone relies on the British fleet, and when Salisbury finds
public opinion of value. What is more remarkable is that the
ideas of Pitt clearly anticipate the dangers of violent nationalism,
the merits of a League to enforce peace, and the necessity for
England to steer a middle course between these alternating
policies.'

It is a fascinating task to read the speeches, despatches, memoranda, and private letters of our prime ministers and foreign
secretaries on all the major issues of peace and war from the
struggle against revolutionary France till the opening of the
twentieth century. Here are the essential documents, such as
the State Paper of 1820 on non-intervention, Russell's eloquent
homage to the Garibaldians in 1860, the Grey Declaration on
the Nile valley in 1895, and Salisbury's impressive reaffirmation
in 1901 of the policy of avoiding Continental commitments.
Equally instructive are the introductions to each document or
group of documents, revealing wide acquaintance with printed

and unprinted materials and a serene impartiality towards the actors who throng the stage. Castlereagh is saluted as the most 'European' of British statesmen. Canning was extremely reluctant to give guarantees, and he never gave one which he could not enforce. Palmerston's championship of constitutional states was his nearest approach to a system. Russell defined the balance of power in Europe as the independence of its several states, and the preponderance of any one Power as threatening that independence. In the same spirit Gladstone pleaded for the acknowledgement of the equal rights of all nations as the very basis of a Christian civilisation. Salisbury was as ready for co-operation as he was disinclined to pledge the country in advance. With the latter's retirement in 1902 a new era began, in which the old quest for security assumed a new form.

A companion volume, *A Century of Diplomatic Blue Books, 1814–1914*, appeared at the same time. The first aim was to discover the exact date of the two thousand publications and the cause of their issue, whether, as was usually the case, at the wish of the Government or in response to pressure from the House. The next question was how far a document or a series is complete. Total reliance on Blue Books at any period, we are warned, would be a cardinal error, for much was always omitted and the text was frequently curtailed. For the general reader the most valuable portions of the book are the introductions on the practice of each successive Foreign Secretary from Canning, who began the system of publicity, to Grey, who, for sufficient reasons, concealed most of the negotiations which led or failed to lead to agreements with other Great Powers. Some of the results of the elaborate investigation were incorporated in an article 'British Secret Diplomacy from Canning to Grey', in the *Cambridge Historical Journal*, 1939. Our diplomacy, it appears, became more secret as our constitution grew more democratic. Canning and Palmerston were less secretive than Gladstone, and Salisbury was infinitely less secretive than Lansdowne and Grey. When we were afraid of no one and could do without allies we could dispense with secret agreements. When we were compelled to abandon our isolation—and Temperley never doubted the necessity—we had to imitate the secrecy and conform to the diplomatic ways of the Continental groups. This practice, however, could be carried too far, as in the case of the secret clauses of the Anglo-French Treaty of 1904, for which Lansdowne is blamed.

After the completion of the *British Documents* Temperley confided to the present writer that he did not intend to undertake any further large-scale editorial tasks, but in two instances he lent effective aid. The *Cambridge Modern History* had been completed shortly before the World War, and there was an obvious need for supplementary volumes; but the flight of time was not the only reason for scholars to bestir themselves. Owing to the opening of the archives of all the Great European Powers except Italy we now know the political mind and face of Europe during the generation before 1914 as we know no other period of history. It was Temperley's idea to inaugurate a new series of volumes, and he explained the purpose of the first (not yet published) in a foreword. There was no desire to rewrite the story of political, social and economic movements described in the closing volume of the original work. Its object was to explain, in the light of the latest information and by the efforts of historians of different nationalities, the origins and causes of the catastrophe. An attempt would be made to tell the story fairly, to supply the reader with a summary of ascertained fact, and to provide the materials of judgment where the facts are still disputed or the issues still in doubt. A few pregnant pages sketch the development of the European system since the foundation of the German Empire and during the World War. The book, which was to be edited by Professors Lillian Penson and Bernadotte Schmitt, was abandoned soon after his death. The second enterprise was the *Cambridge History of Poland*. The Secretary of the University Press describes him as 'the only begetter', and the work is dedicated to his memory. He made several suggestions as to authors, and he was to have contributed the chapter on the Peace Conference.

Temperley used his second sabbatical year to make a journey round the world. His main purpose at each place, writes his wife, was to visit the university, to secure new members for the International Historical Congress, and to bring teachers into touch with the historians of the West. He left Cambridge in June 1936 for California, where he lectured at the Leland Stanford

University for three months and took discussion classes in place of Professor Lutz.   He sailed from Vancouver to Japan, where an old Peterhouse friend, Viscount Kato, opened many doors. Saigon and Mukden were visited on the way to Peking, Nankin, and Shanghai.   After brief halts at Penang and Rangoon he reached India in January 1937, where he found old pupils, made new friends, saw the glories of Kinchinjunga from Darjeeling, and visited the historic cities between Calcutta and Bombay. After breaking the journey in Egypt, the travellers reached home in March 1937.

Temperley's travels, war service, and field of study prepared him to play a leading part in the international organisation of scholarship.   The first Historical Congress was held in Rome in 1903, the second in Berlin in 1908, the third in London in 1913, the fourth in Brussels in 1923.   The Bureau of the International Committee of Historical Sciences, of which Temperley was a member, was founded in 1926.   He headed the British Delegation at the fifth Congress at Oslo in 1928, and at Warsaw in 1933 he succeeded Professor Koht as President.   He attended meetings of the executive at Cracow in 1933, Paris in 1934, and Bucharest in 1936.   He presided at the seventh Congress in Zürich in 1938, where he lectured on 'England and the Dogma of Turkey's Integrity and Independence from Palmerston to Disraeli, 1865-75'. At the close he handed over the reins to Dr. Leland.   In his opening address he reported that forty-four countries or civilisations were now connected with the Congress, and that China, the Vatican City, and Ireland had applied for membership.   'It is difficult to imagine our International Committee without him', wrote Professor Koht, the Norwegian Foreign Minister: 'he had a truly international mind.   He possessed in the highest degree that quality which is found more frequently in the English than in any other nation, the power to free oneself from all national prejudice in the study of international conflicts.   He was in the fullest sense what the English call fair, a man of absolute good faith and serene impartiality.   You could have unlimited confidence in him.'

Professor Lhéritier, the General Secretary, adds that he inspired confidence in his collaborators, impartially arbitrating differences and developing the activity of the Committee to the maximum.

'To him above all we owe the institution of our Commissions extérieures de l'histoire régionale, and the accession of China, India, Egypt, Malta and Ireland.' He liked administrative tasks, was never too busy to attend to details, and had a great capacity for making friends. Elected to the British Academy in 1927, he served on the Council from 1932 to 1938, and acted as Chairman of the Mediæval and Modern History Section from 1933 to 1938. He was a member of the Royal Commission on Historical Manuscripts. His services to history brought him academic honours from Durham and St. Andrews, from Czechoslovakia, Denmark, Hungary, Jugoslavia, Norway, Poland, and Rumania. He was among the official guests at the Sokol celebrations at Prague in July 1938.

In 1934 Temperley became the first President of the New Commonwealth Institute, the object of which was to study the fundamental principles of international relations and in particular the problems of international justice and security. 'It is by discussion and dispute that the truth emerges from darkness', he wrote in his foreword for the first number of the *New Commonwealth Quarterly*. Justice and equity were the desire of the modern world, he declared in the preface to one of the Institute's monographs, and research was the means of attaining them. It was only since the war that the new method of research had been perfected. 'This is to work on international lines, to get the scholars of different countries to contribute their ideas and to pool the results of their labour.' His assistance was particularly valuable, writes the Director, Professor Keeton, in the early years when the need for such an independent and international institute was not universally recognised. 'The fact that this distinguished scholar fully associated himself with the new venture, and gave his unconditional support and unsparing advice, contributed more than anything else to lay the foundation on which the Institute is now firmly based.' From his sick-bed he steered it through a complete reorganisation in 1939.

It was a tribute to Temperley's eminence that he was invited by the B.B.C. to prepare four 'radio-historical dramas' in collaboration with Mr. Lawrence Gilliam. The first and the most striking was entitled 'Twenty Years Ago, or The Outbreak of War', performed for the first time on August 4, 1934, with prominent actors taking part.   The second, 'Twenty-five Years', performed on May 8, 1935, on the Jubilee of George V, summarised the events of the reign.   The third, 'Kitchener, Twenty Years after his Death', was given on June 3, 1936.   The fourth, 'Revolution in Russia, or Twenty Years after the Bolshevik Triumph', was given on December 13 and 14, 1937.   He had no love for the Bolshevists, but he realised that the way for their coming had been prepared by the faults and follies of the Tsarist régime.   His strictures provoked protest in certain quarters, but he was sure of his ground.

Temperley seemed well enough when scholars from many lands met at the Historical Congress at Zürich in August 1938, but he sickened before he reached home.   He went into a nursing home at Cambridge to be treated for a streptococcus infection and was unable to lecture till the middle of the autumn term.   He appeared to make a good recovery and took full duty during the Lent term, though great care was necessary.   At Easter, heart weakness began to cause anxiety, and a specialist ordered several weeks in bed.   'He had the most wonderful resilience of spirit,' writes his wife, 'and never was this shown more than during his illness.   His brain was perfectly clear, he wrote articles and letters, and read omnivorously.'   He had, indeed, every reason to cling to life.   His election as Master of Peterhouse in 1938 was the fulfilment of a cherished ambition, and a singularly happy second marriage had given him a home again.   He made a gallant fight, but the end came quietly on July 11, 1939.

Temperley warmed both hands before the fire of life.   His capacity for work was astonishing.   Possessing an accurate mind, he insisted on accuracy and thoroughness in others.   As a reviewer he was not easy to please.   No British scholar of his time knew more about European diplomacy since the fall of Napoleon.   He was primarily a political historian of the school of Ranke and Seeley, less interested in social conditions and the evolution of thought than in institutions and the relations of states.   His two great books, *The Foreign Policy of Canning* and *England and the Near East*, deserve the highest of all compliments, namely that the work will not have to be done again.   As an editor of documents he was in the first flight.   None of his contemporaries did more to encourage disinterested study and research. His travels and foreign contacts helped him to stand above the battle. A stream of articles and letters to the Press revealed his intensive study of current affairs. Ardent and highly strung, he was ever ready to do battle for his principles and ideas. Professor Ernest Barker has spoken of his rugged greatness. He threw every ounce of his energy into whatever he undertook, and he left his impress on many lives. His death at the height of his powers was felt throughout the academic world, not only as a personal loss, but as a blow to the cause of historical scholarship to which he had dedicated his life.

8

HISTORICAL NOVELS

IN his delightful book, *The Light Reading of our Ancestors*, Lord Ernle defined the historical novel as the imaginative re-creation of the life of the past. No historian would admit that fiction, however conscientious and erudite, could provide a substitute for genuine historical study. What might have been is not the same as what was. If, however, we bear continually in mind that we are only in the outer courts of the temple of truth, that it is the privilege of the author to give rein to his imagination, that his object is rather to stimulate interest than to solve problems, there is no reason why we should not enjoy the feast; for here is History without Tears.

In a striking little book published in 1924 Professor Butterfield offers a vigorous defence of the historical novel. That there is a place for it, he argues, is due to a certain inadequacy in history itself. The chart must be turned into a picture if we are to recover the pulse and processes of life. The imagination of the historian may perform this transmutation for himself as he broods over his materials. But scholars are relatively few, scholars with creative imagination still fewer, and what they see they cannot always transmit to their readers. Moreover, even the expert knows only what his sources can tell him. Our knowledge remains eternally incomplete, for the dead carry most of their secrets with them to the grave. Thus the historian and the novelist work on parallel lines, which never meet, the former telling us what happened, the latter helping us to see it happen. The mind of a great historical novelist is full of the past, as the mind of a musician is full of melodies; he sets history to fiction as the composer sets words to music. The tacit assumptions and values, the atmosphere, the irrecoverable things are recalled, and the past lives again before our eyes. In a word, historical fiction is a supplement to history, not a rival—a twin-brother, to use the phrase of Scheffel, not a usurper. It flourishes in the borderland between history and *belles-lettres*, but it is nearer to the latter than to the former. Thus the proper place for a lecture on the subject is not the Royal Historical Society, but the Royal Society of Literature.

Before the historical novel could be successfully launched the novel itself had to develop, and the great practitioners of the nineteenth century owe to the early masters the fashioning of their tools. From the Elizabethan era onwards writers often staged their story in an earlier time, and recalled famous personages from a vanished world. But the retrospect was incidental, and no serious effort was made to recapture the colour and the rhythm of life. Not until the Romantic Movement substituted a zealous if uncritical admiration of the Middle Ages for the supercilious indifference of the generation of Hume, Gibbon and Voltaire was the soil prepared in which the historical novel could grow. The technique of fiction had been perfected by Bunyan and Defoe, Richardson and Fielding in England, by the Abbé Prévost, Marivaux and Bernardin de St. Pierre in France, by Goethe in Germany. In the closing decades of the eighteenth century the current in Western and Central Europe set strongly towards poetry and romance, and an army of writers hastened to catch the flowing tide.

In 1764 Horace Walpole wrote the first historical novel which is still read. *The Castle of Otranto*, a tale of Italy in the time of the Crusades, was partly a burlesque of the extravagances with which the public taste was beginning to be fed; but the ingredients of his art—spectres, dungeons, tortures—became the bread and meat of the 'novel of terror', and were partially adopted by historical novelists hungering for emotional thrills. The success of his *jeu d'esprit* indicated that the *sæculum rationalisticum*, the reign of so-called 'common sense', was nearing its end, and that imagination was coming into its own.

There were brave men before Agamemnon, as Horace remarked, and there were plenty of historical novelists before Scott. About fifty stories made their appearance in England while the Wizard of the North was growing up. But for practical purposes we may say that he was the first as well as the greatest of the tribe, and that *Waverley* burst upon the world like Minerva from the head of Zeus. The young Scottish laird was a born antiquarian, for the past laid its spell on him while he was still in the schoolroom. At the age of thirteen he forgot his dinner over Percy's *Reliques of Ancient English Poetry*. Madame de Staël said that she would not open her window to look at the Bay of Naples, but would travel leagues to hear a clever man talk. Scott would have gone leagues to see a ruined castle or explore an historic site. He loved the romantic story of his own country, and studied it till its scenes lived again before his eyes. In 1805, the year of *The Lay of the Last Minstrel*, he began his first novel. But the poetic mood was strong upon him, and *Waverley* lay forgotten in a drawer till it was discovered by accident in 1814. He once declared that he gave up poetry because Byron beat him. He now revised, expanded and published his tale, and its instantaneous success determined how he should spend the remainder of his life.

Though some of his most celebrated books are staged in England and France, Germany and the Middle East, his tread is surest north of the Tweed or when he follows a Scot across the border or the sea. With unerring instinct he laid down the lines which the best practitioners have followed ever since. In his hands history becomes the kernel of the book, while the love story and the adventures form the embroidery. No one has ever surpassed him in his power of bringing the illustrious dead to life. To read of the revels at Kenilworth is to visualise Queen Elizabeth in all her masculine strength and feminine weakness. In *The Abbot* we hold our breath as Mary Queen of Scots escapes from Lochleven. What reader of *The Fortunes of Nigel* can ever banish the picture of James I, the wisest fool in Christendom? *The Talisman* stamps King Richard and Saladin on our minds, and Louis XI peers grimly forth from the pages of *Quentin Durward*. The Young Pretender lives in *Waverley*, and no picture of Queen Caroline brings her so close to us as her interview with Jeanie Deans in *The Heart of Midlothian*.

It is idle to discuss which is the greatest of the masterpieces which poured forth like a mountain torrent, for the question involves a combination of literary and historical judgments. Dr.

Trevelyan describes *Ivanhoe* as the first attempt to envisage our distant ancestors as human beings; yet, though it is admittedly the favourite of the crowd, the expert deplores the exaggeration of the antagonism of Norman and Saxon. In my opinion *Old Mortality* was never surpassed, if indeed it was ever equalled. Scott was no more impartial than other mortals, and *Woodstock* is the measure of his inability to understand English Puritanism; but *Old Mortality* presents us with a Claverhouse, the Royalist chief, as real and convincing as Morton, the iron leader of the Covenanters. The great magician has most fully explained and defended his method in the Dedicatory Epistle to *Ivanhoe*. He made his own rules, and his practice has been followed with varying success by the great army of his disciples in every country in Europe. It is his proud achievement not only to have dowered the world with a crop of imperishable masterpieces, but to have created a genre which at its best is capable of rendering equal service to history and to literature. In the opinion of Dr. Trevelyan he did more for history than any professed historian of modern times.

Scott took the world by storm, and nowhere was the welcome warmer than in France. The Romantic Movement had been inaugurated by Rousseau, Bernardin de St. Pierre and Chateaubriand, but it only reached its full stride during the years which witnessed the appearance of the Waverley Novels. In his admirable volume on Scott's influence in France Maigron describes the rapturous excitement in literary circles, the hasty translations, the crude dramatisations, the unending discussions in the *salons* and the Press. Classicism was dead and realism was unborn. The public thirsted for diversion, and every young writer of talent felt his pulse quicken to the call of romance. The literature of the First Empire had been dry and colourless; now winter melted into spring.

When Scott visited Paris in 1826 Alfred de Vigny was presented to him and offered him *Cinq-Mars*, his first and last historical novel. The young conspirator lacks flesh and blood, and Richelieu is an impossible monster; but the atmosphere of the France of Louis XIII is skilfully reproduced, and many of the scenes and characters are instinct with life. History is a novel, he declared, of which the people is the author. A greater success

25

was scored by Mérimée with his *Charles IX*, the fruit of assiduous study of the memoirs and characters of the Wars of Religion. Superior to both in human interest and technical skill must be reckoned *Les Chouans*, in which Balzac paints the civil wars of the French Revolution against the background of the dark forests and fanatical peasantry of the West.   But neither de Vigny, Mérimée nor Balzac continued to work the rich vein they had opened up, and the championship of the historical novel in France passed into other hands.

Victor Hugo's genius is too dazzling to be obscured even by his colossal faults, and his place among the immortals is secure. *Cinq-Mars*, *Charles IX* and *Les Chouans* were cast into the shade by *Notre Dame*, published in 1831.   It was an inspiration to make the old cathedral the pivot of the story, the soul and symbol of the great city, around which surges the life of the France of Louis XI, and with which the fortunes of the actors are mysteriously linked.   If we are forced to admit that Paris is more real than any of its citizens, and if the critical reader is often aware of the author's slender historical equipment, we must pay our tribute to the Venetian colouring, the breathless emotions, the stir and throb of life.   And when the great magician returned in old age to the arena in which he had outpaced his youthful contemporaries, *Quatre-Vingt-Treize* was to reveal that his right hand had not lost its cunning, and that he could evoke the spirit of the French Revolution in its mingling of savagery and idealism with no less power than the fifteenth century.

The most popular of French historical novelists was not Victor Hugo, who only made occasional incursions into the territory, but Dumas.   The French Scott possessed none of the scholarly instincts and nothing of the moral elevation which radiates from the Waverley Novels.   He described himself as a *vulgarisateur*, and no great artist ever carried out his mission with less conscious effort.   His strength lay not in the delineation of character but in the inexhaustible invention of picturesque incident.   He poured out romance as Mozart and Schubert poured out melody.   No historical novelist has such a vast array of wares in his shop-window, for he had Maquet and other 'ghosts' to help him.   It was inevitable that a man who laid all history under contribution, from Nero to Marie Antoinette, should often stumble and fall, yet only a pedant will deny him a place among the supreme masters of his craft. George Saintsbury, in his massive *History of the French Novel*, has truly remarked that he was at his best from the second half of the sixteenth century to the end of the eighteenth. His masterpieces, I think, are *Queen Margot* and *The Three Musketeers*. While the all-round greatness of Scott can only be appreciated in maturity, the appeal of Dumas is above all to the young; and human nature will have to change a good deal before the dashing d'Artagnan and his three gallant comrades cease to enthral.

It is sometimes said that Dumas ruined the historical novel in France by turning it into melodrama, and by seeking in the quarry of history nothing but the picturesque. Whatever the cause, no French writer of the first rank during the second half of the nineteenth century devoted his full strength to this department of literature. Théophile Gautier's *Capitaine Fracasse* attempts to revive the age of Louis XIII without much success. George Sand painted a charming picture of eighteenth-century Venice, of Vienna under Maria Theresa, and of Berlin under Frederick the Great, in *Consuelo*, and its weaker sequel *La Comtesse de Rudolstadt*. Flaubert resuscitated the glittering savagery of Carthage in *Salammbo*, the most celebrated attempt by a French writer at *le roman savant*, but he crushed much of the life out of his book under a load of erudition. Erckmann and Chatrian collaborated in studies of the Napoleonic campaigns which enjoyed immense popularity. Anatole France, the master of subtle irony, recalled the early struggles of Christianity and paganism in *Thaïs*, and the hectic fever of the French Revolution in *Les Dieux ont Soif*. Zola's *La Débâcle* contains almost as much history as fiction, and towers above the volumes in which the brothers Margueritte describe the same unfortunate Franco-German War.

The influence of Scott was felt no less strongly in the Romantic Movement of Italy; and when Manzoni announced himself as a disciple to the master while passing through Milan he received the flattering reply, 'In that case *I Promessi Sposi* is my best work'. *The Betrothed*, published in 1825, is the first and far the greatest of Italian historical novels. Despite its length it is easy to read, for it is suffused with the serene humanity of its author. 'It satisfies us,' remarked Goethe, 'like perfectly ripe fruit.' If some critics complain that the historical element is too prominent, that we hear too much of the war, the famine and the plague which afflicted the Milanese under Spanish rule in the first half of the seventeenth century, others will argue that the balance between truth and poetry, between the historical setting and the personal drama, can be justified by precedents from Scott. The success of *The Betrothed* never tempted the modest author to try his hand again; and though Grossi, D'Azeglio and Cesare Cantú carried on the tradition, their twentieth-century readers echo the exclamation of one of them, 'How far we are behind Manzoni!'

Almost every country in Europe has played its part in working the rich vein opened up by Scott, but in some cases the leaven worked slowly. The creator of the Spanish historical novel, Perez Galdos, narrated the troubled fortunes of his country from Trafalgar to the expulsion of Queen Isabella in two score volumes, which might be seen in the window of every bookshop in the peninsula at the turn of the century. They have taught many Spaniards, who are not a nation of readers, all that they know of the Napoleonic invasion, the odious Ferdinand, the ferocious futilities of the Carlist wars, the short-lived Republic, and the Restoration of 1874. Galdos was a democrat and anti-clerical; but he was above all a patriot, and men of every school enjoy his lively survey of the sufferings and achievements of their sorely tried country. Yet none of his stories grips us so tightly as *The Four Horsemen of the Apocalypse*, in which Blasco Ibañez splashes on to his canvas the boiling passions of the First World War.

The first critical Portuguese historian, Herculano da Carvalho, was a poet and a novelist as well as a scholar, and his name deserves mention among the practitioners, though not among the masters, of historical fiction. His story of the Arab invasion, *Eurich the Priest*, written in 1843, was translated into German by Heine, and may also be read in a French translation. It describes the collapse of the degenerate Visigoths before the Moorish attack, and the retreat of the unconquered Pelagius to the mountains of the north. These dramatic events are linked with the life of the hero who, having become a priest in the despair of frustrated love, re-emerges as 'the Black Knight' to perform prodigies of valour, and rescues his beloved from dishonour in the tent of the conqueror. When, however, all outward obstacles to their union are removed, the vow of celibacy remains; and the story ends with the voluntary death of Eurich and the madness of the broken-hearted Hermengard.

The separation of Belgium from Holland in 1830, and the attainment of an independence which her people had never known, gave an impetus to research and prepared the soil for the historical novel. The opportunity was seized by Hendrik Conscience, a Fleming who wrote in his own tongue, but who nevertheless gave both races of his countrymen the patriotic nourishment they craved. *The Lion of Flanders*, published in 1838, extols the miracle of deliverance wrought at the battle of Courtrai in 1302, when Philip the Fair was flung back and, according to tradition, his proud knights left their golden spurs on the field. The writer keeps close to the chronicles, but his ship carries sails as well as cargo, and the contrast between the haughty chivalry of France and the opulent burghers of Bruges is finely drawn.

Far more important is *Tyl Ulenspiegl*, published in 1869, that full-blooded reconstruction of the epic struggle of the Low Countries against the Spanish yoke, so familiar to English readers from Motley's *Rise of the Dutch Republic* and Miss Wedgwood's biography of William the Silent. The prankster of popular farces was transformed by the genius of Charles de Coster into the resourceful patriot. His adventures and stratagems, his sufferings and sorrows, are skilfully woven into the pattern of tremendous events. Philip II, the torturer of captive animals in youth and of his subjects when he grew to manhood, cold, unsmiling, fanatical, unloving and unloved, served only too zealously by the Duke of Alva and the Spanish Inquisition, is the villain of the piece. The book throbs with patriotic emotion and burns with hatred for the foreign oppressors and their monstrous cruelties. Never has this work, unquestionably one of the greatest historical novels ever written, been more eagerly read by Belgians than during the long agony of German occupation in the two World Wars.

The Romantic Movement and the 'Ritterromane' which floated like froth on its surface had prepared the soil of Germany when the name and fame of Scott were borne across the North Sea. The appetite for the Waverley Novels was insatiable, and many a young author lit his torch at the glowing flame. Hauff's *Lichtenstein*, which he described as a romantic saga from Württemberg history, may claim to be the first real German historical novel. No author reproduced the master's touch in his lifetime with greater fidelity. Hauff follows the favourite plan of inventing his hero and launching him into the stream of events. Georg Sturmfelder, a young soldier of fortune, joins the army of the Swabian League which desires to prevent Ulrich of Württemberg from regaining his throne. He quickly changes sides, for the father of his sweetheart, Marie von Lichtenstein, is a leading supporter of the Duke. The varying fortunes of the antagonists in the early days of the Reformation form the background for the adventures and the love story of the hero. Had he not died at twenty-five, Hauff might have realised his dream of earning the proud title of the German Scott.

The vacancy was partially filled by Willibald Alexis. Volunteering at seventeen for the Waterloo campaign, he reached the front too late to join in the fray, but the gesture was an emblem of the ardent patriotism which inspired his life. His first novel, *Walladmor*, is at once a curiosity of literature and a tribute to the spell of Scott. Written as a parody of what he regarded as the master's failings, the story, which was described as a translation, was universally believed to be a new work by the author of *Waverley*. Sailing under a false flag it won instantaneous success in Germany, and was translated into English and several other languages. Scott described it as the boldest hoax of the age, a description welcomed by the author as the highest praise.

The Roland of Berlin is the best of his books, and despite its prolixity the interest never flags. The stone figure of Roland outside the town hall of cities which possessed exclusive rights of judicature was the symbol of dignity and independence, but the conflict of Berlin with the second Hohenzollern is presented with a decided leaning to the wise and virtuous Margrave. For the Elector Frederick II strives to regain some of the power which had been lost to the towns during his father's struggle with the nobility. 'You are lord of the land, but not of our town,' argues Rathenow, the old Burgomaster, after the victory of the Margrave; 'we were defending our ancient privileges.' 'My right is to see that justice is done to all,' retorts the ruler. The Roland is broken to pieces in token of the loss of justiciary rights, and the Burgomaster, broken but unbent, goes into voluntary exile. The picture of the turbulent life of a fifteenth-century city, proud of its privileges but weakened by class distinctions and the fickleness of the crowd, is no mean achievement.

The passion of Willibald Alexis for the old core of the Prussian State was shared by Fontane, whose *Wanderungen durch die Mark Brandenburg* is a popular classic. *Vor dem Sturm*, a story of 1812–13, claims a place in the short list of first-class German historical novels. Fontane, whose strength is in character and atmosphere rather than in incident, makes no attempt to hurry over his tale, and the length of the book is a burden to impatient readers. We find ourselves in the Oderland, where memories of Frederick the Great and his desperate struggles are still fresh, and where men are bracing themselves for the reckoning with Napoleon. The invasion of Russia has failed, and hope has dawned in northern Germany that the fetters may at length be broken. But the French garrisons are still strong, and the narrative closes with a premature attack by the little group whose lives and thoughts we have shared. Fontane was wise in leaving the drums and trumpets of the War of Liberation to others, and in confining himself to a study of the people who were to rise against the aggressor.

While Willibald Alexis and Fontane wrote on Prussia for the Prussians, a greater man recalled the long story of the German people in symbolic form to the citizens of the new-born Empire. In his entertaining *Autobiography* Gustav Freytag relates how the victorious campaign of 1870, in which he accompanied the Crown Prince Frederick to the front, gave rise to visions which were one day to be embodied in the cycle entitled *The Ancestors*. The whole history of the race seemed to unroll itself before his eyes like a map. 'I was always deeply interested in the con-nexion of man with his ancestors,' he wrote, 'in their mysterious influence on body and soul. What science cannot fathom the poet may attempt.' He worked out a plan by which a single

family should take part in the decisive events of German history.
The first volume dealt with the Roman invasion, the second
with the Slavonic inroads, the third and fourth with the rise
and fall of chivalry.   The fifth brings us to the Reformation,
mirrored in the career of a merchant of Thorn living under
Polish rule but German in feeling.   The sixth portrays the
Thirty Years War, the seventh the reign of Frederick William I,
the last the Wars of Liberation.   Freytag described his work as
a symphony in eight parts.   Though the pearls are strung on an
almost invisible thread, the series derives a certain unity from
the pervading atmosphere of national sentiment.   Read with
avidity during the years succeeding the wars of unification, *The
Ancestors* helped to make the citizens of every part of the new
Empire conscious of their kinship.   The work grew out of the
author's earlier volumes, *Pictures from Germany's Past*, as Schiller's
Wallenstein dramas had grown out of his *History of the Thirty
Years' War*.   Freytag's novels did more to interest German
men and women all over the world in their own history than
the writings of any other man of his generation.   But despite
their scholarly character none of them belong to the first or even
the second rank, for his characters are too symbolic to have
much vitality.

Two other German writers of the middle of the century found
their inspiration in widely different periods of history.   Fresh
from the resounding triumph of *Der Trompeter von Säckingen*,
Scheffel cast his net once more into the storied waters of the
upper Rhine.   The novel *Ekkehard*, like the poem, went
straight to the heart of the German people, and may claim to
have been the most popular work of German historical fiction
in the nineteenth century.   The tale of the monastic chronicler
of St. Gall was suggested by studies of South German law in the
tenth century undertaken in hopes of an academic career.   Scheffel
assures his readers that there is little in his tale that is unsupported
by the *Monumenta Germaniæ*.   The book breathes a gentle charm.
The beautiful landscape of Lake Constance is lovingly reproduced, and the raid of the Huns is told with considerable spirit.
The figures of Ekkehard, the handsome young monk, and the
imperious Duchess of Swabia are cleverly sketched.   But the
work lacks muscle, and a certain conventionality of treatment

renders it impossible for modern readers to recapture the enthusiasm of 1855. Very different in character is *The Amber Witch*, in which Meinhold, a Pomeranian pastor, exposes the superstition and savagery of north Germany during the Thirty Years War. The grim strength of this unadorned tale grips the reader, and Professor York Powell used to say that there had been nothing like it since the Elizabethans. But the subject is repulsive and neither it nor its still more disagreeable successor *Sidonia* has ever been a popular favourite.

While Freytag was employing the historical novel to stimulate patriotism, two German professors were engaged in creating a type which the French describe as 'Le Roman Savant', the dominant purpose of which is to impart information. Felix Dahn devoted his long and laborious life to the 'Völkerwanderung', the period of the migration of the peoples which separated the fall of the Roman Empire from Charlemagne. His massive historical works are known only to scholars, but the novels in which he has presented the same materials in popular form carried his name all over the German-speaking world. He relates in his *Autobiography* how the conflict of the Ostrogoths with Belisarius fired his imagination, how as a young man of twenty-five he wrote the first part of his most celebrated work, how he put it aside for many years in doubt as to its value, how he resumed his task in middle life, how he soaked himself in the atmosphere of Ravenna, 'the city of the great dead', and how *A Struggle for Rome* finally appeared in 1876. The book took Germany by storm. Readers of Hodgkin's monumental *Italy and her Invaders* do not need to be reminded of the fascinating story of the Gothic Kingdom of Ravenna, the internal collapse after the death of Theodoric, the landing of Belisarius, and his gallant defence of Rome, the triumph of Justinian's arms in the capture of Ravenna, the final flicker of Gothic fortunes with the radiant figure of Totila, the disgrace of Belisarius, and the defeat and death of Teias, the last of the Goths, at the hand of Narses, the eunuch. Closely following Procopius, on whom he had published an admirable monograph some years before, Dahn leads us from Ravenna to Naples, from Naples to Rome, from the Tiber to the Bosphorus. Some critics complained that Cethegus, the fictitious protagonist, was an impossible monster, others that the Empress Theodora is painted too black; but, whatever reserves may be made on minor points, no student of the period can fail to admire the author's grasp of its problems, and no lover of literature can be blind to the power of the work. The popularity of *A Struggle for Rome* led Dahn to write a long series of successors, of which *Attila* and *Felicitas* are among the best, but he never found another subject so fully worthy of his powers. Dahn is the only professional historian who has produced historical fiction of the first class, for the expert as a rule prefers solid ground under his feet.

While Dahn interpreted the centuries of the 'Völkerwanderung' to his countrymen, Ebers chose Ancient Egypt for his province. He began his studies when Lepsius was giving the world the twelve gigantic volumes on the results of his first historic journey to the valley of the Nile, and it was to Lepsius that he took the manuscript of his first novel with a timid request for his verdict. The first great German Egyptologist opened it with reluctance, fearing that his beloved science was about to be vulgarised; but he was gripped from the start and returned the book with warm words of congratulation. *The Egyptian Princess*, like *A Struggle for Rome*, was an instantaneous success, and its pictures of the intrigue-ridden court of Cambyses and the Persian monarch's invasion of Egypt are as fresh to-day as when they were painted. It is a curious fact that though the author was to make repeated visits to the land of his dreams, and though he produced a long series of novels embodying his learning in popular form, he never repeated the triumph of the young enthusiast who knew the gorgeous East from books alone.

When the generation which had welcomed Freytag was passing away and the glamour of Dahn and Ebers had begun to pale, the historical novel lost its vogue in Germany for a couple of decades. Ricarda Huch's pictures of the *Risorgimento* keep almost too close to history, and read more like a record than a tale. The First World War, the defeat and the revolution turned the thoughts of young and old to the trials, the glories and the lessons of the past. The revival was inaugurated by Walter von Molo, whose full-length portrait of Schiller appeared between 1912 and 1916. The atmosphere in which it was conceived was already electric, and the picture of the poet-patriot was warmly welcomed in the last years of peace and the first years of war; but the volumes enjoyed their greatest popularity as a work of edification in the dark era which followed the collapse. Scarcely less successful from the point of view of sales was the trilogy which carries us from Frederick the Great to the War of Liberation. *Fredericus*, published in 1918, exhibits the king in the crisis of the Seven Years War, when dreams of victory had vanished, and his utmost hope was to save Prussia from annihilation. The picture of Frederick amid the tense horrors of the battlefield is boldly drawn, and the curtain falls on the sensational announcement that with the death of the Tsarina Elizabeth Russia is ready for peace. The second volume, *Luise*, describes the struggle at the court of the helpless Frederick William III, on the eve of the Jena campaign, between the party of peace and the party of action led by Prince Louis Ferdinand, Stein and the radiant Queen. The third volume, *Das Volk wacht auf*, sketches the beginnings of the War of Liberation, and displays Scharnhorst, Blücher and Gneisenau at work. A later effort, *Brother Luther*, the narrative of a single day, revives the emotions of the Diet of Worms. Yet to-day Molo may be counted among the extinct volcanoes.

The most sensational triumph of German historical fiction since the First World War was scored by Feuchtwanger, whose *Jew Süss*, a study of princely misrule in eighteenth-century Württemberg, owed as much of its world-wide acclaim to its unflinching realism as to its narrative power. Another best-seller was *Der Teufel*, by Alfred Neumann, who dared to enter into competition with Scott and Hugo by resuscitating Louis XI and his merry men. A smaller but more discriminating public was charmed by Bruno Frank's *Days of the King*, three vignettes of Frederick the Great of exquisite literary workmanship, and by *Lotte in Weimar*, in which Thomas Mann recaptures the atmosphere of the little capital bending in reverent homage before Goethe, the greatest of its sons.

The writings of Conrad Ferdinand Meyer, the Swiss novelist and poet, have won the admiration of connoisseurs rather than the plaudits of the crowd; but his masterpiece, *Jürg Jenatsch*, published in 1874, is among the half-dozen classics of historical fiction in the German language. He describes it as 'neither history nor biography nor even a psychological novel, but a sort of fresco'. He chooses a minor episode of the Thirty Years War, the liberation of Graubünden from the Spanish yoke, and keeps close to his authorities. It is a tragedy born of the conflict between ambition and patriotism, in which his countrymen are finally compelled to free themselves from their liberator. In striking contrast to Jenatsch, a Nietzschean superman 'beyond good and evil', stands the stainless figure of Rohan, the Christian knight who trusted and was betrayed.

There is no better illustration of the mixture of history, patriotism and romance than in the Hungarian Scott. During the dark years that lay between the ill-starred insurrection of 1848 and the 'Ausgleich' of 1867, Maurus Jokai kept the flame alight by the historical novels which he poured forth with a rapidity only excelled by Dumas himself. He had taught himself English in order to read *Ivanhoe*, and he evaded the perils of the Austrian censorship by choosing for his earliest flights the period of Turkish rule; but he had Austria in mind, and his readers knew it. His message to his fellow-countrymen was that they had survived worse tyrannies than the yoke of Schwarzenberg and Bach. Elected to the Diet in 1861 and a member of the Hungarian Parliament for thirty years after the Compromise of 1867, Jokai gloried in the resurrection of the country he had striven so manfully to serve.

Like Scott, he is at his best in his own country. *The Strange Story of Rab Raby* is an excellent specimen of his art. The hero, a high-minded and well-educated young man, appalled by the incompetence and corruption of the administration, attempts to reform it. Finding the task beyond his unaided strength he seeks the help of Joseph II, whose moral standards are as lofty as his own. But the patronage of the Emperor proves a hindrance, not a help, and the whole countryside rallies to the defence of Magyar officials and Magyar abuses. The authority of Joseph is openly flouted in Budapest, and the hero, tormented and vilified by the rough people he is labouring to serve, has to fight for his life. The story ends with the withdrawal of the reforming Emperor's centralising edicts just in time to save Raby from death. We meet Joseph II at fleeting intervals in the Hofburg and in his Hungarian capital, but he scarcely emerges as a man of flesh and blood. Jokai had no talent for the delineation of character, but his snapshots of Hungarian history help us to understand the meaning and the strength of Magyar nationalism. Though not a man of learning, he cast his net wide, and some of his most popular stories carry us to distant centuries and climes. *Halil the Pedlar* is a stirring tale of rebellion in Constantinople in 1730, when the Janissaries, led by the hero, an Albanian sailor, dethrone the nerveless Sultan. Halil rules Constantinople for six weeks till he is murdered by order of the new Sultan whom he had enthroned. Another favourite is *The Lion of Jannina*, a vivid tale of Ali Pasha, the old Albanian chief whose ferocity is still a living tradition in the Near East. Jokai's books are never too long, and the interest aroused on the first page is held to the end by exciting incidents following one another in breathless succession. The pace, however, is too hot and the colours are too crude to win him a place among the immortals.

Now let us turn to Russia. Pushkin, the father of Russian literature, tried his hand at the historical novel in *The Captain's Daughter*, a tale of the rebellion of Pugatcheff in the reign of Catherine the Great, and Gogol recalled the savage Cossack wars of the seventeenth century in *Taras Bulba*; but their best work lay in other fields. Tolstoy's *War and Peace*, on the other hand, ranks among the great novels of the world, and perhaps no other writer has so fully succeeded in conveying the confused delirium of battle as in his picture of Borodino. Yet, though the background of the story is the national saga of the invasion of 1812, with Alexander and Kutusoff, Napoleon and Murat tramping across the stage, his main interest lay in the children of his fancy; and his masterpiece, as Percy Lubbock has argued in his book, *The Craft of Fiction*, belongs more to literature than to history. Merejkowsky, on the other hand, has produced a series of studies in which fiction is rather the sauce than the joint. *The Emperor Julian* portrays the last struggle of the Pagan Empire against the flowing tide of Christianity. *The Forerunner* resuscitates the superman Leonardo da Vinci, to whom art was only one of the many competing interests of life. *Peter and Alexis*, the most impressive of the series, recalls the foundation of St. Petersburg, and paints a convincing picture of the greatest figure in Russian history. A fourth volume, *The Decembrists*, depicts the abortive attempt of a few unpractical talkers to seize power in the brief days of confusion which followed the death of Alexander I in 1825.

The historical novel has meant more to Poland than to Russia, and during the dark years of partition and persecution the vestal fire of Polish patriotism was tended by pious hands. Kraszewski, the father of the Polish novel, grew to manhood while Scott was still alive. Banished on the eve of the insurrection of 1863 for his political activities, he settled in Dresden, where he discovered in the archives rich material for the history of his country during the period when two Electors of Saxony were also Kings of Poland. Augustus the Strong lives again in *The Countess Cosel*, a realistic picture of the Dresden Court and of the rise and fall of one of the innumerable favourites of the most dissolute ruler in Europe. Scarcely less vivid is the description of the Court of his successor Augustus III in *Count Brühl*, the unscrupulous page who grew to be the real ruler of the land and one of the makers of modern Dresden. Kraszewski's passionate devotion to Poland was shared by his younger contemporary Sienkiewicz, who took more time over his books and produced work of more enduring worth. The insurrection of 1863 broke out when he was seventeen, and the disappointment at its failure inspired him to seek consolation in the past. The greatest of Polish novelists chose his main themes from the history of his race, illustrating the fierce mediæval struggles of Teuton and Slav in his *Knights of the Cross*, and depicting the terrible conflicts of the seventeenth century in his trilogy *With Fire and Sword*, *The Deluge* and *Pan Michael*. These stories of almost unbearable horrors appealed above all to his fellow-countrymen, and helped to keep the soul of Poland alive till a body could be created in which it might dwell; but in *Quo Vadis?* he addresses the world. Since *The Egyptian Princess* no historical novel had enjoyed such world-wide popularity as this picture of Nero's Rome, where the champions of dying paganism and nascent Christianity meet and grapple in deadly embrace. No grander drama offers itself to the creative artist; and, though it has tempted many pens, Sienkiewicz alone possessed the alchemy to transform the rich ore into a nugget of shining gold.

America's notable contributions are comparatively few in number, perhaps because her background is so short. The Waverley Novels were welcomed with enthusiasm, and America's earliest novelist modestly described himself as nothing more than a chip from Scott's block. With the publication in 1821 of *The Spy*, a tale of the War of Independence, Fenimore Cooper woke up to find himself famous; and *The Pilot*, a study of the adventurous career of Paul Jones, earned the commendation of Scott himself. Though he lives above all as the interpreter of Red Indian character, his later stories merely confirmed the fame he had won as the romantic historian of the white man. Of far higher quality are Hawthorne's subtle studies of Puritan New England in *The Scarlet Letter* and *The House of the Seven Gables*, perhaps the most exquisite products of American fiction, even if they can hardly be described as historical novels in the narrower sense. Not till our own day has America made further important additions to the world's store. The transatlantic Winston Churchill painted a stirring picture of the Colonial era and the War of Independence in *Richard Carvel*, and in *The Crisis* he brought vividly before our eyes the struggle of North and South, with the radiant figure of Abraham Lincoln dominating the stage. The same titanic conflict inspired Margaret Mitchell's *Gone with the Wind*, America's best seller since *Uncle Tom's Cabin*. A life-like portrait of Alexander Hamilton, the most dazzling figure in American history, was painted by Gertrude Atherton in *The Conqueror*, which, though it contains more history and less fiction than any of its rivals, is as readable as a work of romance, and is perhaps the finest historical novel grown in the soil of the New World.

After this rapid survey of the achievements of Scott's spiritual progeny on the Continent and in the New World, let us return to our own shores; and here we can be brief, for we are on familiar ground. Almost every writer of fiction of the Victorian era tried his hand at the game. Lytton scored the first resounding success with *The Last Days of Pompeii*, the best of his many ventures, though as a boy I loved *Rienzi* and *The Last of the Barons* almost as much. Kingsley scored with *Westward Ho!*, Charles Reade with *The Cloister and the Hearth*. George Eliot entered the lists with *Romola*, Thackeray with *Esmond* and *The Virginians*, Dickens with *A Tale of Two Cities*, Meredith with *Vittoria*, Blackmore with *Lorna Doone*, to say nothing of the more facile triumphs of Charlotte Yonge, Harrison Ainsworth and the legion of caterers for the appetite of schoolboys. Cardinal Wiseman painted in *Fabiola* a picture of the persecutions that was deservedly admired throughout the Catholic world, and Cardinal Newman sketched the sufferings of Christian converts in Roman Africa in his rather lifeless story *Callista*.

Our best historical novels have been written because their authors were in love with their subject. But which are the best? When Kingsley sat down to write *Hypatia* he was an Anglican parson in his surplice; but when *Westward Ho!* was on the anvil he was transformed into an Elizabethan, filled with Protestant fury against the Popish dogs of Spain, his pulse tingling with the hot blood of the age of Raleigh and Drake. Yet Kingsley's star, which shone so brightly in the mid-Victorian heavens, has been sadly dimmed, and a good deal even of *Westward Ho!* has lost its relish. Thackeray had steeped himself in the literature of the age of Queen Anne, and felt perfectly at home in the company of Addison and Steele; but his art is of far higher quality, and *Esmond* is perhaps our greatest historical novel since the death of Scott. *The Virginians* possesses some admirable scenes, but the book is too long and illustrates anew the relative failure of sequels. It is the fashion nowadays to argue that *Romola* lacks life and atmosphere, but for many readers it remains a treasured picture of the Florence of Lorenzo and Savonarola. *The Cloister and the Hearth* is in some degree marred by its didactic purpose. *The Last Days of Pompeii* survives by its dramatic theme and its author's dazzling abilities. No one would reckon *The Tale of Two Cities* or *Barnaby Rudge* among the masterpieces of Dickens, though the story of the Gordon Riots in the latter is finely told.

At the end of the nineteenth century we may note Stevenson's unfinished *Weir of Hermiston* and Stanley Weyman's *Under the Red Robe*, the finest of his evocations of French history. The stories of Marjorie Bowen may be read with pleasure, and Naomi Mitchison's scholarly pictures of Greek and Roman life deserve their reputation. Maurice Hewlett's *Richard Yea and Nay* possesses distinction of style, and E. F. Benson's *The Vintage* presents a picture of the early stages of the Greek War of Independence full of knowledge and local colour. George Moore's *Héloise and Abélard* revives one of the great love stories of the world, and the same tragic theme has tempted the scholarly pen of Helen Waddell. Mrs. Steel recalls the horrors of the Indian Mutiny in *On the Face of the Waters*. Mrs. Woods brings Swift and his ladies to life in *Esther Vanhomrigh*, and the young Wordsworth in *A Poet's Daughter*. If *Marius the Epicurean* is to be numbered among historical novels it must claim high rank; but Pater's elaborate analysis of Roman life and thought in the second century, with its shadowy figures, is perhaps more correctly classified as a philosophical romance. Monsignor Hugh Benson's *Come Rack, Come Rope*, a study of the Elizabethan martyrs, is a work of passionate but powerful propaganda. In *The Flight of the Eagle*, presented by its author 'not as a romance but an actual historical episode,' Standish O'Grady painted a picture of Elizabethan Ireland based on careful study of the sources. George Gissing's *Veranilda*, unfortunately never completed, revives the age of St. Benedict and the Gothic kingdom in its decline. More recently the Claudius novels of Robert Graves have found many readers. But I must not allow a lecture to degenerate into a catalogue; many are called, but few are chosen.

No English historical novel has been subjected to such minute analysis as Shorthouse's *John Inglesant*, which for countless readers made the life of seventeenth-century England and Italy strangely real. The mellow charm of the book was irresistible; and the religious and political issues with which it dealt claimed the attention of serious minds which cared little for the noise of drums and trumpets. But it exposed a wide surface to attack, and Gardiner promptly detected some of the mistakes in the field he had made his own. Acton told Mary Gladstone that he had read nothing more thoughtful and suggestive since *Middlemarch*, but he added a formidable list of errors and contradictions, particularly in the Italian portion, which reduced the author's academic claims to very modest dimensions. A later Catholic critic, Baron von Hügel, attributed its fascination to its author's 'all-penetrating sense of the massiveness, the awful reality, of the life within the Roman Catholic Church'. This was its only

26

merit, he added, though a great one, to set against its misleading portrait of Molinos and other faults. Later still an article in the *Quarterly Review* revealed the fact, which all the learned critics had overlooked, that many passages had been lifted from well-known seventeenth-century writers with scarcely the change of a word. The discovery, while confirming its veracity as a picture of certain aspects of English life, stamps the work as a skilful mosaic, a coloured photograph, a literary curiosity unique in the annals of historical fiction.

At the close of this bird's-eye view of an enormous territory I may be allowed a few words of reflection and recapitulation. Firstly, the historical novel is the child of the Romantic Movement. Secondly, in the whole field of nineteenth-century litera-ture no influence compares in world-wide significance with that of Scott. Thirdly, the masterpieces of the new *genre* have added fair treasures to the opulent heritage of mankind. Fourthly, a mass of fruitful knowledge has been assimilated by millions who have neither time nor inclination for serious historical study. If it be objected that the fictitious element may implant false ideas, I reply that readers of professedly historical works have also to be on their guard against prejudice and inaccuracy, and that the danger in the latter case is all the greater since the author professes to be a purveyor of nothing but the truth. Fifthly, historical novels have repeatedly given an impetus to scientific study by awakening youthful interest in a period or a movement, a country or an individual, and evoking the desire in the reader to discover for himself what relation the story bears to the real character of actors and events. In one of the precious fragments dictated in his old age Ranke declared that his discovery of the difference between the portraits of Louis XI and Charles the Bold in *Quentin Durward* and the memoirs of Philip de Commines constituted an epoch in his life. 'I found by comparison that the truth was more interesting and beautiful than the romance. I turned away from it and resolved to avoid all invention and imagination in my works and to stick to facts.' Thus the greatest of historical novelists had a share in the making of the greatest of modern historians. Finally, historical fiction has played an active part in reviving and sustaining the sentiment of nationality, which for good or evil has changed the face of Europe in the nineteenth

and twentieth centuries. A department of literature for which
so many claims can be justly advanced is not to be dismissed as
mere chicken-feed, an occupation for tired minds or idle hours.
Here is something for us all. The wind bloweth where it listeth.
Men of genius must be allowed to choose their own medium
and to work with their own tools. There is still plenty of sap in
the noble tree planted by Walter Scott. Let us gratefully salute
the masters of the craft as among the benefactors of mankind,
and hope that many others in many lands will follow in their
footsteps.

9

OUR HERITAGE OF FREEDOM

OUR heritage of freedom, the most treasured of our possessions, rests on three stout pillars—the independence of the
nation, the self-determination of the people, the rights of the
individual. All are of equal value, and each is a blessing beyond
price. None of them has fallen into our lap like manna from
heaven, though they have become so much a part of our existence
that we take them as a matter of course. They have had to be
fought for—by arms, by speech, by pen, by heroism, by sacrifice.
The more we know of that wonderful record the greater is our
sense of obligation to the brave men who gave us what we need
only less than our daily bread. The story has been summarised in
an admirable book, *Liberty and Tyranny*, by Francis Hirst. How
can we show our gratitude, how can we prove ourselves worthy
of such privileges? Only by clinging to them tenaciously, by
resisting attempts to undermine their appeal, by widening the
range of their application. To quote the familiar couplet of
Goethe:

> 'He alone has a right to liberty,
> Who has to fight for it from day to day.'

The independence of the nation comes first in chronological
order, for the flowers of freedom cannot bloom under a foreign
yoke. The last time England was conquered was in 1066, and
the Normans were slowly digested by the sturdy Anglo-Saxon
stock. The last time Continental troops set foot on English soil,
except as prisoners of war, was in the troubled reign of King John.
Since then we have had to fight for our existence on four occasions—against the Spanish Armada, against Napoleon, against
Germany in 1914 and 1939. We have engaged in many other

wars, and our Empire, like others, has been created partly by the sword; but in these four crises of our fate we strove not for territory but for survival. At the height of our conflict with revolutionary France, Pitt was asked in the House of Commons what we were fighting for. 'I can answer in a single word,' he replied: 'Security.' We may say the same to-day, for we have no more territorial aims.

Geography is the mother of history, and our island position has made it easier to defend ourselves than if we had land frontiers subject to sudden attack. Thus we were able to concentrate attention on the navy, and when we became a Great Power under the Tudors we learned the vital need of wooden walls. 'What shall we do to be saved in this world?' asked Halifax in 1694. 'There is no other answer but this: Look to your moat. The first article of every Englishman's creed is that he believeth in the sea. Our Trimmer is far from idolatry in other things, in one thing only he cometh near it—his country is in some degree his idol. For the earth of England to him there is divinity in it, and he would rather die than see a spire of English grass trampled down by a foreign trespasser.'

In the eighteenth century James Thomson expressed the national resolve in a poem which may be read in full in the Pelican book, *Forever Freedom*, compiled by Josiah Wedgwood and the American Professor Allan Nevins, and of which two lines are as familiar to us as *God save the King!*

> 'When Britain first, at Heaven's command,
> Arose from out the azure main,
> This was the charter of the land
> And guardian angels sung the strain:
> "Rule, Britannia, rule the waves;
> Britons never will be slaves."
>
> Thee haughty tyrants ne'er shall tame;
> All their attempts to bend thee down
> Will but arouse thy generous flame,
> But work their woe, and thy renown.'

The Battle of Trafalgar, though fought a thousand miles away, was as much an effort of self-defence as the destruction of the Armada which was visible from the Dover cliffs. Everyone knows the famous sentence of Mahan: 'The Grand Fleet, on which Napoleon's armies never looked, alone stood between him and the mastery of the world.' Cobden, the most peaceable of men, recognised as clearly as any of his contemporaries the necessity of a navy capable of keeping our communications open and our shores inviolate. The submarine, the aeroplane and the directed missile have complicated the technical problem, but our will to survive is as strong as ever. While zealously striving for a new international order which will end aggression as we have ended civil war centuries ago, we remain prepared to defend ourselves and our partners in the Atlantic Pact, for we possess treasures worthy of defence. In the First World War the democracies stayed the course better than the autocracies, and in the Second the Anglo-Saxons rescued Western civilisation from its brutal Nazi foes. That the willing co-operation of free men in defence of their way of life produces strength, not weakness, is a truth which Dictators seem unable to grasp.

Since national independence is compatible with domestic tyranny, the struggle for freedom has had to be waged against foes within no less than foes without. The sovereignty of the people does not by itself provide for all the needs of the citizen, since a majority, elected or unelected, may be as despotic as any oligarchy or autocrat; yet freedom in the fullest sense is radically insecure when sovereignty is located elsewhere than in the community itself. If good autocrats—when they can be found—may make concessions, bad ones can take them away. The winning of constitutional self-government has been a slow process, beginning with Magna Carta and the creation of Parliament in the thirteenth century, and reaching the final goal in the establishment of adult suffrage in our own day. The outlines of modern England began to emerge under the Tudors; but whereas in the sixteenth century the executive power was in the hands of the Monarch, in the nineteenth and twentieth it rests with a Parliament freely elected by the whole people. Not every country has the government it deserves, but free communities are rightly held responsible for the choice and the doings of their rulers. Like other mortals we have made mistakes, yet we have found by experience that there is a better chance of obtaining and maintaining liberty and internal tranquillity when the pyramid stands not on its apex, but on its base. England is not merely the mother of Parliaments but the chief architect of ordered liberty. It is indeed her chief contribution to the welfare of mankind.

The sovereignty of the people, as A. J. Carlyle has shown in his erudite treatise, *Political Liberty*, was widely proclaimed by writers of the Middle Ages, though it hardly materialised outside the Swiss Cantons. The power of the great nobility was a check on despotic and unpopular rulers; yet feudalism was rather an obstacle than a help to political freedom, for which we have to thank the towns and the bourgeoisie. Despite some anticipations of constitutional principles in the parliaments of the fifteenth century—above all no taxation without representation and the redress of grievances—it was not till the second half of the sixteenth that Englishmen began to grapple in a practical way with the problems of self-government. Though most of the leading Reformers—Luther and Melanchthon, Calvin and Knox —were as intolerant as their Catholic foes, the spirit of the Reformation, which substituted the ideal of the priesthood of believers for that of ecclesiastical authority, was fundamentally individualist. If it is going too far to say with Montesquieu that Catholicism has an innate affinity with monarchy and Protestantism with republicanism, the idea that underlies the exaggeration is substantially correct. The one stresses tradition, the other private judgment. Both conceptions have their merits and their perils. The significance of the Reformation as an emancipating influence is to be found in its long-range political and intellectual consequences, as Troeltsch reminds us in his suggestive book, *Protestantism and Progress*. The refusal to take orders from anybody in regard to the deepest convictions and decisions of life set in motion forces which gradually leavened the whole of our national life. Stout-hearted Puritans, poring over their Bible in the mother tongue and owning obedience to conscience alone, were not prepared to bow the knee to Stuart Kings who claimed to rule by Divine Right and exalted the royal prerogative above the common law. By an easy transition religious Independents became political democrats. Democracy and the freedom of the spirit have taken much firmer root in the soil of the Protestant North of Europe, and in the great American Republic which is its child, than in the Catholic South. For practical purposes our heritage of freedom begins with the century of the Reformation.

In the constitutional struggles of the first half of the seventeenth century the Puritan Ironsides were reinforced by the growth of an educated and prosperous bourgeoisie, as Professor Laski has shown in his illuminating book, *The Rise of European Liberalism*. By 1640, when the Long Parliament met, the modern Englishman was rapidly taking shape. His sturdy independence rejected the theory and practice of autocracy, but he was ready to obey the behests of a freely elected Parliament. A law-abiding individualist and a firm believer in the *juste milieu*, he had as little taste for anarchy as for subservience. Moderation, he felt, was the beginning of wisdom. The notion of Whig historians that there was a cut-and-dried constitution and that the first two Stuart kings deliberately broke it is no longer accepted, for the juridical situation was still partly fluid and both camps could appeal to precedents. Falkland and Hyde, who changed sides when they saw Parliament challenging the whole range of the royal authority, were as worthy of respect as Hampden and Pym, who were out for a fight to the finish. Moreover, the Parliamentary leaders themselves who fought under the banner of popular rights occasionally threw law to the winds, as when they sent Strafford and Laud to the block. Before we condemn them for the execution of Charles I we must find a satisfactory answer to the practical issue which confronted them: what else could be done with the man who had unleashed not only the first civil war but the second, and had invited the Scots to invade England? After three hundred years of controversy opinion remains divided. What is not in doubt is that the scaffold at Whitehall was a plain warning that our rulers could no longer do exactly as they liked. Despite the ensuing royalist reaction the grim lesson was not in vain. No one sensed the atmospheric change more clearly than Charles II, who resolved never to go on his travels again.

Cromwell's contribution to our heritage of freedom was both positive and negative. Since Charles I would probably have won the Civil War but for his iron resolve and military genius, he stands in the front rank of our benefactors. On the other hand, the five years of the Protectorate, which was only another name for government by the Army, implanted a national resolve as strong as that which had been generated by the fires of Smithfield: Never again! No one could take our greatest man of action for a democrat. We have only to read his speeches, the army debates published in the *Clarke Papers*, the angry *Memoirs* of Ludlow and the pungent pamphlets of Lilburne, to discover the deep distrust felt by the Protector and the Radicals for one another. He was well aware of the distaste for personal government in general and his own military autocracy in particular, but he could find no way out. Though he had rendered incomparable services, almost everyone was glad to see the end of an experiment which had been doomed from the start. Our first Dictator was also the last. Since his death we have had three successful soldiers in the highest place, Marlborough, Stanhope and Wellington, but none of them dreamed of challenging constitutional government. The lesson of Cromwell's career is clear enough: No more autocrats in England, crowned or uncrowned!

Constitutional monarchy was rendered possible by the Civil Wars, but it was not established till the bloodless revolution of 1688, perhaps the most satisfactory in history since it embodied the wishes of the whole country. Its decisive contribution to our heritage of freedom, so justly stressed by Macaulay nearly a century ago, has been more briefly defined in Dr. Trevelyan's little book, *The English Revolution of 1688–89*. 'At the end of Charles II's reign nothing seemed less probable than that England would soon become either a powerful State or a free and peaceful land. The violence of her factions for half a century past had reduced her to prostration before a royal despotism in the pay of France. Nothing could really have saved England except the apparently impossible—a reconciliation of Tory and Whig, Church and Dissent. That miracle was wrought by the advent of James II, who united against himself the old antagonists. The eleventh-hour chance thus given to our ancestors was neither missed nor abused. It was the victory of moderation, a victory not of Whig or Tory passions, but of the spirit and morality of Halifax the Trimmer. The settlement of 1689 was in its essence the chaining up of fanaticism alike in politics and religion.'

No further revolution in England was necessary. Since 1688 the barometer has risen steadily instead of veering with every gust of wind. With the gradualness characteristic of our easy-going empirical temperament the sovereignty of the people has become ever more solidly established. The wise provision by which the pay of the army had to be voted annually made it necessary that Parliament should meet every year. We have governed ourselves, not always wisely, yet without the convulsions which no other European Power has escaped. The royal veto was exercised for the last time by Queen Anne and then on a trifling issue. That George I was a foreigner and could speak no English when he arrived aided Walpole to inaugurate the system of Cabinet Government under a recognised Parliamentary head. That the four Hanoverian Kings were drab figures facilitated the transfer of the executive power from the monarch to the people. 'George, be a King!' exclaimed his mother to her son when he succeeded his grandfather in 1760, and he did his best to follow her advice; but his attempt to play the part of Bolingbroke's Patriot King was a short-lived experiment. When Pitt took the helm in 1783, after the loss of the American colonies, he strengthened the principle that Parliament and the Cabinet, not the King, decides the course of the ship.

But for the French Revolution, which frightened the propertied classes almost out of their wits, the rule of the territorial aristocracy would have ended before 1800, for the Industrial Revolution rendered a widening of the basis of power inevitable. The enfranchisement of the middle classes in 1832 was followed by that of the urban manual worker in 1867 and of the agricultural labourer in 1884. The demand for woman suffrage was logically irresistible in a democratic State, for women are as useful citizens as men. The legalisation of Trade Unions and the rise of a Parliamentary Labour Party ensured that the vote should not be an empty symbol but an effective instrument for the expression of opinion and the shaping of policy. In his celebrated brochure on Fascism, reprinted from the *Encyclopedia Italiana*, Mussolini described Liberalism, by which he meant democracy, as a failure, since it rested on the illusion of perfectibility. The Century of Hope, to employ Marvin's illuminating phrase, had been succeeded, according to the Duce, by the Century of Fascism, the ideal of liberty by the ideal of discipline. Englishmen reply that the proof of the pudding is in the eating; that on the whole our belief in the common man has justified itself; that we have blended tradition and experiment with considerable success; that dictatorships have no roots and usually perish as the result of aggressive war; that democracy, as we understand and apply it, means a sharing of responsibility; that in Great Britain and the Dominions the sovereignty of the people has come to stay.

Experience teaches that popular sovereignty, like the independence of the nation, is a presupposition but not a guarantee of liberty. Lecky wrote a big book over fifty years ago on the thesis that democracy is its enemy, not its friend. We may admit that the temptation of majorities to bully minorities, of the mass mind to discourage individuality, of the State to claim omnipotence is strong. Absolute power, as Acton declared, corrupts absolutely. The only way to counterwork these evil tendencies is by cutting up power into little bits. No individual, no class, no party, no Church should claim or possess a monopoly. In his celebrated eulogy of the British Constitution in *L'Esprit des Lois*, written in the middle of the eighteenth century, Montesquieu selected for special praise the separation of powers between the Executive, the Legislature and the Judiciary. Since his time the Executive and the Legislature have been combined, and the search for safeguards against the abuse of power has been made along other lines. Compared with most other modern States our efforts in this direction have met with a fair measure of success.

The range of State action, here as elsewhere, has enormously increased during the last century, for the needs and demands of a community, material and immaterial, wax with the growth of population, education and wealth. Some think that the process has not gone nearly far enough. Others believe that it has already gone too far, particularly in regard to the control of industry, and that a large measure of private enterprise is essential to the prosperity and initiative of our people. Fortunately the intellectual and emotional attitude of the average citizen towards the State remains substantially unchanged. What the French call *étatisme* has never been popular. Throughout the English-speaking world there is nothing of the almost mystical reverence of Hegel for a mysterious entity claiming to be higher and wiser than ourselves. There is no echo of Treitschke's slogan: ' The State is power.' That is not our way. We are a prosaic people. Society, we admit, is more important than the individual, but society is not the State. We do not believe in blank cheques. The machinery of State is obviously essential to our safety and welfare, but it is worked by human agents as fallible as ourselves and in case of need we call them to account. It is our servant, not our master. *Droit administratif*, as Dicey reminded us in a famous book, does not exist in England. We pay obedience to the laws which we make for ourselves; if we disapprove them we strive for their amendment or repeal.

Democracy at its best is not only government by discussion but government by consent. Political liberty was defined by Ritchie as the right of a minority to transform itself by argument into a mjaority if it can. We have come to feel that it is our State, not because we approve everything it does, but because we know that in the main it carries out the national will in the making of which every adult citizen has a responsible part. In politically immature countries there might be a danger of an unwritten constitution leading to a perpetual chopping and changing, of laws made one session and repealed the next, of a perpetual uncertainty as to what is coming next. Looking back over the past three centuries, during which we have been learning how to govern ourselves, we are struck by the fact that beneficent changes have often been made too slowly, rarely too quickly; that even the most hotly contested decisions have been loyally accepted by the defeated party; that the cool blood and horse sense of the British people have kept us from pushing things to extremes. The average citizen is neither a slave nor a rebel. He clamours for what he believes to be his rights, but he usually realises that nothing he could obtain by extra-constitutional methods would be worth having since it could never be secure. Direct Action, as recommended by Georges Sorel, is a risky game at which two can play, a game in which the victor of to-day may well become the victim of to-morrow.

The three main lines of advance in our struggle for the rights of the individual have been towards the supremacy of the law, freedom of expression, and religious equality. The conception of law as embodying not merely the will of the ruler but the ideal of justice derives from the great Roman jurists, was generally accepted during the Middle Ages, and survived into modern times under the guise of the Law of Nature. This venerable formula was defined in different ways and was appealed to on behalf of competing interests, yet the conception of a moral and intellectual standard by which laws and institutions should be tested played a fruitful part in the development of our liberties. For though what we call civil rights do not by themselves constitute liberty, they provide the only framework within which it can exist. Here is the noble tribute of our great Elizabethan Richard Hooker at the end of the First Book of his *Laws of Ecclesiastical Polity*: 'Of law there can be no less acknowledged than that her seat is the bosom of God, her voice the harmony of the world. All things in heaven and earth do her homage, the very least as feeling her care, and the greatest as not exempted from her power, both angels and men and creatures of what condition soever though each in different sort of manner, yet all with uniform consent, admiring her as the mother of their peace and joy.'

The champions of Parliamentary Government in the seventeenth century, led by Coke and Selden, appealed to the common law, statute law and precedent against the excessive claims of the royal prerogative. The chief victories in the campaign for the protection of the individual citizen have resulted from specific perils at a particular time. The Petition of Right was the reaction of Parliament to the first encroachments of Charles I. After the excitements of the Popish plot, the old dictum, 'The Englishman's house is his castle', received legislative sanction in the Habeas Corpus Act, perhaps the stoutest of our bulwarks against oppression by the Executive. The Bill of Rights was a comprehensive reply to the antics of James II. That part of the so-called Revolution settlement which decreed that judges should be irremovable *quamdiu se bene gesserint* resulted from the subservience of certain magistrates to the despotic wills of the Stuart Kings, and gave us the independent judiciary which has become an essential element of our national tradition. During the dark days of reaction at the close of the eighteenth century Erskine's courageous speeches in the treason trials helped to protect the citizen against the panic-stricken ruling classes. It is sometimes asserted by champions of the economic interpretation of history that even to-day our judges are subconsciously biased by class feeling in cases where the social and economic *status quo* is involved. That is a suspicion that can neither be proved nor disproved, but nobody believes them to be the tools of the Executive, like their terrified brethren in totalitarian states. Any citizen may bring the Government into court, and if he has a good legal case he can win it. Our judges have inherited a noble tradition which they are resolved to transmit untarnished to their successors. Our non-party and incorruptible Civil Service inspires no less well-merited confidence.

The second line of advance is towards the freedom of the Press, or, to use President Roosevelt's phrase, freedom of expression. The twenty years between the meeting of the Long Parliament and the Restoration witnessed such a spate of pamphleteering as we have never seen again. Among the pamphleteers was Milton, who, in addition to proclaiming his republican faith, set forth in *Areopagitica* in his organ tones the case for unlicensed printing. The exordium defends the right of free comment on the double ground that it is at once a privilege of citizenship and a benefit to the State. He proceeds to lodge an emphatic protest against the war on books. 'For they are not absolutely dead things, but contain a potency of life in them to be as active as that soul whose progeny they are. As good almost kill a man as kill a good book. Who kills a man kills a reasonable creature; but he who destroys a book kills reason itself, the image of God. Many a man lives a burden to the earth, but a good book is the precious life-blood of a master-spirit, embalmed and treasured up on purpose to a life beyond life.' Frankly admitting that there is evil in many books, he refuses to praise 'a fugitive and cloistered virtue that never sallies out and sees her adversary'. A wise man, like a good refiner, can gather gold out of dross, and will make better use of an old pamphlet than a fool of Scripture. When God gave man reason he gave him freedom to choose, for reason is but choosing. 'Give me the liberty to know, to utter and to argue freely according to conscience above all liberties.' That the censorship lay like a dead hand on the intellectual life of a nation had been brought home to him by his visit to Italy, 'where nothing had been written these many years but flattery and fustian. There it was that I found and visited famous Galileo grown old, a prisoner of the Inquisition, for thinking in astronomy otherwise than the Franciscan and Dominican licensers'. In

England we have permitted no Inquisition and no Index of Prohibited Books.

The savage penalties of the seventeenth century, such as cutting off Prynne's ears and whipping Lilburne through the streets, stimulated instead of silencing criticism, for Englishmen were determined by this time to say what they thought. 'Above everything liberty!' wrote the learned Selden in Greek in the books of his library. The burning of the *Leviathan* and other political treatises in 1683 in Oxford, the home of reactionary royalism, was equally futile as a deterrent. Defoe was pilloried and imprisoned, but only death could stay his busy pen. A welcome advance was made by Fox's Libel Act, which referred to a jury the decision on what constituted libel. Since 1832 our right to express ourselves has become uncontested except in time of war. Subject to the three justifiable exceptions of libel, indecency, and attempts to sap the loyalty of the armed forces, we enjoy the full liberty of utterance which a civilised community deserves. Nowhere has the freedom of teaching and research produced more fruitful results than in our Universities. 'Parliamentary freedom,' writes Count Sforza in his *European Dictatorships*, 'is a form of freedom. But the essential freedom, without which a people is doomed to decline, is freedom of thought, of speech, of the Press, of association.'

The third line of advance is in the field of religious freedom, a better because a more comprehensive term than freedom of worship. We rightly desire not only to worship as we like but to teach and to learn. Most of us believe in what William James in a celebrated book calls the varieties of religious experience. People have different needs. In a pregnant aphorism Acton declared the emancipation of conscience from authority to be the main content of modern history. Like Frederick the Great, most of us feel that every one should be allowed to go to heaven in his own way. Here again we look back with gratitude to the wise and fearless thinkers of the seventeenth century in England and abroad who argued and often suffered for the blessings we now enjoy. The founders of the doctrine of religious liberty were not the Fathers of the Reformation but the courageous Nonconformists who rebelled against their yoke. In fighting for their own existence the Socinians in Poland, the Arminians in Holland, and the minority sects in England were pioneers of the spiritual liberty of the world. In England no notable champion of toleration emerged before the seventeenth century, when not only Nonconformists, but Broad Church Anglicans, such as Hales, Chillingworth, Jeremy Taylor, and the Cambridge Platonists joined in the demand. Yet they were voices crying in the wilderness, for toleration seemed to most people both wicked and dangerous. The Commonwealth proved as narrow-minded as the Monarchy.

Everyone knows Spurgeon's celebrated jest: the only sect which had never persecuted was that of the Baptists, to which he and his congregation belonged. When the applause died down, he quietly added: 'and they never had the chance'. That was true enough of England, but not of America, where the Welsh Baptist Roger Williams practised what he preached. Though but a speck on the map, and the smallest of the American Colonies, Rhode Island stands out in history as the first place where complete religious liberty was both proclaimed and applied. The Quakers, needless to say, worked for the good cause, for to the believer in an inner light coercion was a spiritual outrage. 'The Tower,' as William Penn put it, 'is to me the worst argument in the world.' The Revolution of 1688 was followed by the Toleration Act, which, imperfect though it was, registered a definite advance. Though it excluded Catholics from its scope and only relieved Dissenters from the penal laws on certain conditions, such liberty as it gave was a permanent conquest since it rested on the assent of Parliament and public opinion. Even Locke, in his celebrated *Letters on Toleration*, recommended the exclusion of Catholics on the ground of their allegiance to a foreign prince and of their teaching that faith is not to be kept with heretics. Atheists were also excluded on the ground that covenants could have no hold upon them. We have moved cautiously towards our goal by steps which have never had to be retraced.

In his suggestive little book, *Persecution and Toleration*, Bishop Creighton argued that the main cause of the decline of religious intolerance in modern times was the growth of indifference, the diminishing intensity of religious conviction. What Lecky called the secularisation of thought was admittedly an important factor, for we are no longer so certain as our ancestors that ultimate truth has been or can be attained. Yet there were other causes at work. The rapid growth in the numbers and social influence of Nonconformists, the recognition of their shining private virtues, the gradual discovery that there was nothing to be feared from law-abiding citizens, the domination of the Anglican Church by the Latitudinarians between 1688 and the Oxford Movement—all these played their part. The granting of the vote to Irish Catholics, the opening of the Universities to Nonconformists, the admission of Jews to Parliament, are among the nineteenth-century landmarks in our advance from limited toleration to full religious equality. If, to quote Acton once more, the provision made for minorities is the best test of the standard of civilisation, England should rank high among the nations of the world. Anti-Semitism has never shown its ugly face, and (except in war-time) everyone is now presumed to be a good citizen till the contrary is proved. Such respecters of individuality have we become that, like our spiritual progeny in the United States, we allow bona fide Conscientious Objectors to stand aside from desperate conflicts in which their fellow-citizens are struggling for survival against naked aggression. Apart from the small number of people who regard it as a valuable discipline, conscription is accepted only as an unwelcome expedient to meet a grave emergency.

Here are six names in the list of our political oracles—Hobbes, Locke, Halifax, Burke, Bentham and Mill. It is indicative of the general pattern of English thought that only the first was authoritarian. Books can exert a profound and lasting influence even if they are not read by the common man, for their ideas filter through other minds and become part of the air we breathe. That we should doubtless have won our liberties without their aid does not diminish our debt to prophets and pioneers.

Our view of political and spiritual self-determination reflects our ideology like a face in a mirror. Those who think meanly of human nature, like Machiavelli and Hobbes, cry aloud for the strong arm of the Prince and the Great Leviathan to prevent us from cutting each other's throats, and consequently endeavour to keep us behind steel bars. If, on the other hand, we entertain a relatively favourable view of the average man, if we believe in his capacity to learn from his mistakes, we are disposed to grant

27

him the maximum of opportunity and to impose the minimum of restraint. Hobbes's rules of government were simple enough, for they embodied his view of the unchanging imperfections of the human animal. Loving intellectual liberty as much as any of his contemporaries, he was convinced that self-government was a prize for ever beyond our grasp. Order, he argued, was heaven's first and only law, and anarchy could only be kept at bay by an autocrat's lash. France of the Absolute Monarchy, where he took refuge during the Civil Wars, not Puritan England, was his spiritual home. His pessimism made him the father of modern totalitarianism, as the optimism of his contemporary Grotius made him the pioneer of International Law.

The state of nature, according to Hobbes, had proved intolerable, for no man's life or possessions were safe. Hence the decision of primitive communities to create a state of civil society under a sovereign to whom the useless right to all things possessed by individuals was irrevocably transferred. Man being by nature incorrigibly selfish, and indeed little better than a wild beast, the ruler's main task is to prevent his subjects from robbing and murdering each other. Leviathan is simply a policeman of superhuman size with a truncheon in his hand. Hobbes did not care whether he was a legitimate monarch or a usurper, an individual or a council. All that mattered was that his authority should be unchallenged and unchallengeable whatever he did, for to oppose it would be to relapse into the anarchy from which the community had found it necessary to escape. Though subjects are bound to obey the ruler by the contract made with each other, he is in no way bound to them; for no conditions were made or could be made when he received his power. To complaints that our ancestors might thus have jumped out of the frying-pan into the fire Hobbes retorts that the greatest evils of misgovernment are trifles compared to the calamities of civil war or anarchy inevitable in the absence of effective coercive power. Bad laws are better than none.

Nothing is more revealing or more satisfactory in the history of political thought in England than the failure of Hobbes to secure disciples during his life or after his death. Englishmen rejected the totalitarian gospel as emphatically as its theological equivalent, the Divine Right of Kings. That human beings had deliberately parted with all their rights and that the sovereign could do whatever he liked was an affront to common sense. No unconditional surrender of natural rights could have occurred, for men would not have been such fools. Moreover, the picture of man outside civil society as a lawless savage was a caricature, for primitive communities think in terms of the group, not the individual.

The most effective reply to Hobbes came a generation later from Locke, who in his *Treatises on Government* accepted the notion of a contract between subjects and their ruler but interpreted it in a completely different way. Starting from the assumption that men—even primitive men—are at any rate partially rational beings, he saw no compelling reason for them to surrender their uncovenanted rights without making or even attempting to make conditions. 'All the compact that is or needs be between the individuals that enter into or make up a Commonwealth,' he declares, 'is barely agreeing to unite into one political society.' These contracts or compacts, of course, were legal fictions, for they had never occurred, the transition to civil society taking place gradually, not in a single jump. Yet the practical value of the conception was unaffected by this fact, for its purpose was to define the relationship between the community and the sovereign. This aim was achieved to the satisfaction of his contemporaries and their descendants by the Revolution of 1688.

Since the community existed before the ruler it could make whatever terms it wished. What was needed was not an irresponsible autocrat but a trustee with limited powers: if he failed to discharge his duty a new trustee should be chosen. To Hobbes anarchy, by which he meant the absence of or disobedience to a recognised ruler, was the supreme evil; to Locke the worst thing was misgovernment. Why should we suffer torments from what we could change? When estates, liberties, lives were in danger, perhaps religion too (he was thinking of James II), resistance was a duty as well as a right. Knowing how much his easy-going countrymen would stand without making a fuss, he trusted them only to assert their rights and exert their power in case of desperate need. If any political thinker deserves the proud title of the philosopher of common sense, it is Locke. His fundamental assumption is that in a serious dispute between the sovereign and the people the latter is most likely to be in the right. Since, however, it is not always of one mind, the majority must decide. Being also aware that the majority may abuse its rights, he recommends the division of the functions of government into executive, legislative and judicial. His two Treatises on Government have been justly described as the Bible of the Revolution of 1688. With equal justice they may be called the voice of England.

They were also to become the voice of America. 'We hold these truths to be self-evident,' runs the Declaration of Independence, 'that all men are created equal, that they are endowed by their Creator with certain inalienable rights, that among these are life, liberty and the pursuit of happiness. That to secure these rights Governments are instituted among men, deriving their just powers from the consent of the governed. That whenever any form of Government becomes destructive of these ends, it is the right of the people to alter or to abolish it, and to institute a new Government, laying its foundation on such principles and organising its powers in such form as to them shall seem most likely to effect their safety and happiness. Prudence indeed will dictate that Governments long established should not be changed for light and transient causes; and accordingly all experience hath shown that mankind are more disposed to suffer, while evils are sufferable, than to right themselves by abolishing the forms to which they are accustomed. But when a long train of abuses and usurpations, pursuing invariably the same object, evinces a design to reduce them under absolute despotism it is their right, it is their duty, to throw off such government and to provide new guards for such security.' These famous sentences are pure Locke, of whom Jefferson, like the other founders of the United States, was a diligent student. It is a source of legitimate pride to Englishmen that the American torch of liberty was kindled at the parent flame.

Halifax was a statesman by profession, not a philosopher, but the agitating experiences of the Restoration era brought him to much the same position as that of Locke. Making no reference to the law of nature or the social contract, he contents himself with expressing his own opinions in simple form. At the height of his influence, during the struggle over the Exclusion Bill, he pleased neither Whigs nor Tories; he was not a party man, yet he found himself the representative of the average citizen. Like Locke he was a convinced apostle of the *juste milieu*, to which his *Character of a Trimmer*, written in 1684 and published in 1688, is the finest tribute in the language. 'Our Trimmer owneth a passion for liberty, yet so restrained that it doth not in the least impair or taint his allegiance. He taketh it to be the foundation of all virtue and the only seasoning that giveth a relish to life. Our climate is a Trimmer between that part of the world where men are roasted and the other where they are frozen. Our Church is a Trimmer between the frenzy of fanatic visions and the lethargic ignorance of Popish dreams. Our laws are Trimmers between the excesses of unbounded power and the extravagance of liberty not enough restrained. True virtue hath ever been thought a Trimmer, and to have its dwelling midway between the two extremes. Even God Almighty Himself is divided in His two great attributes, His mercy and His justice. In such company our Trimmer is not ashamed of his name, and willingly leaveth to the bold champions of either extreme the honour of contending with no less adversaries than nature, religion, liberty, prudence, humanity and common sense.' If John Bull were an intellectual he would define his political creed in very similar terms, for he instinctively prefers the middle of the road.

Though Burke is more often regarded as the founder of philosophic Conservatism than as the champion of the Revolution of 1688, he always considered himself an orthodox Whig. No one was more deeply convinced of the salutary character of that memorable event, and no one was less inclined to revert to the bankrupt system of personal government. His first literary masterpiece, *Thoughts on the Present Discontents*, published in 1770, exhorted the nation to combine against 'a faction ruling by the private instructions of a court against the general sense of the people'. The sovereignty of the people is assumed, but caution is enjoined in the exercise of its rights. 'Our constitution stands on a nice equipoise, with steep precipices and deep waters upon all sides of it. In removing it from a dangerous leaning towards one side there may be a risk of oversetting it on the other. Every project of a material change in a government so complicated as ours is a matter full of difficulties, in which a considerate man will not be too ready to decide nor a prudent man too ready to undertake.' These words might have been written by the Trimmer himself.

This note of caution is reiterated in louder tones in the *Reflections on the French Revolution*. His analysis of the causes of the upheaval in France is vitiated by ignorance, as Mackintosh and Tom Paine immediately pointed out. The permanent value of the treatise lies in the discussion of the method and justification of political change, a theme involving the still wider problem of the nature of human society. His thesis, which was developed at greater length in the *Appeal from the New to the Old Whigs*, is that the events of 1688 exemplified the principles by which alone revolutions could be justified. Since the thoughts and instincts of ninety-nine in every hundred persons are those of their environment, reforms should be gradual. Shocks are as bad for the community as for the individual. Rejecting the atomic view that society is merely an association of individuals bound together by a contract for certain specific purposes, he presents the conception of a living organism whose character is determined by its history, whose members are linked to one another and to the whole by innumerable unseen ties. In this clear recognition of continuity and solidarity lies his claim to rank with the founders of what is called the Historical School and with the greatest political thinkers of all time. Society, he taught, is a partnership in all science, in all art, in every perfection, a partnership between those who are living, those who are dead and those yet to be born. The belief of the imaginative Irishman that there was an element of mystery in the cohesion of men in society made little appeal to Englishmen, and his almost morbid dread of rapid change reflected the panic caused by the stupendous events in France. Happily we have been able to take just as much of his teaching as we want, and most of us realise that the ship of state needs ballast as well as sails.

If Burke is the posthumous offspring of the Revolution of 1688, Bentham is the forerunner and indeed the spiritual father of the Reform Bill of 1832. No two men and no two gospels could be more dissimilar. Burke accepted the rule of the aristocracy, though it snobbishly excluded him from high office. Bentham, sprung from the same middle class, was a fearless reformer, ever ready to experiment and take risks. The one was gratefully conscious of the wisdom of our ancestors, the other was obsessed by the crying needs of the present. Burke cannot be accused of disbelief in human nature, but he had no use for the common man. To employ nineteenth-century terms, he was a conservative, while Bentham in his later years was a radical. When changes were proposed Burke was inclined to ask: Why should we? The reaction of Bentham was: Why should we not? Men are at bottom so much alike, he argued, their needs so fundamentally similar. Every one of us craves for happiness and seeks to avoid pain. Laws and institutions should be tested, not by their antiquity, but by their results. People were right to desire happiness, and in his opinion it was the duty of the State to help them to get it. He was not interested in such legalistic formulas as the social contract, and he sharply attacked the philosophical assumptions underlying the Declaration of the Rights of Man: the task of the legislator was not to argue about first principles but to remove injustices and abuses. If vested interests stood in the way they must be brushed aside, since the needs of the many must in fairness prevail over the privileges of the few.

Bentham's unwearying campaign on behalf of the common man places him among the founders of modern democracy and the benefactors of mankind. Every one, he proclaimed, was to count for one, no one for more than one, a maxim involving adult suffrage and equality before the law. The aim of the State, as of society, is to secure the greatest happiness of the greatest number, a slogan borrowed from Priestley. Though as a lawyer he spoke with special authority about the reform of the criminal law, the impact of his challenge was felt in many fields, and reformers such as Romilly and Brougham hailed him as their chief. His utilitarianism as an ethical philosophy has had its day, for his psychology was superficial; yet, next to Locke, he was perhaps the most useful and influential of British publicists. Hobbes was chiefly interested in the authority of the sovereign, Locke in the sovereignty of the people, Burke in the solidarity of society, Bentham in the needs of the individual citizen. The fearless struggle against abuses, the perpetual adjustment of our laws and institutions to new circumstances, is essential to the preservation of our liberties. No community racked by discontent is safe from revolution and despotism. If it is complained that such publicists speak less of duties than of rights, we reply that the citizen is more likely to perform his duties loyally and efficiently when he has secured what he believes to be his elementary rights.

Next to Darwin, Mill was the most influential of our great Victorian thinkers, and our debt to his writings is beyond price. The saint of rationalism, as Gladstone called him, thought with his heart as well as his head, and an unselfish devotion to humanity breathes through all his works. Inheriting his individualism from Bentham and his father James Mill, he gave it a richer content and a warmer tone. In his *Utilitarianism* he argued that the conception of utility, properly interpreted, embraces our loftiest emotions as well as our obvious needs. The essay *On Liberty* is the most characteristic of his books and, as he foretold, the most enduring; it ranks with the *Areopagitica* as a confession of faith in the spiritual worth of the individual citizen. Mill started from the assumption, not that we are all wise and good, but that we are moral and rational beings. Every one, he taught, should have the fullest opportunity of developing his powers within the limits of the law and without infringing the right of others to similar self-realisation: only thus can we make our maximum contribution to the welfare of the community. It is a gospel of service, not of selfishness.

That opinions might be wrong, or might be thought so at the time, was irrelevant. 'The peculiar evil of silencing the expression of an opinion is that it is robbing the human race; posterity as well as the existing generation; those who dissent from the opinion, still more those who hold it. If the opinion is right, they are deprived of the opportunity of exchanging error for truth; if wrong, they lose, what is almost as great a benefit, the clearer perception and livelier impression of truth produced by its collision with error.' No majority, however large, has the right to suppress the opinions of a minority or even of an individual. 'I deny the right of the people to exercise such coercion either by themselves or by their Government. The power itself is illegitimate. The best Government has no more title than the worst.' Mill lacks the splendour of Milton's prose, but his grasp of principle, his fearlessness, the nobility of character stamped on every page, place the book among the finest creations of the human spirit. *The Subjection of Women*, the most impressive plea for equal citizenship ever written, carried the argument for self-realisation into a field which had been strangely neglected. *Representative Government* discussed how the difficult experiment of democracy could be most successfully operated, and how the rights of minorities could be secured by Proportional Representation and in other ways.

Though, as he confesses in his *Autobiography*, Mill came to favour State ownership of monopolies, he never abated his detestation of a mechanised bureaucratic state. Entertaining the loftiest view of the potentialities of the human spirit he pleaded that no obstacles should be placed in the way of rising to the height of our stature. Pupils, he reminded us, would never advance if the schoolmaster did all their lessons for them. Like Herbert Spencer he has been accused of thinking too meanly of the State and too highly of the citizen. Sir James Stephen vigorously attacked this optimistic ideology in his powerful book, *Liberty, Equality, Fraternity*, a defence of what he and his disciples would call political realism. In such controversies neither side ever scores a complete victory, for our views of the human animal are the result of temperament and experience, not of argument. Mill appeals to Libertarians, not to Authoritarians. His profound belief in the capacity of the common man to make good use of his opportunities is a stimulus to render ourselves worthy of his trust.

'Les révolutions changent tout sauf le cœur humain,' declared Pascal. Since human nature is sadly imperfect, our creations are stamped with its imperfections. Yet the assumption throughout this address is that man—at any rate the Anglo-Saxon variety—is a teachable animal rather than the chained gorilla that he seemed to Taine after witnessing the horrors of the Paris Commune. Carlyle, the only prominent Englishman of the nineteenth century who liked Dictators, sourly described England as a country of thirty millions, mostly fools. To-day we should say: fifty millions, mostly good citizens. We have no valid reason to envy other countries their record or their stock. Looking back across the ages some observers emphasise our slow progress, the disappointing use we have often made of our chances, the abuse of power by the territorial aristocracy in the eighteenth century, the greedy industrialists in the nineteenth, the trade unions in the twentieth. Others are encouraged by the achievements of what Wordsworth calls 'man's unconquerable mind', his ingenuity and persistence, his triumphs over formidable obstacles, his irrepressible yearning for the three ultimates—the true, the beautiful, and the good. After all, he has created civilisation. In Emerson's phrase, we are still at cockcrow and the coming of the dawn. That democracy asks more from the common man than any other political system, that, to use Montesquieu's term, it requires more virtue than its rivals, is to one type of mind its condemnation, to another the core of its appeal. That democratic forms without a fairly high standard of education and civic conduct are bound to fail we have learned by very recent experience. Happily British democracy is an organic growth, not a sudden improvisation or a hothouse plant. It has secured general acceptance for the simple reason that rival systems have been weighed in the balance and found wanting. Neither Fascism nor Communism has struck roots.

Lord John Russell used to say that there is nothing so conservative as progress, and progress requires unceasing effort. We must struggle against what Bury calls the illusion of finality. Of Franklin Roosevelt's four desiderata for civilised mankind we in England can boast of three—freedom of expression, freedom of worship, freedom from want. Economic democracy is on the way. The bitter taunt that 'bourgeois' liberty means liberty for the manual worker to starve has become meaningless since the establishment of the finest system of social security in the world and the acceptance by all parties of the doctrine of a minimum standard of life. The twentieth century, as Henry Wallace phrases it, is the century of the common man. Every year we witness an advance in the levelling down of privilege and the levelling up of opportunity. Freedom from fear, on the other hand, still eludes our grasp, and the maintenance of our heritage of liberty depends on the political and economic organisation of the world. How can we expect the flowering of personality in a regimented community perpetually racked by wars or the threat of war? *Inter arma silent leges.* Though Continental conditions are widely different from our own, the ease with which the principles and practices of Western civilisation have been trampled underfoot in many countries, first by the Nazis and later by the Bolshevists, is a solemn warning to us all. Even more clearly than our fathers and grandfathers we realise that the price of ordered liberty is good citizenship and eternal vigilance.

INDEX

A

Acton, Lord, 272-3, 319-23; on history, 335-6; on the Christian Church, 336-7; on representative government, 337, 340 ff.; on America and the Puritans, 338, 342-3; on France, 338-9; on autocracy, 339-40; on religious liberty, 343-6

Adelaide of France, 124, 126, 130, 131, 149

Aiguillon, Duc d', 71, 129, 136; dismissal, 149, 150, 156-7

Aix-la-Chapelle, Peace of, 3

Albert of Saxe-Teschen, 91, 105

Alexis, Willibald, 390-1

Amelia of Parma, 38

America, and liberty, 338, 342-3, 344

American War of Independence, 80, 108

Andlau, Comtesse d', 182

Artois, Comte d', 126, 134, 143, 151, 152, 153, 158, 166, 169, 171, 196, 211, 212, 215

Artois, Comtesse d', 192

Aulard, François Victor Alphonse, 240-1, 270-2, 277, 280, 284, 286, 289-90

Austrian Netherlands, 81, 85, 86, 200

Austrian Succession, War of, 2, 120

Austro-French Alliance, 55, 80, 102, 121

B

Babylon, discoverers of, 250-1

Balzac, Honoré de, 386

Bancroft, George, 248-9

Baronius, Cesare, 220

Bartenstein, Baron von, 3, 7

Batthyany, Count, 6-7

Baur, Ferdinand Christian, 254

Bavarian Succession, War of, 77 ff., 197 ff.

Beccaria, Marchese di: *Crimes and Punishments*, 41

Bentham, Jeremy, 422-4

Besenval, Baron de, 164, 168, 180, 208

Bodin, Jean, 223

Boeckh, August, 226, 227-8

Bossuet, Jacques Bénigne, 224

Brissac, Duc de, 139

Brockett, Laurence, 303-4

Brown, P. A., 292

Brunswick, Duke of, 281

Bryce, Lord, on Acton, 335

Bukovina, Austrian acquisition of, 65, 79

Burke, Edmund, 141-2, 421-2

Burnet, Gilbert, Bishop, 223

Bury, J. B., 323-7, 369-70

Butler, J. R. M., 330-1

Butterfield, Professor, and historical novels, 382-3

Byzantine Empire, history of, 253

C

Cabinet government, 410

Campan, Madame, 145

Campardon, E., 282

Carignan, Prince de, 176

Carlyle, Thomas, 243-4, 264, 265

Caroline of Naples, 38, 123, 137, 138

Carvalho, Herculano da, 388-9

Catherine the Great of Russia, 56, 60, 62, 65; conversations with Joseph II, 104 ff.

Chamberlain, Sir Austen, 370-1

Charles I of England, 408, 413

Charles III of Spain, 16

Charles VI, Holy Roman Emperor, 2, 3, 4, 8, 121

Charles VII, Holy Roman Emperor, 16

Chartres, Duc de, 171, 180, 196-7, 210

Chimay, Princesse de, 177, 178

Choiseul, Duc de, 71, 72, 103, 121, 124, 126; dismissal, 129; episode at Rheims, 158, 159, 180

Church history, 253 ff.

Clarendon, Earl of, 223

Clark, G. N., 330

Clement XIV, Pope, 45-6

Clothilde of France, 126

Cobentzl, Comte de, 105, 111, 112

Cobentzl, Philip, 107

Coigny, Duc de, 179, 208

Conscience, Hendrik, 389

Constituent Assembly, writings on, 279-81

Convention, the, writings on, 287

Cooper, Fenimore, 399

Coster, Charles de, 389

Coulanges, Fustel de, 238-9

Cromwell, Oliver, 408-9

D

Dahn, Felix, 393–4
Danton, Georges, 283, 284
Danzig, 65
Daun, Count von, 12
Deffand, Madame du, 128, 129
Dillon, Madame, 179
Directory, the, writings on, 287 ff.
Döllinger, J. J. I., 344, 345
Dorislaus, Isaac, 298
Droysen, J. G., 233–4
Du Barry, Madame, 70, 125, 129; and
Marie Antoinette, 130 ff.
Dumas, Alexandre, 386–7

E

Ebers, G. M., 394
Ecole des Chartes, 238
Egyptologists, 250
Eichhorn, K. F., 226, 228
Eight Years' War, 4
Elizabeth Charlotte of the Palatinate,
120
Elizabeth of France, 126
Elizabeth of Wolfenbüttel, 15
England, Catherine the Great's opinion
of, 110
Ernle, Lord, and historical novels, 382
Esterhazy, Count, 208, 211
Eugene of Savoy, 3, 64

F

Ferdinand of Lombardy, 66
Ferdinand of Naples, 38
Ferdinand of Parma, 38
Fersen, Count H. A. von, 168, 175
Flacius Illyricus, Matthias, 220
Fontane, T., 391
France: Catherine the Great's opinion
of, 110; and liberty, 338–9
Francis of Lorraine, 1–2, 17, 120
Frederick the Great, 2, 4, 21, 30, 64, 65,
66, 120; conversation with Joseph,
57–61; uneasiness over Bavaria, 79–80;
invades Bohemia, 89, 201; negotiations
with Maria Theresa, 94; Treaty of
Teschen, 102
Freeman, Edward, 245–6
Freytag, Gustav, 391–2
Froude, J. A., 244–5

G

Galdos, Perez, 388
Galicia, Austrian acquisition of, 65, 66
Galitzin, Prince, 104
Ganganelli. See Clement XIV
Gardiner, Samuel, 247

Gibbon, Edward, 225
Gibson, Edmund, Bishop, 298–300
Gierke, O. von, 235
Giesebrecht, W. von, 232–3
Gooch, G. P., and Temperley, H.:
Documents on the Origins of the War,
370–3
Gottschalk, L. R., 285
Grant, A. J., and Temperley, H.:
Europe, 366–8
Gray, Thomas, 302, 303, 304–7
Greece, historians on, 251–2
Green, J. R., 246
Greville, Fulke (Lord Brooke), 297
Grimm, Jacob, 229–30
Grimm, the brothers, 229
Guéménée, Princesse de, 178, 179, 182,
186, 187, 193, 203
Guicciardini, Francesco, 219
Guines, Duc de, 72, 164–5, 208, 211
Guizot, François, 236–7

H

Halifax, Charles Montagu, 1st Earl of,
420–1
Hallam, Henry, 242–3
Hardwicke, Lord, 304
Harrach, Count, 32
Harris, Samuel, 300–2
Hauff, W., 390
Haugwitz, Count von, 4; and the Ten
Years' Recess, 5, 6, 11
Hawthorne, Nathaniel, 399
Henry IV of France, 125
Henry of Prussia, 62, 97
Herder, Johann, 229
Historical Association, Temperley's
services to, 362–3
Hobbes, Thomas, 417–19
Hooft, Pieter, 223
Hubertusburg, Treaty of, 12
Hugo, Victor, 386
Hume, David, 224
Hungary, 2, 3, 6; Temperley's services
to, 350–2, 359–60

I

Independence, Declaration of, 338
Industrial Revolution, 410
Institute of International Affairs, 357–61
International Historical Congresses,
377–9, 380
Isabella of Parma, 7–8; death, 11

J

James II of England, 409, 413
Jaurès, Jean, 269–70

Jenkins' Ear, War of, 353
Jesuits, 344–5; campaign against, 42, 45–6
Jokai, Maurus, 396–7
Joseph II of Austria: birth, 6; marriage, 7; suggestions for reforms, 8–11, 21–8, 42, 68; King of the Romans, 12; remarriage, 16–17; relations with his brother, 18–21, 39; financial policy, 29; difficulties as Co-Regent, 34–6, 39, 43–5, 46–8, 53–5; views on a third marriage, 39; on religious toleration, 49–54; foreign policy and Frederick the Great, 57–61, 62, 63 ff., 78, 91–2, 95; and Marie Antoinette, 69, 70, 71–2, 72–5, 75–7, 160–1, 184 ff., 187–90; and Catherine the Great, 103 ff., 114–15

K

Karl of Zweibrücken, 79
Karl Theodor, Elector Palatine, 77, 79
Kaunitz, Prince, 4, 12, 17, 18, 27, 30, 41, 42, 48, 56, 57, 62, 63, 66, 67, 78, 84, 85, 96, 117, 122, 139; and rapprochement with Russia, 103 ff.
Keith, Robert, 114
Khevenhüller, Count von, 30, 31
Kingsley, Charles, 315–17
Kraszewski, J. I., 398

L

Lacy, Field-Marshal, Count, 18, 30, 39, 41, 42, 78, 104
Lamballe, Princesse de, 72, 163, 173, 175–84 passim, 203, 210
Lassone, Dr. J. M. F., 182, 194, 195, 203
Laudon, Marshal, E. G., 92–3
Lavisse, Ernest, 260, 268–9, 273–4
Law, supremacy of, 412–14
Lea, Henry Charles, 321
League of Nations, 361
Lecky, W. E. H., 219, 323
Lefebvre, G., 276, 277–8, 287
Legislative Assembly, writings on, 281
Leopold of Tuscany, 1, 11, 12, 17, 31, 38, 63, 64; discord with brother, 18–21; and occupation of Bavaria, 80, 81; grief at mother's death, 116
Lieven, Princess, 366
Locke, John, 419–20
Long Parliament, the, 408
Lords, House of, reform of, 352–3
Louis XV of France, 70, 122, 123, 124, 128, 130; death, 141

Louis XVI of France, 74, 75, 76, 124, 130, 184; accession, 142, 146; coronation, 155; and Bavaria, 199, 204; and the Queen's measles, 208, 209; and gambling, 211; and grant to Polignac, 214
Louise of France, 125
Louise of Parma, 16
Luxembourg, Chevalier de, 180

M

Mabillon, Jean, 222
Macaulay, Lord, 243, 311–12
Machiavelli, Niccolo, 219
Madelin, E. L. M., 273, 287–8
Mahan, Admiral, 249, 323
Maistre, Joseph de, 294
Maitland, F. W., 246–7
Malesherbes, Chrétien de, 149, 162, 163; dismissal, 165
Marat, Jean Paul, 283, 284, 285
Marche, Comtesse de la, protegée of Princesse de Lamballe, 180
Marczali, H., and Hungarian history, 350–2
Maria Antonia of Saxony, 7, 46
Maria Josepha of Bavaria, 16
Maria Josepha of Saxony, 126
Maria Leczinska of France, 126
Maria Theresa of Austria; and religion, 28, 45–6, 49–54; has smallpox, 31; differences with Joseph as Co-Regent, 34–8, 39–41, 44–5, 46–8; her health, 49; and foreign affairs, 62–3, 65–6, 78–9, 81–4, 85, 86, 88, 197 ff., 207; and Frederick the Great, 85, 86, 89, 91, 95–6, 98, 100; death, 115–16; parting Memorandum to Marie Antoinette, 122–3; advice on Marie Antoinette's accession, 147; rebukes to Marie Antoinette, 129, 132–3, 136, 137, 139, 170–1, 172–3; opinions on Marie Antoinette's insufficiency and insta- bility, 142–3, 148–9, 152, 159–60, 166, 174; attacks her over La Polignac, 214, 215
Marie Antoinette of France: and her brother Joseph, 71–2, 191–2; birth and childhood, 120–2; marriage, 125–6; and the Du Barry, 130 ff.; formal visit to Paris, 139–41; and the pursuit of pleasure, 146, 150, 154, 168 ff.; and d'Aiguillon, 156–7; and her favourites, 168 ff.; pregnancy, 203; birth of daughter, 204–5; and measles, 208–9; grief at mother's death, 216

Marie Christine of Austria, 8
Marie de Medici, 146
Marie Louise of Spain, 16
Martineau, Harriet, 309–10
Marx, Karl, 256, 258
Masson, Frédéric, 241
Mathiez, A., 241, 274–6, 277, 284, 285, 288, 289, 290
Maupeou, R. N., dismissal of, 149
Maurepas, Count, 70, 149, 152, 157, 163, 164, 181, 199–200, 202, 213, 216
Maximilian of Austria, 71
Maximilian Joseph of Bavaria, 16, 77, 78
Mercy-Argenteau, Comte de, 69, 71, 96, 104, 119–120; reports to Maria Theresa on Marie Antoinette, 125–213 *passim*; rebuke to Marie Antoinette, 161; advice to her, 204; waning of influence, 217
Merejkowsky, D. S., 397–8
Mérimée, Prosper, 386
Meyer, Conrad Ferdinand, 395–6
Michelet, J., 235–6, 265, 283
Mignet, François, 237–8, 263
Mill, J. S., 424–5
Milman, Henry, 255
Mirabeau, Comte de, 279
Mohilev meeting, the, 104 ff.
Molo, Walter von, 394–5
Mommsen, Theodor, 252
Moravia, religious antagonism in, 49, 52
Morley, John, 323
Mortimer-Ternaux, L., 283–4
Moscow, Joseph's visit to, 109–10
Müller, Otfried, 227–8
Muratori, Ludovico, 222

N

Necker, Jacques, 185, 213, 215, 216, 262
Neisse meeting, the, 57–61
Neustadt meeting, the, 62
New Commonwealth Institute, 379, 380
Niebuhr, B., 226–7
Noailles, Comte de, 123, 124
Noailles, Comtesse de, 123, 124, 131, 176, 178

O

Ottoman Empire, the. *See* Turkey

P

Pallavicino, Cardinal, 221
Panin, Count, 104, 106, 108, 111
Pariset, G., 274

Paul of Russia, 106, 108, 112, 114
Penson, Lillian, 363, 371, 375, 377
Penson, L. and Temperley, H.: *Foundations of British Policy from Pitt to Salisbury*, 375–6; *A Century of Diplomatic Blue Books*, 376–7
Penthièvre, Duc de, 175, 178
Pergen, Count, 12, 46
Pertz, G. H., 230
Peter III of Russia, 113
Pius IX, Pope, 344, 345
Poland, Partition of, 41, 62 ff.
Polignac, Comtesse Diane de, 178
Polignac, Comtesse Jules de, 163, 164, 167, 175, 177–8, 181, 182, 210; claims for land and money, 212, 213–14
Pompadour, Madame de, 126, 129, 149
Potemkin, Prince, 105, 106, 107, 109, 110, 111, 112
Pragmatic Sanction of 1713, 3
Press, the, freedom of, 414–15
Provence, Comte de, 126, 134, 135, 137, 139, 143, 152, 157, 188
Provence, Comtesse de, 143, 152, 157
Prussia. *See* Seven Years' War *and* Frederick the Great
Pufendorf, Baron von, 223

R

Ranke, Leopold von, 219–20, 230–2, 233
Religion, freedom of, 415–17
Richelieu, Duc de, 126, 129
Right, Petition of, 413
Rights, Bill of, 413
Rights of Man, Declaration of, 338–9; controversy on, 278–9
Robertson, William, 224–5
Robespierre, Maximilien, 283, 284, 285
Rosenberg, Count, 71, 72, 158, 159, 177
Russia: Prussian fears of, 60; as mediating power in Bavarian Succession War, 101–2; and advances from Austria, 103 ff.
Russo-Prussian Treaty, 103
Russo-Turkish War, 62–3, 65

S

Sagnac, Philippe, 273–4, 276
St. Petersburg, Joseph's visit to, 110
Sarpi, Paolo, 221
Savigny, Friedrich von, 226, 228–9
Scheffel, J. V. von, 392–3
Schmitt, Bernadotte, 377

Scott, Sir Walter, 383–5
Seeley, Sir John, 247, 317–19
Ségur, Marquis de, 262
Serbia, Temperley's interest in, 349–50, 354, 355–6
Seton-Watson, Professor, 350, 356, 370
Seven Years' War, 4, 5, 7, 11, 12, 29, 32, 55–6, 60, 61, 121
Shorthouse, J. H., 401–2
Sienkiewicz, Henryk, 398
Silesia. *See* Seven Years' War
Slovaks, the, 349–50
Smyth, William, 309–11
Sophie of France, 126
Sorel, Albert, 239–40, 267–8, 269, 280, 296
Soubise, Marshal, 179
Spengler, O., 258
Stanislas of Poland, 60, 62
Starhemberg, 31, 36
State control, 411–12
Stein, Baron vom, 230
Stephen, Sir James, 312–15
Strauss, David, 254
Stubbs, William, Bishop, 245, 246
Sweden, Catherine the Great's opinion of, 110
Swieten, Dr. van, 5, 7
Switzerland, 342–3
Sybel, H. von, 233
Symonds, John, 308–9

T

Taine, Hippolyte, 265–7, 280
Tanucci, Marchese di, 38
Temperley, Harold: *Life of Canning*, 348–9; and the *Cambridge Modern History*, 349, 377; *Senates and Upper Chambers*, 352–3; *Frederick the Great and Kaiser Joseph*, 354; and the *Cambridge Historical Journal*, 362; *Foreign Policy of Canning*, 363–6; *The Victorian Age in Politics War and Diplomacy*, 368; *Research and Modern History*, 368–9; *England and the Near East*, 373–4; and the *Cambridge History of Poland*, 377; and B.B.C. historical dramas, 379–80
Temperley family, the, 348
Terray, Abbé, dismissal of, 149
Teschen, Treaty of, 102

Therese of Austria, 32
Thiers, Adolphe, 238, 263
Thompson, Dr. M., 285
Thugut, Baron von, 91 ff.
Tillemont, S., 221
Tocqueville, Alexis de, 239, 260–1
Toleration Act, 416–17
Tolstoy, Count Leo, 397
Tourzel, Madame de, 120
Townshend, 2nd Viscount, 298–300
Toynbee, Arnold, 258
Treitschke, Heinrich von, 234–5
Trevelyan, G. M., 327–30
Turgot, A. R. J., 7, 149, 185, 223, 262; dismissal, 162–5
Turkey: Austria's policy towards, 62–3; problem of, 64–5; Catherine the Great's opinion of, 110
Turner, Shallett, 302–3

U

Ultramontanism, 344, 346

V

Valla, Lorenzo, 219
Vandal, Albert, 241–2
Vaudreuil, Comte de, 183, 212, 215
Vergennes, Comte de, 76, 81, 149, 199–200; Marie Antoinette's hostility towards, 165
Vermond, Abbé, 121–2, 125 ff., 136, 138, 142, 148, 152, 155, 156, 162, 166, 167, 172, 182, 185, 193, 206, 213; rebukes Marie Antoinette, 183
Victoire of France, 126, 132, 134
Vigny, Alfred de, 385
Voltaire, 69, 70, 224, 256
Vossius, Gerard, 297

W

Wallon, H. A., 282
Walpole, Horace, 128, 129, 146, 305–6, 307, 383
Ward, Sir Adolphus, 349, 361
Weger, Abbé, 6
Westphalia, 200

Z

Zips, Austrian occupation of, 62